Psychology's Territories

Historical and Contemporary Perspectives from Different Disciplines

⇥ ⇤

Psychology's Territories

Historical and Contemporary Perspectives from Different Disciplines

Editors

Mitchell G. Ash
University of Vienna, Austria

Thomas Sturm
Max Planck Institute for the History of Science, Germany

Berlin-Brandenburg Academy of Sciences and Humanities

LAWRENCE ERLBAUM ASSOCIATES, PUBLISHERS
2007   Mahwah, New Jersey   London

This publication is the result of the interdisciplinary working group "Psychological Thought and Practice" at the Berlin-Brandenburg Academy of Sciences and Humanities. It has been made possible with the kind assistance of the Department of Science, Research, and Culture of the Senate of Berlin, and the Ministry of Higher Education, Research and Culture of the State of Brandenburg.

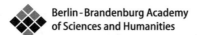 Berlin-Brandenburg Academy of Sciences and Humanities

This volume is dedicated with deep respect to Paul B. Baltes (1939–2006)

Lawrence Erlbaum Associates, Inc., Publishers
10 Industrial Avenue
Mahwah, New Jersey 07430
www.erlbaum.com

Cover design by Tomai Maridou

Library of Congress Cataloging-in-Publication Data

Psychology's territories : historical and contemporary perspective from different disciplines / editors, Mitchell G. Ash, Thomas Sturm.
    p.   cm.
Includes bibliographical references and index.
ISBN 0-8058-6136-X (cloth : alk. paper)
ISBN 0-8058-6137-8 (pbk. : alk. paper)
ISBN 1-4106-1490-5 (e book)
1. Psychology. 2. Psychology—History. I. Ash, Mitchell G. II. Sturm, Thomas.
BF121.P86 2006
150.1—dc22   2006016213
                                                       CIP

Books published by Lawrence Erlbaum Associates are printed on acid-free paper, and their bindings are chosen for strength and durability.

Printed in the United States of America
10 9 8 7 6 5 4 3 2 1

Contents

Instruments at Disciplinary Frontiers:
Psychology and the Neurosciences

Instruments as Metaphors for Psychological Objects

Conclusion

Foreword

Paul B. Baltes

This volume is the final publication of the Interdisciplinary Working Group, "Psychological Thought and Practice in Historical and Interdisciplinary Perspective," sponsored by the Berlin-Brandenburg Academy of Sciences and Humanities from October 2000 until March 2004. To set the stage for this volume, I would like to make a few observations about the history and workings of the group.

Interdisciplinarity and historical analyses are at the center of the work of most major academies of sciences around the world. This certainly has been true for the primary sponsor of this Working Group, the Berlin-Brandenburg Academy of Sciences and Humanities or, in brief, the BBAW. Let me begin by expressing the gratitude of the Working Group to the Berlin-Brandenburg Academy of Sciences and Humanities not only for supporting this enterprise with financial and infrastructural resources, including funds for conferences and stipends for graduate students, but especially also for the intellectual context, ambience, and input that the structure and membership of the BBAW have provided. It is part of this Academy that any project undergoes careful planning and evaluations with participation of groups at several levels of discourse. Aside from this intellectual support, it's especially notable that generous financial support continued, although the finances of the BBAW came under severe constraints due to a budget crisis of the city-state of Berlin which occurred during the life of the group. In light of these budgetary constraints, we are also very grateful to the German Academy of Science Leopoldina and the Heckmann-Wentzel-Stiftung, which generously provided additional funds to help cover impending budgetary shortfalls and to enable especially the younger participating scholars in the group to move forward with their work.

At least two other institutions deserve mention and our gratitude for their cooperative spirit in launching and completing this project: the Max Planck Institute for Human Development and the Max Planck Institute for History of Science (in particular its co-director Hans-Jörg Rheinberger). At critical moments they made two of the projects of the Working Group parts of their respective intellectual agendas. Such co-sponsorships speak to the high level of respect and collegial collaboration that the Berlin-Brandenburg Academy of Sciences and Humanities enjoys as an institution. By giving away its intellectual and financial resources, it also receives.

The Working Group came to life in the late 1990s, when a Planning Group of the BBAW for the Millennium Year 2000 met, of which I was a member. This Planning Group met several times to explore special projects with interdisciplinary character and a connection with Berlin, intended in part also to commemorate the three-hundredth anniversary of the founding of the Prussian Academy of Sciences. At that time, and with the informal advice of Mitchell Ash, I suggested that the Academy consider a project on the external contextual and interdisciplinary connections of psychology. I am not an historian of psychology. However, when presenting the idea to that Committee, I mentioned the role of Berlin in the history of psychology, and also two additional factors that could serve to legitimate such a project.

It was my first impression that present-day German academies of science had not acknowledged the increasing presence of the discipline of psychology under the umbrella of the sciences, broadly defined. There were no special sections in these academies devoted to that discipline. Across the German republic, and not only in the BBAW or the Leopoldina, there were few members of academies of sciences who were psychologists. I thought that these millennium activities might contribute in a small way to remedying this apparent historical lag in recognizing that psychology had arrived as a serious discipline.

My second argument was more intuitive than evidence-based. My intuition was that this relative neglect was the more surprising since it suggested a departure from the past. Not being a historian of psychology, my impression was that this relative lack of representation of psychology in German academies of sciences was not true for the previous, the nineteenth, century. With my limited knowledge of the historical state of affairs, I speculated that during these earlier periods, the subject matter of psychology seemed to figure much more prominently on the agendas, for instance, of the mother academy of the BBAW, the Prussian Academy of Sciences.

However, when contemplating this possibility of a marked discrepancy between the significance of psychology in modern times and its seeming decline in German academies, I was enough of a realist to wonder whether there would be solid evidence for my supposition if the matter were studied more carefully. At the same time, and after conversations with historically better-informed colleagues such as the late Friedhart Klix and Wolfgang Schönpflug, I was reasonably sure that intuition had some basis in fact. As to the importance of interdisciplinary perspectives, I knew, having just completed co-editing, with Neil Smelser, the *International Encyclopedia of Social and Behavioral Sciences,* which contains several chapters on the history of these fields, that there was more to the evolution of a given discipline than developments within the discipline itself. Social, institutional, and professional contexts did matter—that was the argument in most of the relevant chapters in that encyclopedia.

In any case, when I presented this rationale to the Year 2000 Planning Group and pointed to Mitchell Ash as a possible leader, there was support. With no other psychologists present, who could object, based on substantive grounds? Of added significance was that the Millennium Planning Group liked the focus on Berlin, and Berlin indeed had been one of the centers where experimental psychology had been established in Germany. Therefore, the Planning Committee supported the idea of establishing a working group, the task of which would be to study the historical, contextual, and interdisciplinary factors that shaped the formal and informal evolution of psychology in the last century. Berlin and Germany were expected to be at the core of the group's work, and the historical research was to concentrate on the period from 1850 to 1950, but there would be no objection if the activities were to include a larger context and more recent times as well.

Launching the Working Group was facilitated by two events. One was related and ongoing work by Friedhart Klix, who edited an excellent collection of journal articles on the history and current situation of German psychology during this time. This became part of the series of special issues of the *Zeitschrift für Psychologie* devoted to "Psychologie 2000" (Vol. 207, No. 3–4, 1999; Vol. 208, No. 1–2, 2000; Vol. 209, No. 1, 2001) The second related event was the election of Professor Mitchell Ash as a member of the Berlin-Brandenburg Academy of Sciences and Humanities. Ash's expertise as a general historian, a historian of science, and a historian of psychology made him an ideal leader to undertake a project that the Millennium Planning Group had only envisioned in rather rough terms. His work on the history of psychology shines by its concern with interdisciplinarity, contextualism, and commitment to general societal and cultural perspectives. Thus, under his leadership a working group was formed to explore historical, contextual, and inter-disciplinary processes in the shaping of psychology and related disciplines. The group included historians of science, psychologists, philosophers, engineers, and medical researchers. The majority were psychologists and historians of science. (A list of the Working Group's members is presented in Appendix II to this volume.)

Under the guiding mind of Mitchell Ash, the Working Group articulated a threefold, triangulated program. We were first interested in providing a better understanding for what we called the institutional differentiation of the subject matter of psychological objects. Which disciplines, in which sequence, with what emphases, declared themselves interested in psychological topics, why and to what purpose?

Second, we asked, to what degree was this interest in psychological subject matter dictated or influenced by questions of empirical methodologies, especially the availability, constraints, and development of instruments and instrumentation? This is partly a question of theory-method alignments but it is also a question of disciplinary power and preferences. Who is in control of instruments, who has the financial resources to develop new methods, for what purpose? What is the long-range consequence of the availability of such instrumentation for psychological work in theory and practice—how does this impact concretely on research agendas?

As a third avenue towards understanding the role of interdisciplinarity, interprofessionalism and historical-institutional contexts in the history of psychology, we explored the question of applications and technology. This emphasis highlights the fact that psychology is not only driven by forces located within the core of the discipline or profession. On the contrary, we asked to what degree even the evolution of psychology in the narrow sense was driven by external forces, and to what degree groups outside the discipline of psychology proper became involved, as recipients and agents of change. This topic, of course, resonates well with the current-day issues of the competitive and synergistic dynamics between the cognitive neurosciences and psychology.

Perhaps I might be permitted to make one final observation. Often, what is presented in public settings such as this is a rather abstract distillation of internal deliberations. Using terms from the psychology of emotion, it is cold rather than hot. To counterbalance this coldness, but also to spice up our dialogue, I would like to report on some of the hotness and humidity.

The workings of the Committee were an excellent illustration of the saying that for science to advance, it needs to be at the same time a matter of war and a matter of love. It became clear to us that there was quite a separation between our respective preferences and criteria of relevance. The views and bodies of knowledge of the Working Group's members were far from being the same. For some of us, this was especially conspicuous when historians of science interested in psychology and psychologists tried to communicate. Neither side was ready to give the other much credit. There were schisms and occasionally lack of mutual respect. Often the historians enjoyed each other's views of psychology, while the psychologists turned away in utter despair about the seeming lack of knowledge about psychology that was reflected in what the historians were saying. Occasionally, the psychologists thought that these historians and philosophers of science had constructed their own territory of psychology, or that they lacked knowledge about the institutional contexts that really matter to working scientists. The reverse, of course, was equally true. Historians wondered about how contextually and institutionally naïve these psychologists seemed to be. Could it really be that they, the psychologists, did not understand that scientific thought is heavily conditioned by broader cultural and institutional influences, their constraints and opportunities? Some of us on both sides of the aisle, of course, felt that they knew better. Perhaps such feelings were the real problem.

Yet, these initial and temporary mutual disenchantments were exactly the source from which productive thought and new insights streamed. Moreover, having to deal with such multiple streams of thought and knowledge demonstrated that the original reasons for forming this Working Group were more than a fleeting idea. Even some of the psychologists in the group began to consider the possibility that work by psychologists on the history of psychology is less informed by contextual and interdisciplinary factors than is desirable. Psychologists writing their own history, it became increasingly clear, thought from within their discipline, and had little understanding of the societal and professional contexts that shaped psychology from the outside. On the part of historians, my assumption is that they also began to understand that what they viewed as the subject matter and methods of psychology occasionally bore little similarity to what psychologists thought psychology was all about, and which contexts shaped their behaviour as scientists. With time, the mutual benefits of the dialogue grew in depth and scope. This was a working group where learning rather than pontificating became the gist of the discourse—true to the spirit of an Academy working group.

The special challenge of this volume is to take this project to a new level of discourse, the international scene. How far we have come in our efforts, you, the readers, will be able to judge. I, for one, am sure that the ground has been laid for battle, but also for cooperation and efforts at integrative thoughts and conclusions. Let us hope that both occur, and each at a higher level and with better means than before. For myself, I continue to be confused about some of the core issues that are so clear in the heads of my historian colleagues; this includes the question whether good historical knowledge facilitates or hinders scientific advances in a given field. The correct answer is probably some of both. My confusion about this and other related issues, however, no doubt exists at a much higher level of sophistication than before. Even states of confusion can grow in mindfulness.

About the Contributors

Mitchell G. Ash is Professor of Modern History and Head of the Working Group in History of Science at the University of Vienna, Austria. He was speaker of the Interdisciplinary Working Group "Psychological Thought and Practice" at the Berlin-Brandenburg Academy of Sciences and Humanities from 2001 to 2004. Since 2002, he has been President of the "Gesellschaft für Wissenschaftsgeschichte" (Society for History of the Sciences and Humanities). He has published extensively on the history of modern psychology, and his research now focuses on the relations of the sciences to politics, society, and culture in the 19th and 20th centuries. Selected publications: *Gestalt Psychology in German Culture 1890–1967: Holism and the Quest for Objectivity* (1995); *Forced Migration and Scientific Change: Emigre German-Speaking Scientists and Scholars after 1933* (edited with A. Söllner, 1996); "Scientific Changes in Germany 1933, 1945 and 1990: Towards a Comparison." *Minerva*, Vol. 37 (1999); "Psychology," In *Cambridge History of Science, Vol. 7: The Modern Social and Behavioral Sciences* (Eds. D. Ross & T. Porter, 2003); and "Innovation, Ethnicity, Identity: German-Speaking Jewish Psychologists and Social Scientists in the Interwar Period" *Jahrbuch des Simon Dubnow Instituts*, Vol. 3 (2004).

Address: Mitchell G. Ash, Department of History, University of Vienna, Dr. Karl Lueger Ring 1, A–1010 Vienna, Austria
Telephone: +43-1-27 74 08 37
E-mail: mitchell.ash@univie.ac.at
URL: www.univie.ac.at/Geschichte/_ash.html

Paul B. Baltes was Emeritus Director of the Center of Lifespan Psychology at the Max Planck Institute for Human Development, Berlin, Germany, and Honorary Professor of Psychology at the Free University of

Berlin. Baltes was interested in advancing a life span view of human ontogenesis that considers behavioral and cognitive functioning from childhood into old age in a changing society. Substantive topics include work on historical cohort effects, cognitive development, a dual-process conception of life span intelligence, and the study of wisdom. His interests also include models of successful development (including aging) and the cross-cultural comparative study of self-related agency beliefs in the context of child development and school performance. Selected publications: *Successful Aging: Perspectives From the Behavioral Sciences* (edited with M. M. Baltes, 1990); *The Berlin Aging Study: Aging From 70 to 100* (edited with K. U. Mayer, 1998); "On the Incomplete Architecture of Human Ontogeny: Selection, Optimization, and Compensation as Foundation of Developmental Theory," *American Psychologist*, Vol. 52 (1997); "Wisdom: A Metaheuristic (Pragmatic) to Orchestrate Mind and Virtue Towards Excellence" (with U. M. Staudinger), *American Psychologist*, Vol. 55 (2000); and *International Encyclopedia of the Social and Behavioral Sciences* (edited with N. Smelser, 2001).

URL: http://www.baltes-paul.de
  http://www.maxnetaging.mpq.de
  http://www.mpib-berlin.mpg.de/en/forschung/lip/index.htm

Rainer M. Bösel is Professor of Psychology at the Free University of Berlin. His research interests include attention, electroencephalography, and topics in cognitive and social neuropsychology. Selected publications: *Denken* (2001); "Focusing of Visuospatial Attention" (with C. Pesce), *Journal of Psychophysiology*, Vol. 15 (2001); *Einführung in die Psychologie* (with D. Ulich, 2005).

Address: Rainer M. Bösel, Arbeitsbereich Kognitive Neuropsychologie, Habelschwerdter Allee 45, D-14195 Berlin, Germany
Telephone: +49-(0)30-838 55733
E-mail: rboesel@zedat.fu-berlin.de
URL: http://web.fu-berlin.de/kogpsy/Kogpsych/rboesel.html

Jochen Brandtstädter is Professor of Psychology at the University of Trier, Germany. Substantive topics in his research include adult development, action theory, goal definition processes across the life span, self-regulatory processes, dynamics of goal commitment and disengagement, theoretical psychology, statistical methods. Selected publications: "Apriorität, Erfahrung und das Projekt der Psychologie" (with T. Sturm), *Zeitschrift für Sozialpsychologie*, Vol. 35 (2005); *Entwicklung—Intentionalität—Handeln* (2001); "Emotion, Cognition, and Control: Limits of Intentionality," In W. J. Perrig & A. Grob (Eds.), *Control of Human Behavior, Mental Processes, and Consciousness* (2000).

Address: Jochen Brandtstädter, Fb I—Psychologie, Universität Trier, Tarforst, Gebäude D, D-54286 Trier, Germany
Telephone: +49-(0)651-201 29 69
E-mail: brandtst@uni-trier.de
URL: www.psychologie.uni-trier.de/personen/jbrandtstaedter/

James H. Capshew is Associate Professor in the Department of History and Philosophy of Science at Indiana University. At present, he is working on a synthetic history of psychology in the 20th century. Selected publications: *Psychologists on the March: Science, Practice, and Professional Identity in American Psychology, 1929–1969* (1999); other publications in *Osiris, Technology and Culture,* and the *American Psychologist,* among other places.

Address: James H. Capshew, Department of History and Philosophy of Science, Indiana University, 1011 East Third Street, Goodbody Hall 130, Bloomington, IN 47405, USA
Telephone: +1-812-855-3655
E-mail: jcapshew@indiana.edu
URL: www.indiana.edu/~memento/

Kenneth J. Gergen is the Mustin Professor of Psychology at Swarthmore College and the Director of the Taos Institute. He is a leading figure in the development of social constructionist thought and practice and has been an active contributor to dialogues on the historical and cultural lodgement of conceptions of self. Selected publications: *Realities and Relationships* (1995); *The Saturated Self* (1991); *An Invitation to Social Construction* (1999); *Social Construction in Context* (2001); with C. -F. Graumann he also edited *Historical Dimensions of Psychological Discourse* (1997).

Address: Kenneth J. Gergen, Department of Psychology, Swarthmore College, 500 College Avenue, Swarthmore, PA 19081, USA
Telephone: 001-610-328-8434
E-mail: kgergen1@swarthmore.edu
URL: www.swarthmore.edu/SocSci/kgergen1

Gerd Gigerenzer is Director of the Center for Adaptive Behavior and Cognition at the Max Planck Institute for Human Development, Berlin, Germany, and Honorary Professor of Psychology at the Free University of Berlin. His main research interests include models of bounded rationality; social intelligence; ecological rationality; the heuristics of scientific discovery; and the philosophy, history, and methodology of social sciences. Selected publications: *Cognition as Intuitive Statistics* (with D. Murray, 1987); *The Empire of Chance: How Probability Changed Sci-*

ence and Everyday Life (with L. Krüger et al., 1989); *Adaptive Thinking: Rationality in the Real World* (2000); and *Calculated Risks: How to Know When Numbers Deceive You* (2002).

Address: Gerd Gigerenzer, Max-Planck-Institut für Bildungsforschung, Lentzeallee 94, D-14195 Berlin, Germany
Telephone: +49-(0)30-82406-460/461
E-mail: sekgigerenzer@mpib-berlin.mpg.de
URL: http://www.mpib-berlin.mpg.de/en/forschung/abc/index.htm

Horst Gundlach is Professor at the Institute for the History of Psychology at the University of Passau, Germany. His research focuses on the history of psychology, especially in the 19th and 20th centuries, the interaction between theoretical and applied psychology, and the role of instruments in psychology. Selected publications: "Psychoanalysis & The Story of "O": An Embarrassment"; *The Semiotic Review of Books 13* (2002); "Die Psychophysik und Fechner," *Teorie & Modelli* (1999); *The First to Thirteenth Congress Proceedings of the International Association of Applied Psychology* (Ed., 1988); *Apparative Psychologie: Geschichtliche Entwicklung und gegenwärtige Bedeutung* (Ed. with D. Albert, 1997).

Address: Horst Gundlach, Institut für Geschichte der Psychologie, Universität Passau, Leopoldstr. 4, D-94030 Passau, Germany
Telephone: +49-(0)851-56 09 86 11
E-mail: gundlach@uni-pasau.de
URL: www.phil.uni-passau.de/igp/

Michael Hagner is Professor for Science Studies at the ETH Zurich, Switzerland, and was Senior Fellow at the Max Planck Institute for the History of Science in Berlin, Germany. He is a leading historian of brain research, and his current research concerns the history of cybernetics and the strategies of visualization in the life sciences. Selected publications: *Homo cerebralis. Der Wandel vom Seelenorgan zum Gehirn* (1997); *Ecce cortex. Beiträge zur Geschichte des modernen Gehirns* (Ed., 1999); *Ansichten der Wissenschaftsgeschichte* (Ed., 2001); *Mindful Practices: On the Neurosciences in the Twentieth Century* (Ed. with C. Borck, 2001); and *Geniale Gehirne. Zur Geschichte der Elitegehirnfoschung* (2004).

Address: Michael Hagner, Chair for Science Studies, ETH Zürich, Rämistr. 36, CH-8092 Zürich, Switzerland
Telephone: +41-1-632 4050
E-mail: hagner@wiss.gess.ethz.ch

Michael Heidelberger is Professor of Logic and Philosophy of Science at the University of Tübingen, Germany. He has a wide interest in topics related to causality and probability and measurement and experiment and also specializes in the history of the philosophy of science, especially of the late 19th and early 20th centuries. Selected publications: *Die innere Seite der Natur* (1993) and *Experimental Essays—Versuche zum Experiment* (Ed., with F. Steinle, 1998).

Address: Michael Heidelberger, Philosophisches Seminar, Universität Tübingen, Bursagasse 1, D-72070 Tübingen, Germany
Telephone: +49-7071-2974347
E-mail: michael.heidelberger@uni-tuebingen.de
URL: www.uni-tuebingen.de/ philosophie/heidelberger/index.htm

Hans-Jochen Heinze is Professor and Director at the Department of Neurology II at the Otto-von-Guericke-Universität Magdeburg, Germany. Selected publications: "Alterations of Continuous MEG Measurements During Mental Activities," *Neuropsychobiology* (2000); "Kognition und Denken," In *Lehrbuch Vorklinik, Teil B* (ed. Birbaumer, Kurtz, Schartl, Unsicker, 2003); and "Asymmetrical Activation in the Human Brain During Processing of Fearful Faces" (with others) *Current Biolology* (2005).

Address: Hans-Jochen Heinze, Otto-von-Guericke-Universität Magdeburg, Klinik für Neurologie II, Haus 60/B, Leipziger Straße 44, 39120 Magdeburg, Germany
Telephone: +49-(0)391-6713431
E-mail: hans-jochen.heinze@medizin.uni-magdeburg.de

Sven Lüders received a PhD in sociology from the Free University of Berlin, Germany, and was a student associate of the Interdisciplinary Working Group "Psychological Thought and Practice" of the Berlin–Brandenburg Academy of Sciences and Humanities. He now works for the Humanistische Union, a German civil rights organization.

Address: Sven Lüders, Humanistische Union, Haus der Demokratie und Menschenrechte, Greifswalder Straße 4, D-10405 Berlin, Germany
Telephone: +49-(0)30-20 45 02 56
E-mail: lueders@humanistische-union.de

Sabine Maasen is Professor for Science Studies at the University of Basel, Switzerland. Her recent research interests include the social construction of sexual selves; and the dynamics of knowledge, particularly as regards the notion of consciousness; as well as the dynamics of knowledge between different scientific and nonscientific discourses. Selected publications: *Genealogie der Unmoral. Zur Therapeutisierung sexueller Selbste*

(1998); *Metaphors and the Dynamics of Knowledge* (with P. Weingart, 2000); *Voluntary Action: On Brains, Minds, and Sociality* (with W. Prinz & G. Roth, 2003).

Address: Sabine Maasen, Wissenschaftsforschung, Universität Basel, Missionsstr. 21, CH-4003 Basel, Switzerland
Telephone: +41-61-260 21 99
E-mail: sabine.maasen@unibas.ch
URL: www.unibas.ch/mgu/semprog/WS0203/maasen.htm

Jill Morawski is Professor of Psychology at Wesleyan University, where she also is a faculty member of the Science in Society Program and the Women's Studies Program. Her research in the history and theory of psychology includes studies of early 20th-century experimental psychology and gender theory in psychology. Her current projects entail a study of the formation of subjectivities in experimentation and a history of representations of sperm in 20th-century American culture and science. Selected publications: *The Rise of Experimentation in American Psychology* (ed., 1988); *Practicing Feminisms, Reconstructing Psychology* (1994); "Men Crazy: Making Theories of Masculinity" (2003); "The History of Modern Social Psychology" (with B. Bayer, 2003); and "White Experimenters, White Blood, and Other White Conditions: Locating the Psychologist's Race" (1998).

Address: Jill Morawski, Department of Psychology, Wesleyan University, 207 High Street, Middletown, CT 06459–0408, USA
Telephone: +1-860-685-2344
E-mail: jmorawski@wesleyan.edu
URL: www.wesleyan.edu/psyc/jmorawski.htm#contact

Thomas F. Münte is Professor for Neuropsychology at the Otto von Guericke University of Magdeburg, Germany. His main research interests concern cognitive processes in neuronal lesions, the neuronal basis of working memory, action, temporal aspects of selective attention, and neurolinguistics. Selected publications: "Specialization of the Specialized: Electrophysiological Investigations in Professional Musicians," *Annals of the New York Academy of Science*, Vol. 999 (2003); "Cognitive Changes in Short-Term Hypothyroidism Assessed With Event-Related Brain Potentials" *Psychoneuroendocrinology*, Vol. 29 (2004, with others); and "Kognitive Potenziale" (with J. Rössler), in *Evozierte Potenziale, neurovegetative Diagnostik, Okulographie: Methodik und klinische Anwendungen* (Ed. by H. Buchner & J. Noth, 2005).

Address: Thomas F. Münte, Institut für Psychologie II, Lehrstuhl für Neuropsychologie, Universitätsplatz, Gebäude 24, D-39106 Magdeburg, Germany

Telephone: +49-(0)391–6718475
E-mail: thomas.muente@medizin.uni-magdeburg.de

Wolfgang Prinz is Director of the Max Planck Institute for Psychological Research, renamed Max Planck Institute for Human Cognitive and Brain Sciences in 2004. His main research interests are perception, action, attention, and consciousness. Selected publications: *Kopf-Arbeit. Gehirnfunktionen und kognitive Leistungen* (Ed. with G. Roth, 1996); *Common Mechanisms in Perception and Action* (Ed. with B. Hommel, 2002); and *Voluntary Action: Brains, Minds, and Sociality* (Ed. with S. Maasen & G. Roth, 2003).

Address: Wolfgang Prinz, Max Planck Institute for Human Cognitive and Brain Sciences, Department of Psychology, Amalienstr. 33, D-80799 Leipzig, Germany
Telephone: +49-(0)341-9940 286
E-mail: prinz@cbs.mpg.de

Gerhard Roth is Professor of Zoology and the Chair of Behavioral Physiology in the Department of Biology and Chemistry at the University of Bremen, Germany, where he is also the Director of the Brain Research Institute. Since 1997 he has been Rector of the Hanse Institute for Advanced Study of the German States Bremen and Lower Saxony, located in Delmenhorst. His fields of research are the anatomical and physiological basis of visually guided behavior in vertebrates, neurobiology of emotions, developmental neurobiology of amphibians, and theoretical neuroscience and neurophilosophy. Selected publications: *Das Gehirn und seine wirklichkeit. Kognitive Neurobiologie und ihre philosophischen Konsequenzen* (1997) and *Fühlen, Denken, Handeln—Wie das Gehirn unser Verhalten steuert* (2001/2003).

Address: Gerhard Roth, Hanse-Wissenschaftskolleg, Lehmkuhlenbusch 4, D-27753 Delmenhorst, Germany
Telephone: +49-(0)42 21-916 00
E-mail: zkwroth@uni-bremen.de
URL: www.h-w-k.de/fsdeu2.htm

Norbert Schwarz is Professor of Psychology at the University of Michigan, Ann Arbor, Research Professor at the Survey Research Center and the Research Center for Group Dynamics of the Institute for Social Research, Professor for Survey Research in Michigan's Program in Survey Methods, and Professor for Marketing at the University of Michigan Business School. His research interests focus on human judgment, broadly conceived, including the interplay of feeling and thinking; the role of conversational processes in reasoning; and the cognitive and communicative underpinnings of self-reports of attitudes and behaviors. He was the winner of the Wilhelm Wundt Medal of the American Psychological Association in 2004. Selected publications: *Thinking About Answers: The Application of Cognitive Processes to Survey Methodology* (with S. Sudman & N. Bradburn, 1996); *Cognition and Communication: Judgmental Biases, Research Methods and the Logic of Conversation* (1996); *Well-Being: The Foundations of Hedonic Psychology* (with D. Kahneman & E. Diener, 1999); and *Cognitive Aging: A Primer* (Ed. with D. C. Park, 2000).

Address: Norbert Schwarz, Institute for Social Research, 426 Thompson Street, Ann Arbor, MI 48106-1248, USA
Telephone: +1-734-647-3616
E-mail: nschwarz@umich.edu

Fritz Strack is Professor of Psychology at the University of Würzburg, Germany. His areas of research include social cognition, judgment, and the psychology of survey response. Selected publications: "Response Processes," In R. S. Wyer & T. K. Srull (Eds.), *Handbook of Social Cognition* (1994); "Reporting Recollective Experiences: Direct Access to Memory Systems?" (with J. Förster) *Psychological Science*, Vol.\ 6 (1995); "'Erkenne Dich selbst!' Einige Überlegungen und Befunde zur Selbsterkenntnis als Methode und Gegenstand psychologischer Forschung" (with L. Werth & J. Förster), in W. Schneider & W. Janke (Eds.), *100 Jahre Würzburger Schule* (1999).

Address: Fritz Strack, LS Psychologie II, Universität Würzburg, Röntgenring 10, D-97070 Würzburg, Germany
Telephone: +49-(0)931-31-2877
E-mail: strack@psychologie.uni-wuerzburg.de
URL: wy2x05.psychologie.uni-wuerzburg.de/strack/

Thomas Sturm was coordinator of the Interdisciplinary Working Group "Psychological Thought and Practice" at the Berlin–Brandenburg Academy of Sciences and Humanities from 2002 to 2004 and is currently Research Fellow at the Max Planck Institute for the History of Science, Berlin, Germany. His main research interests concern Kant's philosophy of science, the history and philosophy of perceptual illusions, and philosophical problems of rationality. Selected publications: "How Not to Investigate the Human Mind: Kant on the Impossibility of Empirical Psychology," In E. Watkins (Ed.), *Kant and the Sciences* (2001); "Apriorität, Erfahrung und das Projekt der Psychologie" (with J. Brandtstädter), *Zeitschrift für Sozialpsychologie*, Vol. 35 (2005); *Lorenz Krüger: Why Does History Matter to Philosophy and the Sciences?* (Ed. with W. Carl & L. Daston, 2005); and "Roles of Instruments in Psychological Research" (with M. G. Ash) *History of Psychology*, Vol. 8 (2005).

Address: Thomas Sturm, Max Planck Institute for the History of Science, Boltzmannstraße 22, D-14195 Berlin, Germany
Telephone: +49-(0)30-22667-236
E-mail: tsturm@mpiwg-berlin.mpg.de
URL: http://www.mpiwg-berlin.mpg.de/en/mitarbeiter/members/tsturm

Members of the Interdisciplinary Working Group "Psychological Thought and Practice in Historical and Interdisciplinary Perspective"

Mitchell G. Ash*, Speaker (Department of History, University of Vienna)

Paul B. Baltes*, Vice-Speaker (Max Planck Institute for Human Development, Berlin)

Jochen Brandtstädter (Department of Psychology, Universität Trier)

Gerd Gigerenzer* (Max Planck Institute for Human Development, Berlin)

Horst Gundlach (Institute for History of Modern Psychology, University of Passau)

Michael Hagner (Chair of Science Studies, ETH Zürich)

Michael Heidelberger (Department of Philosophy, University of Tübingen)

Hanfried Helmchen* (Psychiatric Clinic and Policlinic, Free University of Berlin)

Reinhold Kliegl* (Institute for Psychology, University of Potsdam)

Gerhard Roth* (Hanse-Wissenschaftskolleg, Delmenhorst; Brain Research Institute, University of Bremen)

Wolfgang Schönpflug (Department of Psychology, Free University of Berlin)

Lothar Sprung (Department of Psychology, Humboldt University Berlin)

Günter Spur* (Institute for Machine Tools and Factory Organisation, Technical University of Berlin)

Bernhard Wilpert (Institute for Psychology, Technical University of Berlin)

---

* Members of the Berlin–Brandenburg Academy of Sciences and Humanities

Coordinator:

Thomas Sturm (Coordinator of the Working Group, Berlin–Brandenburg Academy of Sciences and Humanities, Berlin; now at Max Planck
Institute for the History of Science, Berlin, Germany)

Student Associates:

Martin Eberhardt (Berlin–Brandenburg Academy of Sciences and Humanities, Berlin)

Sven Lüders (Berlin–Brandenburg Academy of Sciences and Humanities, Berlin)

Sören Wendelborn (Berlin–Brandenburg Academy of Sciences and
Humanities, Berlin)

List of Illustrations

Psychological Thought and Practice: Historical and Interdisciplinary Perspectives

Mitchell G. Ash
University of Vienna

Wilhelm Wundt (1907/1908) thought that psychology should become the foundational discipline for the human sciences. Instead, two rather different but related things have happened. Psychology has become a protean discipline that occupies a peculiar place among the sciences, suspended between methodological orientations derived from the physical and biological sciences and a subject matter extending into the social and human sciences. At the same time, modern societies and cultures have become permeated with psychological thinking and practices, much of which relates tenuously at best to what goes on in the discipline. So, we may well ask, what are psychology's territories, and where might they be located? And if psychology actually *has* such territories—meaning not only institutions, but concepts and research practices used exclusively within such institutions—then how did such territories come to be established, how have they changed over time, and how do they compare with psychological concepts and research practices used elsewhere? The following remarks are an effort to discuss these questions in historical and interdisciplinary contexts. In so doing, attention is paid to the fact that the contributors to this volume have taken different roads. Some, including the author of this chapter, wish to explore the possibilities for a social and cultural history of psychological thought and research. Others, although not denying the usefulness of an historical understanding of psychology's contested territories, try to address these issues from more systematic points of view.

Psychology's boundaries have continuously been contested in various ways—by neighboring disciplines, by everyday psychological viewpoints, and by practical approaches to solving psychological problems coming from outside the field. Traditionally, questions concerning the identity of psychology and its demarcation from other domains have been discussed by referring to psychology's subject matter or method; but the obvious multiplicity of the discipline's subjects and methods makes this approach difficult to sustain. The authors of this volume take a novel approach to this issue by focusing on a broad range of specific questions: How have psychological concepts been understood in different disciplines such as psychology, philosophy, neuroscience, or the social sciences, as well as in daily life? What instruments have been used in research on the mind, coming from what sources, and with what potentials and limits for defining and solving specifically psychological problems? And how have applications of psychological thinking and research worked in various technological and personal contexts? Using focused historical and contemporary case studies, the authors reflect critically on traditional images of psychology as a scientific discipline and as a professional practice. The volume thus has a dual agenda: to make historical and philosophical studies of psychology relevant to contemporary concerns, and to show how psychology can profit from better interdisciplinary cooperation, thus improving mutual understanding between different scientific cultures.

The time is ripe for such an effort, but there is no clear agreement on how to proceed. The historiography of psychology, for example, has become part of the general history of science, due in large part to the common efforts of historically aware psychologists, general historians and historians of science to contextualize the discipline's varied development in different places and times (for surveys, see Ash, 2003, and Smith, 1998). In turn, the history of science has professionalized at a rapid pace in the past 20 years. Scholars in the field now generally recognize that research in this area cannot be limited either to technical histories of individual scientific disciplines, as constructed by the members of these disciplines (although such studies continue to be of value); nor can it be limited to the histories of scientific disciplines as institutions, of the kind most familiar to general and social historians, and often practiced by historians of psychology as well. Alongside these approaches, a vast variety of contextualizations of science has appeared, ranging from studies of cultures of scientific research at the micro-level to cultural histories of central scientific concepts, including even the concept of objectivity, at the metalevel.

By themselves such contextualizations have, and must have, the effect of questioning, even dissolving long-held distinctions between "internal" and "external" histories of scientific disciplines, including psychology. Whether that dissolution is actually accepted by nonhistorian members of a given discipline is another matter entirely. Among psychologists, in so far as they take any interest in history at all, it seems that "internal" history—meaning the stories psychologists tell one another about the development of their discipline—is still very much alive. This is particularly true of the many textbooks on history and systems of psychology produced for required courses in the subject, but not only there. Such histories often edit out precisely the contextual dimensions that historians of science and general historians find most relevant. In addition, they either ignore or construct barriers against the stories other nonpsychologists tell about the subject matter of the discipline.

Quite similar tensions appear when psychologists and philosophers, or psychologists and neuroscientists attempt to discuss what may appear at first to be similar topics. There have been countless disputes about the nature and workings of the mind, or the relations of mental processes to the operations of the brain. And often enough it seems as though what academic psychologists have discovered or find interesting bears little relation to what nonpsychologists want to know or discover about themselves. A common and understandable, but entirely unhelpful and scientifically unproductive response is to circle the wagons and stick to the tried and true, either paying no attention to what outsiders may say, or declaring such viewpoints uninteresting or even unscientific.

While introducing the approaches taken in the contributions to this volume, I would like to present a thematically oriented approach combining historiography of psychology in its present form with certain broader considerations from the history of science and general history (see also Ash, 1992). My belief is that such an approach will contribute to clarifying the social and cultural situation of contemporary psychological and social science research. In the case of psychology, this approach seems particularly appropriate, in view of the number of disciplines employing psychological methods of various kinds as well as the wide variety of psychological doctrines and practices outside academic settings.

FOUNDATIONS

The approach taken here is based on three propositions:

1. *The history of psychological thought cannot be reduced to that of the discipline called psychology, narrowly constructed.* Psychological thinking in the broadest sense—including conceptions of human nature and subjectivity—has played a fundamental role in the formation and history of every discipline that deals with human affairs. Because many of these disciplines emerged before psychology did and have often developed quite independently of psychology, limiting our perspective to the internal history of academic psychology is insufficient to the task at hand. All forms of psychological thinking, wherever they may be located institutionally, could and should be included in principle within the purview of the analysis proposed here, although of course a comprehensive survey is not possible. Similar considerations also apply to the multiple interrelationships between the psychological disciplines and the use of psychological vocabularies by non-academics, which have their own history.

2. *The common assumption that methodologically controlled use of research tools effectively insulates psychology both from other disciplines and from lay practices can and should be questioned, for two reasons.* First, as recent historical research has shown, the same tools have been made to work in varied disciplines over time, whereas the uses and meanings of such tools change in various ways while they "travel" from one context of use to another (see, e.g., Benschop & Draaisma, 2000; Schmidgen, 2005). Their belongingness to a particular discipline is thus determined not only by specificities of machine design, but also by contexts of use (Gundlach, chap. 9, this volume; see the following section). Second, the history of research practices in any science is as important as the history of concepts and theories, because the two can be quite independent of one another. Ian Hacking (1992), Hans-Jörg Rheinberger (1997a, 1997b), and others have shown, for example, that experimentation has a history of its own, which may not be limited to the confirmation or refutation of theories (for further discussion see Sturm & Ash, 2005). Moreover, as Lorraine Daston (1992, 1995) has argued, the belief that methodologically controlled use of research tools guarantees objectivity did not become established until the 19th century. If that is the

case, then the concept of objectivity itself has a history, of which the historical development of research practices and the changing uses of various kinds of instruments are a part.

3. *The common view that applied science is derived in a linear way from basic science has rarely been correct in psychology, and may not work very well for any science. Rather, it is more precise to speak of "psychology in practical contexts," rather than "applied psychology"* (Ash & Sturm, 2004a). Speaking in this way acknowledges that the practical realm, too, has a history of its own, and—far from being only on the receiving end of academic work—has had specific impacts on basic science (Schönpflug, 1992). Changes in society and culture have created practical problems that generated demand for psychological as well as other kinds of knowledge, whether or not basic science was prepared to meet that demand. Sometimes academic psychologists have tried to adapt existing research practices to meet this demand; at other times new techniques have been created by practitioners—who often enough were not psychologists—quite independently of developments in basic science. But at the same time, enhanced public attention to particular social problems led to the development of new methodological instruments, such as intelligence tests and personality inventories, that have had significant feedback effects on research in academic psychology.

Thus, both in theoretically oriented and practical areas, interactions between academic, psychology, and other fields, and also between psychology, culture ,and society have taken place, in which psychology has not only been the giving, but often enough the receiving discipline; as a result, the breadth and scope of the discipline have changed continuously. Put in the terms of this volume, the territories of psychology are not fixed, but fluid. This is not a cause for hand-wringing, but rather a historical fact that is true not only of psychology, but of all of the human sciences. The contributions to this volume support this view and develop its implications in detail.

TRANSDISCIPLINARY THEMES

The breadth and complexity of the issues at stake plainly require an interdisciplinary approach. Just as war is too important to be left to the generals (as a former general, Dwight David Eisenhower, once said), historical forms of psychological thought and practice are too varied and widespread for their study to be left to psychologists. In any case, an interdisciplinary approach works best when the topics considered are transdisciplinary in the first place. Such transdisciplinary themes have guided the discussions of the Berlin-Brandenburg Academy of Science's interdisciplinary working group "Psychological Thought and Practice in Historical and Interdisciplinary Perspective," selected results of which are presented in this volume. (For overviews of the group's program and research, see Ash, 2001; Ash & Sturm, 2002, 2003, 2004b, and the Web site of the group on the homepage of the Academy: http:www/bbaw.de/bbaw/Forschung/Forschungsprojekte/psychologie/en/Startseite).

Three transdisiplinary themes have guided the group's discussions:

1. Meanings of psychological concepts in different disciplines, and in everyday life;
2. Roles of instruments in psychological research;
3. Technological and personal applications of psychology.

Previous results of the group's work on psychology in practical contexts have been presented in a special issue of the German journal, *Zeitschrift für Psychologie* (Ash & Sturm, 2004a). Results of the group's work on the roles of instruments in the history of psychological research have appeared in a special issue of *History of Psychology* (see Sturm & Ash, 2005). This volume presents results relating to all three themes, with emphasis on the first and second topics. As will soon be clear, each theme has two dimensions.

PSYCHOLOGICAL CONCEPTS IN DIFFERENT DOMAINS: SHARED OR DIVIDED MEANINGS?

Interdisciplinary collaboration occurs more often in some fields of psychology than in others, but there is general agreement that cooperation with the biological sciences on the one hand and the social sciences and humanities on the other could be intensified. One obstacle to such cooperation is that psychological concepts appear to have different meanings in different disciplines. Sometimes it almost seems as though neuroscientists, philosophers, or historians, for example, use psychological terminology without checking first to see how psychologists may have refined the meanings of such terms during decades of research and discussion. Do the psychological concepts used in these disciplines in fact have the same meanings, or do the same terms have different meanings in different disciplines? And how are these differences to be evaluated?

Similarly, though "psychobabble" is everywhere in popular culture and the media, its impact on psychological thinking as it occurs within the discipline, if any, needs clarification. Just what are the relationships of academic and non-academic psychology? How much is scientific psychology affected even today by pre- or nonscientific concepts of human thinking, feeling, and action? To what extent can or should psychology "liberate" itself from or even replace everyday psychology? Can the concepts of everyday psychology be retained, but made more precise with the help of scientific research? Perhaps it will be helpful to divide this vast thematic domain into two subtopics: meanings of psychological concepts in different disciplines; and shared uses of concepts in academic psychology and in the surrounding cultures.

Meanings of Psychological Concepts in Different Disciplines. Much of the sociological literature on the differentiation of scientific disciplines or of professions from one another assumes that the establishment of new fields either resulted in, or was based on, a clear distinction of that field's subject matter from that of other disciplines (Abbott, 1988; Gieryn, 1999; Stichweh, 1994). Historical research over the past few decades has given us a much better appreciation of the intellectual and institutional struggles that were necessary in specific circumstances to achieve such differentiations. Thomas Gieryn (1999) has called such struggles "boundary work." A related but different view is that such distinctions are artifacts of the need to define scientific (sub)communities, rather than of discoveries about how things actually are. In the case of experimental psychology in 19th-century Germany, at least, things indeed began this way. Wundt and others limited psychology to the study of the processes of consciousness, and those who did this with experimental techniques and brass instruments plainly distinguished themselves from humanist philosophers like Wilhelm Dilthey or Heinrich Rickert, for whom the sort of sophisticated everday psychology familiar to educated Germans was more than sufficient for the practice of history or other human sciences (Ash, 1995; Ash, 1999). But even this definition of the new discipline did not prove to be binding for long, even in Germany (see Danziger, 1990).

Perhaps it is more correct to speak not of one, but of many conceptual "objects" of psychological thought, for example soul, consciousness, emotion, cognition, behavior, voluntary action, motivation, personality, or social interaction. Whether the subject matter is single or multiple, the constructions of these psychological "objects" have plainly changed over time, their relative weight within the discipline of psychology has always been controversial, and they have always been discussed in rather different ways by nonpsychologists as well as psychologists (Danziger, 1997). It might be noted here in passing that this is by no means true only of psychology; scientific "objects" in other fields of knowledge have also had complex careers (Daston, 2000, 2004).

In order to understand how this works in fields outside psychology, consider, for example, the well-known construct called *homo oeconomicus*. This concept, like that of the "reasonable person" in legal theory, is based on a theory of the subject or of "human nature," but that theory differs considerably from the concepts of personality or motivation that have come to be used in academic psychology (Kirchgässner, 1991; Bowler, 2005). Seen historically, one could make the point this way: In the early modern period (from the 16th through the 18th centuries), particular constructions of the subject became metatheoretical foundations of disciplines and professions with central roles in the construction of modern society. Because these constructs—not empirical hypotheses about what and how humans are and how they behave, but rather normative assumptions about what the theorists in questions wished humans ideally to be—were foundational to the disciplines and professions in question, they were insulated from empirical examination of any kind, and thus also from disproof by psychologists, once that discipline emerged in the late 19th century.

Recent histories of psychology sometimes provide thorough accounts of these early modern conceptions of human nature and the subject, but then leave off further discussion of the topic once they reach the founding era of the discipline (see, e.g., Schönpflug, 2004). In my opinion this is a serious mistake. If we imagine for a moment the ways in which such constructs—normative beliefs about "human nature"—actually shape the behavior of professional practitioners in court rooms or in the formation of economic policy, we can see that the relationship—or lack of relationship—between such beliefs and the approaches of modern psychology is not only an academic issue in the pejorative sense of that word, but one that has practical relevance for our understanding of the ways modern society works, or fails to work.

Some further remarks about *homo oeconomicus* might help to clarify this point further. Ordinarily, economic behavior is supposed to be based on a very specific form of rationality—calculations of comparative advantage or marginal utility. But how "rational" was Adam Smith's original "economic man"? Emma Rothschild (2001) and others have shown that what Smith called "moral sentiments" were just as central to prevailing concepts of human nature in the Enlightenment as supposedly objective rationality. For Smith (2000/1776), for example, people wish by nature to engage in economic dealings, and also wish these dealings to be fair, meaning satisfactory to both parties. Plainly this is not a way of thinking that posits the profit motive as a human universal and the individual as a profit maximizer at others' expense. The reduction of the concept of value to economic value in the narrower sense appears to have happened long after *The Wealth of Nations* was published, and then attributed back to Smith. Only in this way could efforts to develop quantifiable models of marginal utility be viewed as part of a tradition that Smith began.

As a result, the psychological dimension of economic theory has sometimes been reduced to the behavior of groups, for example the entrepreneurs discussed by Joseph Schumpeter (1987/1942), whose behavior is regarded as being deviant from the accepted normative model and thus in particular need of explanation. The Austrian theorist Ludwig von Mises (1949, 1981/1933) understood that any economic theory was also a theory of intentional action, and that efforts to explain such behavior at the level of individual decisions with mathematical models might be futile. In reaction to such scepticism, Neumann and Morgenstern (1980/1944) developed game theory—efforts to discover basic rules of economic behavior at the level of individuals' interactions with one another—which, in turn, has led in recent years to fruitful cooperation of economists and psychologists, as well as to Nobel Prizes for outstanding economists using this approach. Gerd Gigerenzer (2001) and others have made productive use of Herbert Simon's (1997) concept of bounded rationality, meaning an empirically grounded concept of rational choice different from that of the model builders. The relevant point here is that psychological concepts of some kind have never disappeared from economic thought; only different constructions of the psychical have been involved.

Topics such as learning, memory, or intelligence have also been defined differently in different disciplines, even though the same words continue to be used in each case. This is particularly clear in the case of memory (see, e.g., Draaisma, 2000). When historians talk about "places of memory" (Koshar, 1998; Nora, 2001), they refer to a concept of collective cultural remembrance that is plainly different from the concept of memory as a cognitive process in individuals as studied by psychologists, or the notion of unconsciously repressed memories allegedly recovered by victims of childhood abuse (Hult, 2005). Nonetheless, the tension between memory as a process of storage and retrieval on the one hand and remembering as a process of cognitive or cultural (re)construction is common to both discourses (Assmann, 1997). Historical research can help us learn how this came to be so, and also to discover whether and how such parallel or shared vocabularies may become sites of interactions between psychology and other disciplines. Even within psychology, controversies over memory led to changes in the territory of the discipline; as Danziger (2001) has shown, Wundt and Ebbinghaus differed not only over whether memory could be studied by experimental means, but presupposed different conceptions of memory itself.

***Interactions Between Academic and non-Academic ("Everyday")
Psychology.*** The psychological thinking of ordinary people has been a topic in cognition research for some time. The term in German is *All-*

tagspsychologie, which plainly refers to psychological concepts as used in daily life and is best translated as "everyday psychology." The corresponding term in English, *folk psychology*, seems to me to be quite misleading in comparison with the German term. Be that as it may, researchers recognize that many psychological concepts, such as intelligence or anxiety, are themselves part of everyday language. Given that language is plainly a social institution, it is a short step from here to the thesis that everyday psychology itself is a social construction (Kusch, 1999). Issues of this kind often create opportunities for "boundary work" in the discipline: In the process, highly specific, sometimes rather strange-sounding vocabularies proliferate within psychology, in part to establish discursive communities linked by common use of sophisticated-sounding psychological terms deemed more precise than, and therefore superior to, "naïve" everyday psychology. Rather than simply repeating such boundary work or joining long-standing and widespread critiques of proliferating neologisms in psychology, it might be more useful in this context to consider the varied ways in which mutual interactions, translations, or feedback between academic and non-academic discourses about psychical phenomena take place. What we have learned about such interactions suggests that the popularization of psychological research results and theories is only one such relationship among many.

Here as well, historical reflections offer potentially promising insights. Two concepts shared by academic and everyday psychology for which historical studies are already available are "intelligence" and "character."

In the case of "intelligence," John Carson (1993) has shown that during the mass use of intelligence tests in the United States Army during the First World War, the interaction of two emerging professions—applied psychology and the professional officer corps—reshaped both the aims of intelligence testing, the test instrument itself and ultimately conceptions of the object being assessed. Intelligence became not intellectual or problem-solving capacity alone, but a sum of skills and (presumed hereditary) aptitudes for certain kinds of learning (see also Zenderland, 1998).

In the case of "character," systematic studies of so called "characterology" (in German: *Charakterologie* or *Charakterkunde*) have been pursued since the 18th century by both scholars and laypeople. Popular in the late 18th and early 19th century was an approach called "physiognomics," which purported to be able to "read" personal qualities from facial and bodily expressions. During the 1920s this field reemerged in Weimar, Germany and became a site of competition between, and cooperation among, academics and non-academics (for the following, see

Hau & Ash, 2000). For example, psychiatrist Ernst Kretschmer's effort to correlate personality and body types was taken up quickly by experimental psychologists in an effort to determine whether styles of behavior or cognition might also be linked with "character" types. At the same time, racial theorists like Hans F. K. Günther and Ludwig Ferdinand Clauß developed their own intuition-based inventories of facial features, body types, behavioral styles and personality characteristics allegedly "typical" of the various German and non-German peoples (Hau, 2003). Another trend of the period involved academic and nonacademic approaches to character diagnostics under the heading of expression studies. These were initially promoted in explicit opposition to "school psychology" by the self-styled philosopher and handwriting expert Ludwig Klages, but the notion of personality-specific facial expressions, for example, was soon incorporated into character diagnostics by Philipp Lersch and others. All of these approaches fed into the personality diagnostics used in officer selection by the German military, which ultimately became central to the professionalization of psychology in Nazi Germany—while "race psychology" was discarded because it failed to work in the practical contexts involved (Ash, 2002; Geuter, 1992).

The chapters in Part I of this volume focus primarily on the ways that psychological concepts have been and continue to be treated in different disciplines, as well as on the relations between psychological and everyday constructions of mental concepts. Three such conceptual fields have been selected for discussion here: attention, intentional action or will, and the self. In each of these areas there has been and continues to be strong interaction between academic and everyday psychology. Indeed, these studies suggest that a cyclical interaction occurs. Everyday mental concepts are taken up and operationalized, while everyday techniques of prediction and explanation are investigated and modified by academic psychology. Through applications, for example in therapies, journalistic writings and popular scientific literature, these concepts then find their way back into public discourse and often enough modified yet again, and the cycle continues.

In his chapter on "fluctuations of attention," Sven Lüders (chap. 1, this volume) presents a concrete example of the cyclical interaction of everyday and scientific psychological concepts by showing how the everyday concept of attention was operationalized in two sciences, physiology and experimental psychology, in the first third of the 20th century, and how both scientific and everyday language constructions of the concept affected its use in applied psychology. In the process, he critiques the claim by cultural theorist Jonathan Crary (2000) that such scientific technologies of observation, as Crary calls them, were formative of modernity itself.

In the following chapters, Jochen Brandtstädter (chap. 2, this volume), Wolfgang Prinz (chap. 3, this volume), Michael Heidelberger (chap. 4, this volume), and Sabine Maasen (chap. 5, this volume) investigate philosophical, psychological, and daily life explanations of mental phenomena such as intentional action and what is generally called *free will*. Maasen's chapter is discussed in the final section of this introduction. Brandtstädter takes a nonreductionistic position. Although the idea of intentionality—that is, the directed or intentional character of consciousness and action—may even be constitutive for psychology's definition of itself as a discipline, Maasen argues, the emergence and development of intentional phenomena, such as attitudes, opinions, ideas, wishes or actions, cannot actually be explained from the standpoint of intentionality. Rather, as, studies of the genesis and control of mental states and other psychological phenomena show, intentional and non-intentional aspects affect one another.

Wolfgang Prinz (chap. 3, this volume) argues in his chapter that the idea that the human will is free is incompatible with the program of a scientific psychology. Nonetheless, people (at least nowadays and in so-called "Western" culture) feel and understand themselves as being free agents. Prinz outlines two psychological research questions connected to this fact that, however, have rarely been pursued: (1) Why do people feel free in their choices and believe that they are free, although recent brain research appears to show that they are not—that is, that relevant neurophysiological processes actually occur before, and not in response to, subjects' seemingly volitional commands; and under which conditions does this intuition arise? (2) What role does the intuition of freedom play for the persons who develop it? What psychological, social, and cultural effects do these intuitions encourage? Prinz argues that in both of these contexts, we should not understand free will as a naturally given mental capacity but, rather, as a social institution.

In response to Prinz's position (in particular to the more radical version of it in Prinz, 1996), Michael Heidelberger (chap. 4, this volume) offers a scathing philosophical critique of recent challenges to the belief in free will by brain researchers and cognitive neuroscientists. Far from being a defense of everyday psychological notions of free will, however, Heidelberger's position is a call for philosophical rationality. As he argues, such attacks on free will are inconsistent with the beliefs the same scientists hold while doing their own experiments, and thus undermine both the scientific enterprise itself and the claims of science to improve society by providing it with better knowledge. In addition, he argues, they could have a disastrous impact on the fruitful cooperation between philosophers of science and cognitive scientists that has been developing for decades.

Finally, the chapters by Jill Morawski (chap. 6, this volume), Kenneth Gergen (chap. 7, this volume), and Thomas Sturm (chap. 8, this volume) focus on the concept of self. General historians have recently taken up this topic by asking whether different political regimes implicitly posit, or in some cases even try to create, different kinds of "selves," meaning citizens as objects of political power relations (see, for example, Egighian, 2004). Jill Morawski approaches the topic by investigating the history of the ways in which psychologists talked about themselves as researchers, and about their subjects as producers of material for scientific treatment, during the early history of academic psychology in the United States. As Morawski argues, by introducing techniques such as quantification, aggregate statistical methods, and nominal classification of subjects, psychologists transformed the objects of their analysis, replacing particularities about subjects, their sensitivities and subjectivities with subjects rendered anonymous and purportedly passive actors, their thoughts and behaviors represented solely through experimenters' terms or numbers. In parallel to this process experimenters emerged who no longer themselves generated objects of analysis or engaged in self-reflection (introspection) but, rather, came to regard themselves largely as scientific practitioners of objective research techniques. Thus, psychologists dealt with the problematic relations between scientific and everyday psychology by constructing two kinds of self-concepts that were in tension with one another. Strack and Schwarz (chap. 10, this volume) consider the methodological issues involved here in Part II of this volume, with particular reference to the use of questioning in research. Morawski places this complex transformation of self concepts in the context of changing conditions of personhood and identity in American culture during the early 20th century.

Kenneth Gergen (chapter 7, this volume) shows that the cyclical interaction of everyday and academic psychology has worked particularly prominently in the case of so called "mental deficits." As psychological concepts like "depression" have been used more frequently in ordinary life, Gergen argues, people have come to been seen—and to see themselves—more often and more easily as mentally ill. As they seek professional help more frequently, psychology reacts to this increasing demand, and the cycle continues. Gergen explains such cycles by arguing that psychological phenomena are socially constructed in any case, and that such constructions depend in turn on intellectual and financial interests. However, though he calls the process "colonization," he acknowledges that it need not result from deliberate strategies by psychologists in order to be effective.

Thomas Sturm (chap. 8, this volume) argues that there is a conceptual fragmentation in talk about "the self" between psychologists and philosophers. One way to resolve it is to compare philosophical and psychological perspectives on phenomena such as self-knowledge or self-control, in order to clarify how the self, or rather talk about the self, figures in such phenomena. Sturm applies this approach to self-deception. One could imagine a disciplinary division of labor between philosophical analysis of the everyday concept of self-deception on the one hand and empirical psychological studies of the origins and functions of self-deception on the other hand, but such a convenient division has problems of its own. As Sturm argues, it is not possible to establish a single correct concept of self deception with philosophical analysis alone; indeed, some philosophers have seriously doubted that such a thing as self-deception is logically possible. Nonetheless, psychologists and philosophers still have areas for fruitful discussion, for example the question of the rationality or irrationality of the phenomenon.

THE ROLES OF INSTRUMENTS IN PSYCHOLOGICAL RESEARCH

What relevance do research instruments have for this discussion? A link between this issue and topic area one becomes clear when we acknowledge that instruments and the systematic introduction to their use also forms an important aspect of the "boundary work" of the discipline, in that it separates authorized from non-authorized practitioners of psychological science. Psychologists working in basic science often appear to assume that the methodologically organized, and in this sense disciplined and replicable, use of instruments assures scientific objectivity and thus insulates, even liberates science from the vague intuitiveness of everyday usages. This belief appears to hold whether the instruments involved are large, expensive pieces of equipment or paper tools such as questionnaires and personality inventories. Researchers may assume, further, that instruments are no more than neutral tools, and that problems with them can be solved simply be improving their functioning, in a way analogous to difficulties with machines that need repair. Recent work in history and philosophy of science suggests, however, that instruments and their uses are shaped by researchers' theoretical commitments, and in some cases may even determine research agendas (Sturm & Ash, 2005). What implications do answers to such questions have for the interaction of psychology with other disciplines, such as the neurosciences, and what implications could such technical-sounding debates possibly have for wider cultural issues?

The term *instrument*, as it is used here, includes all means employed to achieve repeatable, standardized production of specific phenomena or effects. Apparatus as well as routinized methods of observation and data interpretation can and should be included in this broad definition of the term, whether these involve metal, plastic, or paper tools. Viewed in this wide sense, instruments can be and frequently are employed both in research as well as in professional practices in psychology. The chapters in Part II of this volume look more closely at two particular issues within this broad field of study: instruments as organizers of psychological research practices, and instruments as metaphors for the "objects" of psychology itself. In both cases, tools can serve and have served as mediators between disciplines as well as between psychology and its wider cultural context. At times a cyclical process appears that is surprisingly analogous to the circulation of psychological concepts discussed in Part I.

Instruments as Organisers of Psychological Research Practices. Recent literature on the history of research practices in the natural sciences and the "experimental systems" organized around them has shown convincingly that new apparatus—as small as a microcentrifuge or as large as a particle accelerator—can initiate or even organize research programs just as well as theories can (Hacking, 1992; Rheinberger, 1997b). Moreover, and contrary to a more traditional view in philosophy of science that limits the use of instruments to theory testing, this literature emphasizes the basic openness of "experimental systems"; scientists follow them wherever they may lead, and the theoretical issues involved, if any, may turn out to follow the apparatus rather than the other way around. In psychology as well, terms like *data-driven* or *apparatus-driven research* have become familiar. The implications of such processes—doing something because the instruments are there to do it with—and the concomitant fixation on the data that measuring apparatus can produce are often discussed and criticized, but seldom placed in historical context.

On the basis of a large number of examples taken mainly from the "brass instrument" psychology of the turn of the 20th century, Horst Gundlach (chap. 9, this volume) asks a deceptively simple question: What are psychological research instruments? By this, Gundlach means to ask not only what instruments psychologists have used, but also what makes them *psychological*, rather than physiological, neuroscientific, or other kinds of instruments. His answer is that this question is decided not only by technology or instrument design, but also by the contexts in which such instruments are used. Of course, the context of use includes, but need not be limited to, the (psychological) questions that the data produced by the instrument are alleged to answer, and the inferences to be drawn from the data, in this case inferences about psychological processes alleged to cause the responses being measured.

The article sets the agenda for this part of volume by focusing on interactions between psychology and other scientific disciplines as mediated by research instruments and the practices associated with them.

As already noted, instruments that are used in psychological research are not always made of brass or other hard substances, but can be and indeed very often are paper tools. Fritz Strack and Norbert Schwarz (chap. 10, this volume) discuss the use of questioning as a research method, and thus focus on the paper tools that have long been predominant in academic and applied psychology. Given that asking questions is also a common way of obtaining information in everyday life, they also address indirectly the relations of scientific and everyday psychology. As Strack and Schwarz show, the influence of the order and the concrete formulations of questions on the behavior of subjects can be demonstrated, and they argue that psychological testing theory must take such findings into account. They then discuss different models with which these demonstrated influences can be brought under theoretical control.

Part II continues with three chapters on the roles of instruments in the interaction of psychology and neuroscience. These combine both aspects of the broader issues raised in this part of the volume. As Paul Baltes cogently states in his Foreword to this volume, the degree to which interest in psychological subject matter is influenced by the availability, constraints, and development of instrumentation "is in part a question of theory–method alignments, but it is also a question of disciplinary power and preferences. Who is in control of instruments, who has the financial resources to develop new methods, for what purpose? What is the long-range consequence of the availability of such instrumentation for psychological work in theory and practice, and how does this impact concretely on research agendas?"

Instrumentation from brain research, such as the EEG, has played a significant role in cognition research for decades, in combination with other methods taken from experimental psychology (Rösler, 2005). At the same time, brain researchers have long claimed to have privileged access to the psyche (Hagner, 1996). Current brain research, and particularly neuroimaging and other visualization techniques, are now having such a major impact on cognitive science that a leading segment of the field has been renamed cognitive neuroscience. In addition, at least some brain researchers clearly want to argue that their instruments can or will soon make psychological processes visible; if there is anything to such controversial claims, they would have fundamental implications for any model of or metaphor for the mind.

Gerhard Roth with collaborators Thomas F. Münte and Hans-Jochen Heinze (chap. 11, this volume) and Rainer Bösel (chap. 12, this volume) consider from different standpoints the question of what phenomena can in fact be "captured" or made visible with neuroscientific techniques. As Roth and collaborators write, modern neuroscience maintains that all affective-emotional processes are coupled to neural processes in specific brain regions. Though they acknowledge that attempts to delineate the neurobiological foundations of affective-emotional states and of psychiatric disorders with the aid of structural and functional imaging methods are still at very initial steps, they nonetheless maintain that states of the "psyche" can be visualized by modern neuroimaging methods. In this case, one might well ask two questions: first, what in fact is being "imaged," psychical or neuronal processes; and second, are the techniques in question only instrumental or also rhetorical? Are psychological processes now being made visible by neuroscientific apparatus, as Roth and collaborators argue, or are pieces of equipment and spectacular images being used as tools in a rhetorical strategy to make people *believe* that this has happened?

Rainer Bösel (chapter 12, this volume) counters such suspicions by arguing that, although one can indeed achieve far more today with imaging and other techniques than before, we are still far away from being able to provide sufficient neuronal explanations for all psychical phenomena. Specifically, Bösel argues that that there is an important time lag between neurological processes and corresponding conscious acts, not because free will is an illusion, as Prinz (chap. 3, this volume) argues elsewhere in this volume, but because voluntary acts are coordinated according to the history of subjective experience and previously established strategies. This suggests that unless psychologists and neuroscientists work more closely together, the successes of the neurosciences might literally change the subject. New answers to new questions might thus be discovered, whereas the classical questions psychologists have asked about the relation between mental and neuronal events would remain unanswered.

In strong contrast to the technology-centered discussions of Roth and coworkers as well as Bösel, Michael Hagner (chapter 13, this volume) presents a perspective from cultural history. As he shows, hopes of making mental processes directly visible are very old indeed, and have been expressed—or satirized—most vigorously in fictional literature, for example by the avant-garde German writer Georg Büchner, who was himself a physician by training. Hagner then discusses how literary and scientific discussions of this question have interacted continuously from the nineteenth century to the present. Finally, he provocatively describes what he calls the "fictional" elements in current (over)confident proclamations by neuroscientists and by their allies in the media. In Hagner's view, poetic dreams about brain mirrors and mind reading have been kept alive mainly by the sense of uncanny possibility that they evoke. The simple fact that a category mistake is involved—that the metabolic processes in the brain being recorded by neuroimaging techniques obviously do not "think" in any coherent sense of the word—suggests, in his view, that the current controversy may say more about the need to make exaggerated claims in order to gain media attention, and thus to use cultural resources to attract research support, than they do about the science involved.

Instruments as Metaphors for Psychological "Objects".　Instruments have not only been central to the organization of psychological research programs, but in certain cases their functioning has often been taken as a model or metaphor for psychological operations. An example of what is meant from the period of the emergence of natural scientific psychology is research on the senses as "apparatus" in the 19th century, described by Crary (1990), Hoffmann (2001) and others. In the same period, the "sensitivity" of sensory discrimination was considered to be analogous to the calibration of machine tools (Gundlach, chap. 9, this volume). Seen in this light, it is not a coincidence that the notion of what Lorraine Daston (1992) has called "instrumental objectivity" emerged during the industrial age in the 19th century, which even contemporaries called an age of machines. In this and other cases (see Ash, 2003) the use of instrument metaphors links science and culture quite directly. The cultural impact of new technologies leads researchers to talk about psychological processes in new ways, and such talk is more easily accepted because it makes the technologized life world of modernity seem more natural.

Such ways of talking, and such analogies between the workings of the mind and those of machines, have hardly been limited to the formative period of the human sciences. Indeed, it might be suggested that these disciplines have always taken cues in their thinking from the leading technologies of their time and place. Classical examples of such transformations in the 20th century are the role of the telephone network as a metaphor or analogy for the central nervous system, or the functioning of the computer as a metaphor for perception and thought processes (Gigerenzer & Goldstein, 1996). Examples in which not a piece of equipment, but a "soft" technology is involved are cases in which a calculation or a (statistical) assessment technique have taken over such a metaphorical role, such as intelligence or personality concepts based on the factor analytic techniques used to treat the research results, and the concept of humans as "intuitive statisticians" based on the Baysian statistics employed to assess the significance of research data in cognition research (Gigerenzer, 1992).

In their contribution to this volume, Gerd Gigerenzer and Thomas Sturm (chap. 14, this volume) focus primarily on the ways in which, since the so-called "cognitive revolution" of the 1960s, the human mind itself has been theoretically described as an instrument, for example as an "intuitive statistician" or as a computer program. They argue that such theories have been strongly inspired by specific tools—inferential statistics and the digital computer—that were introduced into psychological research somewhat before the spreading of such theories within the psychological community, and suggest that some psychological research tools can provide metaphors for psychological theories whereas others do not. As they show, such metaphors can be advantageous, but using them can also raise the danger of self-vindication.

TECHNICAL AND PERSONAL APPLICATIONS
OF PSYCHOLOGY

What does it mean when we speak of "applied psychology"? The word "application" in ordinary language—and in contemporary computer software lingo—suggests a practical extension of already established knowledge from basic research, as in a software program. However, this relationship is by no means as linear as generally supposed. Applications-oriented research may use many of the same instruments and techniques as so called basic research, but it turns out to have its own history (Schönpflug, 1992). Could it be that the line of influence flows just as often from contexts of application to basic science as the other way around? More provocative still: Are the many uses of psychological techniques in personal life discussed in popular culture, symbolized by injunctions to "work on a relationship" or engage in "self management," also examples of applied psychology; and if not, then what do they represent? Such questions are clearly connected with the problem of the relationship of academic and everyday psychology, raised in Part I.

From this starting point the working group has considered two topic areas: "psychotechnics," meaning the methods developed from the turn of the 20th century onward to optimize production of individuals and factory units in industry and elsewhere by paying more attention to the "human factor"; and the myriad reflexive applications of psychological techniques in personal life. As just mentioned, discussions of the first aspect of the topic have been published in a special issue of the German journal, *Zeitschrift für Psychologie* (Ash & Sturm, 2004). The chapter by Lüders in Part I also addresses this topic area. Several other chapters in the volume discuss personal applications of psychology. Seen from the perspective of social and cultural history, both kinds of applications of psychological knowledge belong to the history of what Perkin (1996) has called the expert society.

"Mind games" of various kinds have been around for a very long time. A random list of examples would include Zen practices, the spiritual exercises of St. Ignatius de Loyola, the agonized "soul-searching" of English and American Puritans, as well as the passionate introspections of Karl Philip Moritz and his colleagues in the *Magazin für Erfahrungsseelenkunde* in the late 18th century (Moritz, Pockels & Maimon, 1783–1793). In the 1920s, approaches emerged that could be called reflexive or self-applications of psychology, which were offered to wider publics and not only to the adepts of sects. One example is the autosuggestive relaxation technique developed by the German psychotherapist Johannes Heinrich Schultz (1991/1932), which he called "autogenic training," and which is still in use.

From such modest beginnings, an entire field of reflexive practices has emerged, with particular intensity since the 1960s, in which everyday psychological knowledge(s) have been given the appearance of technical tools and put on offer by a wide variety of practitioners to improve productivity through self-knowledge or group awareness in management training workshops, to raise the quality of childrearing, or to increase individual well-being in numerous kinds of psychotherapy (Herman, 1996, 2003; Moscowitz, 2001; for historical background, see Richards, 2002; Shamdasani, 2005).

Nikolas Rose (1990, 1996) and others have suggested that these techniques, and the "work on one's self" they all claim to involve, have become a fundamental feature of late modern societies and cultures. Precisely because it is so diffuse and widespread, Rose argues, psychological knowledge shapes the practices of welfare states and justifies them with a rationale, according to which individuals are required to be free, and feel obligated to correct or repair defects if they fail to cope on their own. In this view, technical and self applications of psychology are two sides of the same coin: both involve "optimization," albeit from two rather different perspectives.

In Part I of this volume, Sabine Maasen (chap. 5, this volume) contributes to this discussion by comparing the self-help literature of the 1920s and that of today, focusing particularly on constructions of the concept of will in the two periods. As Maasen argues, in modern life the government of others is closely linked with practices in which free individuals are enjoined to govern themselves as both free and responsible subjects. To this end, self-help manuals do not themselves prescribe any particular action or values, but 'train' us to decide for ourselves. This self-help literature often refers to psychological knowledge and the practices of counseling and psychotherapy, but it also draws from other sources, such as manuals designed to refine manners and educate virtues. Whereas, in the 1920s, self-help manuals aimed to help male employees establish strong, fixed identities, today's self-help books and techniques advocate (male and female) "enterprising selves," capable of managing various tasks efficiently.

In his concluding chapter James Capshew (chap. 15, this volume) combines such considerations with the history of psychology as a discipline when he describes the increasing emphasis on what he calls "reflexivity" in psychology since World War II. By "reflexivity" Capshew means, first, the awareness that psychologists are themselves part of the subject matter of their own discipline, and, second, that working on people's selves, meaning their identities and personal problems, has become an increasingly important purpose of psychological practice. Thus, his chapter describes developments in postwar American psychology that parallel, but cannot be equated with, those described in Maasen's contribution, and also connects with Morawski's discussion of psychologists' selves and those of their subjects self included in Part I. As Capshew shows, reflexivity in the first sense—the awareness that psychologists are part of their own research—was initially suppressed during the formative period of academic psychology, but has become an increasingly acknowledged feature of psychological thinking within the discipline since the 1940s. One reason for this, he shows further, is the increasing demand for reflexivity in the second sense—the emergence of what Roger Smith (1998) has called "psychological society," and the corresponding need for expert assistance in self-improvement, or for expert repair of damaged selves. Capshew concludes his analysis by suggesting that culture-oriented narrative approaches can complement what he calls "paradigmatic," natural, or social science oriented approaches.

Self-oriented applications of psychology often evoke mixed feelings. Some may think that the enormous popularity and wide circulation of self-help literature harms the image of the discipline, but others point out that psychology cannot simply ignore the well established and rapidly growing societal demand for such "knowledge." In any case, it is certainly appropriate to ask why certain uses of psychology in practical contexts, such as those employed in industry, are widely ignored in public discourse, whereas others, such as intelligence testing and self-help literature, attract almost obsessive attention in the media and thus have continued to shape the public image of psychology from the early twentieth century until the present.

CONCLUSION: DILEMMAS SOLVABLE AND UNSOLVABLE

The restaurant chapters in this volume outline a number of routes into a potentially vast field of research. As I stated at the beginning of this introduction, psychology has become a protean discipline, suspended between methodological orientations derived from the physical and biological sciences and a subject matter extending into the social and human sciences. One of the obvious dilemmas this discipline has faced from the outset might be called the limits of scientism. Liam Hudson's *The Cult of the Fact* (Hudson, 1972) is a polemical book title that stands for an ever-renewed accusation: By limiting itself to what it can do with "scientific" methods, psychology makes itself ever less relevent to broader human concerns. A common reply to such critiques is a countercritique—that efforts to address such concerns without sufficient grounding in scientific method have distinguished themselves often enough by their pretentious vagueness, nonfalsifiability, and sloppy approach to empirical data. Interestingly enough, both of these viewpoints have found expression during the recent controversy on Loren Slater's popular book on psychological experiments in the 20th century (Slater, 2004), which shows that even ostensibly historical accounts have become resources for such arguments.

Perhaps more fruitful than such debates are sophisticated efforts by researchers like Herbert Simon and Gerd Gigerenzer, described above, to incorporate critiques of scientism productively by using concepts like "bounded rationality" to broaden the reach of scientific psychology. The use of implicit psychologies in other human sciences, as described earlier in the case of economics, are efforts to resolve this dilemma in different way.

A second and perhaps more discomfiting dilemma might be named by posing another often-asked question: Who is an expert if everybody is an expert? Psychologists and others like nowadays to talk about "expert systems," but that is not what is meant here. The fact that the psychology and the self-help sections in American bookstores are usually located next to one another—if they are separated at all—seems to me to indicate something more than the (admittedly) widespread foolishness of soft-headed consumers. I would suggest, instead, that this is one symptom of a dilemma that is probably unresolvable in principle, for the simple reason that it is built into the construction of the human sciences, and not only of psychology.

One could take this point still further and suggest that this dilemma is a subset of a paradox that is central to the history of modern thought, society and culture since the Enlightenment. Historians have detailed the ever-widening reach of expertise in modern society (Perkin, 1996; Porter, 1995). But the more widespread and sophisticated expert knowledge has become, the less respect nonscientists have for experts. This is true to some extent for all the sciences, but it is especially true in fields like psychology and the social sciences, where everyone from whose behavior the knowledges in question are derived and to whose behavior these knowledges are then "applied" in the form of policy thinks they already know something about what they think, feel and do.

The only serious answer to this dilemma currently on offer is the constantly repeated admonition to engage in a reflexive interaction between "experts" and "clients" that regards the latter as autonomous subjects who have some idea of what they want and who deserve respect. Ulrich Beck speaks in this context of "reflexive modernization," which includes the constant evaluation and self-evaluation of science and politics as well as quality control in the business world (Beck, Bonss & Lau, 2003; Beck, Giddens & Lash, 1994). Whether such reflexive processes can actually fulfill the Enlightenment's dreams of democratization, as Beck appears to hope, remains to be seen.

The material in this volume clearly has implications for many questions of current concern, for example the following: How can psychology respond to both the challenges from the neurosciences and other fields as well as to the continuing threats to its standing due to loose talk about psychological issues in popular culture? That all these issues have histories should also be clear. The authors believe that greater historical awareness and deeper theoretical reflection might help, on the one hand, to place current concerns and dilemmas in perspective, and, on the other hand, to deepen understanding of the complex interactions involved.

REFERENCES

Abbot, A. (1988). *The system of professions: An essay on the division of expert labor.* Chicago: University of Chicago Press.

Ash, M. G. (1992). Historicizing mind science: Discourse, practice, subjectivity. *Science in Context, 5,* 193–208.

Ash, M. G. (1995). *Gestalt psychology in German culture 1890–1967: Holism and the quest for objectivity.* New York: Cambridge University Press.

Ash, M. G. (1999). Psychologie in Deutschland um 1900: Reflexiver Diskurs des Bildungsbürgertums, Teilgebiet der Philosophie, akademische Disziplin [Psychology in Germany around 1900: Reflexive discourse of the educated middle class, subdiscipline of philosophy, academic discipline]. In C. König & E. Lämmert (Eds.), *Konkurrenten in der Fakultät. Kulturwissenschaften um 1900* (pp. 78–93). Frankfurt am Main: Fischer Verlag.

Ash, M. G. (2001). Arbeitsgruppe Psychologisches Denken und psychologische Praxis in wissenschaftshistorischer und interdisziplinärer Perspektive [Working group "Psychological Thought and Practice in historical and interdisciplinary perspective"]. *Berlin-Brandenburgische Akademie der Wissenschaften, Jahrbuch 2000* (pp. 283–290). Berlin: Akademie-Verlag.

Ash, M. G. (2002). Psychologie. [Psychology.] In F.-R. Hausmann (Ed.), *Die Rolle der Geisteswissenschaften im Nationalsozialismus* (pp. 229–264). München: Oldenbourg Verlag.

Ash, M. G. (2003). Psychology. In D. Ross & T. Porter (Eds.), *Cambridge history of science, Vol. 7: The modern social sciences* (pp. 251–274). Cambridge, U.K.: Cambridge University Press.

Ash, M. G., & Sturm, T. (2002). Arbeitsgruppe Psychologisches Denken und psychologische Praxis in wissenschaftshistorischer und interdisziplinärer Perspektive [Working group "Psychological Thought and Practice in historical and interdisciplinary perspective"]. *Berlin-Brandenburgische Akademie der Wissenschaften, Jahrbuch 2001* (pp. 299–314). Berlin: Akademie-Verlag, 2002.

Ash, M. G., & Sturm, T. (2003). Arbeitsgruppe Psychologisches Denken und psychologische Praxis in wissenschaftshistorischer und interdisziplinärer Perspektive [Working group "Psychological Thought and Practice in historical and interdisciplinary perspective"]. *Berlin-Brandenburgische Akademie der Wissenschaften, Jahrbuch 2002* (pp. 267–280). Berlin: Akademie-Verlag.

Ash, M. G., & Sturm, T. (2004a). Die Psychologie in praktischen Kontexten— Einführende Bemerkungen [Psychology in practical contexts – introductory remarks]. *Zeitschrift für Psychologie, 202,* 177–182.

Ash, M. G., & Sturm, T. (2004b). Arbeitsgruppe Psychologisches Denken und psychologische Praxis in wissenschaftshistorischer und interdisziplinärer Perspektive [Working group "Psychological Thought and Practice in historical and interdisciplinary perspective"]. *Berlin-Brandenburgische Akademie der Wissenschaften, Jahrbuch 2003* (pp. 262–265). Berlin: Akademie-Verlag.

Assmann, A. (1997). *Erinnerungsräume. Formen und Wandlungen des kulturellen Gedächtnisses* [Spaces of remembrance: Forms and changes of cultural memory]. Munich: C. H. Beck.

Beck, U., Bonss, W., & Lau, C. (2003). The theory of reflexive modernization: Problematic, hypotheses and research programme. *Theory, Culture and Society, 20,* 1–33.

Beck, U., Giddens, A., & Lash, S. (1994). *Reflexive modernization. Politics, tradition, and aesthetics in the modern social order.* Stanford, CA: Stanford University Press.

Benschop, R., & Draaisma, D. (2000). In pursuit of precision: The calibration of minds and machines in late nineteenth-century psychology. *Annals of Science, 57,* 1–25.

Bowler, R. (2005). Sentient nature and human economy: The "human science" of early *Nationalökonomie. History of the Human Sciences, 18,* 23–54.

Carson, J. (1993). Army alpha, army brass and the search for army intelligence," *Isis, 84,* 278–309.

Crary, J. (1990). *Techniques of the observer. On vision and modernity in the nineteenth century.* Cambridge, MA: MIT Press.

Crary, J. (2000). *Suspensions of perception. Attention, spectacle, and modern culture* (2nd ed.). Cambridge, MA: MIT Press.

Danziger, K. (1990). *Constructing the subject: Historical origins of psychological research.* New York: Cambridge University Press.

Danziger, K. (1997). *Naming the mind: How psychology found its language.* London: Sage.

Danziger, K. (2001). Sealing off the discipline: Wilhelm Wundt and the psychology of memory. In C. G. Green & T. Teo (Eds.), *The transformation of psychology: Influences of nineteenth-century philosophy, technology and natural science* (pp. 45–63). Washington, DC: American Psychological Association.

Daston, L. (1992). Objectivity and the escape from perspective. *Social Studies of Science, 22,* 597–618.

Daston, L. (1995). The moral economy of science. In A. Thackray (Ed.), *Constructing knowledge in the history of science* (Vol. 10; pp. 1–27). Chicago: University of Chicago Press.

Daston, L. (Ed.) (2000). *Biographies of scientific objects.* Chicago: University of Chicago Press.

Daston, L. (Ed.) (2004). *Things that talk: Object lessons from art and science.* Brooklyn, NY: Zone Books.

Draaisma, D. (2000). *Metaphors of memory. A history of ideas about the mind* (P. Vincent, Trans.) Cambridge, U.K.: Cambridge University Press.

Egighian, G. (2004). The psychologization of the socialist self: East German forensic psychology and its deviants, 1945–1975. *German History, 22,* 181–205.

Galison, P. (2004). Image of self. In L. Daston (Ed.), *Things that talk: Object lessons from art and science* (pp. 257–294). Brooklyn, NY: Zone Books.

Geuter, U. (1992/1984). *The professionalization of psychology in Nazi Germany.* (R. Holmes, trans.). New York: Cambridge University Press. (Original work published 1984)

Gieryn, T. (1999). *Cultural boundaries of science: Credibility on the line.* Chicago: University of Chicago Press.

Gigerenzer, G. (1992). From tools to theories: Discovery in cognitive psychology. *Science in Context, 5,* 329–350.

Gigerenzer, G. (Ed.). (2001). *Bounded rationality: The adaptive toolbox.* Cambridge, MA: MIT Press.

Gigerenzer, G., & Goldstein, D. G. (1996). Mind as computer: Birth of a metaphor. *Creativity Research Journal, 9,* 131–144.

Hacking, I. (1992). The self-vindication of the laboratory sciences. In A. Pickering (Ed.), *Science as practice and culture* (pp. 29–64). Chicago: University of Chicago Press.

Hagner, M. (1996). Der Geist bei der Arbeit: Überlegungen zur visuellen Repräsentation cerebraler Prozesse [The mind at work: Considerations on the visual representation of cerebral processes]. In C. Borck (Ed.), *Anatomien medizinischen Wissens* (pp. 259–286). Frankfurt am Main: Fischer.

Hau, M. (2003). *The cult of health and beauty in Germany: A social history, 1890–1930.* Chicago: University of Chicago Press.

Hau, M., & Ash, M. G. (2000). Der normale Körper, seelisch erblickt. [The normal body, viewed from the soul]. In S. Gilman & C. Schmölders (Eds.), *Gesichter der Weimarer Republik. Eine physiognomische Kulturgeschichte* (pp. 12–31). Cologne: DuMont.

Herman, E. (1996). *The romance of American psychology.* Berkeley: University of California Press.

Herman, E. (2003). Psychologism and the child. In T. M. Porter & D. Ross (Eds.), *The Modern social sciences: The Cambridge history of science* (Vol. 7, pp. 649–662). Cambridge, U.K.: Cambridge University Press.

Hoffmann, C. (2001). Haut und Zirkel, ein Entstehungsherd: Ernst Heinrich Webers Untersuchungen "Über den Tastsinn." [Skin and compass, a place of origin: Ernst Heinrich Weber's study "On the sense of touch"]. In M. Hagner (Ed.),

Ansichten der Wissenschaftsgeschichte (pp. 191–226). Frankfurt am Main: Fischer.

Hudson, L. (1972). *The cult of the fact: A psychologist's autobiographical critique of his discipline.* New York: Harper & Row.

Hult, J. (2005). The re-emergence of memory recovery: Return of seduction theory and birth of survivorship. *History of the Human Sciences, 18,* 127–142.

Kirchgässner, G. (1991). *Homo oeconomicus: Das ökonomische Modell individuellen Verhaltens und seine Anwendung in den Wirtschafts-und Sozialwissenschaften* [Economic man: The economic model of individual behaviour and its application in the economic and social sciences]. Tübingen: Mohr.

Koshar, R. (1998). *Germany's transient pasts: Preservation and national memory in the twentieth century.* Chapel Hill, NC: University of North Carolina Press.

Kusch, M. (1999). *Psychological knowledge: A social history and philosophy.* London: Routledge.

Moritz, K. P., Pockels, K. F., & Maimon, S. (Eds.). (1783–1793). *Gnothi sauton magazin für Erfahrungsseelenkunde* (Vols. 1–10). Berlin: A. MyLius.

Moscowitz, E. (2001). *In therapy we trust: America's obsession with self-fulfillment.* Baltimore: Johns Hopkins University Press.

Nora, P. (Ed.) (2001). *Rethinking France: Les lieux des memoire, Vol. 1: The state.* (M. S. Trouille, Trans.). Chicago: University of Chicago Press.

Perkin, H. (1996). *The third revolution: Professional elites in the modern world.* London: Routledge.

Porter, T. M. (1995). *Trust in numbers: The pursuit of objectivity in science and public life.* Princeton, NJ: Princeton University Press.

Prinz, W. (1996). Freiheit oder Wissenschaft? [Freedom or science?] In M. von Cranach & K. Foppa (Eds.), *Freiheit des Entscheidens und Handelns. Ein Problem der nomologischen Psychologie* (pp. 86–103). Heidelberg: Asanger.

Rheinberger, H.-J. (1997a). Plädoyer für eine Wissenschaftsgeschichte des Experiments [Argument for a scientific history of the experiment]. *Theory Bioscience, 116,* 11–31.

Rheinberger, H.-J. (1997b). *Toward a history of epistemic things: Synthesizing proteins in the test tube.* Stanford, CA: Stanford University Press.

Richards, G. (2002). The psychology of psychology. A historically grounded sketch. *Theory and Psychology, 12,* 7–36.

Rösler, F. (2005). From single-channel recordings to brain-mapping devices: The impact of electroencephelography on experimental psychology. *History of Psychology, 8,* 95–117.

Rose, N. (1990). *Governing the soul.* London: Routledge.

Rose, N. (1996). *Inventing our selves: Psychology, power and personhood.* New York: Cambridge University Press.

Rothschild, E. (2003). *Economic Sentiments: Adam Smith, Condorcet, and the Enlightenment.* Cambridge, MA: Harvard University Press.

Schmidgen, H. (2005). Physics, ballistics, and psychology: A History of the chronoscope in/as context, 1845–1890. *History of Psychology, 8,* 46–78.

Schönpflug, W. (1992). Applied psychology: Newcomer with a long tradition. *Applied Psychology: An International Review, 42,* 5–30.

Schönpflug, W. (2004). *Geschichte und Systematik der Psychologie: Ein Lehrbuch für das Grundstudium* (2nd, Rev. ed.). History and systematic account of psychology: An introductory textbook. Weinheim: Beltz.

Schultz, J. H. (1991/1932). *Das Autogene Training: Konzentrierte Selbstentspannung. Versuch einer klinisch-praktischen Darstellung.* Stuttgart: Thieme. (Original work published 1932)

Schumpeter, J. A. (1942). *Capitalism, socialism, democracy.* New York: Harper.

Shamdasani, S. (2005). "Psychotherapy": The invention of a word. *History of the Human Sciences, 18,* 1–22.

Simon, H. (1997). *Models of bounded rationality: Empirically grounded economic reason.* Cambridge, MA: MIT Press.

Slater, L. (2004). *Opening Skinner's box: Great psychological experiments of the twentieth century.* London: Bloomsbury Press.

Smith, A. (2000/1776). *The wealth of nations.* New York: The Modern Library.. (Original work published 1776)

Smith, R. (1998). *The Norton history of the human sciences.* New York: W. W. Norton.

Stichweh, R. (1994). *Wissenschaft, Universität, Professionen: Soziologische Analysen.* Frankfurt am Main: Suhrkamp.

Sturm, T., & Ash, M. G. (2005). The roles of instruments in psychological research. *History of Psychology, 8,* 3–34.

von Mises, L. (1981/1933). *Epistemological problems of economics* (G. Reisman, Trans.). New York: New York University Press. (Original work published 1933)

von Neumann, J., & Morgenstern, O. (1980/1944). *Theory of games and economic behavior.* Princeton, NJ: Princeton University Press. (Original work published 1944)

Wundt, W. (1907/1908). *Logik. Eine Untersuchung der Prinzipien der Erkenntnis und der Methoden wissenschaftlicher Forschung.* (3rd ed., Vols. 1–3). [Logic: A study of the principles of knowledge and the methods of scientific research]. Stuttgart: Enke.

Zenderland, L. (1998). *Measuring minds. Henry Herbert Goddard and the origins of American intelligence testing.* New York: Cambridge University Press.

Part I

Psychological Concepts in Different Domains: Shared or Divided Meanings?

⊁ ⊀

1

The "Fluctuations of Attention" Between Physiology, Experimental Psychology and Psycho-Technical Application

Sven Lüders
Humanistische Union, Germany

FLUCTUATING SENSES AND RETROSPECTIONS

In the summer of 1875, Viktor Urbantschitsch (1875) reported in the *Centralblatt fuer die medicinischen Wissenschaften,* "Ueber eine Eigenthümlichkeit der Schallempfindungen geringster Intensität" (On a peculiarity of sound sensations of smallest intensity): "The ticking of a watch, at some distance to the ear, is not at all perceived consistently, but the perception of sound occasionally shows ups and downs"[1] (p. 625).

---

[1]"Das Ticken einer Taschenuhr, welche sich in einiger Entfernung von dem Ohre befindet, wird keineswegs gleichmäßig vernommen, sondern es zeigt sich zeitweise eine Zu- und Abnahme in der Schallperception."

First, Urbantschitsch wanted to rule out the possibility that his observation was dependent on the characteristics of the clock he had used. With a weak jet of water and a tuning fork, he was able to produce the same phenomena—the weak noises disappeared and were noticed again at regular intervals shortly afterward. Therefore Urbantschitsch attributed this effect to the functioning of our hearing organ and stated that "… our ear is not capable of perceiving weak acoustic stimuli consistently, but is initially affected by a temporary, later by a permanent fatigue."[2] (Urbantschitsch, 1875, pp. 626–627) In further studies Urbantschitsch tried to find out which part of the hearing organ is responsible for this quick fatigue. He found enough test subjects in his medical practice for ear medicine in Vienna. Step by step he excluded all sound-transmitting components of the ear (eardrum, auditory ossicle, head bone) as causes of the phenomenon. Therefore, he concluded that a fatigue of the auditory nerves had to cause the fluctuations.

At the end of his short report, Urbantschitsch compared this phenomenon with a peculiarity of optical perception already described by Hermann von Helmholtz in his physiological optics (Helmholtz, 1896). In a discussion of the validity of Fechner law in the area of visual perception, Helmholtz describes how the perception of smallest shade differences (in photographs) depends on the luminous intensity of the environment. According to Helmholtz, one can observe this phenomenon particularly well with a rotating disk as used by Masson: if such a disk is set in motion, grey rings of different contrast appear.

Helmholtz's formula for the computation of the brightness of a grey tone on the moved disk is as follows:

$$b = 1 - \frac{d}{2\pi r}$$

h—brightness of ring
d—thickness of line
r—distance from center of disk

The formula can be understood more easily if one keeps in mind that the term $\{2\pi r\}$ corresponds to the perimeter of the grey ring in respective distance r from its center.

According to Helmholtz, one recognizes the circles of different grey shades better "… if one takes a reciprocating glance at the different areas of a circle, as if one holds it fixed at a point; in the latter case, the weaker circles swiftly disappear again, even if one has seen them be-

---

[2]"… dass unser Ohr außer Stande sei, schwache akustische Reize gleichmäßig zu empfinden, sondern dabei anfänglich von einer vorübergehenden, später von einer andauernden Ermüdung befallen werde."

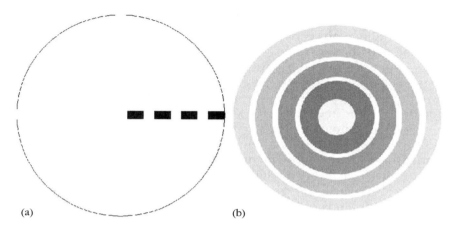

(a) (b)

Figure 1–1.   Pattern of a Masson disk at rest (a) and in motion (b).

fore."[3] (Helmholtz, 1896, p. 391) Helmholtz describes here an extremely volatile phenomenon, which would quickly stabilize itself as an experimental fact and initiate the beginning of experimental psychological investigations of attention.

In 1885, Nicolai Lange took up these observations of fluctuating sensations in order to determine their cause. He had already studied this phenomenon in a book published in Russia, but neither he nor other authors referred later to his early work (see Külpe, 1897). He thought two theories to be possible: the first would try to explain the phenomenon by attributing it to the fatigue of auditory nerves (as Urbantschitsch had done). In Lange's opinion, there are four objections against such a peripheral cause (see Lange, 1887, pp. 396–400):

1. Why should weak stimuli tire out sensory nerves so fast, while the fatigue of motor nerves takes much longer?
2. Why does it come to periodic fluctuations and not to a complete disappearance of the sensations?
3. Why are these fluctuations not observed with strong stimuli, which fatigue the nerves much more?
4. Why does the combination of two different kinds of stimuli (with different fluctuation periods) generate a new overall rhythm according to which both sensations vary together?

---

[3]"... wenn man mit dem Blicke zu den verschiedenen Stellen eines Kreises hin- und hergeht, als wenn man eine Stelle fixiert; im letzteren Falle verschwinden die schwächeren Kreise schnell"

Because of these objections, Nicolai Lange preferred a second possibility, a central nervous explanation of the phenomenon. In his view, the fluctuation of the sensations with small stimulus intensities points to fatigue symptoms caused by strained attention. Lange then carried out tests using optical, acoustic, and tactile stimuli in order to support his hypothesis. His test subjects were instructed to press a key if the sensation disappeared and release the key again as soon as the sensations returned. A chronograph registered the closing and opening of the electric circuit and thus the fluctuations of sensations. From the recorded curves, Lange subsequently determined the period length of the fluctuations. But, from his data, Lange could only draw some phenomenological conclusions (see Lange, 1887, p. 405): Fluctuations occur with different kinds of stimulation; their rate is individually different and sense-specific, but within one kind of sensation the fluctuation periods are relatively constant (with an average variation of max. 1/4 of the period length).

Lange's first results thus reveal little about the origins of the fluctuations. At this point we find an interesting change in his argumentation: in order to obtain a theoretical explanation for the fluctuations, he considers a stair figure by Schroeder.

Such tilting figures are well known because, in the longer run, the perception oscillates between two pictures (in this case: wall and stairs). Here two different things are noteworthy: on the one hand, this case is no longer an optical stimulus at the threshold of sensation, like the grey rings of the Masson disk or the other stimuli used by him. Lange's selection of this example had profound effects on the examined object: it was more than a mere exchange of one exemplary case for another. With the tilting figure, Lange left the level of volatile sense experiences where Urbantschitsch and von Helmholtz had originally located the phenomenon; the fluctuations became a general psychological phenomenon of perception. Moreover, the illustration has no relation to Lange's preceding investigations or measurement results.

Nevertheless, Lange uses this illustration and its effects as the starting point of his further considerations, thus showing that experimental work and a speculative way of thinking can very well be consistent with one another. He states that the fluctuations in the perception of this picture can only be based on a fluctuation of the pictures kept in the mind. Because the illustration (the objective stimulus) is continuous, the fluctuation must be produced by a subjective additive that Lange sees in the memorized pictures (wall/stairs) associated with the illustration. The fluctuations of sensations are ultimately due to the fluctuations of such pictures. Lange calls the resulting mechanism *active apperception* or *sensual attention*.

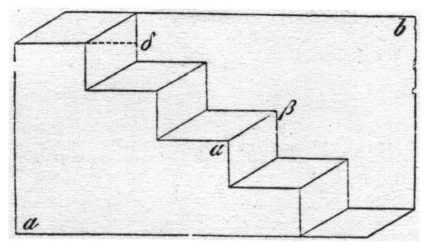

Figure 1–2.   Tilting figure (according to Lange, 1887, p. 406)

One may argue about what was more crucial—Lange's experimental work or his exceptional theses, which are only roughly summarized here. In any case, one should keep in mind that with the concept of sensual attention, a sensory-physiological phenomenon became a subject of experimental psychological investigations (for a good summary of experimental accounts in American psychology see Guildford, 1927). Now I would like to follow the further career of this topic. In doing so I emphasize the following question: How did psychological accounts differ from other approaches to the scientific object called "attention"? In other words: How did experimental-psychological investigation influence the problem?

FLUCTUATING ATTENTION: PSYCHO-PHYSICAL PHENOMENON OR PSYCHOLOGICAL OBJECT?

Nicolai Lange's theses about sensual attention met with some interest. At the end of the 19th century, we find several investigations about the significance of attention for sense impressions, most of which referred to Lange's work. Hugo Münsterberg (1889) endorsed the claim that the fluctuations are of peripheral origin. However, in contrast to Lange, whose theory about the central origins of fluctuations could not (or not directly) be experimentally proved, Münsterberg advanced a psychological thesis that also made detailed physiological claims about this phenomenon. In doing so Münsterberg focused exclusively on fluctuations of optical stimuli which he could reproduce in his own experiments. His explanation assumes an increasing insensitivity of the retina, resulting from long fixation and continuous accommodation of the eyes while looking at the Masson disks. A decreasing accommodation with increasing fatigue of the eye muscles causes an unintentional diversion of the gaze, so that the picture is sidetracked on lateral, more sensitive parts of the retina and disappears. Münsterberg's contribution initiated lively discussions of the question. In 1893, for example, Edward Pace insisted that Münsterberg's theses about the influence of retina sensitivity cannot apply. As he showed, the sensation of a grey ring on a black disk varies likewise, though it should not do so according to Münsterberg's theory (Pace, 1893).

Pace's criticism encouraged numerous experimental attempts to discover the causes of this phenomenon. It became more and more probable that the fluctuations may actually be different phenomena (see Eckener, 1893; Wiersma, 1901). From today's perspective, what happened could almost be called a deconstruction of attention in psychological laboratories. Nicolai Lange had introduced the fluctuations of weak stimuli from the periphery of volatile sense phenomena to the range of (more or less stable) psychological facts. Now these phenomena disintegrated under the eyes of the experimenting psychologists into numerous underlying processes. It became obvious that the fluctuations arose only under very special conditions of observation (which had already been noticed by Helmholtz), that they depend strongly on the daily form of the test subjects (whatever influenced them—see Wiersma, 1901) and are overlaid by fatigue symptoms. An investigation presented by Bertil Hammer (1906) shows clearly the disintegration of the object. Obviously bothered by the numerous speculations of his predecessors, Hammer presented some results of his own, in which the fluctuations turned out to be a consequence of an insufficient control of experimental conditions. Thus, he could show that numerous clocks had barely noticeable rhythms in their operation sounds, whereas in other cases a gradual adaptation of the sensory organs was observable. Finally the fluctuation disappeared completely when the acoustic stimuli were modified! So, what was left of attention as a psychological object?

Following Jonathan Crary (2000), we could take the disappearance and reappearance of optical phenomena attributed to fluctuating attention as indications for a special modern "precariousness, contingency, and insubstantiality" (p. 45) characteristic of a cognitive faculty that turns back on itself. In the investigations presented herein, attention does not appear any longer as the mental faculty that guaranteed *a priori* the unity of consciousness; nor does it represent a moral category or civic virtue that should contribute to the perfection of personality. These two classical meanings of attention had become obsolete. In psychophysical discourse, attention was subject to an interplay of internal and external forces, whose experimental control turned out to be extremely difficult. To this extent, attention had now become an extremely unstable object. This instability had profound effects: Michael Hagner (2001) has pointed out the close connection between attention and techniques of introspection and self-experiment. For him, attention is a "condition of the possibility of self-observation and self-experiment as such"(Hagner 2001, p. 242). The fragility of the psychological object "attention" led to general doubts concerning the reliability of the attentive reaction as an instrument of psychological research. Given the impossibility of verifying the fluctuations of attention experimentally, Bertil Hammer (1905), for example, asks the heretical question: "How is it possible, with the registration switch in the hand, to mark the moment where the attention stops?"[4] (p. 365).

The same skepticism was expressed by Edgar Rubin (1926) in a lecture at the Ninth Congress for Experimental Psychology in Munich. There, he argued for the psychological non-existence of attention and demanded that the term be deleted from the vocabulary of psychology without substitution. Both authors, Hammer and Rubin, took up an old objection of Kant against the possibility of an introspective observation of attention. Kant saw a constitutive gap between a scientific, logically arranged description and the unordered sequence of internal events, which, for him, cannot be overcome. For Kant, this gap undermines the value of any kind of introspection (Kant 1786/1900). In their rejection of introspective methods, some psychologists probably would have liked to give up attention as a methodological instrument altogether.

THE EXPERIMENTAL ADJUSTMENT OF ATTENTION

Despite the uncertainties about the nature or even the existence of the psychological object called *fluctuating attention*, the term nonetheless continued to attract active interest in experimental psychological contexts. Curiously, Wilhelm Wundt—the "mentor" of the experimental method—played a decisive part in this development because attention was a central factor in his theory of apperceptions. Wundt assumed that different sensations can reach the center of consciousness only by a special act of the will, which he called *apperception* (Woodward, 1982, pp. 175, 178). For him, the totality of mental objects, that can be registered

---

[4]"Und man darf billig fragen: wie ist es möglich, die Registriertaste in der Hand, den Moment zu markieren, wo die Aufmerksamkeit—aufhört?"

by consciousness, forms a field analogous to the visual field of the eye. Comparable to an internal spotlight, the attention could, according to Wundt, glide across this internal field and thereby shift the focus of consciousness (that point of highest concentration) onto different perceptions or images (*Vorstellungen*):

> "The internal focus can now turn successively to the different parts of the internal field of consciousness. At the same time however, the internal focus, quite different from the focal activity of the eye, can narrow and widen itself, whereby its intensity in turn always increases and decreases. Strictly taken, it is thus not a focal point, but a field of a somewhat variable extension. Yet this field of apperception always forms a unitary image (*Vorstellung*), by connecting the individual parts of the same to one whole." (Wundt, 1887, p. 236)[5]

This metaphor of attention as an internal spotlight of consciousness is remarkable. On its face, it conflicts with the self-understanding of psychology geared to accurate measurement of physiological and psychological factors. But Wundt *Grundzüe der Physiologischen Psychologie* was more than a collection of experimental facts and tasks; it also has to be seen as a programmatic work. The use of the term *attention* here can only be understood, in my opinion, if we recognize its role in Wundt's psychological system. Wundt used the term *apperception* (as a description of a psycho-physiological process), or alternatively *attention* (as a description of the associated sensory-psychological process), in order to gain a second dynamic process level beyond the associative, stimuli-bounded dynamics for the course of perceptions (*Vorstellungen*). In Wundt's concept of psychology, the term *attention* marked the strategic goal of supplementing the dominant descriptions of our mental world as passive and associatively formed by an active, volitional aspect of mental life.[6] To this extent the term *attention* results from a necessity of Wundt's psychological system and was not connected to Wundt's experimental psychological research program. Nonetheless, out of this metaphorical complex (and its implications) he developed a coordinate system of experimental questions, to which attention was later subjected in his laboratory. The quotation just cited indicates the three tasks

---

[5]"Der innere Blickpunkt kann sich nun successiv den verschiedenen Theilen des inneren Blickfeldes zuwenden. Zugleich kann er sich jedoch, sehr verschieden von dem Blickpunkt des äußeren Auges, verengen und erweitern, wobei immer seine Helligkeit abwechselnd zu- und abnimmt. Streng genommen ist er also kein Punkt, sondern ein Feld von etwas veränderlicher Ausdehnung. Immer jedoch bildet dieses Feld der Apperception eine einheitliche Vorstellung, indem wir die einzelnen Theile desselben zu einem Ganzen verbinden."

[6]I am grateful to Horst Gundlach for this reference to the strategic significance of the term in Wundt's writings; but see also Woodward (1982).

of an experimental study of attention, on which Wundt and his students concentrated in their following investigations:

- The determination of the scope of attention as a quasi-elementary quantum of consciousness: How many elements can simultaneously come into one's internal field of vision?
- The rate of attention switches: How quickly can attention switch between different elements of the field?
- The verification of the limitation of consciousness, that is, the proof that only one apperception (one psychological act) at a time could become the subject of consciousness.

The term *attention* itself thereby remains strangely indefinite. As we have just seen, it is taken by Wundt to be an internal activity, with which consciousness directs itself to individual perceptions (*Vorstellungen*). Wundt here combines a notion of apperception taken from Leibniz with a volitional interpretation, which regards attention as an internal act of the will. For Wundt, the crucial criterion for the manifestation of an activity of attention is the clarity of the mental contents connected with it—a characteristic that, up to that point, had been described mainly in sensualistic interpretations of attention. According to Wundt, one can assess the degree of attention on the basis of the different levels of clarity of mental contents. But this is only an apparent specification of the object, for what is to be understood by the clarity of mental contents differs even in Wundt's own writings. Hans Henning (1925) found six different definitions of the term: Clarity is sometimes seen as having to do with the temporal relations between the individual conceived ideas, at other times as connected to the degree with which one image or idea (*Vorstellung*) is marked off from other mental contents. In his later work, finally, Wundt described clarity as the third fundamental characteristic of sensations (besides their quality and intensity). Especially the fact that he held on to the idea of a center of apperception located in the human brain resulted in numerous criticisms of Wundt by contemporary psychologists. What attention or that process of apperception exactly was, thus remained the subject of speculative discussions rather than a result of experimental research.

Perhaps more decisive than these speculations for the shaping of the term in experimental psychology was another distinction, by which Wundt introduced attention into the field of response time experiments. Due to observations by Nicolai and Ludwig Lange, he assumed that differences in the response times of the same person could be explained by the direction of her attention. For that purpose, Wundt divided the process of psychologically simple reactions into three phases or five sections, respectively (see Wundt 1887):

- perception (excitation time of the stimulus and becoming aware of it)
- apperception (formation of a clear impression)
- volition-time (building up of motor excitation for switch response).

If attention is directed at the required movement, the registering switch could be triggered in a reflex reaction after the subject becomes aware of the stimulus. In this special kind of response, which Wundt called *muscular reaction*, the apperception time and the formation of the volitional impulse drop-out of the overall response time. Accordingly, the reactions occur faster than under normal conditions. In contrast, if attention is directed completely to the stimulus that was to be expected, the response time was extended by the necessary act of apperception. According to Wundt, muscular and sensory reaction types should be distinguishable from each other based on specific indicators. In the case of sensory reactions, one could observe a tension of the sensory organs. In the case of muscular reactions, in contrast, often false or precipitate reactions occur, which never appear with reactions of the sensory type.

However, more important than the absolute difference of about 0–1 sec in response times on average, which Ludwig Lange had detected, was the fact that attention thereby became the criterion for whether an experiment had psychological significance at all. Wundt regarded the shortened muscular reaction as a brain reflex, in the process of which no psychological elements were involved except for becoming aware of the stimulus. The physiological phases of the reaction process could be determined primarily by muscular adjusted reactions. Only attention directed to the sensory stimuli guarantees that also a psychological event is measured in this reaction (Wundt, 1887). Thus, for Wundt, experiments in which the direction of attention and possibly arising changes of it were not considered, for Wundt have "… generally the value of subjective opinions, which one could form just as well before as after the tests were done …" (Wundt, 1900a, p. 314).[7]

We can conclude, therefore, that in this work, attention became a methodologically relevant variable that determined the scientific value of psychological experiments. Still, I would not go as far as Jonathan Crary (2000) in the evaluation of this development. Crary takes the problem of attention to be the core of classical psychological ap-

---

[7]"… im allgemeinen den Werth subjectiver Meinungen, die man sich ebenso gut vor wie nach der Anstellung der Versuche bilden könnte…"

proaches to response time. But the goal of Wundt's investigations, in connection with which this problem arose, was to find "general laws of the process of mental ideas" (Wundt, 1887, p. 261). Besides attention, numerous other factors (association laws, complication conditions, etc.) played an important role in this project. Furthermore, it was the special conditions and problems of psychological experiments that aroused the interest of Wundt and his students in attention. The investigations of attention by experimental psychologists took place in a scientific climate where the development and refinement of experimental apparatus and techniques was seen as a criterion of scientific and methodological quality. From these efforts, a set of experimental parameters arose under which attention could be observed with as little interference as possible. Among them were the following five techniques (see Wundt, 1891, Wundt, 1900a, 1900b):

- the placement of the stimuli in the center of the perceptual field
- attuning test subjects to the stimuli by pilot signals and given fixed points
- the elimination of interfering stimuli (daylight, dropping noises, etc.)
- simple rules for reaction
- simple response actions, mostly operating a switch.

Thus, the adjustment of attention became a *component of an experimental technique*. Should we therefore talk about experimental techniques of attention control, as Crary's (2000) description of tachistoscopic experiments suggests? Crary sees the experimental practices of disciplined observation as the core of a social standardization of attentional performance:

> The tachistoscope was part of a broad-ranging project to acquire knowledge that would allow a rationalization of a perceiver and the management of attentiveness, but it did so through a fragmentation of vision perhaps even more thorough than anything in early forms of cinema and high-speed photography. (Crary, 2000, p. 306)

However, we should be aware that this "experimental technology" has two fundamental limitations. First, it is closely connected to the establishment of psychological laboratories. This means, first, that the perceptional and attentional experiences presented in the experiments were only available to the test subjects. The typical test subject of psychology in the 19th century was a student, psychologically educated and trained in experimental practice for many years—a rather small and carefully limited social group. This limitation of the laboratory also reveals itself in the fact that the distinction between muscular and sensory direction of attention could not be transferred from reaction experiments to other fields. That was quite obvious for the persons involved. James McKeen Cattell, for example, pointed out that the "rules" of directed attention in everyday routine actions are completely different than in Wundt's analysis of experimental response times:

> In the practiced automatic movements of daily life, attention is directed to the sense impression and not to the movement. So, in piano playing, the beginner may attend to his fingers but the practiced player attends only to the notes or to the melody. In speaking, writing and reading aloud, and in games and manual work, attention is always directed to the goal, never to the movement. In fact, as soon as attention is directed to the movement, this becomes less automatic and less dependable. (Cattell, 1947, pp. 252–253)

Second, Wundt's distinction is only an analytic instrument for the dissection of response times, but not in itself a psychological technique. The distinction alone could thus hardly justify a transfer of techniques of control and rationalization of attention. If we take Crary's claim seriously that we are dealing with a process of standardization and control of attention, which was justified by experimental psychology, then we would, first of all, have to find out on which material techniques this process was based. Thus, we would have to distinguish between analytic descriptions and practicable psychological techniques. Next, we should identify those special techniques of experimental work, which allow a transfer of the direction of attention from scientific context to other social areas. Maybe there were some tricks in experimental contexts in order to obtain the direction of attention that was desired in the particular situation. But in this regard, we only find vague suggestions. Crary himself draws on an analogy between tachistoscopic experiments, which offer meaningless stimuli detached from all experience, and the "atomized character" of modern industrial and mass consumptive reality, and the "perceptual shocks" that arise from it. Yet this analogy reveals little about the causes for such a development. It can hardly support Crary strong thesis of a standardization of attention resulting from psychological research.

But even in the published sources of experimental psychologicy, we find only a few examples of techniques for the successful control of attention. One is provided in Ernst Westphal's thesis on primary and secondary tasks in reaction experiments (Westphal, 1911). In this investigation, he used so-called vexing stimuli (*Vexierreize*). These are frequently used in reaction experiments as control items. They are placed between the stimuli that are really of interest in order to exclude automatic (muscular) reactions. Now Westphal chose stimuli, on the basis of which subjects could not accomplish the observation task they were asked to perform. By using vexing stimuli in this way he wanted to redirect the attention of his test subjects to their own behavior, because it was their self-observation that particularly interested him. Westphal (1911) described the underlying mechanism of the experiment as follows: "If one is prepared to behave a certain way and one is confronted with an inadequate object for such behavior, then attention will always automatically jump to the behavior itself; the behavior is experienced as behavior because there is nothing at the object to be experienced" (p. 235).[8]

In my opinion, this trick is a real psycho-technique. Westphal used the automatic excitation of attention, which was caused by unexpected unsolvable problems, as a method of eliciting a specific kind of behavior from his subjects. But among those who tried to control attention in experiments, this was rather exceptional. How unstable the experimental practice was is also revealed by the consistently arising doubts whether in this or that experiment the direction of attention really was of a sensory or motor kind (for Müsterberg's investigations see Martius, 1891). I therefore have my doubts about how Wundt distinction could have possibly developed the kind of broader social or cultural effect imagined by Crary under these conditions.

BETWEEN EXPERIMENT AND APPLICATION

Now I would like to consider the significance of attention within psycho-technical activities in contrast to the academic-psychological accounts treated before. If one takes the programmatic statements of psycho-technicians at face value, their interest in this aspect of human activity was quite pronounced. In all of their larger publications we find a reference to this topic, and most of the authors understood that the relief of constant pressure on attention within the workplace was a substantial goal. The passage from Hugo Müsterberg's *Psychology and Economic Efficiency* may illustrate this:

> In industrial establishments in which the smallest disturbance in the machine is at once remedied by a mechanic in order that the greatest possible economic effect may be secured, frequently nobody takes any interest in the most destructive disturbances which unnecessarily occur in the subtlest part of the factory mechanism, namely, the attention apparatus of the laborers. (Muensterberg, 1913, p. 206)

---

[8]"Wenn ein Verhalten eingenommen ist und diesem Verhalten ein inadäquates Objekt gegenübertritt, so pflegt die Aufmerksamkeit stets unwillkürlich auf das Verhalten selbst überzuspringen; das Verhalten wird als solches erlebt, weil an dem Gegenstande nichts zu erleben ist …"

Thus we can assume that psycho-technicians were interested in the topic of attention. Yet how does the situation look when we go beyond these programmatic statements? Given the instability of attentional fluctuations and the difficulty of actually controlling attention in the laboratory just described, on what could psycho-technicians actually rely on in this undertaking? If one starts with the three classical procedures of psycho-technics (the best organization of workflow, the optimal use of work equipment and the best selection of the fittest workers), then it is conspicuously clear that the psycho-technique of attention concentrates almost exclusively on the selection task. The organization of work or of working equipment based on attentional criteria was obviously a larger problem. For instance, Walter Moede's textbook of psycho-technics (Moede, 1930) presents under the label of "attentional performance" (*Beachtensleistung*) test procedures for four different functions of attention:

- reliability, e.g. necessary repetitions during the realization of several stimuli
- the noticing of changes
- the search for certain characteristics
- capacity for sorting.

These tasks lead to the question of how far they are connected to increased attention or to other psychological functions. Thus, for instance, sorting tasks can be solved particularly quickly and without large attentional demands if test subjects have knowledge of the suitable sorting algorithms. It becomes clear how difficult it is to determine the contribution of attention in such complex tasks if we consider the indicators for (decreasing) attention used by Moede. He mentions among other things a decreasing quantity and quality of the output and a rising number of errors (see Moede, 1930, pp. 154–165). The same items were already used 30 years earlier by Emil Kraepelin in his ergographical studies of work and fatigue curves, which were precisely not concerned with attention but with fatigue (see Kraepelin, 1902). And this is not just a problem in Moede presentation. His criteria, like the quantity of the output, how easily the tasks are executed, or the number of errors, appeared in numerous psycho-technical investigations about the strain on attention (see Sachs, 1920).

This confusion of attention with fatigue also becomes clear in a criticism of the procedure for the control of attentional performance in multiple task work, which Walter Moede and Curt Piorkowski developed together (Piorkowski, 1920). In this test, the subjects had to keep in mind a story told before, and multiply triple-digit numbers at the same time. Their results were compared with their performance on single-task work. From the relation between multiple-task and single-task performances, Moede and Piorkowski deduced an ability to distribute attention. Several things were methodologically crucial in this procedure. For example, it was not recognizable whether an above-average performance was really based on fast changes of attention or simply on special talents for the tested tasks. Thus, from the perspective of an experimental psychologist, such tests were simply "not adequate" to draw reliable conclusions about the abilities for the distribution of attention or the qualification for multiple-task work (see Sterzinger, 1927, p. 195). But even this critic granted that such a methodologically false procedure had a certain legitimacy for the practical purposes of qualification tests:

> "For the qualification test, it is after all not important whether the actual performance comes about one or the other way; i.e. whether by real attention distribution or by rapid change, or more by remarkable specific talent for the individual activities. The main thing is and remains the quantity of the output."[9] (Sterzinger, 1927, pp. 195–196)

The simple transfer of experimental questions and techniques into a psycho-technical context was obviously difficult. The experimental rules listed above could not so easily be transferred into an industrial context. I therefore mention briefly some of the difficulties arising in a psycho-technical account of attention.

First, we can discern different interests in the work of academic psychologists and psycho-technicians. As we have seen, Wundt was only interested in psychologically complete reactions, for example reactions with a sensory direction of attention. The pure length of a reaction time was of no interest for him insofar the psychological structure of this reaction was not decomposable. Otherwise, techniques that would increase the speed of working movements became the center of interest for psycho-technical researchers. In the context of industrial application, there was no concern about whether this would be achieved by psychological actions or physiological reflex-like reactions. This difference in scientific interests and the aims of rationalization cannot simply be neglected.

Also, it is obvious that experimental psychologists and psycho-technicians were concerned with quite different dimensions of time and space. On the one hand, the fluctuations of attention, the rate of its changes, and its part in overall response times—all these objects of ex-

---

[9]"Für die Eignungsprüfung ist es im Grunde gleichgültig, ob die schließliche Leistung so oder so zustande kommt, d.h. ob durch wirkliche Aufmerksamkeitsverteilung oder durch raschen Wechsel oder mehr durch auffällige spezifische Begabung für die einzelnen Tätigkeiten. Die Hauptsache ist und bleibt die Größe der Leistung."

perimental work focused on periods between a few milliseconds and a few minutes. On the other hand, we find industrial work conditions that extended over several hours a day. Furthermore, Haber pointed out that the reaction performance at the tachistoscope and in ordinary industrial arrangements were quite different; in a larger field, the reaction performances were partly better than at the tachistoscope (Haber, 1929, 1932). This discrepancy can also be observed for the involved reactions. Fritz Giese summed up the difference between pressing a registration switch and a work situation: "... in everyday life, only a few people might be waiting with the hand on the button in order to react"[10] (as cited in Haber, 1932, p. 230).

Last but not least, there was a fundamental quarrel between experimentalists and practitioners about the status of individual differences in attentional capabilities. Experimental psychologists were inclined to treat the performance of attention (its extent, rate, or duration) as a fundamental item of consciousness, which could not be enhanced by training (Feilgenhauer, 1912; Mager, 1920, 1925; Pauli, 1930; Wundt, 1909). This is even more remarkable because the different investigations measuring the range of attention exhibited a considerable variance, between 4 and 12 elements. This may be one reason why Wundt considered applied psychology to be a danger for the development of the discipline, due to the problem of hasty generalizations resulting in a schematized formation of concepts (Wundt, 1909). But in the case of the problem of attention, the charge of hasty generalization applied just as well to academic experimental psychology.

For psycho-technical practitioners, such interindividual discrepancies constituted the differences in capabilities that made effective selection possible *and* desirable (see Piorkowski, 1919, pp. 17–19). In addition, the success of the rules for obtaining increased output was, in the long run, the very criterion for measuring the value of their work. This was a primary factor behind the discussion of a "crisis of psychotechnics" in German-speaking Europe at the end of the 1920s. In that discussion, two central criticisms of psycho-technics were advanced: (1) conflicting aims (for whom did psycho-technicians actually work?) and (2) increasing doubts about the validity and effectiveness of test procedures and improvement techniques (see Metraux, 1985). Many psycho-technicians saw the solution to these problems in the achievement of methodological validity; they hoped this would improve the reputation of psycho- technics and, at the same time, increase the usefulness of psycho-technical methods for companies and workers. (For a different perspective on the crisis of psycho-technics see Vatin, 1998). Thus, it is

---

[10]"... mit der Hand am Taster verharren im Leben die wenigsten, um zu reagieren."

understandable that many attempts to diagnose and enhance attentional performance originated in psycho-technical contexts (see Kindler, 1929).

CONCLUSION

Psychological investigations by Wundt and his students showed that the problem of attention occupied experimental psychologists around 1900 more than any other period. Attention was treated first as a sensory-physiological phenomenon before it became a methodological criterion in the practice of psychological experimentation. Particularly the direction of attention was regarded as a central characteristic that crucially affected the psychological value of experiments. However, the theoretical significance of attention in experiments contrasted with its conceptual fuzziness and a certain loss of control over its definition. Most of the experimental psychologists were not up to the development of theoretical concepts that would explain attention beyond the limits of direct experiential evidence. Some attempts at conceptual stabilization even led to the disintegration of attentional phenomena (e.g., the fluctuations of attention) into diverse psychological processes. Yet their interaction remained unsettled. The control of the effects of attention also represented a large practical obstacle, as the attempts to control the direction of attention just described show. What was missing in experimental discourse was conceptual clarity with regard to the object "attention"—not to mention a measure for attention.

Can we actually talk about attention as a scientific object or a psychological technology, given that the interest in attention was mainly based on questions concerning methodology and experimental practice? If we assume that to talk about a scientific object presupposes a certain isolation and independence of that very object from other objects, then I dare to say that attention did not represent such an independent object of psychological research. In experimental contexts attention became more or less a strategic notion, used for the formation of the psychological concepts of (apperceptive) consciousness and their experimental verification.

The social-technological use of an economy of attention in psychotechnics also presents itself as problematic. Numerous difficulties arose when concepts of attention were transferred to the field of psycho-technical diagnosis and the organization of industrial work. On the one hand, these problems refer us back to the point of origin of attention-psychological concepts—the psychological laboratory experiment with its special conditions. At the same time, they mark an existing gap between the experimentalists' goal of identifying and defining attention and the requirements of industrial practice. Due to this gap, it appears unclear how a dominating social technology of attention control could have developed from the experimental investigations into attention, as Jonathan Crary (2000) suggests. In practice, the effects of attention could hardly be distinguished from the effects of fatigue. How should a psycho-technician even use a criterion that experimental psychologists regarded as the indicator for attention: the clarity of mental contents? It was already difficult to operationalize this term for psychological experiments, but it was even less suited as a psycho-technical measure for attentional performance.

REFERENCES

Cattell, J. M. (1947). Attention and reaction. In J. M. Cattell (Ed.), *Man of Science* (Vol. 1, pp. 252–255). Lancaster, PA: The Science Press. (Original work published in 1983)

Crary, J. (2000). *Suspensions of perception. Attention, spectacle, and modern culture* (2nd ed.). Cambridge, MA: MIT Press.

Eckener, H. (1893). Untersuchungen über die Schwankungen der Auffassung minimaler Sinnesreize [Investigations on fluctuations in perception of minimal sense-stimuli]. *Philosophische Studien, 8,* 343–387.

Feilgenhauer, R. (1912). Untersuchungen über die Geschwindigkeit der Aufmerksamkeitswanderung [Investigations about the speed of movements of attention]. *Archiv für die gesamte Psychologie, 25,* 350–416.

Guilford, J. P. (1927). Fluctuations of attention. *American Journal of Psychology, 38,* 534–583.

Haber, A. (1929). Zur Bestgestaltung des Aufmerksamkeits-Reaktionsfeldes. Beachten und Greifen in Abhängigkeit vom Blickraum, von der Reizstärke und der Ablenkung [On best practice of the attention-reaction-field. Notice and grab in dependence on field of vision, intensity of stimuli and distraction]. *Industrielle Psychotechnik, 6,* 316–328.

Haber, A. (1932). Beachtung—Aufmerksamkeit—Reaktion in einem größeren Sehfeld [Observance—attention—reaction in larger field of vision]. *Industrielle Psychotechnik, 9,* 229–245.

Hagner, M. (2001). Psychophysiologie und Selbsterfahrung. Metamorphosen des Schwindels und der Aufmerksamkeit im 19. Jahrhundert [Psychophysiology and self-awareness. Metamorphosis of swindle and attention in 19th century]. In A. Assman & J. Assmann (Eds.), *Aufmerksamkeiten. Archäologie der literarischen Kommunikation* (Vol. 7, pp. 241–263). München: Wilhelm Fink.

Hammer, B. (1905). Zur experimentellen Kritik der Theorie der Aufmerksamkeitsschwankungen [On experimental critique of theories about fluctuations of attention]. *Zeitschrift für Psychologie und Physiologie der Sinnesorgane, 37,* 363–376.

Hammer, B. (1906). Zur Kritik des Problems der Aufmerksamkeitsschwankungen [On critique the problem of fluctuations of attention]. *Zeitschrift für Psychologie und Physiologie der Sinnesorgane, 41,* 48–50.

Helmholtz, H. v. (1896). *Handbuch der physiologischen Optik*. [Handbook of Physiological Optics] (2nd rev. ed.). Leipzig: Voss.

Henning, H. (1925). *Die Aufmerksamkeit*. [The Attention]. Berlin/Wien: Urban & Schwarzenberg.

Kant, I. (1786/1900). *Metaphysische Anfangsgründe der Naturwissenschaft*. [Metaphysical Foundations of Natural Science]. In I. Kant (Ed.), *Gesammelte Schriften* (Vol. IV, pp. 465–466). Berlin: De Gruyter.

Kindler, H. (1929). Über die bedingenden Faktoren und die Erziehbarkeit von Aufmerksamkeitsleistungen [On causal factors and educationability of attentional performance]. *Archiv für die gesamte Psychologie, 70*, 257–310

Külpe, O. (1897). Zur Lehre von der Aufmerksamkeit [On apprenticeship of attention]. *Zeitschrift für Philosophie und philosophische Kritik, 110*, 7–39.

Lange, N. (1887). Beiträge zur Theorie der sinnlichen Aufmerksamkeit und der activen Apperception [Contributions to theory of sensual attention and active apperception]. *Philosophische Studien, 4*, 390–422.

Mager, A. (1920). Die Enge des Bewußtseins [The constriction of consciousness]. *Münchener Studien zur Psychologie* und Philosophie, 1, 497–657.

Mager, A. (1925). Neue Versuche zur Messung der Geschwindigkeit der Aufmerksakeitswanderung. [New trials measuring the speed of movements of attention]. *Archiv für die gsamte Psychologie, 53*, 391–432.

Martius, G. (1891). Ueber die muskuläre Reaction und die Aufmerksamkeit [On muscular reaction and attention]. *Philosophische Studien, 6*, 167–216

Métraux, A. (1985): Die angewandte Psychologie vor und nach 1933 in Deutschland [Applied psychology before and after 1933 in Germany]. In C. F. Graumann (Ed.), *Psychologie im Nationalsozialismus* (pp. 221–262). Berlin: Springer.

Moede, W. (1930). *Lehrbuch der Psychotechnik*. [Textbook of Psychotechnique]. Berlin: Springer.

Münsterberg, H. (1889). Schwankungen der Aufmerksamkeit [Fluctuations of attention]. In H. Münsterberg, *Beiträge zur Experimentellen Psychologie* (Vol. 2, pp. 69–124). Freiburg: Mohr.

Münsterberg, H. (1913). *Psychology and economic efficiency*. New York: Houghton Mifflin (Original work published in 1912)

Pace, E. (1893). Zur Frage der Schwankungen der Aufmerksamkeit nach Versuchen mit der Masson'schen Scheibe [On the question of fluctuations of attention according to experiments with Masson's disks]. *Philosophische Studien, 8*, 388–402.

Pauli, R. (1930). Die Enge des Bewußtseins und ihre experimentelle Untersuchung [The narrowness of consciousness and their experimental investigation]. *Archiv für die gesamte Psychologie, 74*, 201–257.

Piorkowski, C. (1919). Die psychologische Methodologie der wirtschaftlichen Berufseignung [Psychological methodology of economic profession-capability]. *Zeitschrift für angewandte Psychologie, Beiheft, 11*.

Piorkowski, C. (1920). Über Methoden zur Erkennung und Schulung der Konzentration [On methods of detection and training of concentration]. *Praktische Psychologie, 1*, 167–174.

Rubin, E. (1926). Die Nichtexistenz der Aufmerksamkeit [The non-existence of attention]. In K. Bühler (Ed.), *Bericht über den IX. Kongreß für experimentelle Psychologie in München vom 21–25, April 1925* (pp. 211–212). Jena: Gustav Fischer.

Sachs, H. (1920). Studien zur Eignungsprüfung der Strassenbahnführer. Erste Abhandlung: Methode zur Prüfung der Aufmerksamkeit und Reaktionsweise [Studies on capability of conductors. First Treatise: Method of testing attention and reaction]. In O. Lipmann & W. Stern (Eds.), *Schriften zur Psychologie der Berufseignung und des Wirtschaftslebens* (Vol. 15). Leipzig: Barth.

Sterzinger, O. (1927). Über die sogenannte Verteilung der Aufmerksamkeit [On the so called distribution of attention]. *Zeitschrift für angewandte Psychologie, 29,* 177–196.

Urbantschitsch, V. (1875). Ueber eine Eigenthümlichkeit der Schallempfindungen geringster Intensität [On a peculiarity of sound sensations of smallest intensity]. *Centralblatt für die medicinischen Wissenschaften, 1875,* 625–628.

Vatin, F. (1998). Arbeit und Ermüdung. Entstehung und Scheitern der Psychophysiologie der Arbeit [Work and fatique. Rise and breakdown of psychophysiology of work]. In P. Sarasin & J. Tanner (Eds.), *Physiologie und industrielle Gesellschaft* (pp. 347–368). Frankfurt: Suhrkamp.

Westphal, E. (1911). Über Haupt- und Nebenaufgaben bei Reaktionsversuchen [On main and ancillary tasks in reaction trials]. *Archiv für die gesamte Psychologie, 21,* 219–434.

Wiersma, E. (1901). Untersuchungen über die sogenannten Aufmerksamkeitsschwankungen [Investigations on the so called fluctuations of attention]. *Zeitschrift für Psychologie und Physiologie der Sinnesorgane, 26,* 168–200.

Woodward, W. R. (1982). Wundt's program for the new psychology: Vicissitudes of experiment, theory and system. In W. R. Woodward & M. G. Ash (Eds.), *The problematic science: Psychology in nineteenth-century thought* (pp. 167–197). New York: Praeger

Wundt, W. (1887). *Grundzüge der physiologischen Psychologie* [Principles of Physiological Psychology] (3rd rev. ed.; Vol. 2). Leipzig: Engelmann.

Wundt, W. (1891). Ueber die Methoden der Messung des Bewusstseinsumfanges [On methods of measuring the range of consciousness]. *Philosophische Studien, 6,* 250–260.

Wundt, W. (1900a). Zur Kritik tachistoskopischer Versuche [On critique of tachistoskope experiments]. *Philosophische Studien, 15,* 287–317.

Wundt, W. (1900b). Zur Kritik tachistoskopischer Versuche. Zweiter Artikel [On critique of tachistoskope experiments. Second article]. *Philosophische Studien, 16,* 61–70.

Wundt, W. (1909). Über reine und angewandte Psychologie [On pure and applied psychology]. *Psychologische Studien, 5,* 1–47.

2

Causality, Intentionality, and the Causation of Intentions: The Problematic Boundary

Jochen Brandtstädter
University of Trier, Germany

Human organisms are physical (biochemical, neurobiological) systems that are subject to physical causality; at the same time, human beings like to see themselves as reflexive, intentional subjects whose actions can be explained and predicted with reference to mental states, and as responsible agents to whom notions of rationality and morality apply. The boundary work and disciplinary identity of psychology have been, and continue to be, shaped by this basic ontological tension, as well as by the methodological and theoretical orientations that are related to these different points of view. I need to mention here only the traditional debates revolving around presumed dichotomies such as explanation versus understanding, freedom versus determinism, causes versus reasons, and the like. Although psychologists today tend to take a relaxed, if not neglectful, attitude toward these traditional controversies, it can hardly be denied that—despite many attempts to deconstruct the dualisms—the basic ontological tensions are far from being resolved. It rather seems that we are dealing with a kind of ambiguous ontological figure or *Kippfigur* (comparable to the well-known duck vs. rabbit drawing) where none of the conflicting perspectives can claim to be *the* true or correct one, and where any such claims appear "essentially contestable" (Gallie, 1955).

Of course it is uncontroversial that mental phenomena are linked to, or "supervenient" on, neuronal and physiological processes, although the notion of supervenience does not elucidate *how* physical systems instantiate mental states—if they do (cf. Kim, 1993, 1997). Wundt (1894) already emphasized the "complementarity and mutual interpenetration of psychic and physical causality" (p. 81); he noted that "on the basis of psychophysical relations ... contents of consciousness [emerge] that are not motivated in the concurrent or antecedent internal processes" (p. 111). At the same time, however, he posited a categorical difference between mental and physical causality (*anschauliche Kausalität vs. begriffliche Kausalität*). For him this not only legitimated the existence of psychology as an independent discipline, but also as a program of peaceful coexistence with the natural sciences (see Heidelberger, 2003). It is worth noting, however, that quite different conclusions can be drawn from rather similar premises. Freud (1969) at first seems to echo Wundt when he notes that, according to common agreement, mental contents or processes "do not form unbroken sequences" (p. 14), but then he takes a different tack: "Whereas the psychology of consciousness never went beyond the broken sequences that were obviously dependent on something else, the other view, which held that the psychical is unconscious in itself, enabled psychology to take its place as a natural science like any other" (p. 15).

Consciousness as a process exhibiting causal gaps: This is of course far from being a clear notion. In the following, I try to illustrate where, and in what sense, causality and intentionality "complement and interpenetrate" each other, and I also highlight some limitations of the corresponding explanatory stances. I focus on the following issues: (a) The nonintentional genesis of intentional states; (b) the problem of controlling one's mental states; (c) the puzzles of self-deception and motivated reasoning; (d) problems of action explanation; and (e) the relationship between psychology and "folk psychology."

THE NONINTENTIONAL GENESIS
OF INTENTIONAL STATES

In psychology as well as in everyday contexts, we explain human actions by relating them to the agent's intentional states—that is, to his or her expectancies, volitions, and goals. Actions or decisions appear rational to the extent that they can be derived as a practical consequence from cognitive and evaluative orientations of the agent. This basic explanatory scheme corresponds to Aristotle's model of practical syllogism (see von Wright, 1971), and it recurs in modern theories of action and decision (e.g., Ajzen, 1991; Harless & Camerer, 1994). Although highly successful in research and everyday life, this explanatory scheme is seriously incomplete.

Its scope is limited, above all, because the mental states or processes we refer to in intentionalist action explanations cannot themselves be explained—at least not in any comprehensive sense—within the intentionalist format. Our intentions, beliefs, or decisions basically do not originate from an intentional act or decision. Of course, one may develop particular intentional attitudes toward one's intentional states; for example, a person may develop a wish of having, or not having, particular volitions or beliefs ("second-order volitions"; Frankfurt, 1971). We would be caught in an infinite regress, however, if forming an intention would again require an intention. Likewise, our beliefs and insights do not result from a decision to hold a particular belief or to consider a particular proposition as plausible or true; no argument could be compelling if accepting or rejecting it were a matter of choice. That the originating conditions of mental states are not—and cannot—themselves be represented in consciousness is not a Freudian discovery, but was already noted, for example, by Leibniz, Hume, and Kant (see Hartmann, 1873; Leary, 1982). Of course, the nonintentional genesis of mental states opens up possibilities of subtle manipulation. Experimental research in social and motivational psychology has amply demonstrated how particular intentions and behavioral tendencies—for example, aggressive or altruistic tendencies, endorsement of stereotypes, achievement of motivation—can be induced in ways that bypass reflexive attention, so that the person does not feel any heteronomous influence (for overviews, see Bargh & Ferguson, 2000; Wegner & Bargh, 1998).

Similar arguments apply to emotions. Emotional states implicate particular cognitions; colloquially, we often say that the person had reasons to feel jealous, surprised, or worried, but this, of course, does not mean that such "reasons" would have motivated a decision to have that particular emotion. Although not intentionally originated, emotions and mood states modulate intentions and action tendencies because they engage specific mindsets and influence the cognitive availability of particular arguments and beliefs. When we are in a particular mood state, for example, the cognitive system tends to generate "mood-congruent" thoughts and memories (e.g., Blaney, 1986); when in a positive mood, we are more prone to accept, or be persuaded by, weak arguments and are more liable to stereotyped thinking (cf. Bless et al., 1996; Park & Banaji, 2000). Of course, we have some degree of control over our emotional life; we may deliberately seek or avoid situations that tend to produce particular emotions, and we can critically examine the beliefs that emotionally affect us (see also Averill, 1980; Gordon, 1987). Obviously, emotions are a central target area of self-control and self-cultivation. But the fact that we have some control over the conditions under which a particular emotion occurs does not render the emotional reaction itself an intentional act.

As these findings demonstrate, intentional and "conscious" states are linked to, or generated by, subpersonal or preintentional processes; to put it with Ricoeur (1950), they attest to the "unity of the voluntary and the involuntary." The well-known distinction between "controlled" and "automatic" processes (Shiffrin & Schneider, 1977) does not quite capture these intrinsic relations, because even intentionally and reflexively controlled processes appear to be rooted in automatisms. Of course we experience our behavior as personally controlled when external causal influences are not salient (Rée, 1885; Wegner & Bargh, 1998), and when we feel that it conforms with our wants and beliefs, that experience should not simply be dismissed as illusory (e.g., Frankfurt, 1988).

We may summarize the arguments so far by stating, perhaps somewhat apodictically, that *there is no intentionality behind intentionality*. But this brings me to a second can of worms: The control of mental states and processes.

THE PROBLEM OF CONTROLLING ONE'S MENTAL STATES AND PROCESSES

As already intimated, humans not only have particular emotions, wishes, and beliefs, but they can take a critical attitude toward these intentional states. As cultivated persons, we are capable of developing the wish to have, or not to have, particular wishes, emotions, or beliefs, and we should be able to modify our behavior and emotional life according to such secondary volitions. Thus, we are held responsible not only for our actions, but also, to some extent, for the mental states and processes from which our actions ensue. It is important to note that the inherent dialogical structure of self-observation and self-critique problematizes notions of a homogenous self or identity. As Davidson (1982) has noted, "the agent has reasons for changing his own habits and character, but these reasons come from a domain of values necessarily extrinsic to the contents of the views and values that undergo change" (p. 105).

The question of how we can control our thoughts, feelings, and emotions has become trendy, and answers to that question fill the shelves of bookstores (cf. Baumeister, Heatherton, & Tice, 1994; Karoly & Kanfer, 1982). The flourishing market for self-management techniques hints that it may be easier to control the mental life of other persons than one's own. Of course we can exert control over our mental processes, for example, by turning our attention to a particular situation, by actively remembering particular events, by vividly imagining some desired scenario, and so on. But self-regulatory efficiency is basically limited by the actual situation and its particular enticements or distractions; interestingly, prolonged resistance against some strong action tendency appears to drain resources of self-control (Baumeister, Bratslavsky, Muraven, & Tice, 1998). Intentional regulation of attention is impaired when processing resources are reduced, for example, by stress or fatigue or under conditions of "divided attention." Intentional attempts to suppress some particular thoughts even tend to produce counterintentional rebound effects; such "ironic" effects (Wegner, 1994) can arise because the corresponding intention already involves a representation of the undesired thought content. Generally, it appears that producing some particular thought, idea, or insight cannot be an intentional act if the intention already implies the cognitive content that it intends to generate (cf. Brandtstädter, 2001; Müller, 1992).

Obviously, some of the processes that guide and motivate intentional action are themselves not subject to direct intentional control. This also holds for the processes of forming a commitment to, and of disengaging from, particular goals, which are basic to action regulation. Although relinquishing a blocked goal or barren project alleviates feelings of depression and hopelessness, we cannot voluntarily do so in order to avoid such feelings; this makes depression such a recalcitrant problem. Of course we can form a decision to disengage from goals that are beyond our control; such a decision, however, would require a change in preferences that would have to occur *prior* to the decision (see also Brandtstädter & Rothermund, 2002). Theories of rational action and decision notoriously have difficulties with integrating such preintentional or predecisional dynamics. There are, however, attempts to fill the theoretical gaps; for example, the influence that affective states and anticipated emotional consequences may have on decisions is increasingly heeded (e.g., Kahneman & Tversky, 2000; Loewenstein, Weber, Hsee, & Welch, 2001).

It appears paradoxical that we cannot intentionally originate those mental states that form the very core of our intentionality and personhood—our beliefs, insights, creative ideas, and preferences. Intentional processes seem to some extent themselves shielded against direct intentional control. As far as we have control over these processes, it is often of an indirect or technical nature only; the use of self-management techniques attests to these limitations. The point then is not "that desires and beliefs aren't ever in an agents control, but rather that coming to have them isn't something an agent does" (Davidson, 1980, p. 73).

SELF-DECEPTION, MOTIVATED REASONING, AND "SPLIT MINDS"

That mental states are not generated by an intentional act does not mean, of course, that motives and intentions play no role in this process. Early experimental work of the Würzburg School already demonstrated that associative processes, for example, are modulated by "determining tendencies" that are induced by current tasks and goal orientations (Ach, 1905; Bühler, 1908). In a similar vein, recent action-theoretical findings show that different phases of action regulation (planning an action, forming and executing intentions, disengagement from blocked goals) each involve particular cognitive tendencies or "mind sets" (cf. Brandtstädter & Rothermund, 2002; Heckhausen & Gollwitzer, 1986; Klinger, 1987; Kuhl, 1987). That the processing of information, and, accordingly, the construal of truth, reflects personal values and preferences has been documented amply by social-psychological research: Arguments and evidence that conform with our interests and have positive implications for our self-view and well-being tend to be more easily accepted (except perhaps among depressed people); we tend to select or construe the evidence that supports or rationalizes preferred conclusions (cf. Elster, 1983; Kruglanski & Webster, 1996; Kunda, 1990; Nisbett & Ross, 1980).

In everyday parlance, we often refer to the mentioned phenoma as "wishful thinking," "self-deception," and the like. Such notions, however, lead to paradoxes that once more highlight limitations of an intentionalist explanatory stance (see also Greve, 1996; Lockard & Paulhus, 1988; Mele, 1987). As "wishful thinking," we denote the case where a proposition X is held to be true by a person apparently because it would have positive implications for him or her if X were true. We speak of "self-deception" when the wishful thinker appears to have evidence that X is not the case. But how can we bring ourselves to believe something that contradicts our beliefs? And would the self-deceptive maneuver not be compromised by having insight into its defensive purpose?

These paradoxes apparently force us to drop the notion of a coherent, self-transparent self that intentionally deceives itself (see also Rorty, 1988). One might consider, for example, separating the self into a deceiving partial self A and a deceived partial self B, so that self A has superior knowledge but discloses it from B, which apparently would imply that A be intransparent to B. However, translating in that way the model of deception from the interpersonal to the intrapersonal realm creates new inconsistencies: How can self *A* influence the beliefs of self *B* without *B* noticing it or somehow playing along? Does *A* act in its own interest, in the interest of self *B*, or does it simply like lying, and so on (see also Johnston, 1995)?

It seems that these inconsistencies cannot be resolved unless we consider the mentioned phenomena as resulting, not unlike visual illusions in that respect, from the interplay of relatively autonomous and specialized modules or subsystems that are not orchestrated by an intentional master-self. The interplay between these subsystems can be disturbed; for example, conflicts between different goals or between intentional and automatic action tendencies may lead to particular lapses or action slips (e.g., Reason & Mycielska, 1982). Such disturbances attest to the fact that information processing and action regulation engage processes that autonomously organize themselves. Obviously, the boundary between strategic and automatic processes, or between causality and intentionality, is blurred or permeable—as we should perhaps expect when mental phenomena are instantiated by neurophysiological systems.

PROBLEMS OF ACTION EXPLANATION

Not surprisingly, the mentioned ontological ambiguities also breed confusion in contexts of action explanation. Human cognition and action is embedded in causal structures, but also integrated in symbolic relations and systems of meaning (e.g., Brandtstädter, 1985, 1998; Greve, 1994; Harré, 1986). Actions involve causal processes and generate causal effects, but they cannot simply be equated to physical events: In different cultural symbolic contexts, in different situations, or on different developmental levels, acts such as greeting, aggression, and so on, can be instantiated physically in quite different ways, and commonalities between such instantiations often can only be found when heeding the conceptual structure of the particular type of action.

The concepts that we use in contexts of describing, explaining, and predicting actions are thus embedded in semantic structures; these structural constraints, however, exclude particular combinations of events as not "co-predicable" (Keil, 1986). For conceptual rather than for causal reasons we can exclude, for example, that *memories* refer to *future* events, that one could feel *proud* in the face of *failure*, or that one could be *surprised* if something that one has *expected* happens; empirical counterclaims would be suspect of conceptual confusion or invalid observational procedures. This problem recurs in controversies about the causal status of action explanations (e.g., Heil & Mele, 1991). We typically require of a causal relation that it does not already follow from logical or conceptual relations, so that antecedents and consequents can be independently verified. Action explanations that refer to the agent's desires, wishes, beliefs, expectancies, and so on, do not seem to easily satisfy this requirement. This becomes more readily apparent when we try to cast them in accordance with the covering-law format of explanation. We might then eventually come up with some law-like generalization L such as the following (see Churchland, 1970, p. 221):

(L) If
1.   Person P *wants S*, and
2.   *believes* that action A is under the given circumstances a way to bring about S, and
3.   there exists no other action A of which P *believes* that it would be suitable to reach S and that appears to P at least as equivalent to A, and
4. P has not other *wishes* that override S, and
5.   *knows* how to carry out A, and
6.   is *capable* to do A, then
7. P *does* A.

Can such an argument pass as an empirical law that could yield a causal explanation? There are reasons to doubt this. Obviously, L represents a part of the "language game" or conceptual framework that relates concepts of wanting, acting, believing, being able, and so on, so that a particular component of L cannot be identified without presupposing that conceptual structure. For example, to find out whether somebody holds the belief that a particular act is instrumental to achieve some desired outcome, we would have to look whether he or she performs that action when the various hedging conditions mentioned in L apply. Within the semantic system on which L is predicated, particular combinations seem to be not co-predicable and thus can be excluded *a priori*: for example, observing that P acts in a particular way conceptually excludes that P is not capable to perform that act. As Churchland (1970) admits, it would be difficult to contest L without undermining the conceptual systems in which explanations, predictions, and descriptions of human actions are embedded.

Of course we can take steps to enrich L with empirical meaning to make it more useful in contexts of prediction and explanation. For example, a "wish" may express itself in phenomena such as in selective attention or in the agent's readiness to invest effort in the pursuit of a desired outcome; an action-guiding "expectancy" or "belief" may manifest itself in a particular emotional reaction such as surprise over an un-expected outcome; and, of course, physiological measures such as particular activation patterns of the brain might be considered as indica-tors of mental states or processes. Linking the components of L in that way to a system of "reduction sentences," however, does not completely resolve our problem. The enriched structure may now generate empiri-cal hypotheses that could be put to empirical test, but it appears that not *all* parts of the structure could be dismissed in the light of empirical evi-dence (see Brandtstädter, 1987; Brandtstädter & Sturm, 2004; Stegmüller, 1970).

The considerations converge, to some extent, with the argument of a "logical connection" between actions and mental states, which has been defended by philosophers in the Wittgensteinian tradition (e.g., von Wright, Anscombe, Stoutland; for details, see Beckermann, 1977; Mac-donald & Pettit, 1981; Stoutland, 1970; von Wright, 1979; for a discussion of this argument with regard to psychological theories of action, see also Greve, 2001). The Logical Connection argument casts doubt on the as-sumption that mental states such as expectations or wishes could be causal antecedents of action; at least, it seems to follow that action expla-nations, to pass as causal explanations, would require a format that is not subject to the semantic constraints of everyday language or folk psychol-ogy. To understand the "causal push" of mental states, we obviously have to transcend the intentionalist semantics of folk psychology. But can we leave it behind completely? There are reasons to doubt it.

PSYCHOLOGY AND "FOLK PSYCHOLOGY"

Some of the preceding considerations may appear to be grist to the mill of those who hold the view that psychology will not become a respect-able science unless it emancipates itself from "folk psychology" and its semantic constraints. Whereas some proponents of that position con-sider mentalistic concepts of wanting, expecting, believing, and so on as fictional entities, others argue more modestly that such concepts should eventually be replaced by developed neurophysiological theo-ries (cf. Churchland, 1989; Stich, 1983). The common tenor, however, is that "folk psychology" is a degenerated project that may be of some use in everyday contexts of interaction and communication, but that is woe-fully inadequate when dealing with the deviant, alien, young, or ill (see also Clark, 1989; Kusch, 1999).

This criticism seems legitimate to some extent, as long as one under-stands folk psychology as an intentionalist explanatory scheme. That scheme presupposes principles of rationality and finds its limits in mechanisms and processes that cannot be explained in intentionalist terms; as we have seen, even intentional states cannot be considered throughout as intentionally originated. And as far as we hold psychological research and theorizing to be predicated on that scheme, folk psychology seems contaminated by its limitations. However, even everyday explanations of behavior do not simply refer to beliefs and desires, but also to abilities and skills, to habits and tics, to attitudes and temperamental dispositions (see also von Eckardt, 1997). It seems useful, then, to consider the relationship between psychology and folk psychology somewhat more closely.

At this juncture, however, we must first obviate a possible misunderstanding. As far as human agents rely, to a significant degree, on an implicit folk psychology in contexts of attribution, social perception, and interpersonal behavior, it seems natural for psychological theorizing to take that into account. This, by the way, was precisely the aim of attribution research in social psychology as it was described programmatically by Heider (1958). The point is that theoretical approaches in psychology—and one might include here also symbolic interactionism, script-theoretical approaches in cognitive psychology, and other lines of research—may well refer to the semantic structures of folk psychology without themselves being part of it.

It is nonetheless obvious that many psychological constructs have their roots in folk psychology and its semantic structures: Concepts such as anxiety, aggression, introversion, attention, learning, depression, intelligence, or wisdom were used in ordinary language long before they became the subject of psychological theorizing. Psychological research cannot completely neglect these semantic links: For example, the propositions that prejudice is not based on careful scrutiny, that we can remember only past events, or that altruistic acts imply the sacrifice of some personal advantage cannot be empirically refuted in any straightforward sense; rather, they form a conceptual scaffolding that—in the sense of a "relative a priori"—guides the construction of valid tests and observational methods (see Brandtstädter & Sturm, 2004).

The fact that some core meanings of psychological constructs resist empirical falsification may be seen as a shortcoming that psychology has inherited from folk psychology, and that stands in the way of fruitful theorizing going beyond everyday platitudes. However, this view seems mistaken on several counts. First of all, the recalcitrance or even immunity of theoretical core assumptions against empirical evidence is not specific to psychological theories; we have a similar situation in physical theories, for example (cf. the notion of the "theoreticity" of measurement; Balzer & Moulines, 1980; see also Friedman, 2001; Westmeyer, 1992). Furthermore, even where it partly retains the conceptual structures of ordinary language, psychological research goes beyond them: Psychology has enriched concepts such as depression, anxiety, intelligence, or attention with empirical and theoretical knowledge that goes far beyond folk psychology. Such creative "core extensions" (Herrmann, 1976), for example, include knowledge about etiological factors, physiological implications, diagnostic strategies, and therapeutic approaches.

But couldn't we imagine, and wouldn't it be nice, if eventually the concepts of folk psychology would be completely replaced by more refined, perhaps neurophysiological, explications? For some, this is the kind of psychology we should strive for (see, e.g., Churchland, 1989).

Arguments against such an eliminativism sometimes appear to be fueled by panicky metaphysics; for example, Karl Bühler (1927) feared that a physicalistic psychology would leave us behind "in a desert of meaningless events" (p. 70). There are some more principled reservations, however. First, the "objects" of psychology—cognitions, emotions, intentions—do not appear to be linked in any essential way to particular physical substrate conditions: Just as, for example, economists can deal with demand, supply, interest rates, and so on, without implicating particular physical instantiations, psychologists can theorize about knowledge, communication, meaning, etc. without specific physical or physiological implications (this corresponds to the thesis of a "multiple realizability" of intentional processes; cf. Fodor, 1974; Heil, 1992; Putnam, 1982; Searle, 1983). There is a further reservation that seems even more trenchant: We typically conceive of mental states as having propositional content (he wishes, expects, fears, knows, etc. that X—where X stands for some proposition such as "it rains"); and as long as we do so, we find that mental states cannot be equated with, or reduced to, physiological states or events. For example, assertions such as "she perceives X" or "he knows that X" link a particular mental state with an external condition: We imply that X is the case. Similarly, if somebody "expects that X," this seems to require that the person in question has some semantically structured notion of X that is linked to the semantic order within a discourse community. As Putnam (1975) has put it, "'meanings' just ain't in the *head*" (p. 227; see also Burge, 1986; Pettit, 1986). If the specification of mental states must essentially refer to language, culture, and context, it follows that psychology cannot be dissolved without residue into neurophysiology. Obviously, these are further manifestations of the basic ontological ambiguity to which I have pointed earlier in the chapter.

CONCLUSION

Although I was tempted to do so sometimes, I have made no attempt here to take a position on the ontological conflicts just mentioned; any attempt to settle these questions in short compass would indeed be more than pretentious. The very metaphor of an ambiguous figure, however, appears adequate to suggest that causalist and intentionalist approaches, which since Dilthey (1894) have often been opposed as incompatible or even adversary stances, both have their legitimations and limitations. Considering the boundary work of psychology and the historical transformations of its identity and self-understanding, ontological commitments that, in this way, appear to be "essentially contestable" are of particular interest, as they mark the points where the use of arguments tends to change into nondiscursive strategies of polemics, power, and propaganda. There are reasons to assume, however, that the mentioned ontological ambiguities are *constitutive* to the project of psychology. From that point of view, this discipline is the arena where conflicts between physicalist and personalist perspectives are constantly negotiated—so that the belief that only one of them should finally prevail may already be *bad* psychology.

REFERENCES

Ach, N. (1905). *Über die Willenstätigkeit und das Denken.* [On the activity of the will and thought]. Göttingen: Vandenhoeck & Ruprecht.

Ajzen, I. (1991). The theory of planned behavior. *Organizational Behavior and Human Decision Processes, 50,* 179–211.

Averill, J. A. (1980). A constructivistic view of emotion. In R. Plutchik & H. Kellerman (Eds.), *Emotion. Theory, research and experience. Vol. 1: Theories of emotion* (pp. 305–339). New York: Academic Press.

Balzer, W., & Moulines, C. U. (1980). On theoreticity. *Synthese, 44,* 467–494.

Bargh, J. A., & Ferguson, M. J. (2000). Beyond behaviorism: On the automaticity of higher mental processes. *Psychological Bulletin, 126,* 925–945.

Baumeister, R. F., Bratslavsky, E., Muraven, M., & Tice, D. M. (1998). Ego depletion: Is the active self a limited resource? *Journal of Personality and Social Psychology, 74,* 1252–1265.

Baumeister, R. F., Heatherton, T. F., & Tice, D. M. (1994). *Losing control: How and why people fail at self-regulation.* San Diego, CA: Academic Press.

Beckermann, A. (1977). Handeln und Handlungserklärungen [Action and action explanation]. In A. Beckermann (Ed.), *Analytische Handlungstheorie, Bd. 2: Handlungserklärungen* (pp. 7–8). Frankfurt a.M.: Suhrkamp.

Blaney, P. H. (1986). Affect and memory: A review. *Psychological Bulletin, 99,* 229–346.

Bless, H., Clore, G. L., Schwarz, N., Golisano, V., Rabe, C., & Wölk, M. (1996). Mood and the use of scripts: Does a happy mood really lead to mindlessness? *Journal of Personality and Social Psychology, 71,* 665–679.

Brandtstädter, J. (1985). Individual development in social action contexts: Problems of explanation. In J. R. Nesselroade & A. von Eye (Eds.), *Individual development and social change: Explanatory analysis* (pp. 243–264). New York: Academic Press.

Brandtstädter, J. (1987). On certainty and universality in human development: Developmental psychology between apriorism and empiricism. In M. Chapman & R.A. Dixon (Eds.), *Meaning and the growth of understanding. Wittgenstein's significance for developmental psychology* (pp. 69–84). Berlin: Springer.

Brandtstädter, J. (1998). Action perspectives on human development. In R. M. Lerner (Ed.), *Theoretical models of human development* (Handbook of child psychology, Vol. 1; 5th ed., pp. 807–863). New York: Wiley.

Brandtstädter, J. (2001). *Entwicklung—Intentionalit—Handeln* [Development-intentionality-action]. Stuttgart: Kohlhammer.

Brandtstädter, J., & Rothermund, K. (2002). The life-course dynamics of goal pursuit and goal adjustment: A two-process framework. *Developmental Review, 22,* 117–150.

Brandtstädter, J., & Sturm, T. (2004). Apriorität, Erfahrung und das Projekt der Psychologie. [Apriority, experience and the project of psychology]. *Zeitschrift für Sozialpsychologie, 35,* 15–32.

Bühler, K. (1908). Tatsachen und Probleme zu einer Psychologie der Denkvorgänge. II: Über Gedankenzusammenhänge [Facts and problems of a psychology of thought processes]. *Archiv für die Gesamte Psychologie, 12,* 1–23.

Bühler, K. (1927). Die Krise der Psychologie [The crisis of psychology]. Jena: G. Fischer

Burge, T. (1986). Individualism and psychology. *Philosophical Review, 45,* 3–45.

Churchland, P. M. (1970). The logical character of action-explanations. *Philosophical Review, 79,* 214–236.

Churchland, P. M. (1989). *A neurocomputational perspective.* Cambridge, MA: MIT Press.

Clark, A. (1989). *Microcognition: Philosophy, cognitive science, and parallel distributed processing.* Cambridge, MA: MIT Press.

Davidson, D. (1980). *Essays on actions and events.* Oxford, UK: Clarendon Press.

Davidson, D. (1982). Paradoxes of irrationality. In R. S. Wollheim & J. Hopkins (Eds.), *Philosophical essays on Freud* (pp. 289–305). Cambridge, U.K.: Cambridge University Press.

Dilthey, W. (1894). Ideen über eine beschreibende und zergliedernde Psychologie [Ideas concerning a descriptive and analytical psychology]. (Berliner Akademie der Wissenschaften: Sitzungsbericht 1894; pp. 1309–1407; Wiederabdruck in: W. Dilthey [1968]. *Gesammelte Schriften, Bd. V,* pp. 139–240).

Elster, J. (1983). *Sour grapes: Studies in the subversion of rationality.* Cambridge, U.K.: Cambridge University Press.

Fodor, J. (1974). Special sciences, or: The disunity of sciences as a working hypothesis. *Synthese, 28,* 97–115.

Frankfurt, H. G. (1971). Freedom of the will and the concept of a person. *Journal of Philosophy, 68,* 5–20.

Frankfurt, H. G. (1988). *The importance of what we care about.* Cambridge: Cambridge University Press.

Freud, S. (1969). *An outline of psycho-analysis.* New York: Norton.

Friedman, M. (2001). *Dynamics of reason.* Stanford, CA: CSLI Publications.

Gallie, W. B. (1955). Essentially contested concepts. *Proceedings of the Aristotelian Society, 56,* 167–198.

Gordon, R. M. (1987). *The structure of emotions. Investigations in cognitive philosophy*. New York: Cambridge University Press.

Greve, W. (1994). *Handlungsklärung. Die psychologische Erklärung menschlichen Handelns* [Explicating action: Psychological aciton explanation]. Göttingen: Hogrefe.

Greve, W. (1996). Erkenne dich selbst? Argumente zur Bedeutung der "Perspektive der ersten Person" [Know thyself? Arguments on the relevance of the first-person perspective]. *Sprache & Kognition, 15*, 104–119.

Greve, W. (2001). Traps and gaps in action explanation: Theoretical problems of a psychology of human action. *Psychological Review, 108*, 435–451.

Harless, D. W., & Camerer, C. F. (1994). The predictive utility of generalized expected utility theories. *Econometrica, 62*, 1251–1289.

Harré, R. (1986). The social construction of the mind. In R. B. Marcus, G. J. W. Dorn, & P. Weingartner (Eds.), *Logic, methodology, and philosophy of science VII* (pp. 521–537). Amsterdam: North-Holland.

Heckhausen, H., & Gollwitzer, P. M. (1986). Information processing before and after the formation of an intent. In F. Klix & H. Hagendorf (Eds.), *In memoriam Hermann Ebbinghaus: Symposium on the structure and function of human memory* (pp. 1071–1082). Amsterdam: Elsevier/North Holland.

Heidelberger, M. (2003). The mind–body problem in the origin of logical empiricism. In P. Parrini, W. C. Salmon, & M. H. Salmon (Eds.), *Logical empiricism: Historical and contemporary perspectives* (pp. 233–262). Pittsburgh, PA: University of Pittsburgh Press.

Heider, F. (1958). *The psychology of interpersonal relations*. New York: Wiley.

Heil, J., & Mele, A. (Eds.). (1991). *Mental causation*. Oxford, UK: Clarendon Press.

Herrmann, T. (1976). *Die Psychologie und ihre Forschungsprogramme.* [Psychology and its research programs]. Göttingen: Hogrefe.

Johnston, M. (1995). Self-deception and the nature of mind. In C. Macdonald & G. Macdonald (Eds.), *Philosophy of psychology. Debates on psychological explanation* (Vol. 1; pp. 433–460). Oxford, UK: Blackwell.

Kahneman, D., & Tversky, A. (Eds.). (2000). *Choices, values, and frames*. New York: Russell Sage Foundation/Cambridge University Press.

Karoly, P., & Kanfer, F. H. (Eds.). (1982). *The psychology of self-management: From theory to practice*. New York: Plenum.

Keil, F. C. (1986). On the structure-dependent nature of stages of cognitive development. In I. Levin (Ed.), *Stage and structure. Reopening the debate* (pp. 144–163). Norwood, NJ: Ablex.

Kim, J. (1993). *Supervenience and mind*. New York: Cambridge University Press.

Kim, J. (1997). Supervenience, emergence, and realization in the philosophy of mind. In M. Carrier & P. K. Machamer (Eds.), *Mindscapes: Philosophy, science, and the mind* (pp. 271–293). Konstanz/Pittsburgh, PA: Universitätsverlag Konstanz and the University of Pittsburgh Press.

Klinger, E. (1987). Current concerns and disengagement from incentives. In F. Halisch & J. Kuhl (Eds.), *Motivation, intention, and volition* (pp. 337–347). Berlin: Springer.

Kruglanski, A.W., & Webster, D. M. (1996). Motivated closing of the mind: "Seizing" and "freezing." *Psychological Review, 103*, 263–283.

Kuhl, J. (1987). Action control: The maintenance of motivational states. In F. Halisch & J. Kuhl (Eds.), *Motivation, intention and volition* (pp. 279–291). Berlin: Springer.

Kunda, Z. (1990). The case for motivated reasoning. *Psychological Bulletin, 108,* 480–498.

Kusch, M. (1999). *Psychological knowledge. A social history and philosophy.* London: Routledge.

Leary, D. E. (1982). Immanuel Kant and the development of modern psychology. In W. R. Woodward & M. G. Ash (Eds.), *The problematic science: Psychology in nineteenth century thought* (pp. 17–42). New York: Praeger.

Lockard, J. S., & Paulhus, D. L. (Eds.). (1988). *Self-deception: An adaptive mechanism?* Englewood Cliffs, NJ: Prentice-Hall.

Loewenstein, G. F., Weber, E. U., Hsee, C. K., & Welch, N. (2001). Risk as feelings. *Psychological Bulletin, 127*, 267–286.

Macdonald, G., & Pettit, P. (1981). *Semantics and social science.* London: Routledge & Kegan Paul.

Mele, A. (1987). Recent work on self-deception. *American Philosophical Quarterly, 24*, 1–17.

Müller, A. (1992). Mental teleology. *Proceedings of the Aristotelian Society, 92* (Part 1), 161–183.

Nisbett, R. E., & Ross, L. (1980). *Human inference: Strategies and shortcomings of social judgment.* Englewood Cliffs, NJ: Prentice-Hall.

Park, J., & Banaji, M. R. (2000). Mood and heuristics: The influence of happy and sad states on sensitivity and bias in stereotyping. *Journal of Personality and Social Psychology, 78,* 1005–1023.

Pettit, P. (1986). Broad-minded explanation and psychology. In P. Pettit & J. McDowell (Eds.), *Subject, thought, and context* (pp. 17–58). Oxford, U.K.: Oxford University Press.

Putnam, H. (1975). The meaning of meaning. In H. Putnam (Ed.), *Philosophical papers. Vol. 2: Mind, language, and reality* (pp. 215–271). London: Cambridge University Press.

Putnam, H. (1982). Why reason can't be naturalized. *Synthese, 52*, 3–23.

Reason, J. T., & Mycielska, K. (1982). *Absent-minded? The psychology of mental lapses and everyday errors.* Englewood Cliffs, NJ: Prentice-Hall.

Rée, P. (1885). *Die Illusion der Willensfreiheit* [The illusion of free will]. Berlin: Duncker.

Ricoeur, P. (1950). *Philosophie de la volonté I: Le volontaire et l'involontaire.* [Philosophy of will I: The voluntary and the involuntary]. Paris: Aubier.

Rorty, A. O. (1988). Liars, layers, and lairs. In B. P. McLaughlin & A. O. Rorty (Eds.), *Perspectives on self-deception* (pp. 11–28). Berkeley, CA: University of California Press.

Searle, J. R. (1983). *Intentionality: An essay in the philosophy of mind.* New York: Cambridge University Press.

Shiffrin, R. M., & Schneider, W. (1977). Controlled and automatic human information processing: II. Perceptual learning, automatic attending, and a general theory. *Psychological Review, 84,* 127–190.

Stegmüller, W. (1970). *Probleme und Resultate der Wissenschaftstheorie und Analytischen Philosophie* (Vol. 2). [Problems and results of philosophy of science and analytical philosophy]. Berlin: Springer.

Stich, S. P. (1983). *From folk psychology to cognitive science.* Cambridge, MA: MIT Press.

Stoutland, F. (1970). *The Logical Connection argument* (American Philosophical Quarterly, Monograph No. 4). Oxford, UK: Blackwell.

von Eckardt, B. (1997). The empirical naiveté of the current philosophical conception of folk psychology. In M. Carrier & P. K. Machamer (Eds.), *Mindscapes: Philosophy, science, and the mind* (pp. 23–51). Konstanz: Universitätsverlag.

von Hartmann, E. (1873). *Philosophie des Unbewussten* (5th rev. ed.). [Philosophy of the unconscious]. Berlin: Duncker.

von Wright, G. H. (1971). *Explanation and understanding.* Ithaca, NY: Cornell University Press.

von Wright, G. H. (1979). Das menschliche Handeln im Lichte seiner Ursachen und Gründe [Human action in light of causes and reasons]. In H. Lenk (Ed.), *Handlungstheorien interdisziplinär* (Vol. II; pp. 417–430). Müchen: Fink.

Wegner, D. M. (1994). Ironic processes of mental control. *Psychological Review, 101,* 34–52.

Wegner, D. M., & Bargh, J. A. (1998). Control and automaticity in social life. In D. T. Gilbert, S. T. Fiske, & L. Gardner (Eds.), *The handbook of social psychology* (Vol. 1, 4th ed., pp. 446–496). Boston, MA: McGraw-Hill.

Westmeyer, H. (Ed.). (1992). *The structuralist program in psychology: Foundations and applications.* Seattle: Hogrefe & Huber.

Wundt, W. (1894). Über psychische Causalität und das Princip des psychophysichen Parallelismus [On psychic causality and the principle of psychophysical parallelism]. *Philosophische Studien, 10,* 1–24.

3

A Critique of Free Will: Psychological Remarks on a Social Institution

Wolfgang Prinz
Max Planck Institute for Human Cognitive and Brain Sciences, Germany

From a psychological point of view, discussing free will is like asking a zoologist to lecture on unicorns: Neither phenomena belongs to the science where the expert is at home. Expositions on unicorns are perhaps more suited to cultural, than natural science; for although they have no natural past, these creatures do have a cultural story to tell. Studies in cultural history may reveal how unicorns initially got fabricated, why the notion of them has persevered, and just what people get out of continuing to believe in them.

Allow me to think of free will as we think of unicorns. I discuss freedom of will not simply in terms of it being a theoretical construct in psychology, but more importantly, think of the *notion* of free will as a product of collective endeavor—not the unicorn itself, as it were, but the *notion* of unicorns.

Von der Natur / art vnnd eygen=
schafft der Thier/welcher namen anfahet inn
frembden spachen / darmit sie vonn den alten ge,
nant woden am Buchstaben V.

Vnicornis ein Einhon.

Vnicornis ein Einhorn/ist bei vns ein frembd vnbekandt thier / zim,
licher grösse/doch gegē seiner treflichen stercke zu rechnen/nit groß von leib/
von farben gelbfarb wie buxbaumen holtz/hat gespalten kloen/ wonet im
gebfrg vn hohen wildtnussen/hat voien an der stirn ein sehe lang scharpff
hoen/welches es an den felsen vnd steinen scherpffet/durch sticht darmit die
D iij grossen

Figure 3–1.   Unicorn.

Why do people feel free in their choices and believe that they are, al-though they are perhaps not? Under which conditions do healthy minds develop intuitions of free will? What psychological, social, and cultural effects do these intuitions encourage? These issues veer beyond the iso-lated study of cognitive and volitional functions to explore how the functions themselves are (individually and collectively) perceived. They include, for instance, how functions of free will are seen in social psy-chology, developmental psychology, evolutionary psychology, and psychohistory. I proceed in three steps:

- *Denying free will*: The first section of this paper confronts our quotidian intuition of free will with maxims of scientific psychol-ogy, concluding that the two are not particularly compatible.
- *Explaining free will*: Which psychological and cultural conditions favor the emergence of free will intuitions?

- *In praise of free will*: A look at the psychological benefits and social functions supported by our intuitions of free will.

My perspective is exclusively from a standpoint of psychology, implying primarily that it is not a viewpoint of neuroscience. I do not discuss how freedom of will may be related to brain functions. Secondly, my perspective is also not that of philosophy. I do not discuss just how free freedom of will genuinely is—or whether it must be subjected to constraints in order to comply with other common notions about the world.

DENYING FREE WILL

Idiom of Agency and Intuitions of Free Will

Agency Talk: The Psychological Explanation of Actions. We spend a large portion of our lives thinking about behavior—deliberating our own actions and ruminating over those of others. Thinking about behavior is not only an individual pastime, it is also one of our favorite social hobbies: Everyday conversation consists to a fair amount of communicative exchange relating which people do what and when, why they do it, and what we think about their doing so.

Folk psychology provides a simple explanatory scheme for behavior: Normally we trace actions back to mental states that precede behavior. We say that John washes his car in the belief that doing so will impress his rich aunt. Of course, mental states assumed to be causes of subsequent behavior do not detail just how that action proceeds. But they do specify why a certain behavior occurred at all; assumed antecedent mental states do not indicate *how* an act happens, they indicate *what* the action was for.

The list of mental states that may be seen as causes of behavior includes many different kinds, each evoking its own distinct explanation for that behavior. In simple cases we explain behavior by identifying an *intention* to attain a specific *goal*. Here we have the prototypical case for acting voluntarily: we assume that a person plans an action and then executes it in order to accomplish certain objectives. Were we to inquire why the person did what she did, she would give us *reasons*.

Other explanations for behavior use the logics of *causes*. If you were to smash a vase in rage, common opinion holds that you would not do so for some reason, but that nevertheless, your action was caused: A mental state of anger is understood as causative of destructive behavior, but not as a reason for it. Such acts have no goal that performing them may attain.

Habitual behavior is different from instinctual or voluntary action: If you ask people during their morning grooming routine just why they are now brushing their teeth, the answer will normally not include any immediate reason or cause. Explanations for this type of behavior normally assume that the original causal mental states occurred long ago: At one time they were present, namely, when the person acquired the particular habit, but they faded as the habit gradually gained control. The reasons have not entirely disappeared and can be recalled if necessary: You know why you brush your teeth, but you don't state your reasons every time you do it.

In the following we concentrate on prototypical voluntary behavior and the jargon used in quotidian speech to describe it. Voluntary acts happen because agents want to achieve certain goals and believe that performing certain acts will get them there.

Free Will Vernacular: Morally Evaluating Action. Everyday talk about behavior does not only revolve around reasons for action but also around *evaluations and justifications.* We want to know the *reason* for action, how to *evaluate* it, and finally, whether it is *justified.* Two factors are at work: On one level, we judge the actions themselves, and their consequences. But on another level we also judge the *person* responsible for that action and the ensuing consequences. We hold people *responsible* for their own behavior and we justify that by believing that they are *free* in their decisions for actions.

These underlying convictions permeate our everyday phrases for describing the freedom of will. They are so familiar, that they hardly need explication. We simply assume, in almost all walks of life, that we could act other than we actually do—if only we wanted to. We understand our actual behavior to be an outcome of voluntary decision. Although our decisions are also always shaped by a number of circumstances, of which we are more or less aware, we believe that ultimately each person is himself responsible for his final decision. We, ourselves, are the authors of our decisions and actions. We all experience this authorship and freedom and attribute it to each other. That is the heart of what I call our *intuition of free will*.

One important consequence of our free will vernacular is that we sometimes *waive further explanation.* For instance, when a court judge asks a defendant why he did a certain thing, the accused often details causes and reasons apparently beyond his own control. In other words: A defendant will say that under the circumstances he had no choice but to do as he did, thus turning over the causal responsibility for the actions in question to the circumstances that prevailed. Now, a judge may or may not accept certain factors as influential. When she accepts explanatory reasons and causes that regress further and further back into the past of the defendant she foregoes the option of attributing both the action and the consequences for it to that person—and personal responsibility evaporates into thin air. In order to attribute personal responsibility, a judge must interrupt the chain of causes at some point and dispense with further explanation.

Thus, talk of free will has two sides. On the one hand, we use it to describe fundamental *psychological facts*, that is, to describe the personal experience of free will intuitions that are so seemingly and indubitably self-evident. On the other, the permission it grants to waive further explanation serves an essentially *moral* (or even legal) *purpose*, namely, that of ascribing outcomes of behavior to individual persons. What should we think of it? Hen or egg—what is what? Is free will a basic fact of human mental constitution issuing welcome social by-products? Or is it a social device serving to collectively regulate individual behavior? Do psychological facts precede social institutions—or should we dare to believe that social functions actually produce psychological facts?

Science and Our Intuition on Free Will

How does the notion of free will line up with maxims of scientific psychology? We must be careful to distinguish the empirical fact that we experience an intuition of free will from the theoretical construct of free will itself.

The empirical fact is a phenomenon like any other that can be explored and explained using tools of psychology. No problem. But guidelines for psychological explanation falter when we switch from viewing free will as an empirical phenomenon to thinking of it as a theoretical construct, by believing *that we feel free, because we ARE free*. We run up against two standards of science: first, that we must distinguish between perception and reality; and second, the assumption of causal closure and thoroughgoing determinism.

Perception and Reality. Psychology has a long history of confusing observational facts with theoretical constructs. Cognition, attention, will, feelings—in the past all of these phenomena have mistakenly been promoted up from the ranks of mere observational facts to be seen as explanatory constructs. It happened—and still occurs in some areas of research—because of a deep and stubborn misconception about the status of introspection.

A widespread but false construal says that our awareness of psychological events is unlike our perception of material events. More than a century of research has opened our eyes to the fact that human *percep-*

tion of material events involves realistic constructivism, a somewhat paradoxical term meant to characterize the supposed relationship between perception and reality. The working model underlying research in perception is realistic inasmuch as it relies on the notion that contents of perception refer to genuinely existing circumstances in the real world. But at the same time it is constructivist because it assumes that contents of perception result from constructive procedures in which perceptual systems process input data according to certain categories, using its own means of representation. Among other elements, these constructive processes essentially include:

- Selective representation: only a small quantity of all input data actually gets processed, and only a small amount of what gets processed later actually becomes conscious representation.
- Content focus: perceptual representations include contents only. Underlying constructive processes are not represented themselves.
- Categorical transformation: perceptual contents get organized into categories; they present the outcome of an interaction between current input data and stored knowledge.

There are also other significant elements, but, for present purposes, these three suffice to illustrate that what we perceive is not reality as it is in and of itself, but the result of construal: human perception is highly selective, significantly transformed, and shaped to suit certain categories.

So much is true of how we perceive material events in the world. In contrast, widespread opinion holds that the *perception of psychological events* in our minds is not a normal perceptual process at all, but a mental activity *sui generis*, in which a thinking subject is aware of its own mental goings-on. The perception of mental events is supposedly basically not a process of representation and transformation—therefore it makes little sense to question how perceived contents relate to genuine facts. The perception of mental events is considered an immediate awareness of genuine facts—with no room for error. Percepts and reality are one and the same. This makes it seem legitimate to view mental phenomena, as they present themselves to us, as theoretical constructs from which we can conclude that we *feel free* because apparently we *are free*.

Is this convincing? Is introspection privileged access? We have little evidence for it. On the contrary, on close examination we find that what we do know suggests that our perception of our own mental events is equally construed, transformed, and selectively focused. We must distinguish between reality and our perception of reality for both material and mental events.

For instance, studies on insightful thought indicate that when people think, they are unable to note the actual nature of their thought processes. At best, persons can report their individual thoughts; occasionally they can also reconstruct the direction their thoughts took leading up to a certain insight. But they know nothing about the thought-producing process itself. Here we must rely on theory to identify what the person experienced (and can report late) as a selective output produced by submental mechanisms to which experience has no access. Trying to recall a name one has forgotten is also a good example. When we try to remember a certain name we often experience a disquieting mental state of being altogether unable to retrieve it, or of faintly fathoming some fraction of it. And then, suddenly, the entire name emerges, seemingly from nowhere, and that is all a person can report when asked about what just took place. But theory tells us that more was involved: Once again, theory says that the phenomena accessible at the subjective level are the product of events at the subpersonal level, namely, mechanisms executing a search procedure, scavenging that person's stock of knowledge. The same holds for comprehending written text: Try to watch yourself while reading and you will only notice whether or not you understand the text. The practitioning reader never knows how understanding a text works; the theoretician does.

Our own perception of mental events provides only an inconsistent and incomplete picture of the underlying processes at work. It is a highly selective, content-focused representation of products created by mechanisms that are themselves imperceptible. We are not actually aware of mental processes themselves, we are aware of individual mental states that perhaps reveal something about the underlying processes that caused them. It is not only perfectly respectable, but also actually necessary that we inquire how mental perception relates to reality of the underlying functional mechanisms. Whatever introspection may tell us about the nature of mental events, it itself is the product of selective representation, content focus, and categorical transformation. So the fact that we *feel free* says nothing whatsoever about whether the events underlying that feel are voluntary or determined.

Indeterminism and Waiving Explanation. Another feature making freedom of will incompatible with scientific explanation is that it entices us to accept local gaps of indeterminism in an otherwise deterministic worldview. Although we are accustomed to various sorts of indeterminism—or at least a lack of determinability—in certain areas such as quantum physics and chaos theory, when we examine the case of mental events we find that indeterminism here is more radical than mere breaks in causal chains: We're talking about a kind of determinism deprived of causal antecedents. It is allegedly set into motion by an auton-omous subject deciding on its own—a kind of unmoved mover, as it were. This makes attempts at reconciling the freedom of will with quan-tum physics fuzziness and the non-determinedness of chaotic systems doomed to fail. Free will is not simply an absence of causal determina-tion. The concept of free will is more sophisticated: it demands that we view subjects as the autonomous authors of their actions, equipped with a will and in a position to decide freely.

From a scientific point of view, another equally unacceptable practice is that of waiving explanation. It is incompatible with an enlightened, unconstrained scientific ethos. Accepting the tenets of indeterminism requires that we surrender our practice of explanation. That is a consid-erable demand leaving only one possible conclusion, namely, that scien-tific psychology has no room for a theoretical construct called the freedom of will. Theoretically, then, a psychologist must deny free will, if his work is to be deemed scientific.

EXPLAINING FREE WILL

Adhering, then, to the practices of scientific psychology, the legitimate task to tackle is that of explaining our intuition of free will as a psycho-logical fact. Where do our intuitions of free will come from? Why do sub-jects feel free, although, in fact, they are not? Obviously, in order to answer these questions we need a theory that clearly distinguishes the functional reality of subpersonal volitional mechanisms from a phe-nomenal awareness of personal choices based on free will. We must make a distinction if we want to have both: *a perception of free will* within *a world that is deterministic.*

The Intuition of Free Will

Consider, first: Under which circumstances do we experience an intu-ition of free will? When do we say that something is a matter of free will? Typically, intuitions of free will emerge in situations that involve decid-ing to act in some way. It seems that by their very nature, intuitions are linked to decisions involving action. One wonders why intuitions of free will do not surface to guide our thoughts, our fantasies, moods, or feel-ings—at least not to the extent that they accompany voluntary decisions related to action. This may be related to the second essential condition under which intuitions of free will emerge: the active part played by the self. Although decisions about actions constitute the occasions on which intuitions of free will are articulated, persons are the subjects to whom we attribute the underlying freedom: a decision is not free; the *self*, we say, is free to make a decision. We *ourselves* experience freedom, *we* make decisions, *we* are free to make those decisions, and *we* could decide and do otherwise. It seems as if one's very self is confronted with an interplay of motives, interests, and preferences that influence it, as if it were an autonomous subject; as if the self is aware of all these forces acting on it, but *decides on its own* what it will do. We could also see it the other way around: The ability to make decisions on one's own is a constitutive feature of a self. *Explaining our intuition of free will then, demands nothing less than explaining the role of the self.*

This role is particularly conspicuous when we rank decision-related action on a scale according to the degree with which the self participates in any particular decision-making process. One end of the scale, the pole of emphatic volition, marks paradigmatic acts of will displaying a high degree of self involvement. Our intuition of free will is positioned there. The opposite pole on the scale is for ordinary volition, like habitual behavior or drives. We rarely say that the self is involved in decisions prior to this sort of action, so we rarely claim that it involves an intuition of free will.

What sort of theory could accommodate a thorough distinction between subpersonal causal processes that produce decisions on the one hand and personal awareness of agency, where decisions appear to be the outcome of individual choice, on the other? By raising this very question I assume that the subpersonal production of decision processes is "real," whereas how this reality appears to the individual would have to count as "a perception" of something—at least initially. Thinking of those perceptions as belonging to reality is a step we take later on in the chapter.

Action Decisions

Subpersonal Mechanisms Various fields in psychology explore the events and mechanisms that produce, at an underlying level, what we call decisions about what to do. Among others, motivation psychology, social psychology, evolutionary psychology, and the psychology of economics all investigate the phenomenon of decision production, meaning that we must deal with a wide range of applicable, yet often incompatible, theoretical taxonomies. Nevertheless, I would like to outline a few convergences that do exist. Most theories agree that deciding involves at least three ingredients, which I will call *preferences, action knowledge*, and *situation evaluation*. In order to explain this without excessive details, I have to take recourse to mentalist vocabulary; but the processes outlined can nonetheless be conceptualized as subpersonal mechanisms.

The first ingredient is systems of representation with ordered *preferences* (e.g., drives, needs, motives, interests, and so on). These systems represent hierarchies of objectives, and they do so on various time scales, from very long-term (at most: lifelong) preferential dispositions to short-term and current sets of needs. Current needs are embedded in long-term dispositions, but not entirely determined by them. The reverse is also true: long-term dispositions develop out of current needs, but are not entirely determined by them. Research in this area is focused not only on the general principles underpinning the design of the preference system, but also on individual differences, like the configuration and origin of preferences and preference assignment of varying scales of time, the dynamics of reciprocal effects among scales of time, and last but not least, how preference arrangements are altered through learning and interaction.

The second ingredient is representational systems for *action knowledge.* By this I mean knowledge about how action is related to the effects it brings about. This knowledge is organized in a way that makes it accessible and allows it to be used in two ways: from actions to effects and from effects to actions. Both uses are elements of planning action. Forward-directed models provide information about possible effects of certain actions. The other way around, inverse models provide information about possible actions appropriate for achieving certain goals (intended effects). Action knowledge must also be organized along various time scales, corresponding to the periods that action–effect relationships may last, from mere fractions of seconds up to months and years. Research in this field also focuses on how knowledge of actions originates and is organized and how it is changed through learning. It also addresses the difficult question of whether and how declared knowledge about actions can be exploited for procedural action control.

Third, and finally, action decisions require procedures and algorithms that provide running *evaluations of prevailing circumstances* in terms of current goals and behavioral options. These procedures guarantee that the current situation, in which an agent is involved, gets represented in a format that is commensurable with his or her representational systems for preferences and action knowledge. This guarantees not only that the current situation can be continually evaluated in terms of upcoming decisions, but also that future decisions can be enriched with additional, and more specific, options tailored to the circumstances. A central research concern here is how perception and memory processes are organized to support running updates for the representation of circumstances for various periods of time.

Different theories combine these ingredients in various ways. But no matter how the process itself may be conceptualized in detail, the decisive fact is that decisions for action are a *result*, a product of combined preferences, knowledge about action, and evaluations of circumstances. There is no room left for any personal agent actually making a decision: Decisions happen on their own.

Self: Personal Perception.   So what should we think of the constitutive role of the self in our intuitions of free will? Is it a nice illusion, produced by vain self-deceit? Our answer depends on our concept of what we call the self. What is subjectivity? What is real about our perception of being/having a self? In the following, I distinguish roughly between two types of concepts of subjectivity—one is the widespread classic type, the other is a less well-known type that has recently come to challenge the classical notion of the self.

The *classical view* includes concepts of subjectivity saying that the self is a natural organ of the soul. This organ is the bearer of subjectivity, personality, and individuality. Like the other organs of the body, it is a naturally given feature of the mind developed prior to and independent of experience. Experience does not cause the soul to exist, it merely influences its individual unfolding.

I call the basic notion underlying this concept *self naturalism*, meaning that the self is the natural central organ of the mind; it coordinates and controls the activity of other psychological and mental functions. It is therefore present throughout every aspect of the mind's life: we find it in thought, in feelings, in volition—and in every other psychological function. This intuition is deeply rooted in our quotidian psychological notions. So it is not surprising to find this type of self-naturalistic intuition—in various guises—playing prominent parts even in science, and in psychological as well as in philosophical theories. The doctrine of privileged access to one's own psychological events, a concept that surfaces frequently in both disciplines, is the epistemological flip-side of the ontological doctrine of self-naturalism.

In contrast, the *modern version* of concepts of subjectivity includes theories stating that the self is not a natural organ of the soul, but rather an acquired knowledge structure that serves a special function. The idea is that the self itself is, in principle, a mental content, like other mental contents. The representational structures that support it develop parallel to and in interaction with other representational structures. In other words, the self evolves along with other structures involved in action-related decisions.

The basic intuition supporting this concept is what I would like to call *self-constructivism*: A self is based on knowledge organized in a special way, but its relationship to other representational structures is not predetermined, it is influenced through the learning and socialization events that create patterns of knowledge. So, whenever the self appears to play a central or controlling part in the life of a person, we must ask how this particular role evolved (using standards from evolutionary, developmental, and learning psychology) and which benefits it offers.

This view says, then, that the configuration and the role of the mental self are not primarily given, they are generated secondarily. The self is thus an object of reconstruction or deconstruction of a psycho-historical or development-psychological nature. Returning to my introductory remark, you might say that the self's fate is similar to that of the unicorn. Neither originated in the course of natural evolution, but as a result of historical or social design. This is exactly what our dear unicorn thinks after reading a passage on self-awareness from Hegel's *Phenomenology of Mind*.

Figure 3–2.   The unicorn thinks in Hegel's terms (see Hegel, 1807, p. 108; 1980, p. 127).

Let us return to the question of what to think of the personal interpretation of those outcomes of subpersonal processes that are constitutive of our intuition of free will. If we accept the naturalistic concept, we'll have to diagnose the feeling of free will as an illusion. If we accept both notions—namely, that on the one hand decisions can be entirely explained by underlying subpersonal mechanisms whereas on the other the self is an independent, naturally given organ of the mind, then any self-ascription of decisions involves self-deception. We fool ourselves in thinking that we are autonomous authors of decisions to act.

But if we accept the constructivist concept, talk of illusion becomes meaningless because there is no independent, natural self ascribing things to itself, that do not belong to it. Instead, the diagnosis here is that patterns of knowledge that bear the self are arranged in such a way that preferences, action knowledge, and the evaluation of circumstances intimately reciprocally effect one another. The self unfolds to serve the function of an author of decisions to act, and this authorship is its proper function—the specific function for which it is made—at least in terms of the historical and social conditions that presently prevail. This diagnosis also demands that we explore the origins and benefits of the self understood in this way.

An Excursion Back to the Stone Age

Our answer depends on which time periods we are thinking of in general. The largest scale would be that of the evolutionary development of mental functions. Let us look back to the Stone Age, for a moment, and imagine an evolutionary-psychological scenario that illustrates how the development of autonomous selves may have gotten underway.

Let us start with an intelligent subhuman being having the capacity to evaluate behaviorally relevant implications of its given current situation and to convert that knowledge into appropriate action. Imagine that such evaluation occurs based on complex algorithms that developed over the course of lengthy learning processes, and that additional algorithms guarantee that the outcomes of those evaluations get compared to current priorities and transformed into decisions to act. As complex as these calculations may be, they are subject to one essential restriction: They evaluate only those options related to the prevailing situation. Processes related to remembering past or planning future events are irrelevant: This being is caught entirely chained to the present.

Dual Representation.   How can it escape this imprisonment and achieve, as Edelman (1989) says, freedom from the present? It must develop the ability to generate representations of circumstances or things that are not present in the current situation. Generating such representations has two features: First, it allows to decouple oneself from the current, actual situation. But second, and simultaneously, this decoupling must be limited: Although the subject represents something, its normal perception of the current surrounding situation has to continue to function. A simultaneous processing of re-presented *and* perceptually experienced contents requires a processing architecture that allows re-presented information to be processed up front while current perceptual information continues to be processed in the background. I call this ability *dual representation*.

Naturally, we do not know when, where, how, or how often evolution brought forth mental processing arrangements guaranteeing dual representation. But we can be certain that the ability became necessary for survival when animals started living in groups that relied on symbolic communication because, under such circumstances, individuals normally become recipients of messages related to things lying beyond the presently perceived horizon. Subjects can only understand symbolic messages when they are in a position to generate representations—and they must be able to do so without risking their lives; the design of their mental system must therefore allow for dual representation. Dual representation is thus a prerequisite for symbolic communication to work. And a species like *homo sapiens*, whose evolutionary career is entirely founded on symbolic communication, must possess a highly efficient system of dual representation.

Dual representation and symbolic communication enhance the cognitive potential of living beings in many ways. One of them is to develop a notion of self.

Attributing Authorship.   Up to this point we have only been considering ideas that are set off by receiving verbal messages, that is, re-presentations induced by causes external to the subject. But as soon as a system of dual representation is instated, there is also room for generating internally induced representations like memories, fantasies, and plans. For the sake of brevity, in the following I call these kinds of internally induced representations *thoughts*.

One important feature distinguishes internally induced thoughts from externally induced representations. Externally verbally induced representations are always accompanied by a perception of an act of communication, that is, by a perception of the person who is the author of the message. When internally induced thoughts occur, we have no awareness of an immediate author at work producing them. So how can we link those thoughts to the immediate situation?

In these cases, we naturally also think that the principle of personal authorship applies. But that principle can be construed in a number of ways. One notion, for instance, would be to think that thoughts can be traced back to invisible authors or authorities, like the *voices* of gods, priests, and kings. Another, historically more modern notion is to locate the source of thought in an independent, personal subject bound to the body of the agent: the mental *self*. In both cases the author of the thoughts is not a component of those thoughts, but remains external, related to the thoughts by authorship.

Now, when it comes to explaining volition, this idea can also be applied to thoughts concerning action, like plans and goals. Thus, our hypothetical scenario of attribution leads us to accept selves that not only act as cognitive authors, producing mental contents, but also as dynamic authors, making decisions and setting behavior into motion. We will always meet a dynamic problem of attribution whenever representations of internally induced goals turn up. The solutions available for attributing authorship remain the same—except that here social and political implications of the attribution process become increasingly conspicuous. Because goals guide action, the question of where those goals originate becomes more than simply an intriguing riddle regarding attribution. Goal origins are of considerable social and political importance because they specify where we believe the causes lie that make people behave as they do. The (ancient) notion placed authorship of acts and goals in the hands of invisible personal authorities, external, obedience-demanding forces that somehow informed the agent what to do. The modern solution believes that authorship lies within the personal self, substituting autonomy for subservience.

Attribution Discourse. This scenario says that the mental self is a device for solving the problem of attribution: The self is construed as the author of internally induced representations. This contrivance, of course, is not the heroic deed of single individuals. Instead, it is seen as being socially construed as a part of discourse about subjectivity and consciousness. This happens within a culturally standardized scheme of interpretation that guides the socialization of individuals and, among other things, attributes to them a mental configuration centered around a self.

Discourse about attribution permeates our everyday life at several levels. We negotiate attribution most directly in face-to-face interaction within our microsocial realms, without necessarily using verbal communication. More complex systems of attribution are at work within linguistically bound discourse at the macrosocial level: predominantly, for instance, when using psychological common sense, that set of quotidian psychological constructs employed by cultures and linguistic communities for explaining the behavior of human agents. Thus, modern folk psychology is based on the idea of a subject having an explicit, lifelong identical self at its core. Discourse about morals and rights are no less relevant, when they identify the self as an autonomous source of decisions to act.

Now, when agents in social groups organize their mutual interaction and communication at the micro- and macrolevels in such a way that each one expects all the other co-agents to also have a self, every one of the agents—even new ones—is confronted with a discursive situation that already provides a role for him/her—in the shape of a self. Awareness of other-ascriptions to oneself induces self-ascriptions, and the agent ultimately accepts the role of a self ascribed to him by others. A person thinks of himself as others think of him. Our unicorn, again, tells us this much—after having read Adam Smith's (1759/1976) passage on self perception and evaluation in *Theory of Moral Sentiments*: (see Fig. 3–3).

Micro- and macrosocial discourse is supported, among other things, by *narrative discourse* of varying kinds. Fictional stories in books and movies that we enjoy for filling up our time-out from real events are packed with talk about willing and behaving. We tell stories to our children in order to explain to them just what we mean by *person* and how thought is related to behavior. We thereby provide them with two tools. One is the explicit semantics of the culture in which they live—its customs and practices, values and standards, myths and legends. The other is the implicit syntax of our folk psychology, which specifies how human agents function, what they think and do, and how they are rewarded or punished for their behavior—be it on earth or in heaven.

IN PRAISE OF FREE WILL

Our excursion back to the Stone Age provided a speculative answer to the question of how living beings came to understand themselves as subjects, as authors of cognition and action, while simultaneously developing intuitions of free will. Now we see that free will—as the Cambridge philosopher Martin Kusch (1999) puts it—is a *social institution*, made by people and for people. Intuitions of free will emerge only when individuals learn, in social discourse, to develop a mental self as the source of decisions and actions. And because this self is created predominantly for the purpose of establishing authorship for action and thought, it makes little sense to question whether that authorship is an illusion; for there exists no self prior to or beyond mental authorship (that could wrongly attribute something to itself that in reality is not its own).

Figure 3–3.   The unicorn thinks in Adam Smith's terms (see Smith, 1976, p. 111).

Now, we may ask just what a social institution of autonomous selves equipped with intuitions of free will is good for. What does it offer those individuals psychologically, how does it help them be a social and political community?

Psychological Effects

The psychological effects that the ascription of a self has for an individual depend on which role one sees for the personal interpretation of the subpersonal processes that constitute decision making. Thus far, and for the sake of simplicity, I have described subpersonal processes as being something real and personal processes of interpretation as being the perception of that reality. At this point we must abandon simplicity, because nothing would be worse than to conclude, in reverse, that only so-called reality is effective, whereas the awareness of it is epiphenomenal and inefficacious. Like every other social institution, autonomous selves are not fictions, they are real—*real as artifacts*—as Kusch says. The reality of the artifact is in this case expressed by the fact that the personal perception of subpersonal processes must itself also be supported by representational processes—processes consisting of elements like those of all the other representational processes. This means that personal perception, too, can only develop out of underlying subpersonal processes. If so, there is no reason to view them as less real and efficacious than the outcomes of the subpersonal decision-making events to which they refer.

Various suggestions have been made for explaining how the representational processes that support a notion of self are related to the processes and design of subpersonal decision-producing mechanisms. One suggestion is that the system of the self is superimposed on the rest of the representational system like a special network, converging very closely in some areas, but remaining dissociated at others. A different suggestion, which, however, gives us almost the same result, is that the system of the self establishes itself as a separate system of representation, and then adopts a copy of the rest of the representational systems. Both of these notions view the system of self as not being equally ranked with the other systems, they see it as being something separate with very selective links to those other systems. They comport with a basic authorship relation between the self and mental contents and also allow that relationship to be selective and flexible.

But what could a system of self be good for? An initially plausible idea would be that it creates autonomous systems for preferences, action knowledge and situation evaluation, and that these are superimposed on given structures. But this would mean doubling theoretical constructs without necessity, thus violating the principle of parsimony inherent in Occam's razor. So what is left when we deter such duplication? What remain are *procedural changes*—alterations in the algorithms that operate on those contents with the result of an elaboration of decision-making processes.

Explication and Deliberation. The decisive procedural effect of the system of self is probably to slow down the subpersonal decision-producing system, that itself is designed to be quick and efficient. Delaying decisions to act provides an opportunity for elaboration and *increases the depth of processing* in the representational systems relevant to a certain decision. It allows an expansion of the information base provided for making a decision, and this additional information may modify the decision itself (explication). In-depth processing may also activate additional processing and evaluation procedures, the outcomes of which also influence the decision (deliberation). This perhaps clumsy talk of representations says nothing more than what we have been told all our lives, so often, in fact, that we now advise ourselves: "Take your time; think carefully; know what you really want; study your options," and so on.

Communication and Argumentation. Explication and deliberation may influence decisions, but their power is limited: On the one hand, they only act on information found within one's own representational system—personal preferences, knowledge, and personal evaluations of circumstances. On the other hand, competent language users are in a position to break down that barrier through *communication* and *argumentation*. When individuals communicate and argue for the products of their (initially private) explications and deliberations, they establish reciprocal suggestions for modifying decision behavior, and these are not only related to aspects of procedure, they also include changing the contents that are foundational to the decisions. Communicative exchange, therefore, may have the effect that elaboration initially related to procedures in turn also influences the content of a decision.

Social Functions

Authorship and intuitions of free will influence not only the psychological dispositions of individuals, they also alter the shape of the collective in which those individuals see themselves as a community. It is probably not off the mark to guess that this might be its true achievement—if not even its genuine psycho-historical *raison d'être.*

Regulating Behavior. For one thing, authorship and intuitions of free will influence *discourse and institutions that regulate behavior*— namely morals and rights. As we saw in the previous section, one central achievement of our talk of free will is that it allows us to attribute action and its consequences to the people that do them. We make people responsible for what they do. The attestation of free will terminates any otherwise lengthy regress in explanation. Although we may accept that all kinds of circumstances contributed to some behavior, we do not assume that an individual was helplessly commanded by them. The individual could have done otherwise, and therefore must claim responsibility for the deed. Responsibility is the price of freedom.

In modern societies, this is why our moral and judicial evaluations of behavior are only slightly influenced when a person claims he had to obey the will of a given authority. Modern cultures consider that kind of authority obsolete and have replaced it with behavioral regulation based on the personal autonomy of the agent. Foreign authority is of little importance, personal authorship is significant. A remarkable example for this transition can be found in Bruno Snell (1975) and Julian Jaynes's (1976) studies of how agents acted in the *Iliad* and *Odyssey*. Odysseus is a modern subject—a person who thinks about what he does and then turns his convictions into action. Agamemnon, in contrast, is a tool of the deities, whereas Odysseus is a tool of his own will—a remarkable literary metaphor containing what Jaynes finds reminiscent of the psycho-historical development in which the self replaced the gods.

Vernacular of free will, then, identifies, for both discourse and the institutions with which we regulate behavior, the source that issues decisions to act. It leaves little room for justifying behavior by citing external authorities or circumstances. It identifies the source of decisions as being the same instance that gets sanctioned or rewarded: the person, the agent.

Developing Will.   And finally, talk of free will acts back on discourse and institutions for political development of will. To the extent that agents in social collectives mutually ascribe autonomy and responsibility to one another they will also claim these capacities for the collec-

Figure 3–4.   The unicorn thinks in Niklas Luhmann's terms (see Luhmann, 1984, p. 92).

tive. This makes authoritarian leadership obsolete—and with it also the discourse and the institutions that legitimized and guaranteed it. It gets replaced by mechanisms of collective will development, as we know it from many epochs and cultures, and at various levels in social systems. In the extreme case of modern national alliances they are carried by the ideology of the social contract between equal and autonomous individuals, embodied by democratic forms of will development at various levels of society. The idea of democracy is thus founded in the notion of personal autonomy and free will. If we cherish one, we must praise the other.

So in the end, should we deny free will or praise it? Of course, we must do both. That may seem contradictory, but an elegant solution may be phrased in Luhmann's (1984) diction: Science, observing mental systems from an external perspective, finds no place for free will. And must deny it. But it does have a place within reflections on social systems and within the self-awareness of psychological systems guided by those social systems. We may praise its function as a social and personal behavior regulating mechanism. Of course, it is certainly not always easy to maintain this split perspective. If you find it disquieting, our unicorn was comforted by reading Luhmann's theory of social systems.

ACKNOWLEDGMENTS

This chapter was translated by Cynthia Klohr. A slightly different German version of this essay was presented at the conference "Philosophy and/or Science" organized by the Society for Analytic Philosophy/ Gesellschaft für Analytische Philosophie (GAP), Bielefeld, September 22–26, 2003. It appeared as a slightly shortened version under the title "Kritik des freien Willens: Bemerkungen über eine soziale institution" in *Psychologische Rundschau* and *Theologie der Gegenwart*.

REFERENCES

Edelman, G. M. (1989). *The remembered present: A biological theory of consciousness*. New York: Basic Books.

Hegel, G. W. F. (1807/1980). Phänomenologie des Geistes [Phenomenology of mind]. In G. W. F. Hegel, *Gesammelte Werke* [Collected Works], Vol. 9. W. Bonsiepen & R. Heede (Eds.) Hamburg, Germany: Felix Meiner Verlag).

Jaynes, J. (1976). *The origin of consciousness in the breakdown of the bicameral mind*. Boston: Houghton Mifflin.

Kusch, M. (1999). *Psychological knowledge: A social history and philosophy*. London: Routledge.

Luhmann, N. (1984). *Soziale Systeme. Grundriß einer allgemeinen Theorie.* [Social systems. An outline of a universal theory]. Frankfurt a. M. Main: Suhrkamp.

Prinz, W. (2004). Kritik des freien Willens: Bemerkungen über eine soziale Institution A critique of free will: Psychological remarks on a social institution. *Psychologische Rundschau, 55* (4), 198–206.

Prinz, W. (2004). Kritik des freien Willens: Bemerkungen über eine soziale Institution [A critique of free will: Psychological remarks on a social institution]. *Theologie der Gegenwart, 3,* 162–175.

Smith, A. (1759/1976). The theory of moral sentiments. In A. Smith, *The Glasgow edition of the works and correspondences of Adam Smith*, Vol. 1. D. D. Raphael & A. L. Macfie (Eds.) Oxford, UK: Clarendon Press.

Snell, B. (1975). *Die Entdeckung des Geistes. Studien zur Entstehung des europäischen Denkens bei den Griechen.* [The discovery of mind. Studies on the emergence of European thinking in the Greeks]. Göttingen: Vandenhoeck & Ruprecht.

Whiten, A. (2000). Chimpanzee cognition and the question of mental representation. In D. Sperber (Ed.), *Meta-representations* (pp. 139–167). Oxford: Oxford University Press.

4

Freedom *and* Science! The Presumptuous Metaphysics of Free-Will Disdainers

Michael Heidelberger
University of Tübingen, Germany

Science, however, must be constantly reminded that her purposes are not the only purposes, and that the order of uniform causation that she has use for, and is therefore right in postulating, may be enveloped in a wider order on which she has no claims at all. (James, 1890, Vol. II, p. 576)

The title, "Freedom *and* Science" alludes to one of Wolfgang Prinz's lectures from 1996, called "Freedom or Science" (Prinz, 1996a). That title was, in turn, a spin-off from the German Christian Democratic party's slogan from the 1970s: "freedom, not socialism." Seeing himself as a scientific psychologist, Prinz strikes back at the "metaphysical impertinence" of philosophy, which "takes folk-psychological notions of the freedom of will at face value" (Prinz, 1996a, p. 86). He concludes that "the game of scientific explanation of actions and their causes [...] has no place for the idea of free will. It is misguided to think that freedom of will functions as a theoretical concept in scientific explanation." (Prinz,

89

1996a, pp. 86, 91.) Considering that freedom of will exists merely as something felt and that its existence is thus guaranteed only subjectively, our purported last resort is to declare it "an illusion," as some brain researchers do (cf. Roth, 2001, p. 452f), "a cultural construct" (Singer, 2001, p. 156), or "the product of social construction, a tool for socially regulating actions." (Roth, 2001, p. 452f; see also Prinz, 2003, p. 7; Prinz, chap. 3, this volume).

In response to a manifesto by 11 leading neuroscientists on the present state and the future of brain research, published in the German journal *Gehirn & Geist*, (p. 34f), Prinz (2004; chap. 3, this volume) now dismisses the inadequately reflected naturalism behind many neural researchers' idea of man as in need of revision, and states that brain research is unsuitable as a new model discipline for the human sciences. Prinz also strikes new chords in the third part of an enhanced and reworked version of a paper published in 2004 (Prinz, 2004; chap. 3, this volume). Nonetheless, this chapter takes Prinz's earlier essay as its starting point, because it states most clearly the arguments to which I would like to respond here.

Meanwhile, we have been flooded, especially in Germany, with conferences and papers, newspaper articles, features, and books by experts in brain research, scientific psychology, even science in general, ardently claiming to prove compellingly that man does not and cannot have free will. Fascinated, yet fearful, triumphant and sermonizing, they conjure up the consequences that recent findings in pertinent sciences allegedly have for the traditional idea of man. No end to this controversy is in sight (see Roth, 2001; Roth & Brumlik, 2004; Singer, 2001; Singer, 2003; Singer & Nida-Rümelin; 2004). Interestingly, the rebuttal obviously demands constant repetition. In mathematics, the provision of counterevidence suffices once and for all. But in this case, it seems almost as though the deniers of free will, philosophizing as they please, are haunted by uneasiness; it takes unceasing mutual enthusiasm to revise the idea of man.

Philosophers fall easily into this theme's traps and patterns of argument. One can point out that certain concepts involved are muddled, that its advocates are oblivious to one or the other important philosophical argument and should take note of it, that science includes some methodical maxims that actually *support* the notion of free will, that there are numerous relevant philosophical theories showing how freedom is compatible with determinism, and so on. But all of this is in vain when dedicated scientists thump on their facts like drummers on their drums, arguing that if philosophers cannot refute those (which they can't, because philosophers do not do empirical research), then all philosophical objections are merely "metaphysical impertinence". Philosophers are thus condemned to be hopelessly backward scholars, barred from the tough business of scientifically studying reality, with its "guiding value of truth" (Prinz, 1996a, p. 100).

Can a philosopher approach this topic, avoiding the traps and without an air of defense? If freedom of will is real and is crucial for our actions as humans, that fact must also somehow be mirrored in scientists' actions. If that is the case, then we can turn the tables and present a so-called *tu quoque* argument: *Even you*, my worthy scientist, must, for your own actions, assume that you are free-willed, unless you wish to saw off the branch on which your theory is perched. In denying freedom of will and continuing to sort reflection about the world into two different games, namely the "game of scientific explanation," geared solely to pursuing truth, and the "game of moral evaluation and behavior regulation" (Prinz, 1996a, p. 100), a celebration of social rituals, you demand metaphysics of yourself and revert to an obsolete position.

The *tu quoque* argument implies that if natural science intends to remain an enlightening and significant part of our daily lives, it cannot be in its own true interest to deny freedom of will. Precisely the metaphysical zeal that declares free will to be scientifically meaningless deprives any alleged "proof" of free will's nonexistence of any consequences at all. If scientists, instead of declaring that freedom of will is insignificant for science, thought that (based on relevant findings) fewer individuals exercise free will or that they exhibit it less than we commonly imagine (a pet notion of neurologist Antonio Damasio; cf. Damasio, 2000), then I would immediately agree. That would constrain our notion of free will, but not question it fundamentally; and this would allow scientific arguments to become effective in the first place.

But if, on the contrary, science impedes itself by prematurely denying the freedom of will, taking in stride the detriment to possible allies in philosophy and other disciplines that this causes, that is, indeed, lamentable, even annoying. Considering the current state of science, it might be wise to cooperate with philosophy. Of course, such eye-catching denials of free will might simply reflect a strategy for securing research funds. In that case, polemical opposition to philosophers' alleged backwardness would be part of the strategy and any effort at cooperation would be fruitless.

These points dictate this chapter's outline. I begin with some thoughts on how action and behavior are related, and describe the central components of our intuitions of free will. Next, I show how scientific experiments are based on voluntary action; this is the core of the *tu quoque* argument. There I also bring in Hermann von Helmholtz, who thought it impossible to do experiments without some degree of self-awareness. In the subsequent section, I reply to an objection to the *tu quoque* argument, which attempts to diffuse the difference between action and behavior. Then I show why a metaphysical denial of freedom of will deprives science of any relevance at all for our idea of man and therefore cannot be in the interest of its own advocates. In conclusion, I would like to express why, considering the present joint interests between philosophy and cognitive science, denying free will is particularly regrettable as a research policy.

ASCERTAINING INTUITIONS OF FREEDOM

Before arguing that freedom of will is a real aspect of natural science, I must first clarify our intuition of freedom somewhat and name the phenomena we consider to be indicative of that freedom. The concept of freedom is simply too multifarious for us to assume that when we use it, both speaker and hearer, author and reader, mean and understand the same thing.

Yet before doing this, I must first introduce another thought, about how freedom is related to the concept of action. Prerequisite to freedom are the concepts of *action* and *agent*. Since John Locke, we know that it is not the will that is free, but an action that is in accord with the will, or not. Locke does not deny that human beings have the capacity to set preferences or make choices. To him, though, the concept of will means the power or the ability to choose (Locke, 1690, pp. xxi, 17). By freedom he means the power of a person to execute or not execute actions depending on his or her will. Man is free in this sense, but *actions* must be distinguished from mere *behavior.*

The ancient Greeks distinguished action from behavior; perhaps the distinction has always been an element of occidental language. In *Phaedo*, Socrates, sitting in his cell, ponders, on the side, the concept of the cause of an action. More precisely, he reflects on the *explanation* of action and shows how it goes wrong when we use behavior instead of acts to do so. The occasion is an explanation given by a physicist, who makes a similar mistake:

> It seemed to me that he was just about as inconsistent as if someone were to say 'The cause of everything that Socrates does is Mind' and then, in trying to account for my several actions, said first that the reason why I am lying here now is that my body is composed of bones and sinews, and that the bones are rigid and separated at the joints, but the sinews are capable of contraction and relaxation, and form an envelope for the bones with the help of the flesh and skin, the latter holding all together; and because the bones move freely in their joints the sinews by relaxing and contracting enable me somehow to bend my limbs; and that is the cause of my sitting here in a bent position. Or again, if he tried to account in the

same way for my conversing with you, adducing causes such as sound and air and hearing and a thousand others, and never troubled to mention the real reasons; which are that since Athens has thought it better to condemn me, therefore I for my part have thought it better to sit here, and more right to stay and submit to whatever penalty she orders .... (Plato, 1971, p. 98 c-e)

Whoever turns to bent knees, or—in today's jargon—subpersonal neural processes, to explain why Socrates is sitting in prison, is headed down the wrong road. The real reason for his imprisonment is another. An explanation for an action cannot be given by indicating the causes of behavior; it must be done by giving reasons and must therefore (assuming that they are good reasons) be based on reason. To act, then, means to act for reasons. Naturally, I must not always be aware of those reasons. I get in the car every morning because I want to drive to work, but I need not manifest and update that reason with a conscious mental act every day.

Now we can begin to ascertain our intuitions about freedom. Three components stand out and are at least necessary, if not sufficient, for the concept of freedom. Two of them can be found in most discourses about freedom, whereas the third is not mentioned quite as often. However, the third component is important, perhaps even crucial, for assessing and evaluating Libet's experiments (see the following section). Whether these three components are logically independent of one another or whether one implies the other, cannot be investigated here.

1. *Freedom is the ability to choose between alternative actions (or options); freedom of choice.* When a person acts freely, he or she may also do otherwise. He or she has more than one option. Because omitting to do something is also an action, every positive option automatically implies the option of inaction.

2. *Freedom is the ability to cause one's own actions; genuine authorship.* When a person acts voluntarily, she or he is the author of his or her action. The action is not caused by the will of some other person, or by an event not brought about by the author of the action. The cause of the action in question lies within the person himself and not outside of him; he or she has his or her actions under control, they originate within him/her.

3. *Freedom is the ability to think of oneself as being capable of action; reflexive cognitive ability.* When a person acts voluntarily, he or she thinks of himself—perhaps not at that very moment or in every situation, but basically—as someone who does not just consist of mechanical, movable, body parts, but as someone who is *capable of action*. He or she thinks of herself as a person who can take a stance

towards herself, a being who reflects on her doings. Very young children and probably all animals may be said to have freedom of choice and genuine authorship of their actions (we might say that generally their actions are voluntary), but they are not capable of the awareness of their agency that must be present for a full attribution of freedom. Even the actions of some adults are considered not voluntary, if those persons lack a reflexive awareness of self due to ignorance, overwhelming emotionality, or other powers.

Why, John Locke asks, do we not think that a tennis ball flying through the air or lying on the ground is an object acting according to its own free will; why is it not a free agent, although it is mobile? "If we inquire into the reason, we shall find it is because we conceive not a tennis ball to think, and consequently not to have any volition" (Locke, 1690/1961, pp. xxi, 9). Voluntary action, then, is tied to a very specific cognitive capacity that tennis balls do not possess and that small children and animals cannot summon up to the fullest extent. And the agent himself must think of himself as someone who has just that cognitive capacity.

These three components of freedom: freedom of choice, genuine authorship, and self-reflection apparently constitute the central elements of voluntary action. A drug addict cannot choose among various alternatives, even if he considers himself capable of action and injects the substance himself. A pilot threatened by an armed terrorist is not the genuine author of his action while nose-diving the aircraft, someone acts "in his place". A child who sets a barn on fire may have had a choice among different options and may not have been misled into doing it. And yet we would not say that she acted voluntarily, we would say that she was unaware of the outcome of her actions—she does not yet think of herself as of someone whose actions have consequences for herself and others.

SCIENTIFIC EXPERIMENTS AS VOLUNTARY ACTIONS

Scientists claim, and rightly so, that they have a source of knowledge unavailable to philosophers, namely, experiments, which makes their work in some ways superior to philosophy. But experimenting is an act, it is not simply limb movement or behavior, and it is *the* act through which scientists essentially distinguish their own kind of work from that of others. The question, then, is whether these acts are voluntary or must be voluntary in order to fulfill their purpose. My brief outline of the phenomena of freedom has prepared us to answer both questions in the affirmative. Experimental action is voluntary and would miss the point if it were not. To deny free will, then, is to deny the possibility of experimental natural science!

Consider *freedom of choice*: Part of experimenting is trying out various alternative ways of doing things. In contrast to simple observation, an experimenter deliberates which options are available for varying conditions by different arrangements of an experiment; she selects from among various ways of altering the phenomenon under investigation. If we, as human beings, had no such choices and options for manipulating something, we would be unable to experiment. As Ernst Mach puts it, "The fundamental method of experimenting is *variation*" (Mach, 1905/1980, p. 202).

Consider *genuine authorship*: The *art* of experimenting is to control the effects of systematic and unsystematic disruptive factors on dependent variables: either to cancel them entirely, or, when that doesn't work, to either minimize or keep those factors constant, or to get them under control by randomizing and balancing. An experimenter wants to make certain that the only effects happening are those that *she initiated by manipulating*; she wants to prevent any other causes from being effective, whether unnoticed or caused subconsciously by herself. This means that the experimenter wants to secure *personal authorship* of the desired effect, she wants to see *her own* plan put in effect! Mach put it this way: An experiment is an "intentional, autonomous extension of experience" (Mach, 1905/1980, p. 202).

And consider *reflexive cognitive capability*: The requirement that experiments must be *reproducible* shows us that when experimenting, the experimenter must think of herself as a being who is taking action, as someone who is aware of herself and her actions. In doing the experiment, the experimenter must be capable of being replaced by any other person with appropriate instruction. Autonomy and options may not be used arbitrarily in experiments, they must follow a deliberate plan that is related to the state of the art already achieved in the corresponding field, as well as to previous and established experimental actions. The experimenter must be able to communicate her plan; the act of experimenting includes a cognitive and reflexive relationship to oneself. Ernst Mach continues: "The intentional autonomous extension of experience gained by doing physical experiments, and deliberate observation, are therefore always guided by thought and can never be clearly demarcated or severed from thought experiments" (Mach, 1905/1980, p. 202). It is true that we say small children must experiment with the world around them. But if that is to be more than a metaphor, a child must also have an idea of himself as an experimenter.

The way scientists critically evaluate each other's experiments also immediately reveals that they believe that each of the three components of freedom of action is at work in experimenting. An experimenter made a poor selection, overlooked disruptive factors, neglected the prerequisites or the consequences of her experimental activity—such objections illustrate that colleagues make an experimenter responsible for her actions, they think of her as a person who acts freely. If they did not assume that her actions, although experimenting, were voluntary, then this type of criticism would be irrelevant. This also reveals the methodical openness of natural science in the sense that, as an empirical science unwilling to acknowledge free will, it is incapable of adequately describing its own practices. Science is at liberty to do this within the scope of a philosophy that originates on its own soil (and I consider myself to be one such philosopher), but the authority with which science should do so can never be exclusively the authority of the natural sciences, it must come from another source.

Hermann von Helmholtz also saw experimenting as voluntary action. It is surprising—and grist to my mill—that a scientist so fond of reductive explanation (from biology to physics, for instance) saw a connection between experimenting and self-awareness. And his notion of experimenting is neither purely ornamental nor of no consequence for science; rather, it constitutes the foundation on which he erects his theory of perception as a constructive *interpretation* of sensations from past experience. The pertinent passage can be found in his most important philosophical lecture, "The Facts of Perception" (Helmholtz, 1878). Here Helmholtz takes up a thought expressed 11 years earlier in §26 of his *Handbook of Physiological Optics* (Helmholtz, 1867):

> However, the conclusiveness of any experiment [in which we change an object's appearance] is primarily so very much greater than that of observing a process taking place without our intervention, because during an experiment, the causal chain also runs through ourselves. Through intuition we are familiar with one link of the chain, namely our volitional impulse, and we know which motives made it come about. The chain of physical causes, then, starts with this impelling force we are acquainted with and at a time we know and is effective all the way down to the outcome of the experiment. But an essential prerequisite for the knowledge we want to gain is that our volitional impulse itself is neither already influenced by the physical causes that simultaneously determined the physical process, nor has it, itself, psychologically influenced subsequent perception. (Helmholtz, 1878, p. 241)

By "subsequent perception" Helmholtz means modifications of perception that follow from action taken by the experimenter. Experimenting is not done only by natural scientists. According to Helmholtz, once they are born (perhaps even sooner), all humans experiment with movement and this provides them with perceptions, that is, the interpretation of sensations as signs of spatial objects. So not only the way natural scientists experiment, but even spatial perception, which itself is a result of experimenting, is closely tied to the ability to develop an awareness of self. This is exactly the theory of perception the tradition of which Wolfgang Prinz endorses. He writes: "The contents of perception are the result of constructive processes in which the perceptual apparatus comprehends the initial information using its own categories and means of representation" (Prinz, 1996a, p. 94). Even construed perception contains, to a certain extent, a *judgment* (also about oneself), and it is not a concept that can be captured purely causally. Unfortunately, Prinz has apparently lost sight of how this kind of self-awareness is involved in the work of scientists, including himself. I admit that Helmholtz only mentions a fragment of the phenomenon of self-awareness, but that does not depreciate his argument or its relevance here.

In another text Helmholtz tries to prove that experimental activity understood in this way offers the only way to distinguish between real causal relationships and mere correlation. In his opinion, passive observation alone will never lead to reliable knowledge about causes; it takes conscious intervention on the part of a person doing something. He illustrates this using the simple law that mercury expands when heated:

> When I claim that, if unrestricted, all liquid mercury expands when heated, I know that the mercury's higher temperature and expansion, no matter how often I have observed them together, were not due simply to the effect of some unknown, mutual, third cause, as I might believe if I relied on observation alone. By doing an experiment I know that warmth alone is sufficient to bring about this expansion. I have heated mercury often, at different times. According to my own will [!], I chose [!] the time to start the experiment. So if the mercury expanded at that moment, that expansion was a result of conditions that I [!] brought about through my [!] experiment. I know by this, that heating it up was, by itself, a sufficient reason for expansion, and that no other hidden powers were needed to get this result. By doing relatively few, well arranged experiments I can discover the causal conditions of an event with greater certainty than by observing it a million times, where I am not able to change the conditions at will." [!] (Helmholtz, 1867, p. 451f, exclamation points added for emphasis)

John Stuart Mill does not share Helmholtz's opinion that only experiments (mediated by self-awareness) can be seen as reliable indicators of causality. Mill thinks that each experiment could also be substituted by passive observation; we rely on experiments only because the human life span is limited. Man cannot wait as long as it takes for the relevant observable events to occur in order to enhance his empirical knowledge of natural laws. Mill is right about experiments speeding up insight. But Helmholtz, who otherwise was heavily influenced by his contemporary, Mill, is also right that passive observation alone is insufficient for science, and that experimenter intervention is crucial (see Heidelberger, 1997, for a detailed discussion). Out of touch with areas of knowledge accessible by experiment, other sciences that—for contingent reasons—must rely on observation alone would be unsuccessful (compare the relationship of astronomy to physics since Johannes Kepler). This thought can be broadened to make a fundamental objection to Mill's empiricist approach, but that lies beyond the scope of this chapter.

ACTION AND BEHAVIOR

The paragraphs just discussed show how scientific experimentation must be thought of as voluntary action if it is to be successful. Experiments manifest all of the components found in phenomena we associate with freedom. For present purposes, I understand freedom of will to be the human capacity to set priorities and make choices—to decide from among alternatives. This means that freedom of will is a necessary component of freedom of action. The denial of free will undermines science itself and would make its quintessential activity, the experiment, absurd. The section just discussed also shows that denying freedom of will does not work the same way we abandon a hypothesis in natural science, for instance the way Lavoisier, in chemistry, proved that phlogiston, or Einstein, for classical electrodynamics, proved that ether does not exist.

The only objection I can imagine coming from freedom-denying scientists at this point does not relate specifically to the thesis I advocate, but takes up, in general, the distinction between action and behavior. The objection could be phrased as saying that action must be expressed by intentional vocabulary, which, in turn, presupposes the existence of persons. Future science, so the objection goes, will do entirely without this jargon and will describe all processes related to humans on a subpersonal, that is, neural level. For domestic purposes, we still go along with intentional vocabulary that takes actions and thus persons for granted, for a while. "In order to make myself understood with just a few words," writes Wolfgang Prinz, "I cannot avoid using [...] mentalistically tinted vocabulary. But that does not change the fact that the processes I am sketching can be conceived of as subpersonal mechanisms" (Prinz, 2003, p. 13).

Apparently the claim is not simply that subpersonal processes neither *accompany* nor *realize* processes of an intentional nature, but that intentionality itself is dispensable, or that it is at least reducible without residue to a subpersonal level. "Reality" with respect to human beings is the "functional reality of subpersonal volitional mechanisms" (Prinz, 2003, p. 11). The idea is that subpersonal processes (being the only scientifically tenable hard core of action description) are necessary and sufficient for correctly explaining action. This is why, so the argument goes, we can skip the personal level in explaining action; and in the future we will discover a subpersonal explanation even for the act of experimenting. Prinz (1996b) does say that cerebral processes are "not *sufficient* for explaining the development of consciousness," because they must be complemented by "certain social and political conditions" (p. 453). I find this dilution of the argument inappropriate and insincere, because precisely these conditions are supposed to explain what it is about the self that is construction and illusion!

It appears that we are being asked to explain away any phenomena that steadfastly resist scientific metaphysics. Yet one of the most prominent founders of scientific psychology, William James (1890), insisted that natural science, particularly psychology, is obligated to adopt a "radical empiricism" that takes human reality seriously, and that does not shrug it off as a mere illusion, as "not really" reality (Prinz). It looks as if the skirmish over freedom of will actually reflects a dispute about the reality of intentionality. We are expected to follow presumptuous metaphysics that negates the obvious: the reality of intentionality and its (empirical) success at explaining action. (As just noted, recent work by Prinz is much more cautious in this respect.)

In the best case, arguments that explain intentionality *away*, instead of *explaining* it are mere hand-waving, a promise that in 10 years all will be known. That is the kind of claim that we have also heard from artificial intelligence, gene technology, brain research, and a number of other fields—promises that have meanwhile been mercifully muffled by the cloak of oblivion. And yet one leading neuroscientist, Gerhard Roth, makes precisely such claims: "I believe that in ten years, at least, it will be widespread knowledge that there is no such thing as freedom meaning subjective capacity for guilt. Atoning guilt will become obsolete because a person will no longer be 'guilty' in the traditional sense of the word" (Roth & Vollmer, 2000, p. 25).

With respect to *hand-waving* intentionality: From the fact that when I move my little finger a so-called "readiness potential" *precedes* my conscious "decision" to do so (as indicated by Benjamin Libet's experiments in 1983, and Haggard and Eimer's work in 1999, all of which build on Kornhuber and Deeke's work (1965) in Freiburg and Ulm), it is concluded that all action is controlled subpersonally, such that there is no longer need for a category called "person." "We don't do what we want, we want what we do" (Prinz, 1996a, p. 87; see also pp. 98, 100). Disregarding the fact that moving my little finger is not exactly a prime example of demonstrating voluntary action; besides the fact that, as the evidence lies, not one subpersonal characterization has been found for a process described in terms of intentionality that can achieve fully the explanatory performance that intentional explanation of the same phenomenon accomplishes; to my knowledge no one has ever shown that such a readiness potential is either empirically necessary and/or sufficient for *action*. It might just as well be an expression of the subconscious deliberation process that precedes voluntary, although perhaps fairly automatic, action (cf. Keller & Heckhausen, 1990, p. 360; Zhu, 2003).

In the worst case, such arguments will have to deal with the *frame problem* as known to computer science, particularly from work in artificial intelligence. Any programmer can tell you how difficult it is to design a program that will enable a computer furnished with equipment for perception clearly to discriminate actions in normal everyday situations. To this day, every child is better than any computer at distinguishing, under the appropriate circumstances, physically different kinds of behavior that are one and the same action, and kinds of behavior that physically look alike but are different actions. The more artificially purified the surrounding context, such that a particular action matches only one particular behavior, the easier it is, of course, to design the corresponding program.

It would be hopeless, for example, to program a computer to recognize reliably a certain action as a greeting. There are hundreds of different ways to greet someone, and who knows how many forms mankind has yet to develop? Now, a military greeting may be limited to jerking the right hand towards a visor. A program might accomplish recognizing that, but it only works at the cost of ignoring the generalities and genuine variability of real life—rather like the super-intelligent Martian described by Daniel Dennett (1987), who wholly comprehends the material level, but does not understand the intentional level of action. The trouble is very likely related to the problem of induction and to the difficulty in defining precisely what it means to "follow a rule," analyzed by Ludwig Wittgenstein.

These and similar facts have prompted Jerry Fodor to think that the central processes of the brain, which determine our beliefs, are *not* modular (Fodor, 2000, pp. 64–78). Many cognitive scientists were shocked by this alleged change of opinion, because since *The Modularity of Mind* appeared in 1983, Fodor was seen as a representative of the "massive modularity thesis" (although that publication itself already questioned the thesis, as Fodor notes). According to the thesis, all human cognitive abilities, conceived as encapsulated information process-ing modules, developed under the problem-solving pressure experienced by our Pleistocene progenitors. If this were true, we might, in fact, come to the conclusion that human cognitive abilities can be explained entirely at the subpersonal level.

By objecting to the massive modularity theory for the central part of mind, Fodor has taken a step back toward Descartes. In his *Discours* (1637/1897–1910), Descartes wrote that action based on insight and rea-son is distinct from behavior that results from the design and structure of organs in animals and machines. For precisely this reason human beings are mentally superior to animals and machines: reason is a "universal tool" that "is available in all circumstances, while these organs [in animals, etc.] need a special device for each particular action" (Descartes, 1637/ 1897–1910, chap. 5. 10, p. 56f.). Today, we naturally no longer view ani-mals as Descartes did. But anthropologists and cognitive scientists have be-gun supporting the view that by intentionally understanding the other members of his own species, man came to use symbols and develop cul-ture, which in turn gave him a decisive advantage over his closest relatives in the animal kingdom (Povinelli & Vonk, 2003; Tomasello, Call & Hare). Of course, even if the brain does not function nonmodularly, that does not guarantee that the mind is nonreducible.

Thus, it is more than questionable whether the subpersonal level can provide sufficient descriptions for action, including our entire percep-tion of reality and causal order, as some scientists claim. This is at the heart of the presumptuous metaphysics that present-day disdainers of free will are asking us to endorse.

FREEDOM IN THE INTEREST OF SCIENCE

It cannot be in the interest of natural scientists to deny so radically the freedom of will as seems to be happening today, and in such a metaphys-ical manner. This is true even if one rejects my argument that scientists who disdain freedom of will are eroding the methodological founda-tion of their own science.

I suppose that natural scientists really are interested in their own the-ories being relevant for normal life and human activities, because I can-not imagine what else would justify doing science at all. This interest is legitimate, even very important, and, as I said from the start, something that we must vehemently defend, if we still feel even a trace of the mis-sion of enlightenment within ourselves. And I agree wholeheartedly with Prinz, that "the ethos of enlightenment [...] is constitutive of doing science" (Prinz, 2003, p. 11).

But *nothing* at all follows for our actions from allegedly showing that there is no freedom of will capable of scientific proof. Particularly because this step in itself has such far-reaching metaphysical implications, by proposing it science is tying its own hands and abandoning enlightenment to boot. It is voluntarily foregoing any chance of talking about our idea of man at all. Even the Ancient Stoics knew that metaphysical determinism lacks any consequences; they tell the story of a teacher chastising a lazy pupil by thrashing him with a stick: "Why beat me?" the pupil cries in pain. "All I can do is follow the order of causes laid out in the universe from the very beginning!" "Stop complaining" the teacher replies. "By beating you, all I am doing is following that very same causal order!"

The lesson of this anecdote for the deniers of free will is plain to see. If they desire to be consistent in the future, they too may make no demands of society based on their findings; they may derive no "valuable insights" from their own science for our actions. If there is no such thing as free will, what sense does it make to demand that lawyers and judges abolish their "narrow concept of guilt" (Roth) and revise their practices, that philosophers stop talking about freedom of will, that parents stop admonishing their disobedient children, and so on? According to the theory, not only the agent, but also those evaluating actions, such as judges, philosophers, parents, and others, even scientists themselves are subject to the "conditionality of genes, early childhood experience, and social environment" (Roth & Brumlik, 2004, p. 24) that made them what they are. How then, can a brain scientist, a scientific psychologist, a neural physiologist *demand* of us that we act other than we do, just because we now know about our subpersonal processes?

What can a scientist do who wants to review social practices related to free will effectively? He or she should abandon the unreasonable metaphysical demand that we forsake our notion of free will and acknowledge that free will is an empirically very successful instrument of explanation. Then, and only then, can scientific criticism of free will unfold its full potential and successfully and consistently debunk our illusions. Posthypnotic suggestion and behavioral disturbances in cases of schizophrenia, like the cases Prinz lists along with the Libet experiments as proof of his thesis, can only be seen as *involuntary* if they are contrasted with voluntary (or at least *more voluntary*) actions.

Since the 19th century, forensic doctors, in particular, have unearthed ample evidence that under some circumstances people are not as free as society, particularly philosophers, judges, and scientists have thought. As a result, in court we now take account of circumstances that diminish a person's accountability for particular actions. I imagine that, in the future, brain science, empirical psychology, neurophysiology, and any other relevant sciences will be able to develop solid scientific reasons for revising our legal concept of guilt, in court and elsewhere, making it more precise and thus more useful than it is today. Perhaps it is actually true that we should make people much less often responsible for their acts than we normally do. But that stance, in itself, presupposes that freedom of will is not an illusion, no matter how rare it may be; otherwise, we could not discern more or less of it.

It is incomprehensible that Prinz, on the one hand, demands that science be relevant for enlightenment, but on the other castigates the commingling of "two entirely different social games" governed by differing rules—the game of scientific explanation that has no room for freedom of will, and the game of moral evaluation and action control that "relies on the idea of free will" (Prinz, 1996a, p. 86, 101). This reminds me of Rudolph Wagner, the physiologist, neurologist and brain researcher from Göttingen, who triggered the *Materialismusstreit*, a famous and wide-ranging dispute on materialism with his speech before the "Association of German Scientists and Physicians" on September 18, 1854 (Wittkau-Horgby, 1998). That dispute, which continued until the turn of the century, "almost repeated the spectacle made by the great dispute on religion during the time of the Reformation," writes Friedrich Albert Lange (Lange, 1875, p. 536) in his talented chronicle of the debate.

Wagner (1854) did not deny free will, but rather did just the opposite; he fought for the reality of the immortal soul, which he said was "a product resulting from combining Divine Mind with matter to make an individual, independent being." His reason was religious belief, which he saw as a "new organ of the mind," a new "method for knowledge alongside thinking, natural reason," that science must do without. "For both," he continued, "reason and belief are just as different from one another, [...] as the senses, as vision and hearing" (pp. 18, 14f). As early as 1852, he advocated the idea that belief and science are two different spheres, overlapping only a tiny bit at the periphery. As a scientist, one is sometimes forced to accept insights that contradict belief, but as a believer, one can ignore that (Wagner, 1854, p. 10). An "immaterial individual soul substance" is indispensable for "moral order in the world," even if the natural sciences do not suggest it (Wagner, 1854, p. 21).

In his idiosyncratic style, the philosopher Hermann Lotze, with whom Rudolf Virchow and many other contemporaries agreed, called Wagner's standpoint "a queer sort of double-entry bookkeeping": "To follow this principle in science," he says, "and to compensate for desolation by embracing a *different* result in one's belief, has always seemed to me an unworthy fragmentation of our mental powers" (Lotze, 1852, p. 36). Despite the excesses of the materialism debate, we can be grateful that Lotze, the materialists, and other Forty-Eighters of the 19th century (who were otherwise at odds with each other) criticized Wagner's double-entry bookkeeping as dishonest and that they prevailed in this case, although their political revolution failed. If they had not won this battle, the dispute over the role of Darwinism in German secondary education that took place towards the end of the 19th century (see Daum, 1998) would not have ended as it did; in Germany today (at least), American "creationism" is not taken seriously by anyone—across all circles, and entirely independently of political creed or ideology. This is not an isolated episode, but rather one that characterizes the general attitude of the public at large towards natural science in German-speaking Europe.

But whoever uses double-entry bookkeeping, whether to strengthen and purify science or to defend belief and the immortal soul, *enfeebles* enlightenment and turns back the clock. Is this Prinz's intention? I doubt it. He must, then, give up Wagnerian double-entry bookkeeping and acknowledge the relevance of one game for the other, or—to put it more pathetically—acknowledge that reason is indivisible.

DENYING FREEDOM AND ABANDONING EXPLANATION

To deny freedom of will is not only self-destructive for natural science, of no consequence to our practical lives, and disastrous for the idea of enlightenment, as I have tried to show; in light of the present state of the sciences it is also extremely unfortunate for science policy. This is so for two reasons. First of all, this kind of free will debate plays into the hands of those who advocate a strict demarcation between the humanities and the sciences, especially those who, since the days of Neo-Kantianism, continue to fend off all naturalistic influence on philosophy and want to protect philosophy from convergence with the natural sciences. (By the way: Few scholars take the time any longer to think about the division between the humanities and the natural sciences. It crops up when you ask them to decide whether mathematics (or informatics) belongs to the one or the other group. Mathematics naturally belong among the humanities. Reliance on mathematics thus makes the sciences belong in some measure to the humanities, which shows that the entire demarcation is artificial and inappropriate.)

If freedom of will really has no place at all in science, then the only thing left for philosophers to do is to preach "values" unscientifically. They would become marked as apostles of one or another ethos, allowed to provide their followers with pious sayings and illusions of greater or lesser eloquence. That attitude is obviously inappropriate for building interdisciplinary bridges today; with a single whisk it brushes aside the whole tradition of philosophical enlightenment, which—we should not forget—was the cradle of natural science to begin with.

Another reason why it is unfortunate to exploit debate over free will to stress the divide between philosophy and the biological sciences is this: Present developments in cognitive neuroscience and in philosophy (which has been highly influenced by studies in cognition) are equally favorable for mutual respect and mature cooperation in many areas, including the freedom of will and related topics. In the 19th century, it was common to speak of physiologists and philosophers working on the mind–body problem as miners digging a tunnel from opposite sides of a mountain. Deep in the tunnel, philosophers can now hear the miners knocking out rock on the other side. There are signs that cognitive science, albeit of a more humble nature than that of the free-will disdainers, and philosophy that takes its duty to inform science seriously will some day meet in the middle of the mountain. I ask that we view our initial impression that free will and scientific method do not go well together as a *puzzle*, a scientific challenge that philosophers must also help to master. In fact, to adapt the statement by Lotze quoted earlier, it would be "an unworthy fragmentation of our mental powers" if we did not come together to solve this problem. A bit of modesty on the part of scientists would be welcome, of the kind exhibited by William James, who wrote: "My own belief is that the question of free will is insoluble on strictly psychological grounds ... He who loves to balance nice doubts need be in no hurry to decide the point" (James, 1890, p. 572). Libet's experiments have done nothing to diminish the value of James's argument.

Research cooperation between psychology and philosophy could arise, for instance, in what has come to be known in recent years as the "theory of mind" in cognitive neuroscience, developmental psychology, anthropology, and primate studies (cf., for example, Frith & Frith, 1999). Around the age of 4, children develop a sort of "theory of mind" that acknowledges the autonomy of mental life. This enables them to distinguish their own perspective from that of someone else and thus to understand that people can also act out of *incorrect* beliefs, or, more generally, that mental states (in this case: beliefs) play a causal role in explaining action. When asked where another playmate would look for a ball that was first in a basket, but then secretly placed in a closed box while that playmate was absent for a moment, children under the age of 4 say that the playmate will look in the box. Older children realize that due to a lack of information, the playmate will first look for the ball in the basket. Although chimpanzees do seem to grasp the intentional structure of actions, evidence indicates that they apparently have no, or only a very rudimentary theory of mind of this sort (Tomasello et al., 2003, Povinelli & Vonk, 2003).

In terms of the third component of freedom just discussed, having a theory of mental life is certainly a necessary condition for having a free will. In order to think of oneself as an agent, one must accept that others are independent agents, too; this is a concept that has turned up in many guises throughout the history of the philosophical investigation of self-awareness. We do not consider a tennis ball a thinking being, as Locke says, but we do think of our fellow persons in this way. And we do so, as we could say with Locke, because "we conceive him to think and consequently to have volition." If anywhere, this is where we should look for the freedom of will. It is tempting to go along with Michael Tomasello (1999) and see humans' capacity to think of each other as intelligent intentional beings as the origin of human cultural life, and then to understand human free will *and* the capacity to experiment scientifically from there. Why should we sacrifice the possibilities offered by our theory of mind for very successfully explaining action, and through which evolution has raised us above our purely biological nature, for subpersonal mechanisms, as if they were unreal (cf. Prinz, 2003; chap. 3, this volume)? Denying free will blocks many avenues; it means waiving explanation, which, unreasonably, is exactly what Prinz suspects of those who defend the notion of free will (Prinz, 1996a, p. 92f).

Cooperation between philosophers and scientists, however, requires that the latter be less fascinated by their own methodical determinism, which no one seriously questions, and stop thinking that they own it. Many wrongly believe that philosophers who accept free will automatically deny determinism. The fact is that most contemporary philosophers consider free will and determinism to be compatible, and perhaps even see determinism at the subpersonal level as being *indispensable* for freedom of will. Philosophers who advocate indeterminism are usually aware of the difficulties entailed by rejecting determinism, and bend backward to circumvent them.

The insinuation that philosophy is naïve in this respect is uninformed and unfair. Scientists need not instruct philosophers on determinism (as Prinz does in 1996a, p. 92). This might have been appropriate 150 years ago, when the law of the conservation of energy had just been discovered. But until that time even scientists, particularly physiologists and physicians, took at least physiological indeterminism for granted. If this were not so, the deterministic pathos in Claude Bernard's major work (Bernard, 1865, 2nd pt., chap. 1, § V) would be unintelligible. The number of scientists, by the way, who lately feel called to revive philosophical disputes of yesteryear (most of which were settled in the 19th century) is baffling. Naturally scientists are welcome to voice their opinions on philosophical issues. But they should first inform themselves of the state of the discussion and refrain from inconsistency.

And scientists should stop assuming that philosophers continue to follow Descartes in the belief in a nonmaterial mental substance, "mind stuff" as William James, or "soul substance" as Rudolph Wagner called it. Hardly any colleague asserts that notion any longer. On the other hand, do not forget that it was Descartes who, by distinguishing the nonmaterial from matter and thinking of it as an individual "substance," was the first to overcome Aristotle's doctrine of nature and thereby helped to establish the modern sciences of physiology and psychology (the latter of which, in turn, nowadays has trouble imagining how mind can be in matter)! Even Descartes did not think that the *res cogitans* is a controlling "I" or "self," as the opponents of free will like to imply that he thought, or imagine that philosophers today still think.

CONCLUSION

This chapter has not even touched on the most important question of the freedom of will, namely, how it may be compatible with the causal order of the world. I have also said too little about how the errors in freedom-scorning scientists' argumentation come about—except for criticizing the inappropriateness of reducing intentionality to the neural level. But it was not my intention to do such things. What I want to show is that even in science, as in everyday life, we have no other choice but to accept the existence of free will. Science cannot steal off and avoid the "game" of explaining action, and scientists cannot expect philosophers to keep their hands out of the "game" of science. We are all in the same boat. This essay, then, is more a product of contemplating science—the meaning of its business and its relationship to the world—than of contemplating free will. If science cannot get a grip on how to combine an explanation of action that includes free will with its own convictions about subpersonal processes, then that is science's problem, not the problem of philosophers who have already done quite a lot and have quite a bit to offer towards finding a solution.

In conclusion, I would like to let Socrates speak once more. As the passage previously quoted continues, after rejecting an explanation of action in terms of stretching and extending sinews and muscles because it is "very strange, indeed," he addresses the crucial point, namely our notion of causality:

> If it were said that without such bones and sinews and all the rest of them I should not be able to do what I think is right, it would be true; but to say that it is because of them that I do what I am doing, and not through choice of what is best [... that] would be a very lax and inaccurate form of expression. Fancy being unable to distinguish between the cause of a thing, and

the condition without which it could not be a cause! It is this latter, as it seems to me, that most people, groping in the dark, call a cause—attaching to it a name to which it has no right." (Plato, 1971, pp. 99a, b)

Today we would say that action is realized in subpersonal neural processes—no one doubts that. But it is a category mistake to think that they alone are the *causes* of *action*. The disdainers of free will are "groping in the dark" when they do not distinguish between causes and the material conditions that realize and embody them.

ACKNOWLEDGMENTS

I would like to thank C. Brand, E.-M. Engels, E. Hildt, W. Prinz, J. Sautermeister, G. Schiemann, and the editors of this volume for criticism of an earlier version of this paper, although I have not always heeded their suggestions.

This chapter was translated by Cynthia Klohr, and was first published in German as "Freiheit UND Wissenschaft: Metaphysische Zumutungen von Verächtern der Willensfreiheit." In E.-M. Engels & E. Hildt (Eds.), *Neurowissenschaften und Menschenbild* (pp. 195–219). Paderborn: Mentis.

REFERENCES

Bernard, C. (1865). *Introduction à l'étude de la médecine expérimentale.* [An Introduction to the Study of Experimental Medicine]. Paris: Flammarion.

Damasio, A. R. (2000, October 5). Interview. *Die Zeit, 41*, 43.

Daum, A. (1998). *Wissenschaftspoplarisierung im 19. Jahrhundert.* Bürgerliche Kultur, naturwissenschaftliche Bildung und die deutsche Öffentlichkeit 1848–1914 [Popularization of science in the 19th century. Bourgeois culture, scientific formation and the German public]. München: Oldenbourg.

Dennett, D. C. (1987). *The intentional stance.* Cambridge, MA: MIT Press.

Descartes, R. (1637/1897). *Discours de la méthode pour bien conduire sa raison, et chercher la vérité dans les sciences.* [Discourse on method]. Leyden. In Ch. Adam & P. Tannery (Eds.), *Œuvres de Descartes* (Vol. VI, p. 56f). Paris.

Fodor, J. A. (2000). *The mind doesn't work that way.* Cambridge, MA: MIT Press.

Frith, C. D., & Frith, U. (1999). Interacting minds—a biological basis. *Science, 286*, 1692–1695.

Haggard, P., & Eimer, M. (1999). On the relation between brain potentials and the awareness of voluntary movements. *Experimental Brain Research, 126*, 128–133.

Heidelberger, M. (1997). Ist der Kausalitätsbegriff abhängig vom Handlungsbegriff? Zur interventionistischen Konzeption der Kausalität [Does the concept of causality depend on the concept of action? Remarks on the interventionist view of causality. In: Philosophy of subjectivity and the subject of philosophy]. In R. Breuninger (Ed.), *Philosophie der Subjektivität und das Subjekt der Philosophie. Festschrift for Klaus Giel's 70th birthday* (pp. 106–116). Würzburg: Königshausen & Neumann.

Helmholtz, H. von. (1867). *Handbuch der physiologischen Optik* (Vol. 1) [Treatise on Physiological Optics]. Leipzig: Leopold Voß.

Helmholtz, H. von (1878). Die Thatsachen in der Wahrnehmung [The facts of perception]. In H. v. Helmholtz (1884). *Vorträge und Reden* (Vol. 2; pp. 217–251). Braunschweig: Vieweg.

James, W. (1890). *The principles of psychology* (Vols. 1–2). London: Macmillan.

Keller, I., & Heckhausen, H. (1990). Readiness potentials preceding spontaneous motor acts: voluntary vs. involuntary control. *Electroencephalography and Clinical Neurophysiology, 76*, 351–361.

Kornhuber, H. H., & Deecke, L. (1965). Hirnpotentialänderungen bei Willkürbewegungen und passiven Bewegungen des Menschen: Bereitschaftspotential und reafferente Potentiale [Changes of cerebral potentials in voluntary movement and in passive movements of man: Readiness potential and reafferent potentials]. *Pflügers Archiv für die gesamte Physiologie des Menschen und der Tiere, 284*, 1–17.

Lange, F. A. (1875/1974). *Geschichte des Materialismus und Kritik seiner Bedeutung in der Gegenwart* (2nd ed.; Vols. 1–2). [The History of Materialism and Criticism of its Present Importance]. Frankfurt: Suhrkamp.

Libet, B., Gleason, C. A., Wright, E. W., & Pearl, D. K. (1985). [Time of conscious intention to act in relation to onset of cerebral activity]. *Brain, 106*, 623–642.

Locke, J. (1690/1961). *An essay concerning human understanding* (Vols. 1–2). London: Dent.

Lotze, R. H. (1852). *Medicinische Psychologie oder Physiologie der Seele.* [Medical Psychology or Physiology of the Soul]. Leipzig: Weidmann.

Mach, E. (1905/1980). *Erkenntnis und Irrtum. Skizzen zur Psychologie der Forschung.* [Knowledge and Error: Sketches on the Psychology of Enquiry]. Darmstadt: Wissenschaftliche Buchgesellschaft.

Plato. (1971). *The last days of Socrates* (Hugh Tredennick, Trans.). Middlesex: Penguin.

Povinelli, D. J., & Vonk, J. (2003). Chimpanzee minds: suspiciously human? *Trends in Cognitive Sciences, 7*, 157–160.

Prinz, W. (1996a). Freiheit oder Wissenschaft? ["Freedom or Science?" in: Freedom of Choice and Action: A Problem for Nomological Psychology]. In M. v. Cranach & K. Foppa (Eds.), *Freiheit des Entscheidens und Handelns. Ein Problem der nomologischen Psychologie* (pp. 86–103). Heidelberg: Asanger.

Prinz, W. (1996b). Bewusstsein und Ich-Konstitution [Consciousness and the constitution of the ego]. In G. Roth & W. Prinz (Eds.), *Kopf-Arbeit. Gehirnfunktionen und kognitive Leistungen* (pp. 451–467). Heidelberg: Spektrum.

Prinz, W. (2003). Kritik des Freien Willens. Psychologische Bemerkungen [Critique of the Freedom of the Will: Remarks from the Viewpoint of Psychology]. *5th Congress of the Society for Analytical Philosophy*, September 23, 2003.

Prinz, W. (2004). Kritik des Freien Willens. Psychologische Bemerkungen [Critique of the Freedom of the Will: Remarks from the Viewpoint of Psychology, (revised)] *Psychologische Rundschau, 55*, 198–206.

Roth, G. (2001). *Fühlen, Denken, Handeln. Wie das Gehirn unser Verhalten steuert* [Feeling, Thought, Action: How the Brain Governs Action]. Frankfurt: Suhrkamp.

Roth, G., & Brumlik, M. (2004). Hat der Mensch keinen freien Willen? [Has man free will?] *Chrismon, 9*, 24–26.

Roth, G., & Vollmer, G. (2000, October). Es geht ans Eingemachte [Freedom at Stake] (Interview). *Spektrum der Wissenschaft*, pp. 72–75.

Singer, W. (2001, January 1). Das falsche Rot der Rose [The wrong red of the rose] (Interview). *Der Spiegel, 1*, 154–160.

Singer, W. (2003). *Ein neues Menschenbild?* [A new idea of man?] Frankfurt: Suhrkamp.

Singer, W., & Nida-Rümelin, J. (2004). Gehirnforscher sind doch keine Unmenschen. Aber vielleicht leiden sie an Schizophrenie [Brain researchers are no brutes. But maybe they suffer from schizophrenia]. *Frankfurter Rundschau, Magazin, April 3*, pp. 4–5.

Tomasello, M. (1999). The Cultural Origins of Human Cognition. Cambridge, MA.: Harvard University Press.

Tomasello, M., Call, J., & Hare, B. (2003). Chimpanzees understand psychological states—the question is which ones and to what extent. *Trends in Cognitive Sciences, 7*, 153–156.

Wagner, R. (1854). *Ueber Wissen und Glauben mit besonderer Beziehung zur Zukunft der Seelen. Fortsetzung der Betrachtungen über "Menschenschöpfung und Seelensubstanz.* [On knowledge and belief, with special respect to the future of the soul. Considerations of 'Creation of Man and Substance of the Soul']. Göttingen: Wigand. (Original work published in 1852)

Wittkau-Horgby, A. (1998). *Materialismus. Entstehung und Wirkung in den Wissenschaften des 19. Jahrhunderts.* [Materialism: Origin and Reception in the Sciences and Humanities of the 19th Century]. Göttingen: Vandenhoeck & Ruprecht.

Zhu, J. (2003). Reclaiming volition: An alternative interpretation of Libet's experiment. *Journal of Consciousness Studies, 10*, 61–77.

5

Governing by Will: The Shaping of the Will in Self-Help Manuals

Sabine Maasen
University of Basel, Switzerland

Again, this week has been packed with urgencies: meetings, seminars, and yet another conference to attend. My family hardly sees me anymore, going out with me for a beer is a matter of hard-nosed negotiating, and I know that I missed my lessons at the gym three times already. Last but not least, I'm up for a check-up with my dentist ... geez, I think I'm getting a headache!

If you know inner monologues of that type, this chapter has a wonderful message for you: There are ways to free yourself from endless rushing. The magic word is: self-management. Countless books, brochures, seminars, and coaching-letters are at your disposal. In addition, a host of videotapes and Internet sites gladly assist you with word and deed. Offers concerning time and self-management abound, their promise seems to be irresistible: Change is possible. You just have to do it! To this end, the will, your will, assumes two tasks. First, the will is the initiator for all measures taken to educate and discipline yourself. Second, the will is an important vehicle and therefore a prime target of all those measures taken to educate and discipline yourself. To state it bluntly: In the course of your self-managing efforts you have to find out what you really want, for you actually do only what you really want (see Sprenger, 1997, p. 71).

Such a formulation renders the imperative of getting the knack of your self simply irrefutable. Moreover, this imperative is embedded in a huge variety of practices of learning to act efficiently, with regard to both yourself and others—and the practices on offer address individuals and institutions. "Competence-enhancing seminars" as well as coaching for managers, students, politicians, or secretaries are ubiquitous; quality and change management today are routine procedures for improving the efficiency of administrations or companies. In brief: We are surrounded by a culture of efficiency and efficiency-enhancing procedures, all of which are more or less visibly connected to the will.

The very term, *will*, may seem somewhat awkward, even old-fashioned. And indeed, one needs to go back to the 1920s in order to find the term in a more explicit way. At that time, the predecessors of modern time and self-management manuals were called "schools for the will" (*Willensschulen*) or "guides to success." Ever since, books and manuals have been issued that address topics such as success, happiness, health, or the art of living—yet, at the core of all this self-help literature we find one basic motive: how to learn to educate your will and yourself in a methodical way. However diverse in style and scientific underpinning, each education or training program usually starts with the volitional decision to become more efficient, and it works at and through the will.

All the more reason for the sociologist of knowledge to become curious: Though this genre of self-help manuals may seem inconspicuous, if not altogether lacking in seriousness, it does have far-reaching effects: Not only does it address all of us, but it also teaches us how to work on our selves step by step. It is thus a prescriptive genre with the help of which individuals discipline themselves. It offers knowledge to reflect on yourself, and techniques to realize your self-set goals.

Yet another reason for the sociologist of science to become curious. Though this genre of self-help manuals may seem unscientific, it does seek recourse to science, though it does so decreasingly: In the 1920s, science, notably psychology, was still the prime source for legitimating respective manuals—nowadays, however, we find other sources as well, such as the authority of wisdom or common sense. While the role of science may have changed, it is noteworthy that the genre as a whole is based on, and enforces, systematic reflection and methodical procedures on virtually everybody. In a world that throughout the 20th century has enforced on the individual evermore and increasingly conflicting demands, self-help manuals promise to liberate the self by introducing rational ways of conducting life. Hence, they convey "scientific" modes of living.

This chapter has three goals. First, I show that and how those little helpers for the seekers of success and happiness work as self-technologies (Foucault, 1988). By providing us with detailed notions and techniques for training our will willfully, these manuals offer to assist us in accomplishing ourselves as willing selves. This entails norms and normalizations: The texts constitute socially stabilized behavior, even, and especially, in times that call for increased flexibility. The name of the game is "rationalizing everyday life."

Here is where the second goal of this chapter comes in. Although one may hold that the emergence and recent shape of the self-help genre is a clear case of applied psychology, one should, in my view, be more cautious. For self-help has become a literature *sui generis*; it draws from various literary genres, such as penitentials, manuals designed to educate our manners and virtues, as well as from the practices of counseling and psychotherapy. They all have their own educational and moral projects, albeit different ones in each case (Dryden & Still, 1999). From this perspective, self-help literature forms a distinct hybrid of all those influences without being reducible to any one of them.

Furthermore, self-help relies on evermore types of knowledge: Next to religious notions and knowledge about social etiquette we find esoteric, medical, or (neuro)physiological knowledge. Likewise, the techniques show evermore variation: In addition to psychologically oriented self-monitoring, meditation, wellness, and bodily fitness are top on the list. Again, self-help forms a distinct hybrid of all those influences without being reducible to any one of them.

From the perspective of academic psychology, one may either applaud or reject the (ambivalent) impact of psychology on everyday thought and practice, as well as the impact of everyday thought and practice on (public views of) academic psychology. In contrast to this, I suggest another line of reasoning. My thesis is that the interplay of both types of discourses eventually contributes to both agenda setting in the public (next to the self-management hype see, e.g., the media debate on the will) and the societal diffusion of quasi-scientific procedures (e.g., techniques of self-monitoring). From this perspective, the crucial question is: What are the societal effects of those knowledge dynamics? One effect is: In the course of this happening, a hybrid genre emerges that contributes to making selves and social order. It is a governmental technology, in the sense that it presents quite literally a technique for self-government.

The third goal of this article is thus to show that self-help literature assumes increasing importance in today's knowledge societies—societies that we regard as confusing, demanding, and risky. Therefore, whatever knowledge contributes to this device for orientation and self-control will gain in acceptance—for reasons that may or may not conform to academic variants of this knowledge. Psychological knowledge and techniques are part of constituting modern selves in modern societies, yet they do so neither exclusively nor without considerable modification.

As Nikolas Rose writes: "In the 19th century, psychology invented the normal individual. In the first half of the 20th century it was a discipline of the social person. Today, psychologists elaborate complex emotional, interpersonal, and organizational techniques by which the practices of everyday life can be organized according to the ethic of autonomous selfhood" (Rose, 1998, p. 17). In a nutshell, this is the story of disciplining individuals with the help of psychological knowledge: Disciplining is not opposed to autonomy and freedom. Rather, the notions of autonomy and freedom are embodied in, if not constituted by those practices that are then used to regulate and socialize the individuals choosing to perform them. The double-edged sword of autonomy and regulation can hardly be shown better than in recent popular manuals designed to educate us in "self-management," "life-leadership," or "life-work-balance": By encircling the individual with minute advice in terms of both (psychological) knowledge and techniques, those manuals are busy creating what we today conceive of as autonomous persons governing themselves and others by will.

In this connection, it will be interesting to take a look at another body of instruction books at the beginning of the 20th century. In the 1920s, these books taught their readers how to strengthen their wills by focusing on the act of making a decision and on the processing of that decision. They also relied on a host of techniques, some of which persist until today. However, in contrast to recent manuals they seem to be designed to form a subject with a strong and rather rigid identity, not the "flexible self" that postmodernist accounts hail today. Moreover, although earlier manuals mainly addressed the man at work, today they address everybody, for everybody has to work at oneself. Hence, the changing notion and significance of "work" will be identified as key to understanding form and impact of the recent self-management hype.

Yet before going into the two bodies of instruction manuals from the 1920s and the 1990s, I would like to address the following questions: How did the will get on the agenda again, especially on a social science agenda? How does the will relate to the rationalization of everyday life? After answering these questions, I shall integrate the tentative findings into the topic of governmentality by asking, in which sense could one regard modern self-help as part and parcel of a therapeutic branch of governmentality?

FRAMING AND REFRAMING THE DISCOURSE
ON THE WILL AND SELVES

It is safe to say that in the social sciences the will does not play a major role: We'd rather talk about actors, individuals, selves, or subjectivities, depending on the theoretical framework being employed. Some authors even ask whether there are still such entities as selves. No, it is not the social but the natural sciences that rediscovered the will.

Neurophysiological findings by Benjamin Libet (Libet, 1985) seem to challenge a long-cherished notion according to which we do what we want to. According to Libet, simple intentions are processed only after the action has been initiated unconsciously. He concludes that at the time a person realizes its intention, the brain has already decided what to do. Without going into the details of this experiment and its criticisms, let me simply state the challenge: We don't do what we want but we want what we do (see Prinz). From this view, will or intentions cannot be found in the neurocognitive system. This has led to some disquiet: "What if we are but 'a pack of neurons'?" (Crick).

Although on the basis of these and related findings, various scholars of the natural sciences as well as some philosophers are eager to report the will missing altogether (particularly in the feature pages of leading German newspapers, see Maasen, in press), our initial glances at the self-help literature suggest that, at the same time, there is a whole literature informing us about the will—its necessity and its need for constant training if we want to be successful selves.

The astounding coincidence of a discourse in cognitive neuroscience bidding farewell to the will and a huge body of practices insisting on the existence of will gives rise to the question of what the latter is actually talking about. Although self-help books clearly ignore the neurocognitive challenge and do not provide alternative theories of the will, they keep on *working at* the will—thereby, as we see it, constructing "decision-makers," that is, *willful acting selves*.

Recasting self-help literature as well-received vehicles for constructing selves, I do not try to argue with the challenge of cognitive neuroscience, but rather address a sociological debate, that is, to try to add a new dimension to an existing debate about the self as being late modern or postmodern. In both approaches, the self is understood as its own constructor, yet, they differ as to the question whether or not the subject can dispose of its constructive resources. Although Kenneth J. Gergen seems to accept this possibility of volitional self-construction for late modern selves (Gergen, 1990), postmodern approaches simply deny such an option. On that view, the capacity of selves to be and remain flexible is informed by social practices that dispose of us—not we of them (Welsch, 1991).

Both debates, however, conceive the willing, self-regulating individual as a social institution that is always in need of further forming, strengthening, and disciplining. That is why a sociological perspective is needed here. Therefore, I look at self-help literature educating selves in the minute details of planning their lives. The items in that literature testify not only to the (changing) role of the will over time, but also to the so-called rationalization of everyday life.

Rationalizing is one hallmark of modern society among others, such as individualization, differentiation, the steady increase of (perceived) contingencies, and options for acting. These tendencies strongly affect our everyday life (Voss, 1986). Notably the decrease of traditions, the diversification of norms, and the increasing impossibility of a continuous life-course impose the necessity to structure and stabilize one's life by one's own means. This shows in all dimensions: in the dimension of time (time management), in the factual dimension (employability), in the social dimension (social skills).

It is worth noting that Max Weber already coined the term "rationalization of everyday life" at the beginning of the 20th century (Weber, 1993-1920). However, although he postulated such a tendency only for a small bourgeois élite, a rational way of living has now become the predominant characteristic of virtually all members of Western societies. Weber also emphasized the ambivalences and paradoxical effects connected to this type of societal modernization: All attempts to respond to increasing demands by way of rendering one's actions more efficient are meant to gain more time and options for shaping one's life, yet these efforts at effectiveness constitute a novel moment of force: The flip side of the coin "rationalization of everyday life" is the increase of heteronomy. The increase of autonomy and (self-produced) heteronomy thus go side by side. Self-help manuals are a case in point.

SELF-HELP: A BRIEF STUDY OF A SUCCESS-STORY

Advice books are not a new phenomenon. From the 15th century onward, manuals designed to educate our manners and virtues accompany the modernization of Western societies: The book *On Human Relations* by Freiherr von Knigge (1788) is a very well-known example of learning the rules of behaving in public. Another best-seller addresses a different social group: The *Booklet for Helping Countrymen in Cases of Hardship*, written by the educator Rudolf Zacharias Becker (1787), tries to "redress the distinguished bodily and spiritual necessities of the countryman" (Becker, quoted from Günter, 2001). For that purpose, he expands for 800 pages on moral principles, gives "practical hints," tries to counter superstition, explains how to revive hanged and frost-bitten persons or those struck by lightning. Somewhat closer to modern concerns are Becker's teachings on the so-called order of life for the healthy, the sick, and the convalescent. These and other instruction books address everyday or professional behavior and indicate increasing social mobility, a modernization of manners, as well as an increasing difference between public and private behavior (Elias, 1992). Note, however, that this literature as a whole is more canonical and oriented towards rules; it is not yet based on finding the goal of one's life (1920s) or on continuous decision-making (1990s). In bourgeois society, there is only one decision to be made: to know the rules and to follow them. The dreaded alternative is: disgrace, a kind of social death.

Only in the 1920s do we observe the shift toward a more dynamic and goal-oriented type of advice book, resulting from an increasing complexity and contingency of modern society. Two excursions will show how advice becomes based on will and decision: In the 1920s, instruction books focused on the goal of success in the work sphere and on how to proceed methodically in order to reach this goal. In the 1990s, self-management manuals encouraged their readers to set their goals for themselves, to relate them and again: proceed methodically. However, goals become multiplied and dynamic, hence in need of constant observation and change. Nowadays, the readers should be prepared to change their goals, if inner or outer circumstances require doing so. In other words: Self-help literature is indicative of the ways in which everyday thought and practice co-evolves, with the differentiation of Western societies.

SCHOOLS FOR THE WILL AND GUIDES TO SUCCESS: SELF-HELP MANUALS IN THE 1920s

Schools for the will and guides to success issued in the 1920s regard the will as both amenable to and in need of education: Trained in the right way, the will is the key to a true self. Although their allegedly scientific foundation awards these practices special authority, the style of these books resembles that of penitentials: Martin Fassbender (*Willing—A Royal Art*), for example, is convinced that any instruction for self-education has to follow the natural formation of the will and Christian asceticism.

Among the authors of such manuals, one finds (highly or less reputed) academics, professionals, and freelance writers alike: psychologists, educators, psychiatrists, physicians, theologians, priests, but also parapsychologists as well as authors leaning toward the esoteric-ideological end, most prominently to New Thought. Almost all authors made use of contemporary psychological, pedagogical, and/or philosophical knowledge. When it comes to psychologists, they firmly rooted their writings in psychology and philosophy, and strongly promoted an educational program so as to encourage their readership to work at themselves: "If you want to, you can do anything: You must only be capable of wanting" (Lindworsky, 1927, p. 1). Yet, the author of this formula, the experimental psychologist Johannes Lindworsky, professor at the University of Cologne and later at the University of Prague, was fully aware of the fact that it is not easy to be "capable of wanting," which is why writings on the art of willing are so widespread. Therefore, he and fellow authors engaged in distributing methods of improving motivation, efficiency, and success. However, in contrast to the case of psychotechnics, for instance, the clientele of these instruction books—(young) men—is rarely addressed specifically. In most cases the readership remains unspecific. The authors presumably supposed that well-educated men, in general, would seize the opportunity to become more successful by way of self-instruction.

The book titles of these textbooks for schooling the will signal the need for method and enthusiasm alike: *The Gymnastics of the Will: Practical Instructions to Enhance Energy and Self-control, Invigoration of Memory and Pleasure to Work by Reinforcement of Willpower Without Outside Help* (Gerling, 1920); *School for the Will* (Lindworsky, 1927); *Life According to the Art of Generalship* (Sartorius, 1929); *Power and Action: a Guide to Will, Health, and Power* (Helmel, 1928). Although they all focus on willpower, Lindworsky distinguishes two forms: the act of coming to a decision and the realization of a decision. To be sure, decision making reveals the character—persons with a weak will clearly differ from those with a strong one. The latter can take decisions involving hardship and bitter distress, whereas the weak person resigns as soon as obstacles emerge. And the same strength of will shows in the realization of a decision once made, for it will be realized despite any hindrances that may occur (Lindworsky, 1927, p. 569).

By contrast, the book *Power and Action* by Heinrich Helmel, a nonmedical practioner, while covering the classical subjects, is decidedly pre-fascist in its basic ideas and diction: "Inner and outer health, power and beauty is duty and work on one's self, not only a gracious concomitant phenomena of our existence" (Helmel, 1928, p. 5). The will is the key: It is the "driving-wheel" (p. 10). But: "The will must be trained and skilled so as to delight us with its perfection" (p. 10). Like his colleagues, Helmel suggests concrete techniques to exercise mood, character, will, and concentration. Especially "the forming of the will provides us with consciousness of power and releases undreamt-of energy. Whoever exercises, will be given the power of will" (Helmel, 1928, p. 115). His message is nothing less than a "gospel of power, of will, of permeating spirit" (p. 158).

At the same time, so-called guides to success were published that differed from these textbooks for schooling the will in one crucial aspect: In their view, there is no such thing as "a will"; rather, there are only exercises of will performed on specific objects in order to form special competences and to satisfy concrete needs (Grossmann, 1927, p. 164). Gustav Grossmann, who studied philosophy, economics, statistics, and psychology, yet never worked in academia, built his system on a foundation of "science" because of the latter's almost religious normative power (*Glaubensallmacht*): "The strongest power of belief today is provided by science ... Hence, the proposition is absolutely true and right: 'An objective whose realization I believe in becomes reality.' But it must be point-blank: I can only believe in the realization of an objective insofar I dispose of the means and abilities to realize it" (Grossmann, 1927, p. 327). Based on the model of the natural sciences, one needs "to know the factors of one's work just as the physicist knows the objects and laws of physics ... once we are familiar with the elements of our conscious activities and their biological contexts we can start to build methods made of these elements and create them rationally" (p. 106). Grossmann's book *To Rationalize Oneself. Successful Living Can Be Learnt* became the prototype of the genre "guides to success." His empire of rationalization (Rieger, 2002, p. 88) was republished in no less than 28 editions. The most recent edition was issued in 1993.

The Grossmann-method (called today the *HelfRecht-System*, and still in use) targets the enhancement of work power, the refinement of personal powers and capabilities, the ethos of professional career, as well as individual happiness. Everybody can attain these goals: "In former days, personal success was a matter of luck. Today, personal success is a result of methodical procedures accessible to everyone" (Grossmann, 1927, p. 10). Objects of intervention are the subject's powers, resources, and routines. Of special importance are writing systems such as the how-to-do-it (*Wie-Plan*) or the diary of happiness. The procedure seems simple:

> First, set a goal; second, acquire the means to realize it with the help of a plan, wise and thoroughly thought-through, rendering every job manageable; third, achieve the means to realize the goal; fourth, realize the plan with the help of the diary of happiness.

With that formula, the training of the will turns into pure delight: "There is no higher pleasure than wanting and to spring at the goal driven by the willpower to eliminate any hindrances, to make one's way" (Grossmann, 1927, p. 113). True, it is knowledge that determines our goals, yet it has to be supplemented with exercises of enthusiasm and will.

As one can tell from scattered contemporary reactions, neither academic psychologists nor the general readership confused these self-help books with science. Although psychologists sometimes lamented the lack of psychological knowledge and the exaggerated belief in the changeability of people, they all underscored what they took to be the practical usefulness of this kind of advice.

So we see: To work at one's self is taken very literally. We see rational means that must be applied precisely, methodically, and continuously in every situation and on all matters of organizing one's personal life. Not to forget, "the dietetics of the body and the soul, of the sleep, of the trace minerals, the relationship of will and physiology based on iodine-saturated nutrition. ... Even leisure needs strict organization, because also the management of the weekend as recreation is an art. Not by doing nothing do we recover in the best possible way" (Grossmann, 1993, p. 132, Quoted from Rieger, 2002, p. 92). Of course, the same carefulness is prescribed for the organization of every single (working) day.

In the 1920s—this should not go unnoticed—the will is discussed in the contemporary framework of distinguishing power and fatigue. The crucial question was: If the will is energy, how can the will emerge where there is none? How can energy arise out of nothing? This basic paradox is dealt with by processing it: Key variables are the methods of self-energizing, self-education, planned, effective action, self-enthusiasm, and endurance. Ever-new hindrances have to be overcome by ever-new decisions (Lindworsky, 1927, p. 56)—this seemed to be the only way to defeat the dreaded opposites called "weakness of the will" and "nervousness".

SELF-MANAGEMENT MANUALS FROM THE 1990s

Seventy years later, we find ourselves in the midst of the self-management hype of the 1990s. Instruction books have not only increased in popularity, but the vocabulary has also changed. Though we do find terms like *training of the will* and concepts such as self-management, terms such as *life–work balance* and *life-leadership* now prevail. Although self-help manuals still refer to science, especially to psychology, physiology, and, most recently, to the neurosciences, one also finds other forms of knowledge, such as esoteric religious knowledge as well as notions based on wellness, management, and common sense, often combined together in one manual. At the same time, the authorship has changed drastically: With few exceptions that easily pass unnoticed, academic authors have almost vanished and another type of expert has emerged: the management guru with strong ties to consulting, counseling, and/or business management. It is professional experience and/or wisdom rather than academic expertise that is taken to guarantee authority. The intended readership appears to have expanded and to have become more diverse (e.g., women, children, professionals in specific fields, students); but as was the case in the 1920s, this readership is only rarely addressed explicitly. Instead the literature implicitly targets a broader, at least somewhat educated public. Finally and most importantly, the strong will and the true self seem to have lost significance. By contrast, management manuals hail the flexible self that operates best on a flexible, self-organizing mode. They hence occupy themselves less with the self but with practices of self-management. More than ever the will seems to be called for, as it is only the willing self that may cope with decisions vis-à-vis complex conditions and uncertainties—that is, with life in our postmodern times.

On the surface, one may perceive a huge diversity of issues addressed, methods used, and types of knowledge invoked. However, the underlying order is rather simple and should not be overlooked. Recent self-management manuals adhere to simple, supposedly straightforward principles, that is, to principles of self-management. "Simplify your Life" (Küstenmacher, 2001), the "Eisenhower-Principle" (Bossong, 1991, p. 51; Briese-Neumann, 1998, p. 24; Nagel, 2001, p. 16; Seiwert, 1994, p. 84), the "Pareto-Principle" (Bossong, 1991, p. 21; Briese- Neumann, 1998, p. 23; Hovestaedt, 1997, p. 47; Nagel, 2001, p. 17; Seiwert, 1994, p. 27), and the "Boomerang-Principle" (Seiwert, 2002) are pertinent examples. Authors such as Covey and others maintain that following these principles will help to render one's scheme of living more efficient: "Once we understand the principles and lead our lives accordingly, we are able to quickly adapt to ever-new circumstances, because principles can be applied everywhere" (Covey et al., 1999, p. 46f). Although principles need to be adjusted to specific situations, they are not at one's disposal. To be true to certain principles is not least a matter of willful decision:

> Free will is our capacity to act. It gives us the power to surrender our paradigms, to swim against the current, to change our character and act according to our principles instead of reacting on spontaneous desires. ... We can willfully decide to act on self-consciousness, conscience, and vision. (Covey et al., 1999, p. 53)

Free will, self-consciousness, conscience, and imagination are treated as gifts that can be educated:

> Free will: by making and keeping a promise. Self-consciousness: by keeping a diary. Conscience: by learning, listening, and reacting. Imagination: by educating yourself with the help of visualizations. (Covey et al., 1999, p. 57f)

Only a process of continuous training and encouragement can shape and relate those gifts. For instance, the exercise called "keeping a diary" primarily addresses self-consciousness, but also concerns the imagination, conscience, and free will, because writing has a strong imprint on the memory and helps "to remember your intentions and follow them" (Covey et al., 1999, p. 58). The gift of free will means to keep promises. To this end, the authors strongly suggest to perform a kind of bookkeeping:

> If you make a promise, write it down how you managed to keep it thanks to your free will. If you intend to go to the gym four times a week, scrutinize the factors that helped you doing it—or else the reasons why you didn't keep your promise. (p. 57)

According to these authors, a sharpened perception of the free will contributes to its development. Not unlike physical strength, strength of character is just matter of training (Covey et al., 1999, p. 125).

Although success may be judged differently by different people at different times, instruction books offer exercises that strive for more "objective" measures. The so-called "account of integrity" assumes the status of the ultimate measure of being an integrated self. To keep a promise is rephrased as payment. To miss a goal is rephrased as "withdrawals (from an account) that cause pain." Frequent withdrawals lead to a loss of confidence, and inevitably to cynicism. Accordingly, the path to strength of character implies a well-documented "account of integrity." One is well advised to proceed step by step. Don't promise too much, don't risk a withdrawal from your account. Rather, wait until the strength of your will exceeds your desires (see Covey et al., 1999, p. 125).

The balance sheets over time are very clear on this: "Freedom, autonomy, and responsibility are not simply given, are not just there, they have to be learnt and they have to be acquired time and again" (Sprenger, 1997, p. 16f). The techniques of self-help manuals therefore enforce a continuous monitoring of one's actions, because these actions reveal—incorruptibly—one's own decisions. Reinhard K. Sprenger's book bears the message in the title: "The decision is yours"—"Who says, I can't, really means, I won't" (Sprenger, 1997, p. 30). In order to enhance individual efficiency the manuals make use of all techniques known in psychology to monitor and educate one's self: questionnaires, psycho-tests, checklists, exercises to relax. Note: To have some fun and to "waste" time is allowed, but that is part of the overall goal of managing one's time and oneself more effectively.

To sum up: From ancient times until today, the use of the will is an important means of improving self-management, but major changes have occurred during the 20th century, both in the techniques proposed focusing on the will and the constructions of the will itself. Both bodies of instruction books locate the truth of their advice in its practical effects: Does the reader get better at coping with stress, competing demands, and the like? The evaluation is up to the reader himself. An important discontinuity, however, is to be found in the fact that science appears to have been regarded as highly authoritative in the 1920s, but now has to share its claims to authority with other kinds of knowledge. Another discontinuity concerns the resulting self. Reflections, tests, and trainings may seem similar on the surface, as do the instructions (i.e., keep a diary), yet recent self-management manuals no longer hail the "male, purpose-oriented, self-identical character" (Horkheimer & Adorno, 1969, p. 33) of the 1920s. The order of knowledge that informs the instruction book of the 1990s is based on the efficient organization of the flexible self that needs to meet diverse demands and ambitions; which notes, trains, and controls its stakes and expenses. Following this discursive modification, the dreaded alternative has changed accordingly—now self-help authors attack the "disorganized self," helplessly (albeit, from the authors' point of view, not really) being subjected to its circumstances.

SELF-HELP AS SELF-TECHNOLOGY

Philosophers and psychologists complain time and again about this popular genre named self-help. The former miss critical foundations or reflections on the art of living (Schmid, 1998), the latter reject a quasi-therapeutic practice that lacks seriousness and academic expertise (Castel, 1987, 1988). By engaging in such criticism, psychologists in particular, however, ignore a discursive process that they themselves helped to emerge. Throughout the last two decades, therapeutic talk came to permeate society in various forms and fashions, including self-help and advice rather than therapy. Journals, radio, television, the Internet—wherever one looks one finds yet a new version of (one-way) therapy and counseling. All of the versions on offer imply certain requirements: First, they require of us all the capability of performing a demanding type of discourse called therapeutic communication, meaning the ability to present and solve a problem between an expert and a layperson in various settings (on the couch or on the phone). Second, they require that one knows when to seek professional help and how to choose among various offers on the market (you pick up the phone, click on the self-help chat, or buy a book). Third, in the latter case, you need to be your own expert with whom you have to reach an agreement and who takes care of you meeting the agreement. Diagnosis, goal setting, and change all take place in one person, who is both therapist and client.

In the terminology of Michel Foucault, all forms of therapies and self-management are self-technologies. Self-technologies "permit individuals to effect by their own means or with the help of others a certain number of operations on their own bodies and souls, thoughts, conduct, and way of being, so as to transform themselves in order to attain a certain state of happiness, purity, wisdom, perfection, or immortality" (Foucault, 1988, p. 18). Granted, advice books regularly aim at very mundane goals: success, health, and happiness. Yet, those of us who wish guidance are provided with minute instructions referring to our soul, our behavior, our whole form of existence—hence, to our selves.

By doing so, self-help books contribute to a morality that is not about avoiding moral wrongdoing so as to keep up an empty husk of "shoulds" and "oughts." Nor is this morality fully characterized by exercising the virtues (justice, fortitude, prudence, and temperance) as, for instance, Albert Ellis teaches in his writings (see Ellis, 1994). Rather, this is a morality of decision, commitment, responsibility, that is, an ethics of autonomous selfhood.

GOVERNMENTALITY VIA SELF-HELP

Self-management books and manuals are not only self-technologies, however. Rather, they produce willing selves in a double-movement of individualization and normalization. On the one hand, all books emphasize the individual route to a happy and efficient self, on the other hand they normalize the procedure, they render the self an object of intersubjectively understandable methods of reasoning and acting. The astounding success of the self-help culture shows that we do not talk about individual idiosyncrasies but rather about a cultural practice, a culture of self-practices. Our culture describes itself as one of "individuals, yet this implies that individuals have to discipline themselves accordingly. For one can hardly do without discipline, if social order and reciprocal expectation should remain possible" (Luhmann, 1992, p. 199). Individualization and normalization are thus the two sides of the coin named self-help culture.

By sneaking into the lives of virtually all of us, instruction books not only function as self-technologies but as technologies of self-government as well. Coined by Foucault, the term *governmentality* refers to the capacity and a specific mode of (political) rationality that enables us to conduct our selves and others (Focault, 1991). According to recent studies of governmentality, we are busy working at the "enterprising self" (Miller & Rose, 1995). Whereas the therapeutic discourse of the 1980s hailed the jargon of "inwardness" and the search for the true self, modern governmental discourse uses the jargon of "economization." On this terminology, guiding a self simply equals running a company: Subjectivity is a corporate identity; the communication with oneself operates along the mode of project management. The basic principle of organization is the commitment, the commitment toward oneself. This contractual approach (Bröckling, 2000) seems to be the most recent version of the classical voluntary decision. The old paradox of willing to will is being replaced and multiplied by novel paradoxes: Empower yourself! Motivate yourself! Educate yourself! Each and every incentive to go for more hides the verdict of doing just not enough. The work on your self simply never ends.

On a methodological note, recent self-help literature helps to specify and differentiate some of the political rationalities within which government is articulated: Following Miller and Rose (1993, p. 80), we can see one type of language, within which objects and objectives are construed, the grammar of analyses and prescriptions, the vocabularies of programs, the terms in which the legitimacy of governing self and others is established. The discursive matrix revolves around "goals" and "do what you decided to do!" In this way, self-help books are revealed as one of the microtechnologies by which subjects regulate themselves and others—they are, in fact, governmental technologies. Government by will is particularly efficient, because it is wrapped in the promise of liberating one's self, and also of being a prime expression of autonomy (act according to your own choice). The concept of governmentality thus makes us see the intimate and intricate connection of an abstract political rationality (termed *neoliberalism*) and microtechniques of everyday life.

Frequently we hear the lament: What are self-help books for, if not to express the fact that ideologies of feasibility have entered the domain of individuality (Güntner, 2001)? Indeed, on an abstract level, they impart all relevant dimensions of self-description, the norms to be known, adequate strategies to display authenticity, successful ways of reflecting on one's experience and behavior, acceptable technologies to link one's needs and societal expectations. In other words: Self-help books add new prisms to the panoptical machinery of self-control (Kliche, 2001, p. 123). From the perspective of therapeutic governmentality, however, we identify these "feasibilities" and "stagings" of authenticity as technologies of freedom. According to Thomas Osborne:

> Under neoliberal conditions freedom becomes a technology of freedom … this means that freedom once more is a matter of networks of freedom that are integrated with our existence. This is, of course, no absolute freedom—whatever this could be—but we talk about networks of trust, of risk, of choice. Networks that invite us to overcome the incalculability of our lives by way of entrepreneurship and acts of free will … (on this understanding) freedom has a price: continuous monitoring. Wherever freedom appears in our neoliberal era, there is monitoring, audit, regulation of norms. In other words: *forms of freedom that integrate us with the whole continuum of acceptable forms of (self-) government.* (Osborne, 2001, p. 15; emphasis added)

In view of those tense networks of self-producing and self-disciplining technologies, by which selves are induced to will something at all, it seems a bit awkward to talk about a "trivialization of ways to know yourself," as Charles Taylor does (Taylor, 1995, p. 13). At least, we have to maintain that governing by will has come to be an object of continuous and multifaceted efforts. Whereas in the 1920s, instruction books mainly addressed the will in order to enhance the efficiency and success of males at work, in the 1990s, they render the will into a matter of work for all of us. Perhaps it is no wonder, then, that this technology of governing ourselves that has also become a passion (Maasen & Duttweiler, in press) has just been assigned a novel term: *self-change work*.

ACKNOWLEDGMENTS

I am grateful for thoughtful comments and critique by Barbara Sutter, Stefanie Duttweiler, Thomas Sturm, and Mitchell Ash.

REFERENCES

Horkheimer, M. & Adorno, T. W., (1969). *Dialektik der Aufklärung.* [Dialectic of Enlightenment]. Frankfurt: Fischer Taschenbuch.

Bossong, C. (1991). *Zeit-Management. Mehr leisten in weniger Zeit.* [Time management: Achieving more in less time]. München: Compact.

Briese-Neumann, G. (1998). *10 Minuten Zeitmanagement.* [Ten minutes of time management]. Niedernhausen: Falken.

Bröckling, U. (2002). Das unternehmerische Selbst und seine Geschlechter. Subjektivierungsprogramme und Geschlechter-Konstruktionen in Erfolgsratgebern [The enterprising self and its genders. Programmes of Subjectivation and constructions of gender in how-to books]. *Leviathan, 2*(175–194).

Castel, R. (1987). Die Institutionalisierung des Uneingestehbaren und die Aufwertung des Intimen [The institutionalization of the unconfessable and the upvaluation of the intimate]. In A. Hahn & V. Kapp (Eds.) *Selbstthematisierung und selbstzeugnis: Bekenntnis und Gestandnis* (pp. 170–180). Frankfurt: Surkamp.

Castel, R. (1988). Die fluchtigen Therapien [The transient therapies]. In H. G. Brose & B. Hildenbrand (Eds.), *Vom Ende des Individuums zurr Individualität ohne Ende* (pp. 153–160), Opladen: Westdeutscher Verlag.

Covey, S. R., Merill, A. R., & Merill, R. R. (1999). *Der Weg zum Wesentlichen. Zeitmanagement in der vierten Generation.* [First things first. The fourth generation of time management]. Frankfurt: Campus.

Dryden, W., & Still, A. (1999). When did psychologist last discuss "chagrin"? American psychology's continuing moral project. *History of the Human Sciences, 12*, 93–110.

Elias, N. (1992). *Über den Prozeß der Zivilisation. Soziogenetische und psychogenetische Untersuchungen.* [The divilizing process. Sociogenetic and psychogenetic investigations]. Frankfurt: Suhrkamp.

Ellis, A. (1994). *Reason and emotion in psychotherapy* (Rev. ed.). New York: Carol Publishing Group.

Fassbender, M. (1922). *Wollen—eine königliche Kunst. Gedanken Über Ziel und Methode der Willensbildung und Selbsterziehung.* [Willing—A royal art. On goals and methods of forming the will and self education]. Freiburg: Herder.

Foucault, M. (1988). Technologies of the self. In L. H. Martin, H. Gutman, & P. H. Hutton (Eds.), *Technologies of the self. A seminar with Michel Foucault* (pp. 16–49). London: Tavistock.

Foucalt, M. (1991). Governmentality. In G. Burchell, C. Gordon, & P. Miller (Eds.), *The Foucault Effect. Studies in Governmentality* (pp. 87–104). Chicago: The University of Chicago Press.

Gergen, K. J. (1990). Die Konstruktion des Selbst im Zeitalter der Postmoderne [Self construction in postmodern context.] *Psychologische Rundschau, 41,* 191–199.

Gerling, R. (1920). *Die Gymnastik des Willens: praktische Anleitung zur Erhöhung der Energie und Selbstbeherrschung, Kräftigung von Gedächtnis und Arbeitslust durch Stärkung der Willenskraft ohne fremde Hilfe.* [The gymnastics of the will: Practical instructions to enhance energy and self-control, invigoration of memory and pleasure to work by reinforcement of willpower without outside help]. Berlin: Möller.

Grossmann, G. (1927). *Sich selber rationalisieren. Mit Mindestaufwand persönliche Bestleistungen erzeugen.* [To rationalize oneself. Successful living can be learnt]. Stuttgart: Verlag für Wirtschaft und Verkehr.

Güntner, J. (2001). Die ignorierten Bestseller. Ratgeberliteratur—als Phänomen betrachtet [The ignored bestsellers. The phenomenon of how-to literature]. *Neue Zürcher Zeitung, 65.*

Helmel, H. (1928). *Kraft und Tat: Wegweiser zu Wille, Gesundheit, Kraft* [Power and action: A guide to will, health, and power]. Dresden: Verlagshaus Hera.

Hovestaedt, W. (1997). *Sich selbst organisieren: weg vom Zeitdruck. Wie man sich die Arbeit ersparen kann* [Organizing oneself: Avoiding pressure of time. How to spare work]. Weinheim: Beltz.

Kliche, T. (2001). Das moralisch abgezogene und das kapitalisierte Selbst. Psycho-tests, die Erbauungsliteratur flexibler Normalisierung [The morally deducted and the capitalized self. Psycho-tests as literature of edification in flexible normalization]. In U. Gerhard, J. Link, & E. Schulte-Holtey (Eds.), *Infografiken, Medien, Normalisierung* (pp. 125–135). Heidelberg: Synchron.

Knigge, A. V. (1788/1967). *Über den Umgang mit Menschen.* [On human relations]. Darmstadt: Wissenschaftliche Buchgesellschaft.

Küstenmacher, W. T. (2001). *Einfacher und glücklicher leben.* [Simplify your life]. Frankfurt/New York: Campus.

Libet, B. (1985). Unconscious cerebral initiative and the role of conscious will in voluntary action. *Behavioral and Brain Sciences, 2,* 529–566.

Lindworksy, J. (1927). *Willensschule* [School for the will]. Paderborn: Ferdinard Schöningh.

Luhmann, N. (1992). *Beobachtungen der Moderne.* [Observations on modernity]. Opladen: Westdeutscher Verlag.

Maasen, S. (2006). Neurosociety ahead? Debating free will in the media. In S. Pockett, W. P. Banks, & S. Gallagher (Eds.), *Does consciousness cause behavior?* (pp. 339–359). Cambridge, MA: MIT Press.

Maasen, S., & Duttweiler, S. (in press). Intimacy in how-to books: The passion of self-change work. In E. Wyss (Ed.), *Transformations of passion. The mediatisation of intimacy in letters, postcards, TV, Internet and mobile phone.* Amsterdam/Philadelphia: John Benjamins Publishers.

Miller, P., & Rose, N. (1993). Governing economic life. In M. Gane & T. Johnson (Eds.), *Foucault's new domains* (pp. 75–105). London/New York. Routledge.

Miller, P., & Rose, N. (1995). Production, identity and democracy. *Theory and Society, 24,* 427–467.

Nagel, K. (2001). *Erfolg. Effizientes Arbeiten, Entscheiden, Vermitteln und Lernen.* [Success. Working, deciding, communicating and learning efficiently]. München & Wien: Oldenbourg.

Osborne, T. (2001). Techniken und Subjekte: Von den "governmentality studies" zu den "studies of governmentality." [Techniques and subjects. From governmentality studies to studies of governmentality]. *IWK-Mitteilungen, 2–3,* 12–16.

Rieger, S. (2002). Arbeit an sich. Dispositive der Selbstsorge in der Moderne. [Work in itself. Dispositives of self care in modernity]. In E. Horn & U. Bröckling (Eds.), *Anthropologie der Arbeit* (pp. 79–96). Tübingen: Narr.

Rose, N. (1998). *Inventing our selves. Psychology, power, personhood.* Cambridge, UK: Cambridge University Press.

Sartorius, J. (1929). *Die Feldherrnkunst des Lebens. Eine Willensschule.* [Life according to the art of generalship]. Paderborn: Schöningh.

Schmid, W. (1998). *Philosophie der Lebenskunst. Eine Grundlegung* [Philosophy of the art of living. A foundation]. Frankfurt: Suhrkamp.

Seiwert, L. J. (1994). *Das 1 x 1 des Zeit-Management* [The 1 x 1 of time management]. München & Landsberg: MVG.

Seiwert, L. J. (2002). *Das Bumerang-Prinzip. Mehr Zeit fürs Glück* [The boomerang principle. More time for happiness]. München: Gräfe & Unzer.

Sprenger, R. K. (1997). *Die Entscheidung liegt bei Dir. Wege aus der alltäglichen Unzufriedenheit* [The decision is yours. Ways out of daily discontent]. Frankfurt/New York: Campus.

Taylor, C. (1995). *Das Unbehagen an der Moderne* [The malaise of modernity]. Frankfurt: Suhrkamp.

Voss, G. (1986). *Veränderungen in der Arbeitsteilung der Person. Zur sozialen Stabilisierungs- und Strukturierungsfunktion alltäglicher Lebensführung.* [Changes of labour division of the person. On the socially stabilizing and structuring function of life conduct]. (Sonderforschungsbereich 333 Universität München "Entwicklungsperspektiven von Arbeit," Teilprojekt A1.) Retrieved November 22, 2002, from http://www.tu-chemnitz.de/phil/soziologie/voss/alt/PA1.nat

Weber, M. (1993/1920). *Die protestantische Ethik und der "Geist" des Kapitalismus.* [The protestant ethic and the spirit of capitalism. Bodenheim: Athenäum Hain Hanstein]. *Bodenheim: Athenäum Hain Hanstein.*

Welsch, W. (1991). Überlegungen zur Transformation des Subjekts [Thoughts on the transformation of the subject]. *Deutsche Zeitschrift für Philosophie, 39*(4), 347–365.

6

Scientific Selves: Discerning the Subject and the Experimenter in Experimental Psychology in the United States, 1900–1935

Jill Morawski
Wesleyan University

Modern American experimental psychology requires a minimalist cast of actors, taking what appear to be precisely defined roles. From the 1930s onward, the "experimenter" and "subject" served as its principal actors, for a long period holding the abbreviated titles "E" and "S" in experimental reports. Excepting the introduction of "confederates and machine-technology substitutes" (Bayer, 1998; Morawski, 1998), these prescribed roles have endured. Subjects were rendered anonymous and purportedly passive actors whose thoughts and behaviors have been represented almost exclusively through experimenters' terms or numeric systems, and they were "run" through the factory-like operations of the experiment. By eliminating the participant's subjective observations, dropping the misnomer of calling him or her an "observer," and using the controls of precise laboratory procedures, experimenters aimed to remove subjectivity from the experiment. According to J. F. Kantor, "objectivity, that is, making psychological data into autonomous facts to be observed and described," must include "objectifying attitudes." Kantor affirmed a purportedly incontrovertible distinction between observer and object, consequently insisting that "psychology studies the 'other one'" (1922, p. 431). Indeed, Max Meyer (1921) titled his introductory text *The Psychology of the Other One*. Such codification of scientific participants (in terms of capacities for objectivity) was but one of the techniques for standardizing experiments; other techniques include quantification, scales and tests, and aggregate statistical methods.

Experimenters, by contrast to subjects, came to be seen as beings who no longer themselves generated objects of analysis or engaged in self-reflection (introspection) but, instead, regarded themselves as practitioners of scientific objectivity. Their "aperspectival" vantage constituted a cognitive superiority over other scientific selves, a superiority psychologists themselves came to call the "psychologist's advantage," "psychologist's point of view" or the "psychologist's frame of reference" (e.g., see Allport, 1940; Ladd, 1899). Although this advantage was deemed to be an acquired attribute of the experimental psychologists, even students could "enter the kingdom of psychology," wrote Yerkes (1911, p. 15), once they attained such scientific skills.

These laboratory role distinctions and the tacit psychological attributes associated with them led to ready adoption of J. F. Dashiell's 1929 proposal to standardize the term *subject*. According to Dashiell, the term *subject* was most appropriate for the simple reason that "In many contemporary lines of psychological investigation the so-called 'observer' does no observing" (Dashiell, 1929, p. 550). However, the new articulation of subjects did not incorporate all of the identities found to be inhabiting the psychological laboratory. In his objection to Dashiell's move to standardize the nomenclature and, consequently, certain features of the subject's psychology, Madison Bentley (1929, p. 682) described additional traits of these scientific characters, including that of the experimenter. Regarding the experimenter's "excess" character, Bentley noted an authority borne of suspiciousness, claiming "The point of the objectivist seems to be that he prefers to do all the reporting and recording himself and not to trust another." Behind such standardization were psychological and not scientific motives; these motives, in turn, had unscientific consequences, *including* the fact that "This creature the objectivist prefers to call *the subject,* so overlooking the mild inconsistency between having subjects and rejecting with phobic scorn everything 'subjective'" (Bentley, 1929, p. 682). Bentley astutely detected how these modern experimentalists harbored not only some unacknowledged *self-attributes* but also *other features of the subject*, ones at odds with subject's purported role as routine producers of psychological data. Alongside the belief that (largely interchangeable) naïve or untrained subjects produce objects for analysis, objects that are scientifically superior to those of introspectors, emerged a sense that they are challenging, risky, and even dangerous. Subjects are untrustworthy beings ever prone to deceiving or fooling the experimenter, misinterpreting the experimental commands, or otherwise undermining the experiment. Prior to adopting this new psychology of the subject, psychologists who relied on the subject's (also called observer or reactant) observation took neither the subjects nor the experimenters to be infallible reporters without attentional or cognitive error. However, these psychologists expressed confidence that such problems could be eliminated, typically through training of the subject or skillful interventions by the experimenter. Charles Judd confidently held that "The untrained observer has variations in excessive degree because *he is easily distracted.* He does not know how to give himself up to the observation of what is offered; *he begins to speculate about his error.* He may have chosen an experience so foreign to his ordinary life that its very newness disturbs him. As he becomes more accustomed to experimental work, these disturbances tend to disappear" (Judd, 1907, p. 8; see also Foster, 1923; Titchener, 1902). Carl Seashore believed it possible for the subject to "Be Impartial" and "not self-centered (Seashore, 1908, p. xi).

Most psychologists, however, were or became less confident and undertook what was to be generations' long development of methodological procedures and protocols that specifically averted or contained subjects' unruliness, irrationality, or duplicity—a triad of experimental dangers. Experimental researchers devised means to avoid dependence on subjects' fallible and possibly devious self-reports: these included hiding the intention of the experiment from subjects, selecting subjects who were unlikely to apprehend their intent, and eliminating subjects' ability to respond to experimental stimuli in ways that complicated the desired form of experimental data.

Subjects were not the only dangers in the laboratory: experimenters, too, were found to have problematic features that risked their objective selves (Morawski, 1996), although these self-features were only infrequently examined in scientific discourse. Proper training of experimenters was generally believed to control such problematic features, although eventually double-blind techniques were introduced to contain experimenters' non-objective attributes and actions.

How do we understand these scientific selves that emerged simultaneously and coexisted throughout the remainder of the century? What does it mean that psychologists routinely subscribed to these two types of experimental subjects? From where does the other, more vexing facets of subject and experimenter's selves originate? Some answers to these questions can be found in histories of standardization that describe psychologists' embrace of techno-scientific ideals as a means to generate useful knowledge for regulating individuals and institutions as well as producing efficient and interchangeable products. These histories show how psychologists substituted naïve for trained subjects in order to produce systematic knowledge about classes of people, knowledge that could be utilized by teachers and bureaucrats (for instance, Danziger, 1990; Rose, 1990). Historical studies reveal, too, psychologists' aesthetic appreciation of the techno-scientific ideals of standardization and uniformity (Coon, 1993). However, they do not tell us much about the "excess" or double identities of scientific selves and the psychological attributes circulating through the methodological mandates.

The complexity of the experimental selves that materialized in standardized laboratory methods and persists in contemporary experimental psychology is not examined in standardization histories. The evolution of these selves in the early 20th century, I propose, involved at once psychological and epistemic struggles and coincided with wider cultural struggles about the self, autonomy, and agency in what was perceived to be an increasingly industrialized, de-individualized world. The dialectics of these experimental roles took shape via tensions within modernity, notably tensions of authenticity versus artifice (or the real and the artificial). In the modernity of advanced industrial culture, psychological subjectivity was a ubiquitous notion, an ever presence that architectural historian Mark Jarzombek (2000) has described as the "everywhereness" of the psychological in Western popular culture (p. 12). Many educated Americans, exemplified by psychologist Gordon Allport, nervously contemplated the dehumanization brought by the modern emphasis on self-performance: the culture's plentiful invitations to role taking with their implications for free play of the self pushed against the venerated idea of an authentic self. In historian Ian Nicholson's words, moderns "were fascinated by their subjective experience, and they possessed a heightened awareness of their own transformative potential" (Nicholson, 2003, p. 38). Allport dramatically portrayed modernism's psychological dilemmas in a diary account of his graduate studies at Harvard: "Would you believe it if I told you that for eight hours to-day I have actually been administering monotonous intelligence tests to Portuguese, Lithuanian, Negro, and other miscellaneous children in a public school …? I felt between a drained out school-marm and a relentless scientist who classifies, indexes ever, uses a microscope and tweezers. But that I did, and shall continue for moons to come" (Nicholson, p. 75).

In a culture of modernism that advanced psychological notions of the subjectivity of an autonomous ego, the psychological was regulated and validated by the discipline of scientific psychology, but it is also the case that the culturally generated psychological permeated and influenced the science's core constructs. Jarzombek (2000) found in the psychology attending 20th-century art and architecture that "Psychologizing discourses outfox the very science that grounds its principles" (p. 31). Modernism's psychological discourse infused the very construction of experimentation in early 20th century psychology just as that discipline was undertaking scientific codification of subjects. Exploring these dynamic and reflexive iterations of psychological subjectivities—both in and outside the laboratory—is essential to understanding the aforementioned dualities and inconsistencies of the experimental selves that were being articulated in those laboratories.

The urgent drive to routinize experimental roles, despite responses like Allport's lament of the monotony of experimentation, depended on recognition of disorderly if more genuinely dynamic human selves. That is, the very standardized experimental selves were sustained through a sometimes uncomfortable regard of other features of these selves. In a multiple operation involving projection and compensation, the E and S were devised to reflect a tenuous difference, a bifurcation of psychological agents that was assumed to be necessary to obtain objectivity. The "unstandardized" or excess attributes of these experimental actors likewise rehearsed the psychological dialectics and complications of modernity: The roles compensated for the amoral, monotonous depersonalized laboratory roles and reaffirmed (in a circular fashion) the presumed differences. Experimental psychology thus simultaneously acknowledged the modern psyche and aimed to name and govern that psychology for societal as well as scientific ends. Even when Robert Yerkes still defined psychology as a "subjective science," for instance, he asserted the cultural power of experimental psychology, urging, "The least that any of us can do is to learn to observe psychological processes.... This much we owe to ourselves as educated members of civilized races" (Yerkes, 1911, p. 13).

The traversing and looping of the psychological across cultural lines of science, literature, aesthetics, popular media, and commerce demand historiographical work. Their dynamics invite interrogation of subjectivity discourses beyond those of experimental reports, and this chapter introduces such an investigation. The chapter first excavates the dualities of experimenter and subject roles, using case examples that focus on the location, rhetoric, and hybridizations of these selves. Second, the ascribed attributes of the experimental actors are shown to connect with the larger cultural preoccupation with the psychological, and attributes of these selves can be mapped onto what can be called "axes of difference" and hierarchies of knowing. These connections are evidenced in the correspondences between the epistemic and methodological creeds of experimentation and the psychological premises, structures, and ambitions of realist fiction.

MAPPING HUMAN KINDS THROUGH PSYCHOLOGY'S SCIE NTIFIC SELVES

In his 1890 introductory textbook, *Principles of Psychology,* William James cautioned experimenters about the "Psychologist's Fallacy," the unscientific tendency for the psychologist to assume that the perceiver knows his or her thoughts the way the psychologist knows them. In 1933, Saul Rosenzweig issued another warning of the experimenter's psychological assumptions about experimental participants. Rosenzweig delineated numerous unacknowledged psychological processes beyond those that are explicitly hypothesized in the experiment; in other words, experimental subjects are psychologically more present and cognitively complex than the laboratory methods presume. The two admonitions, issued 40 years apart, raise concerns about largely unarticulated psychological complexities in laboratory activities, yet these very critiques also anxiously affirm the need for regulated conceptions of experimenter and subject (Morawski, 2005). Looking more closely at experimenters' writings about laboratory participants makes evident that anxieties about psychological reflexivity (Woolgar, 1988) underlie both the standardized version of experimental selves and another version looming in those statements; each version intimates a cultural legacy more extensive than the laboratory's history.

The new experimental subject was never more accurately or vibrantly described than he or she was by John Dashiell:

> But by no means are all the problems of psychology concerned with a person's (the "subjects") direct experience; and in the degree that they are problems of his efficiency, of his reactions or reaction tendencies, etc., they are a matter of observation less to him and more to the experimenter. In other words, in many contemporary lines of psychological investigation the so-called "observer" does no observing! (Dashiell, 1929, p. 550)

And,

In like manner for the psychological investigator the self-observations of the subject are of only auxiliary value. Perhaps the subject states that he sees orange-red; he may really be red-green colorblind. He may report himself as tired, only to show, when put to a test, no decrement in efficiency at all. He may sincerely insist that he is the prey to no embarrassment, resentment, or other agitation, while at the same time tell tale evidences may be appearing on the experimenter's dials. He may conscientiously give one reason for his conduct toward a person, whereas careful analysis by laboratory technique may bring to light another and quite different motive—which he himself may ultimately recognize and acknowledge. (Dashiell, 1928, p. 12)

Trained in the ethos of Dashiell's conception of the subject, a conception that soon was to become dominant, psychologist Neville Sanford looked back (at midcentury) to a seemingly distant era when a different human kind entered the laboratory. As Sanford described the pre-subject, Wundtian kinds: "In the experiments that got started in Wundt's laboratory the person whom today we are likely to call a 'subject' was called an 'observer.' These observers were real live persons, key figures in the interaction, who could be counted on to take responsibility for their actions, to tell the truth, to keep their promises" (Sanford quoted in Scheibe, 1988, p. 59). It warrants note that Sanford's nostalgia for a time of authentic people, honest and reliable beings, is reported at a moment of modernism's crisis when many American psychologists, apprehending an artifactual and inhumane atmosphere in culture and science, turned toward humanism for alternative versions of human nature. However, if one were to pause at Sanford's depiction of the subjects and ask how these subjects came into being—ask what transpired from the time of the Wundtian laboratories to the mid-20th century—it would be necessary to search beyond arguments such as Dashiell's in order to locate these irresponsible, untrustworthy and otherwise lacking beings. However bewildering the modern S, and whatever perfidies he or she was inclined to commit, this S comprised a distinct human kind, one purposely described by experimental psychologists who were trying to replace the Wundtian observer.

The S described in Dashiell's proposal differs substantially from E, and their differences can be visualized as lying on several axes. First of these axes is the obvious one of rationality: the rational self-knower occupies one end of the axis and the not-so-rational, at times even wildly irrational, knower occupies the other. Another axis has on its one end, authenticity or veracity of self and at the other, inauthenticity or performance and artifice. A final axis of consciousness extends from hidden or deep (unconscious) to visible and apparent (conscious). These three axes—rational–nonrational, authentic–artifice, and conscious–unconscious—were laid on a tacit, hierarchical grid of (kinds of) persons that had been centuries in the making but was refined and legitimated through the modern sciences. Mirroring dominant cultural typologies of persons, the hierarchy categorized and ranked beings according to the social distinctions of race, religion, ethnicity, sex, class, educational attainment, and age. Animals, children, the uneducated, the non-White or "primitive," and the mentally impaired occupied the lower echelons; the college psychology student occupied a high position on the grid. The grid's segments signaled psychological differences; for instance, kinds of persons placed in the lower echelons were considered less likely to deceive because they were more honest and also were less likely to comprehend the nature of the experiment, given their different consciousness (Morawski, 1997). This hierarchy is simply reflected in Mary Calkins' classification of scientific methods: "Introspective psychology is the study of one's own consciousness; and its immediate and dominant method is introspection. Comparative psychology is the stuff of other consciousness than one's own. The most important objects of its study are the conscious experience of animals, of children and of primitive men" (Calkins, 1901, p. 12). Likewise, in proposing means to control the psychological problems of the psychology experiment, Rosenzweig, although sensitive to the dynamic influence of the experimenter's race, gender, and religion, nevertheless readily ranked subjects according to which kinds were most "naïve," mainly children and "Unsophisticated adults—by which is meant adults who are not well educated, perhaps even below normal intelligence" (Rosenzweig, 1933, p. 346).

These axes of difference were not discovered in the laboratory any more than they were drawn from other psychologies, both informal and formal ones, of the early 20th century. Culturally circulated psychologies increasingly understood individuals to be performers, ad men or con men, at worst; they are ruler followers and multifaceted, fragmented "social" selves, in a more positive sense. The new psychoanalysis, although purportedly the sign of the devil in American experimental psychology, the *sine qua non* of the unscientific approach to human psyches, actually comprised a vital resource in psychology (Hornstein, 1992). Among other things psychoanalysis effectively differentiated authenticity from performance, the real from the posed. Psychoanalytic conceptions of the analyst's stance likewise became instrumental to asserting differences between the consciousness of the experimenters and subjects. Echoing the language of analysis, psychologists increasingly made reference to the inauthenticity, nonrationality, and faulty consciousness of ordinary beings. Designers of tests and measures engaged in complex reasoning about the subject's capacities, and introduced increasingly complicated procedures to divert, eliminate, or otherwise control these capacities.

Pressey and Pressey's (1919) invention of "cross-out" tests (for intelligence and personality) bears such complex detective work. Criticizing standardization as "artificial and unnatural," they alternatively advocated more "natural" methods such as crossing out: "To cross out a mistake is a very natural thing to do. It is a child's own method.... From the subject's point of view the task presented in the tests is thus not at all unreasonable" (Pressey & Pressey, 1919, p. 138). Laboratory precautions ranging from the recruitment of naïve subjects to techniques of secrecy and deception were introduced precisely to control these beings. Common sense and cultural knowledge informed psychologists about their subjects and, consequently, guided their experimental practices. These cultural understandings reverberate with anxieties of the modern age and reveal how the struggles of scientific selves resemble tensions common to an elite class of writers, artists, and intellectuals.

Two psychologies in particular provided phenomenal and discursive material for claiming differences both between experimenter and subject and between experimenter and his/her lower-self. The modern S and E were informed by a psychology of performative role taking sort (the social veneer of individual selves) and another of psychoanalytic or depth psychology. During the period 1900 to the 1930s, psychologists drew on performative as well as psychoanalytic models to introduce the scientific persona of E and S. They designed technical operations—experimental procedures—that secured these persona while also calming their own anxieties about themselves and the reality of these different beings. Such techniques for clarifying and fixing the attributes of E and S greatly benefited the laboratory. Most importantly, the techniques structured relations of research whereby experimenter and subject could perform their respective duties without contamination, contest, or ambiguity: the experimenter would avoid confusing his or her standpoint with the subjects (James' Psychologist's Fallacy) and the subject would restrain or be restrained from displaying any democratic, civic, moral or other agenic actions (Rosenzweig's psychologizing subject).

Several examples can serve to illustrate psychologists' anxious acknowledgment of complex subjectivities and their consequent technical inventions to curb, remove, or hide such complexity. Floyd and Gordon Allport's (1921) empirical study of personality constitutes a classic contribution to the development of personality assessment within experimental psychology; their study grappled with the new subject. The resultant paper establishes the rationale, content, and scoring procedures for an innovative personality inventory. Typical of the emerging rhetoric of scientific psychological reports, Allport and Allport's text began by admonishing earlier scientific efforts to investigate such personality attributes as "truthfulness, neatness, conscientiousness, loyalty, perseverance, tactfulness, and the like" (Allport & Allport, 1921, p. 8). These attributes, the authors' contended, have been inaccurately measured: they were distorted by the peculiarities of the observational situation. More importantly, measurement of these attributes was contaminated by the attributes' superficiality: they fail to detect "more pervasive, more deeply lying, and far less evident, tendencies of the personality" (1921, p. 8). Take their illustration: "Neatness, for example, may be due to such diverse causes as (1) the persistence of the parental ideal, and the passive attitude toward parental authority, (2) a phobia toward dirt, arising as a defense reaction against infantile habits, (3) the compensatory striving of a plain-looking girl to make herself attractive in all ways possible, (4) an extreme sensitivity to the social behavior and attitudes of one's fellows. Thus, we see that the deeper and more pervasive tendencies are of far greater importance than the superficial attributes that themselves are merely the product of more fundamental tendencies in their play on the particular environment" (1921, p. 8). Asserting such a deeper subjectivity makes evident an indebtedness to Freud and psychoanalysis in general (see also Morawski, 2005; Nicholson, 2003).

Moreover, these notions of the subject informed research method as well as theory: endowed with a deeper, less readily accessible and less trustworthy self, the subject in the laboratory must be treated with caution and, unavoidably, it would seem, with manipulative, even deceptive techniques. Allport and Allport (1921) argued that methods must be designed in accord with the assumption that subjects *cannot* be trusted. To use self-report techniques and then "To ask the subject whether he is honest, moral, thoughtful, literary in tastes, etc. or to analyze himself by inward searching, is only to encounter the obstacles of carelessness, rationalization, and defense reactions. The questions asked should be in terms of what the subject actually does in his daily life; let the subject judge himself as another person might—by his habitual behavior" (p. 11). Even with such methodological prophylactics against deceit and concealment, methodological protections that soon were to involve routine deceit on the experimenter's part, the subject's hidden self still posed problems. For instance, the Allports' noted, "A general difficulty lies in the impossibility of knowing whether a certain negative reaction in a test is due to a repression or to an actual absence of that element in the individual concerned. This opposition between Freudian and non-Freudian reactions pervades a great deal of the work in personality study, and renders many apparently ingenious tests almost impossible to interpret" (1921, p. 13). The subject is a bifurcated self, able to more or less freely express one or another self in an experimental situation unless one self or part of one self is constrained by experimental protocols.

Despite their awareness of so-called "Freudian reactions" and recommended techniques for control, the Allports wavered in their trust of the subject. In one section of their personality scale (approximating a projective measure), the subject was "asked to react in a spontaneous, emotional manner to these situations, and to write down immediately the way in which he would conduct himself if faced with the conditions described" (1921, p. 14). Here the two psychologists, unlike many subsequent researchers, displayed a measure of experimental trust, albeit a self-doubting trust for they added "This type of test, to be sure, presupposes the co-operation of the subjects, and an interest on the part of each in actually analyzing and truthfully presenting his own type of behavior rather than in merely making a good impression" (1921, p. 14). Allport and Allport extended this optimistic if noteworthy trust in another section of the test. In the "Insight and Self-Evaluation" section, they postulated that some subjects can see themselves honestly: in other words, some subjects can see themselves as experimental psychologists do. "A person of good insight," they wrote, "is not likely to be deceived by his own rationalization and by the self-extenuation of his acts by refusing to recognize their motives" (1921, p. 19). In fact, human improvement depends on this psychological capacity for "The process of reformation of a criminal or of character improvement in the socialized individual is possible only when one's personality is revealed to one's own eyes" (1921, p. 19). Subjects' insight is literally measured in terms of the psychologist's insight or standpoint: a subject is said to have insight to the extent that his self-rating corresponds with the statistical average of the expert raters' rating of his personality. Here the psychologist's fallacy—that the psychologist takes the subject's mental state to be like his/hers—is inverted and transvalued, rendering the subject's approximation to the psychologist's mental state the ideal. Given the wariness of test makers, and the technical devices they crafted to detect and/or eliminate subjects' so called defense reactions (see also Rosenzweig, 1934), it is not surprising that after several decades these same test constructors eventually found themselves designing measures of test anxiety (Goldberg, 1971).

As suspicious of the subjects' shifting self as were the Allports, Lewis Terman and Catherine Cox Miles (1936), were more so. Engaged during the 1920s and 1930s in a massive project to measure masculinity and femininity, Terman and Miles chided other researchers for their naïvete regarding the experimental subject. Addressing psychologists' practice of honestly reporting the specific aspect of psychology being measured in an inventory, Terman and Miles detected a gigantic opportunity for subjects' subterfuge should they be told what the study was measuring. "One would not need to be a psychologist," they wrote, "to be able to score as fair-minded on the Watson test, extroverted on the Laird C2, or self-sufficient on the Bernreuter inventory, provided one know what the test was intended to measure." Psychologists needed to "keep the subject in the dark with respect to the purpose of the test" (Terman & Miles, 1936, p. 77).

To support their admonitions, Terman and Miles conducted an experiment where the subjects were told that their test assessed masculinity and femininity, and they were instructed to respond either as masculine or as feminine as possible. The results confirmed their suspicions of the subject's duplicity as the male out scored the female subjects on femininity scores and the female out scored the male subjects on the masculinity scores. Such "test faking" undoubtedly confirmed, too, both the performative, role-taking capacities of otherwise ordinary subjects and also the need for the experimenter's surveillance. As Woodworth (1945) described the problem, "To control the external situation is a matter of laboratory technique for example, a dark room may be needed and a piece of apparatus for exposing a picture exactly 1/10 of an second. But how shall E control the conditions that lie within O?" (Woodworth, 1945, pp. 11–12). He then suggested that such control requires deception.

Personality research might be seen as an obvious site to find fragments of a psychoanalytic subjectivity. The situation, however, is no different when we turn to the more conventional experimental studies of mental processes and behavior (studies of learning, forgetting, judgment and the like). Although these latter studies rarely mention psychoanalysis proper, reference to unconscious motives nevertheless is made. More often, evidence is found for the modern trickster or ad man persona that parallels the discourse of play, disguise and management of surface appearances in the early 20th-century culture of consumption (Lears, 1989, 1991; Pfister, 1997). In textbooks, references to the everyday management of appearance, along with a less explicit signaling of unconscious processes, are sometimes made with literary flare, whereas in laboratory reports they appear in experimentalist shorthand. Textbook authors like John Dashiell (1928) liberally invoked the advertiser's or salesman's desire for control, as well as the individual's yearning for self-control: "What boy, practicing stance and grip, has not given a little thought to his future possibilities in the major leagues, and what girl has not at some time attentively scrutinized her costuming, her speech, or her special little proficiencies with a view to making an effective impression?" Acknowledging these human ambitions and simultaneously criticizing them, ironically associating such observations and self-observations with being a "good psychologist," researchers essentially found them faulty because they are *merely* about appearances, not reality.

With heightened caution about the overt-covert and the apparent-real dimensions of personhood, experimenters in the 1920s moved toward more systematic detection (or presuming) subjects' resistances and, in turn, regulated them through apprehending and intervening experimental techniques—through laboratory controls. Introduced were a variety of such techniques for apprehending subterfuge and managing the so-called sophisticated subject. Deception was the most common tactic. Experimenters began by deceiving the subject about the real intent of the study or the actual operative variables and, later, about their very performance on initial portions of the experiment. Experimenters even trained subjects to be sophisticated and conniving. A 1925 experiment compared the performance of naïve subjects with others trained to be "sophisticated": they were made more sophisticated by learning experimental protocols along with tactics for deception—by learning the ways a "guilty person might appear innocent" (Strumberg, 1925, p. 95). This play of deception found that experimenters could not readily detect so-called "crimes" committed by the sophisticated subjects. As the experimenter woefully cautioned, "Could the sophisticated subjects not only prevent detection of the crime, but also prevent detection of their sophistication" (1925, p. 95)? Calling the psychological effects of experimentation either an "experimental attitude" or "experimental posture" (terms that both convey the performative and resistance), some researchers actually conducted experiments to test their concerns about these very psychological phenomena (see Anderson, 1930; Fernberger, 1914).

During the 1920s, psychologists also grew increasingly uneasy about their own hidden selves, voicing concern that the heated debates over contending theories actually indicated their own emotionality and irrationality. In this atmosphere, E. G. Boring (1929), a staunch experimentalist, proposed that heeding psychologists' own split selves is scientifically beneficial. Advocating that psychologists "cultivate dissociation," he announced that "Too much has been said in favor of the integration of the personality, and too little in favor of dissociation. The scientist needs to be a dual personality" (p. 120).

LITERARY PLACES, PSYCHOLOGICAL POSITIONS

In drawing on local psychologies, both professional and indigenous ones, psychologists were doubly reflexive, at once invoking scientific, technical, and cultural concepts to identify the occupants of experiments. They simultaneously labored to differentiate these occupants, at least partly in response to their sense of their own fallibility as human observers. Their reflexive entanglements represent unavoidable complications of a human science whose objects are the self-same creatures as the observers (Flanagan, 1981; Morawski, 1992; Smith, 1997). Viewed from another perspective, psychologists' efforts to decipher experimental participants belong to a larger history of scientific vision: their efforts signal what we know as the objective perspective that (paradoxically) assumes some specific observational position while locating the perceiver outside the space. According to Evelyn Keller, that scientific vision "is a history of erasure, of the progressive disembodiment and dislocation of the scientific observer and author that ultimately became sufficiently complete to permit the comprehensive and apparently subjectless representation of the world that emerges today, in the late 20th century" (1992, p. 138). Subjectless representation was precisely what Yerkes desired when he emphatically urged psychologists to create: "devices that shall free us from the observation imperfections (sic) of the experimenter," enabling a freeing of scientists' attention in order to control urgent matters (Yerkes, 1915, p. 258).

The working psychologies of E and S devised in the early decades of that century made possible the smooth functioning of controlled experiments and heightened psychological confidence in those experiments. Their manufacture comprises a peculiar chapter in the emergence of "subjectless representation" within scientific epistemology. By delineating and refining differences between experimenters and their objects of analysis, psychologists could impose rules of conduct, limit spontaneity and transgressions, and ultimately be sole witnesses to the real and not real, the authentic and superficial, in the experimental situation. The anxieties evident in psychologists' refinements of scientific selves also owe much to the culture of modernism. The distinct human kinds of E and S, each endowed with complicated, bifurcated if not internally strained personalities, resemble other depictions of subjectivity at this cultural moment.

The rise of "realism" in art and intellectual life, with eventual modifications in "naturalism" and their ultimate undoing in the immediately subsequent modernist turn, reverberate in the dense personas of E and S. Intertwined intellectually, socially, and interpersonally with scientific thought (Klein, 1932; Taylor, 1969), literary realism "offered coherent representation of a new social order that seemed increasingly inaccessible and fragmented" (Shi, 1995, p. 100). In Henry James' words, realism "represents to my perception the things we cannot possibly *not* know, sooner or later, in one way or another" (quoted in Shi, 1995, p. 120). Some realists, of course, comprehended too, the distinction between *duplicating* and *representing* the world, and naturalists or "savage realists" aimed not simply to reveal the world but to see the primitive, irrational, and determined features of humanity. Modernism, fomenting at the dawn of the new century, embraced not some superior vision but "perceived" reality: modernism began acknowledging illusion, the made up, the pretend, and pretense as well as the mobility and mutability of subjectivity. The modernist edict that "reality is not always, in fact, what is seen" challenged just as it corroborated scientific vision. So, too, is modernism's very dependence on the autonomous subject who experiences and discerns (Jarzombek, 2000).

The work of literary realists of the period reveals the variations and contradictions available in then current constructs of subjectivity: This period of transitional worldviews and "person views" generated varied ideas about human nature. The ingredients available to describe personhood included rational (realist observational stance), not rational (psychoanalytic models), natural (evolutionary theory), mechanical (new biology and engineering), artifice (culture of consumption), fragmented (psychoanalysis and criticisms of modernity), and as emergent (Bergsonian idealism). Alongside writers, artists, and social commentators, psychologists confronted a plethora of choices and contradictions in understanding the subject positions of their laboratory beings.

The variations of subjectivity appearing in the work of literary critic and writer William Dean Howells bear some striking resemblances to the subjectivities being described and inscribed by experimental psychologists. Adopting the unmarked subject standpoint of an "outsider," Howells held that the realist writer is endowed with "critical faculty" to discern conscious and unconscious life processes. As literary scholar Henry Wonham described Howells' authorial stance, "In order to promote the psychological well-being of his readers and himself, the writer must 'be constantly in the position of an outsider studying carefully his effects.' He must learn to juggle conscious and unconscious material, maintaining 'self-possession and self-control' by treating suppressed anxieties 'as if they were alien'" (Wonham, 1995, p. 704). This authorial stance, described by Howells himself as that of a "psychological juggler," served as the vantage point for objective writing. Howells believed authors should retain "self-control" and he disliked any personality of the author appearing in his or her writing (quoted in Peyser, 1992, p. 24). By contrast, his fictional characters cannot occupy such an objective purchase: they have fragmented selves, (those "other selves" as he once described them), shifting consciousness, and internal tensions (pp. 34–35). Social regulations along with the will, taken to be a restraining mechanism, are embraced as means of holding the self together, containing those "other selves" and thus averting moral, social, and psychological disaster.

Howells' subjectivity differs from those of both Henry and William James, who tended toward celebrating the expansiveness of consciousness (Peyser, 1992, p. 34–5). However, not all of Howells' characters have the capacity to restrain consciousness or control (even partially) the fragments of self. His fictional representations of subjectivity contain another version of selves: the Black characters whose subjectivity is lack or blandness, without adequate critical vision, artificial, and driven by primitive impulses of the unconscious. Howells' "therapeutic objectification" projected onto the Black characters his own psychological difficulties and anxieties about self-control, morality, and authenticity. In analyzing the characters in Howells' fiction, Wonham found that "the savages, barbarians, and children who appear with surprising frequency in his critical prose offer an image of the mind prior to the sorting out of individual identity that becomes possible through the realist's power of objectification, his ability to project unwanted aspects of the self outward and to treat his fears 'as if they were alien'" (Wonham, 1995, p. 714).

Literary analysts have explained Howells' conceptions of the ideal author as one who stands beyond personality—beyond his own self. This abstract authorial self along with his "alien others," or others who cannot fully stand outside their personalities, constitute his notable realist position. Some scholars have interpreted this stark realism as a psychological defense: Howells is understood as defensively responding not only to the social upheaval after the Civil War but also to his own personal life struggles. His realism is defensive, composed through classic psychic projections and splitting. As John Crowley described it, "the psychological juggler, unlike his circus counterpart, did not allow the right hand to know what the left hand was doing: as a writer, Howells was given to splitting off conscious control from unconscious inspiration and allowing his characters to arise as mysterious strangers from his own unacknowledged depths" (Crowley, 1983, p. 49; see also Delbanco, 1993). In the swirling mix of notions about the self and subjectivity, Howells engaged his own anxieties to craft several different, although certainly interdependent selves, ranging from the detached observer to those with less veridical access to will and unification of self.

The struggles and anxieties of subjectivity, internal to individuals as well as cultural, that are detected in early 20th-century fiction illuminates psychologists' scientific project of fashioning two distinct scientific selves. These latter types of selves had a distinctive feature: they are internally double beings, at times capable of either suppressing or expressing unwanted tendencies. They were held to be capable of acting with abandon or cunning or with controlled restraint and proper (ex-

pected) conduct. At the cusp of the aesthetic movements of realism/
naturalism and modernism, psychologists' two selves—the *E* and *S*—
acquired their now orthodox form through a play of difference. The dis-
tinctly realist standpoint accorded the experimenter resembles the realist writer's gaze on a social world of confused characters, and the
complex, primitive if not artificial self accorded the subjects paralleled
realist projects that presaged modernist subjectivity. The triumph of
modernism, with its paradoxical free self and criticality of the very possibility of that self, and with growing emphasis on self-constructions and
experience undeniably troubled the privileged purchase of
experimentalist. In the end, such modernist apprehensions trouble the
objective stance precisely because the very problematics raised by
modernism were acknowledged, incorporated, and sometimes reified
in the dual versions of selves in experimentation.

Both constellations of selves were produced through psychological
(enjoining the moral and epistemic) reflexivity on the part of their producers. Just as Howells drew on the psychology of the day to explain his
writerly style, so experimentalists used the psychologies of a dawning
modernism to examine the psychological experiment. Both the literary
and the techno-scientific productions of selves occasionally endowed
these beings with common cultural markers such as race and gender; as
they did so they confirmed or affirmed the social hierarchies of urban culture. Finally, both productions appear to have been therapeutic for their
creators as well as consumers. Regarding scientific psychology, the laboratory inhabited by *E*, with his anxieties as well as self-control and objectivity, and *S*, with her fragmented, confused if not subversive self, contain
potential therapeutic outcomes for the scientist as well as society.

REFERENCES

Allport, F. H., & Allport, G. W. (1921). Personality traits: their classification and
    measurement. *The Journal of Abnormal Psychology and Social Psychology*,
    16, 6–39.
Allport, G. (1940). The Psychologist's frame of reference. *Psychological Bulletin*,
    37, 1–28.
Anderson, O. D. (1930). An experimental study of observational attitudes. *Ameri-
    can Journal of Psychology, 42*, 345–369.
Bayer, B. (1998). Between apparatuses and apparitions: Phantoms of the labora-
    tory. In B. Bayer & J. Shotter (Eds.), *Reconstructing the psychological subject:
    bodies, practices and technologies* (pp. 187–213). London: Sage.
Bentley, M. (1929). 'Observer' and 'subject.' *American Journal of Psychology*, 41,
    682–683.
Bentley, M. (1930). Another note on the observer in psychology. *American Journal
    of Psychology, 42*, 320.

Boring, E. G. (1929). The psychology of controversy. *Psychological Review, 36,* 97–121.

Calkins, M. W. (1901). *An introduction to psychology.* Norwood: Norwood Press.

Coon, D. (1993). Standardizing the subject: Experimental psychologists, introspection, and the quest for a technoscientific ideal. *Technology and Culture, 34,* 757–783.

Crowley, J. W. (1983). Howellsian realism: A psychological juggle. *Studies in the Literary Imagination, 16*(2), 45–55.

Danziger, K. (1990). *Constructing the subject: Historical origins of psychological research.* New York: Cambridge University Press.

Dashiell, J. F. (1928). *Fundamentals of objective psychology.* Cambridge, MA: The Riverside Press.

Dashiell, J. F. (1929). Note on use of the term 'observer'. *Psychological Review, 36,* 550–551.

Daston, L. (1992). Objectivity and the escape from perspective. *Social Studies of Science, 22,* 597–618.

Delbanco, A. (1993). Howells and the suppression of knowledge. *The Southern Review, 19,* 765–784.

Fernberger, S. W. (1914). The effect of the attitude of the subject upon the measure of sensitivity. *American Journal of Psychology, 25,* 538–543.

Flanagan, O. J. (1981). Psychology, progress, and the problem of reflexivity: A study in the epistemological foundations of psychology. *Journal of the History of the Behavioral Sciences, 17,* 375–386.

Foster, W. S. (1923). *Experiments in psychology.* New York: Henry Holt and Company.

Gigerenzer, G. (1987). Probabilistic thinking and the fight against subjectivity. In L. Krüger et al. (Eds.), *The probabilistic revolution* (Vol. 2; pp. 11–33). Cambridge, MA: MIT Press.

Goldberg, L. (1971). A historical survey of personality scales and inventories. In P. McReynolds (Ed.), *Advances in psychological assessment* (pp. 293–336). Palo Alto: Science and Behavior Books.

Heft, H. (2001). *Ecological psychology in context: James Gibson, Roger Barker, and the legacy of William James's radical empiricism.* Mahwah, NJ: Lawrence Erlbaum Associates.

Hornstein, G. A. (1992). The return of the repressed: Psychology's problematic relations with psychoanalysis, 1909–1960. *American Psychologist, 47,* 254–263.

Howells, W. D. (1891). Editor's study. *Harper's, 83,* 314–316.

Hunter, W. S. (1919). *General psychology.* Chicago: The University of Chicago Press.

James, W. (1890). *The principles of psychology.* New York: Holt.

Jarzombek, M. (2000). *The psychologizing of modernity: Art, architecture, and history.* Cambridge, UK: Cambridge University Press.

Jones, E. E. (1985). Major developments in social psychology during the past five decades. In G. Lindzey & E. Aronson (Eds.), *Handbook of social psychology* (Vol. 1; pp. 47–107). New York: Random House.

Judd, C. H. (1907). *Laboratory manual of psychology.* New York: Charles Scribner's Sons.

Kantor, J. R. (1922). The evolution of psychological textbooks since 1912. *Psychological Bulletin, 71,* 429–442.

Keller, E. F. (1992). The paradox of scientific subjectivity. *Annals of Scholarship, 9,* 135–153.

Klein, D. B. (1932). Scientific understanding in psychology. *Psychological Review, 39,* 552–569.

Ladd, G. T. (1899). *Outlines of descriptive psychology.* New York: Charles Scribner's Sons.

Lears, J. (1992). The ad man and the grand inquisitor: Intimacy, publicity, and the managed self in America, 1880–1940. In G. Levine (Ed.), *Constructions of the self* (pp. 107–141). New Brunswick, NJ: Rutgers University Press.

Lears, T. J. J. (1989). Beyond Veblen: rethinking consumer culture in America. In S. Bronner (Ed.), *Consuming visions: Accumulation and display of goods in America, 1880–1920* (pp. 73–97). New York: Norton.

Lears, T. J. J. (1991). *No place of grace: Antimodernism and the transformation of American culture, 1880–1920.* New York: Pantheon.

Meyer, M. F. (1921). *Psychology of the other-one, an introductory text-book of psychology.* Columbia: The Missouri Book Company.

Morawski, J. G. (1992). Self regard and other regard: Reflexive practices in American psychology, 1890–1940. *Science in Context, 5,* 281–308.

Morawski, J. G. (1996). Principles of selves: The rhetoric of introductory textbooks in American psychology. In C. F. Graumann & K. J. Gergen (Eds.), *Historical dimensions of psychological discourse* (pp. 145–162). Cambridge, U.K.: Cambridge University Press.

Morawski, J. G. (1997). Educating the emotions: Academic psychology, textbooks, and the psychology industry, 1890–1940. In J. Pfister & N. Schnog (Eds.), *Inventing the psychological: Toward a culture history of emotional life in America* (pp. 217–244). New Haven: Yale University Press.

Morawski, J. (1998). The return of phantom subjects? In B. Bayer & J. Shotter (Eds.), *Reconstructing the psychological subject: bodies, practices and technologies* (pp. 214–228). London: Sage.

Morawski, J. G. (2000). Just one more'other' in psychology? *Theory & Psychology, 10,* 63–70.

Morawski, J. G. (2005). Reflexivity and the psychologist. *History of the Human Sciences, 18,* 77–105.

Nicholson, I. A. M. (2003). *Inventing personality: Gordon Allport and the science of selfhood.* Washington, DC: American Psychological Association.

Peyser, T. G. (1992). Those other selves: Consciousness in the 1890 publications of Howells and the James brothers. *American Literary Realism 1870–1910, 25,* 20–37.

Pfister, J. (1997). Glamorizing the psychological: The politics of the performances of modern psychological identities. In J. Pfister & N. Schnog (Eds.), *Inventing the psychological: Toward a culture history of emotional life in America* (pp. 167–213). New Haven: Yale University Press.

Pressey, S. L., & Pressey, L. W. (1919). "Cross-Out" tests with suggestions as to a group scale of the emotions: Studies from the psychological laboratory of Indiana University. *Journal of Applied Psychology, 3,* 138–150.

Reed, E. (1995). The psychologist's fallacy as a persistent framework in William James's psychological theorizing. *History of the Human Sciences, 8,* 61–72.

Rose, N. (1990). *Governing the soul; the shaping of the private self.* London: Routledge & Kegan Paul.

Rosenzweig, S. (1933). The experimental situation as a psychological problem. *Psychological Review, 40,* 337–354.

Rosenzweig, S. (1934). Note: A suggestion for making verbal personality tests more valid. *Psychological Review, 41,* 400–401.

Rosnow, R. L. (1981). *Paradigms in transition: The methodology of social inquiry.* New York: Oxford University Press.

Ross, C. C. (1936). A needed emphasis in psychological research. *Psychological Review, 43,* 197–206.

Scheibe, K. E. (1988). Metamorphoses in the psychologist's advantage. In J. Morawski (Ed.), *The rise of experimentation in American psychology* (pp. 53–71). New Haven: Yale University Press.

Seashore, C. E. (1908). *Elementary experiments in psychology.* New York: Henry Holt and Company.

Seltzer, M. (1992). *Bodies and machines.* New York: Routledge.

Shi, D. E. (1995). *Facing facts: Realism in American thought and culture, 1850–1920.* New York: Oxford University Press.

Smith, R. (1997). *The Norton history of the human sciences.* New York, London: W.W. Norton & Company.

Strumberg, D. (1925). A comparison of sophisticated and naive subjects by the association-reaction method. *American Journal of Psychology, 36,* 88–95.

Suls, J. M., & Rosnow, R. L. (1988). Concerns about artifacts in psychological experiments. In J. Morawski (Ed.), *The rise of experimentation in American psychology* (pp. 163–187). New Haven: Yale University Press.

Taylor, G. O. (1969). *The passages of thought: Psychological representation in the American novel, 1870–1900.* New York: Oxford University Press.

Terman, L. M., & Miles, C. C. (1936). *Sex and personality: Studies in masculinity and femininity.* New York, London: McGraw Hill Book Company, Inc.

Titchner, E. B. (1902). *Experimental psychology: A manual of laboratory practice. Volume I: Qualitative experiments; Part I: Student's manual.* London: Macmillan & Co.

Wonham, H. B. (1995). Writing realism, policing consciousness: Howells and the Black body. *American Literature, 67,* 701–724.

Woodworth, R. S. (1945). *Psychology.* New York: Henry Holt and Company.

Woolgar, S. (1988). *Science: The very idea.* New York: Tavistock.

Yerkes, R. M. (1911). *Introduction to psychology.* New York: Henry Holt and Company.

Yerkes, R. M. (1915). Notes: The role of the experimenter in comparative psychology. *Journal of Animal Behavior, 5,* 258.

7

The Self: Colonization in Psychology and Society

Kenneth J. Gergen
Swathmore College

Although the early Greek exhortation to "know thyself" has resounded compellingly across the centuries, the object of knowledge in this case has been in a state of continuous transformation. Precisely what it is that one is supposed to "know" in this case, and for what reason, remains continuously in flux. With the spread of Christianity across the West, the self was virtually equivalent to the human soul. And it was imperative that the state or condition of the soul be known, for indeed its degree of purity would determine the location of one's eternal residence. However, with the emergence of Enlightenment thought and practice, the soul as the essence of the self gave way to conscious reason. For philosophers such as Descartes, Locke, and Kant, reflexive thought (reason gaining knowledge of reasoning itself) was a means toward a morality, personal integrity, and a coherent life.

I invoke a historical perspective here because we tend at any point in history to presume that our common language maps an independent domain of entities or events. Or more specifically, we tend to presume that our discourse for the self is ontologically secure. The names we share for the domain of the psychological interior refer to states or conditions that exist independently of the names: the spirit or soul in the case of the pre-moderns, and agentive reason with the birth of modernism. By historically contextualizing the discourse of the self in this way, we are prepared to inquire into the functions of such discourse within society. How is the discourse of the self employed within our relationships? Which traditions are sustained and which are marginalized? What are the gains and losses of such use in everyday life" What institutions are benefited by any particular discourse? Finally, what forms of life are rendered dangerous or defective? In effect, through historical relativization of the self, we begin to ask pragmatic and evaluative as opposed to ontological questions (see also Graumann & Gergen, 1996).

A consciousness of historical contingency is central to the issues I wish to address in the present chapter. In my view, the varying traditions of self-discourse have contributed in significant ways to the central institutions of society. Indeed, the assumption of agentive reason has contributed to institutions of democratic governance, public education, the justice system, business, and military organizational structures, and more. This is to say that the constructions of the self have been, and continue to be, of enormous consequence to the conduct of everyday life. Most important, because there are variations in traditions of discourse, and the stakes are so substantial, there is an ongoing competition for control of the discourse. Or more dramatically put, most subcultures stand to gain through the discursive colonization of the self. Self-definition and power relations walk hand in hand.

In what follows I first set the stage by illuminating more fully the problems inhering in the attempt to anchor our discourse of the psychological self in an independent world of states or conditions. I propose instead that all mental discourse is essentially contested, that is, in principle, without a decidable referent. These arguments first enable us to problematize the view that psychological science can terminate the contest of discourse through empirical study. More importantly, this sensitizes us to the ways in which the science actively participates in the conflicts of cultural power. To illustrate the conflicts in motion, I then take up the issue of the "defective self," or more formally, the problem of psychological deficit. Here I propose that psychological science has had enormous success in colonizing Western culture within the past century, and with new coalitions in progress, the stage is set for a virtual elimination of all competing voices and values.

MENTAL DISCOURSE AS ESSENTIALLY CONTESTED

Typically we employ such terms as thought, *emotion, motivation,* and *attitudes,* as if they referred to existing states or entities within the individual. Yet, if we scan both the historical and anthropological literature on discourses of the person, we locate an enormous variety of terms and phrases, many of which do not correspond to those currently circulated either within contemporary Western culture in general or within the science of psychology. What, then, are the grounds for holding one vocabulary (and most especially a scientific one) superior to another?

Consider the emotions. Today we consider the emotional condition of the individual as central to his or her well-being; many forms of therapeutic practice are focused on emotional processes; and the emotions are major objects of study within psychological science. Yet, although the discourse of emotion is fully naturalized, and functions as if it referred to independent processes or states within the brain, there are enormous variations in the conception of emotion across culture and history. Historically, for example, in the second book of the Rhetoric, Aristotle distinguished among 15 emotional states; Later, Aquinas' Summa Theologiae enumerated six "affective" and five "spirited" emotions; Descartes distinguished among six primary passions of the soul; the 18th century moralist, David Hartley, located 10 "general passions of human nature;" and the major contributions by recent theorists, Tomkins (1962) and Izard (1977), describe some 10 distinctive emotional states.

Not only did assays of the mind yield differences in the number of emotions detected, they also detected distinct differences in kinds. For example, Aristotle identified placability, confidence, benevolence, churlishness, resentment, emulation, longing and enthusiasm, as emotional states no less transparent than anger or joy. Yet, in their 20th century exegesis, neither Tomkins (1962) nor Izard (1977) recognize these states as constituents of the emotional domain. Aquinas believed love, desire, hope, and courage were all central emotions, and although Aristotle agreed in the case of love, all such states go virtually unrecognized in the recent theories of Tomkins and Izard. Hobbes identified covetousness, luxury, curiosity, ambition, good naturedness, superstition, and will as emotional states, none of which qualify as such in contemporary psychology. Tomkins and Izard agree that surprise is an emotion, a belief that would indeed puzzle most of their predecessors. However, where Izard believes sadness and guilt are major emotions, they fail to qualify in Tomkins analysis; simultaneously, Tomkins sees distress as a central emotion, where Izard does not.

In effect, although each of these scholars presumably "scanned the internal depths," each secure in his conclusions, there is little agreement in their "findings." It is at this point that we may usefully pause to consider the grounds of knowledge in this case. What is the relationship between ourselves and the object of knowledge that we can justify our conclusions? In the present case, our empiricist tradition suggests that we have two major candidates for justification: self-observation and observation of others. In the former case, we might presume that we can know with confidence about mental states such as emotion because we are intimately acquainted with them. In contemporary parlance, we have metacognitive knowledge of our psychological processes. In the case of external observation, we might presume a warrant for psychological knowledge based on the reasoned conclusions of neutrally positioned observers.

Yet, let us consider the possibility of knowledge through self-observation. A brief scan of both philosophic and psychological analyses suggests that the very concept of internal observation is deeply flawed. To succinctly summarize some of the major problems:

• How can consciousness turn in on itself to identify its own states? How can experience become an object to itself? Can a mirror reflect its own image?

• What are the characteristics of mental states by which we can identify them? By what criteria do we distinguish, let us say, among states of anger, fear, and love? What is the color of hope, the size of a thought, or the shape of anger? Why do none of these attributes seem quite applicable to mental states? Is it because our observations of the states prove to us that they are not? What would we be observing in this case?

• Could we identify our mental states through their physiological manifestations—blood pressure, heart rate, and so on? Do I know I am thinking by checking my blood pressure, or that I have hope by sensing my neurological activity? And, if we were sufficiently sensitive to differing physiological conditions, how would we know to which states each referred? Does increased pulse rate indicate anger more than love, or hope more than despair?

• How can we be certain when we identify such states correctly? Could other processes (e.g. repression, defense) not prevent accurate self-appraisal? (Perhaps anger is eros after all.)

• By what criterion could we judge that what we experience as "certain recognition" of a mental state is indeed certain recognition? Wouldn't this recognition ("I am certain in my assessment.") require yet another round of self-assessments ("I am certain that what I am experiencing is certainty …") the results of which would require additional processes of internal identification, and so on in an infinite regress?

• How could we identify an inner state save through a forestructure of a linguistic *a priori*? Could one identify an emotion in terms that were not already given within the prevailing discourse on emotion? If one identified a mental state with an unfamiliar term, it would be wholly opaque.

Of course, many contemporary psychologists (along with many psychoanalysts) are quite willing to abandon inner observation (or introspection) as a valid source of psychological knowledge. For many, it is the external observer—rationally systematic and personally dispassionate—who is ideally situated to draw valid conclusions about people's internal states. Yet, the past 30 years of poststructural and hermeneutic deliberation leave the presumption of external observation as imperiled as that of introspection. Again in abbreviated form, consider some of the major flaws:

- If we were to base our knowledge on our subjects' descriptions of their internal states (e.g. "I am depressed." "I am angry.") how would we know to what the terms referred within their own mind/brain? We never have access to the states or conditions. What if one person's referent for "love" was another's referent for "anxiety?" Without access to the putative referents, there would be no means of sorting out the differences. Indeed, how can we be certain that mental terms refer to anything at all (e.g. "my soul is anguished")?
- If we abandon introspection as the basis of knowledge, how can the observer trust any self-reports (e.g. "I feel ...," "I aspire to ...," "It is my opinion that ...") to reveal an inner state? An inference? How could an observer know that the conditions, are sufficient for the reports to count as inferential evidence?
- Even if self-reports converge (as in the items making up a depression scale, or "The Big Five"), how would the observer know to what (in the individual's mind/brain) the individual items referred—if indeed they refer to anything (could we not also generate a 12 item scale of "soul anguish"?). How could we trust the subject to know?
- How can we determine the nature of what we are observing, save through the lens of a theory already established? Could we identify "cognitive conservation" without a theory enabling us to interpret a child's action in just this way? Could we observe aggression, moral behavior, altruism, conformity, obedience, or learning, for example, without a pre-understanding (forestructure) that would call our attention to certain patterns of activity as opposed to others? Can we observe a "causal relation" without at least a rudimentary theory of cause already in place? Or, more broadly, aren't all observations of psychologically relevant behavior theory saturated?
- If we propose to identify psychological states through their physiological correlates (as in "the physiology of memory"), how can we determine to what psychological states the physiology provides the underpinning? If we cannot determine when a "memory," "a

thought," or "an agitation of the spirit" has occurred, how are we to establish the physiological correlates?

We find, then, that neither self-observation nor observation of others has referential anchors. There is nothing to which such discourse refers that can constrain the usage of mental language. The character and content of the internal world is open to infinite contestation. For illustration, the reader may wish to consult Mary Boyle's (1991) careful critique of diagnoses of schizophrenia. As she shows, such diagnoses are not evidentially based, but are highly interpretive, and rife with conceptual confusion. See also Wiener's (1991) critique of the concept of schizophrenia. More broadly, this is to say that there is no means of halting the process of cultural colonization through a referentially anchored discourse.

Although this is not the proper context for elaboration, it is worth noting that largely because compelling answers to questions such as the ones earlier discussed have not been forthcoming, many contemporary scholars have moved to an alternative view of psychological discourse. They have replaced the pictorial orientation to mental language with a more pragmatic view. They bracket the view of mental language as a picture of inner states, and consider it as communicative action. Or, with Wittgenstein (1953), it is held that psychological language obtains its meaning and significance primarily from the way in which it is used in human interaction. Thus, when I say "I am unhappy" about a given state of affairs, the term "unhappy" is not rendered meaningful or appropriate according to its relationship to the state of my neurons, emotions, or cognitive schema. Rather, the report plays a significant social function. It may be used, for example, to call an end to a set of deteriorating conditions, enlist support and/or encouragement, or to invite further opinion. Both the conditions of the report and the functions it can serve are also circumscribed by social convention. The phrase, "I am deeply sad" can be satisfactorily reported at the death of a close relative but not the demise of a spring moth. A report of depression can secure others' concern and support; however it cannot easily function as a greeting, an invitation to laughter, or a commendation. In this sense to use mental language is more like a handshake or an embrace than a mirror of the interior, more like a strong grip between trapeze artists than a map of inner conditions. In effect, mental terms are used by people to carry out relationships.

KNOWLEDGE, POWER, AND DISCOURSES
OF THE SELF

Foucault's (1978, 1979) writings on knowledge and power are an effective entry to the present analysis. Language, for Foucault, serves as a major medium for carrying out relations. Because language constitutes what we take to be the world, and rationalizes the form of reality thus created, it also serves as a socially binding force. By acting within language, relations of power and privilege are sustained. And, by engaging in the further circulation of a form of language, the array of power relations is further extended. Thus, as disciplines such as psychology, psychiatry, and sociology are developed, so do they operate as discursive regimes. They specify a world and a normative domain of relevant action. As these languages are further elaborated and disseminated, so then is the configuration of power extended. In this sense, power relations possess a productive capacity. The relevance of this perspective for psychology has been effectively demonstrated in Rose's (1985, 1990) analyses of psychological theory and measurement as forms of cultural control.

Yet, there is a strong tendency in Foucault's (1978) work to treat discursive regimes as unitary forms. That is, regimes tend to be treated as internally coherent and hegemonically accelerated. As Foucault proposes, beginning in the 18th century and extending into the present,

> The formation of knowledge and the increase of power regularly reinforce(d) one another in a circular process .... First the hospital, then the school, then, later the workshop were not simply "reordered" by the disciplines: they became, thanks to them, apparatuses such that any mechanism of objectification could be used in them as an instrument of subjection, and any growth of power could give rise in them to possible branches of knowledge; it was this link, proper to the technological system that made possible within the disciplinary element the formation of clinical medicine, psychiatry, child psychology, educational psychology, and the rationalization of labor. It is ... a multiplication of the effects of power through the formation and accumulation of new forms of knowledge. (p. 224)

This line of argument has also been fortified by much Marxist theory, particularly as inspired by Althusser, of a unified, hegemonic order.

The view I propose, and indeed which might be supported with alternative quotes from Foucault's capillary view of power, is that life within what we take to be the existing regimes is seldom unitary. Rather, regimes themselves are composed of variegated discursive practices, drawn from sundry contexts, ripped from previous ecologies of usage and stitched awkwardly together to form what—with continued usage and considerable suppression—is seen as a coherent view ("a discipline"). Ontologies and rationalities are thus only apparently and momentarily univocal; they harbor multiple tensions and contradictions even for those who dwell within. In a sense, I augment (or shift the emphasis of) a Foucauldian perspective with important theses from

Bakhtin (1981) and Derrida (1976). Whereas Bakhtin points to the hybrid or heteroglossial character of any given domain of language, Derrida's writings emphasize the failure of any language to carry autonomous meanings—to stand independent of its multiple signifying traces. The present analysis agrees, then, with Raymond Williams's (1980) view that "Hegemony is not singular. Its own internal structures are highly complex, and have continually to be renewed, recreated and defended; and by the same token ... they can be continually challenged and in certain respects modified" (p. 38). This view is also reflected in Laclau and Mouffe's (1985) vision of radical politics.

The inability to ground psychological discourse creates a condition in which there is enormous latitude available for creating vocabularies of inner being. The creation of such vocabularies can be highly consequential, owing to their functions or uses within ongoing relations. For example, the rich range of terms for states of attraction (e.g. love, liking, passion, respect) do not index states of mind, so much as they serve to create (justify, perform, sustain) various forms of relationship. In this sense, the objectification of the soul, as a state of the individual mind, sustains a hierarchical relationship between priest and supplicant, in the same way that the presumption of repression is essential to the relationship between analyst and analysand.

In a broader sense it may be said that the realities created by people together are functionally insinuated into their daily relationships. The discursive ontologies and ethics are embedded within normal and normative practices. Or more succinctly, the discourses of daily life are constitutive of living traditions. In this sense, to control the vocabularies of the self within society, is to set the grounds for much of its social activity. Alien traditions are often suspect because their traditions of discourse and action are neither ontologically nor ethically acceptable. Because one lives in a tradition of the real and the good, and other traditions may constitute threats, there is a strong tendency not only to defend one's own tradition, but to expand its perimeters.

When efforts to expand the realm in which one's local vocabulary of the self also serve to enhance the outcomes of one's tradition, we may speak of colonization. For example, the attempt to secure Western psychology a place in the curricula of Indian and Japanese universities, is an obvious form of colonization. When behaviorists extinguished the discourses of phenomenology and introspection, and cognitivists subsequently reduced behaviorist discourse to a historical artifact, colonization was successful within the discipline of psychology. And in the same way, today we find power struggles among cognitivists, humanists, psychoanalytic psychologists, hermeneutic psychologists, critical psychologists, feminist psychologists, and more. Power in such cases depends on such instruments of colonization as control of journal content, research funds, appointment policies, tenure procedures, and award committees.

THE DEFICIENT SELF: COLONIZATION AND CONFLICT

My concern in the present offering is not principally with the internecine conflict within psychological science, but with the relationship of the science to the surrounding culture. The case is an interesting one, and also replete with political and cultural significance. During the 20th century, and the full flowering of modernism, the discipline of psychology slowly (if fitfully and unevenly) established itself as the authority on matters of the individual interior. Through its self-definition as a science—along with its development of experimental methods, statistical analyses, psychological testing, and treatment programs—it displaced all competition in claims to authority. Not only were religious and spiritual assays of the mind reduced to mythology, but so were the argots of myriad folk traditions placed in jeopardy. Even the individual's claims to self-knowledge were no longer to be trusted, as it is only the scientific expert who can offer reliable judgements—for example, in therapy, courts of law, and psychiatric hospitalization. In effect, with no viable or organized resistance, psychological science has achieved the capacity for full-scale colonization of the culture. The common definition of the self is fully within its grasp.

In certain respects, this potential is trivial. So long as the scientific community continues to write primarily for its own—sharing findings, mutual critiques, and abstract theories among themselves—there is little political or cultural consequence. However, when the science attempts to share its knowledge with the public, to influence policy issues, and to sell merchandise (such as psychological tests, books, and educational programs), we confront significant issues of cultural concern. The public resistance to IQ testing, homosexuality as mental illness, and empirical justification for child abuse are only representative of the conflict in discourse—and associated ways of life—that can result when cultural colonization is in motion.

Yet, there is one domain in which broad colonization has been enormously successful, and that now reaches the point at which we, as cultural participants, might indeed wish to join in resistance. My concern here is with the domain of mental illness, or the deficiencies of self. The tendency to attribute undesirable behavior to undesirable states of the mind has a long history in Western culture—from spirit possession, to impure thoughts, to failings in moral character. Within the 20th century, as psychological science (along with psychiatry) became the arbiter of interior, it also fell heir to the opportunity of defining the deficiencies of self. I do not use the word "opportunity" lightly here, because the language of deficit, in particular, is also a language of moral and political control. For example, there is nothing intrinsically wrong with prolonged sadness or lethargy; in themselves they are morally and politically neutral. However to classify these as "mental illness" creates them as undesirable, inferior, and flawed (see also, Sadler, 2004). "Normal" behavior, in this sense, is simply behavior that is socially acceptable. (This was indeed the realization of the gay community when homosexuality was deemed a mental illness.)

Concern continues to mount when we inquire into the uses of this power of definition. For in this case, to define a condition of the self as an illness or a disease, is also to imply that a treatment or cure is possible. And indeed, clinical psychology and psychiatry have also offered scientifically appropriate forms of "intervention." Thus "the business" of cure was established. Or, to put it bluntly, the conditions were created in which the colonization of the culture with respect to deficiencies of the self, served the business interests of the professional community.

I am not at all casting aspersions on the relevant professionals in this case. For the most part, professionals indeed share with the culture a sense of what is unacceptable behavior. Within the profession the political and moral sensibilities are simply removed from view in the earnest attempt to bring science to bear on human problems, and to provide reliable treatments for the anguish most clients bring into the therapy room. Classifying, studying and curing illnesses of the mind, no less than the body, is a noble calling. It is the largely unnoticed, "collateral damage" that concerns me here. For, if we view the case historically, we begin to approach a condition of infinite infirming.

"PROGRESS" IN MENTAL HEALTH

It is useful here to consider the colonization process in terms of phases. Although this is an idealized version of historical change, it does enable us to understand the colonization process and the problems it poses for society.

Phase 1: Deficit Translation

We begin at the point at which the culture accepts the possibility of "mental illness," and a profession responsible for its diagnosis and cure, a condition of ever increasing prevalence since the mid-19th century (Peeters, 1995). Under these conditions, the professional confronts clients whose lives are lived out in terms of a common or everyday language (e.g. "unhappiness," "fear," "loss," "aimlessness"). Because life management seems impossible in terms of everyday understandings the client seeks professional help—or, in effect, more "advanced," "objective," or "discerning," forms of understanding. In this context it is incumbent on the professional to (a) furnish an alternative discourse (theoretical framework, diagnosis, etc.) for understanding the problem, and (b) translate the problem as presented in the daily language into the alternative and uncommon language of the profession. In effect, this means that problems understood in the profane or marketplace language of the culture are translated into the sacred or professional language of mental deficit. A person whose habits of cleanliness are excessive by common standards may be labelled "obsessive compulsive," one who rests the morning in bed becomes "depressive," one who feels he is not liked is redefined as "paranoid," and so on.

Phase 2: Cultural Dissemination

Since the 18th century scientific analysis has placed great importance on classifying the various entities in its domain (e.g. animal or plant species, tables of chemical elements; Bowker & Star, 1999). Emulating the natural sciences, the mental health professions have thus attempted to classify all forms of dysfunction in terms of mental illness. As a result, not only is "mental illness" created as a reality, but all problematic action becomes a candidate for such classification. Further, because people lack knowledge of these illnesses, it becomes a professional—and indeed political—responsibility to alert the public to the fact. They must learn to recognize the signals of mental disease so that early treatment may be sought, and they should be informed of possible causes and likely cures. Early in the century this dissemination process was realized in the United States. in the mental hygiene movement. For millions of people Clifford Beers' famous volume, *A Mind That Found Itself* (going into 13 editions within 20 years of its publication in 1908) first served to substantiate mental illness as a phenomenon, and to warn the general public of the existing threat of such illness. In the same way that signs of breast cancer, diabetes, or venereal disease should become common knowledge within the culture, it was (and is) argued, citizens should be able to recognize early symptoms of stress, alcoholism, depression, and the like.

Although the mental hygiene movement is no longer visible as such, its logic has now been fully absorbed by the culture. Most large-scale institutions provide services for the mentally disturbed—whether in terms of health services, guidance counselors, clinical social workers, or insurance coverage for therapy. University curricula feature courses on adjustment and abnormality; national magazines, newspapers and self-help books disseminate news and information on mental disorder (e.g. depression and its cure through chemistry). And, the National Institute of Mental Health provides a range of authoritative pamphlets and a Web site informing the public of how to recognize the "symptoms" of mental illness. An informative illustration of the way in which the media contributed to the cultural construction of anorexia and bulimia is furnished by Gordon (1990).

Phase 3: The Cultural Construction of Illness

As vocabularies of deficit are disseminated to the culture, they become absorbed into the common language. They become part of "what everybody knows" about human behavior. In this sense, terms such as *neurosis, stress, alcoholism*, and *depression* are no longer "professional property." They have been "given away" to the public. Terms such as *split personality, identity crisis, PMS* (premenstrual syndrome), *attention deficit disorder* (ADD), and *post-traumatic stress* also enjoy a high degree of popularity. And, as such terms make their way into the cultural vernacular, they become available for the construction of everyday reality. Veronica is not simply "too fat," she has "obese eating habits;" Robert doesn't simply "hate gays," but is "homophobic;" and so on.

As deficit terms become increasingly available for making the social world intelligible, that world becomes increasingly populated by deficit. Events that passed unnoticed become candidates for deficit interpretation; actions once viewed as "different" can now be reconceptualized as obsessive, phobic, or repressive. Once terms such as *stress* and *occupational burnout* enter the commonsense vernacular, they become lenses through which any working professional can reexamine his or her life and find it wanting. What was valued as "active ambition" can now be reconstructed as "workaholic;" the "smart dresser" can be redefined as "narcissistic," and the "autonomous and self-directed man" becomes "defended against his emotions." As we furnish the population with hammers of mental deficit, everyone can take a pounding.

Nor is it simply deficit labeling that is at stake here. For as forms of "illness" are described in the media, educational programs, public talks, and the like, the symptoms come to serve as cultural models. An individual under stress or in anguish is presented with models for action. It is in this vein that Szasz (1960) has argued that hysteria, schizophrenia, and other mental disorders represent the "impersonation" of the sick person stereotype. Mental illness, in this sense, is often a form of deviant role playing, requiring a form of cultural knowhow to break the rules.

Sheff (1966) has made a similar case for many disorders serving as forms of social defiance. As Sheff proposes, others' reactions to the rule-breaking behavior are of enormous importance in determining whether it is finally labeled as "mental disease."

As people's actions are increasingly defined and shaped in terms of mental deficit language, there is also an increasing demand for mental health services. Counseling, weekend self-enrichment programs, and regimens of personality development represent a first line of dependence; all allow people to escape the uneasy sense that they are "not all they should be." Others may seek organized support groups for their "incest victimization," "co-dependency" or "obsession with gambling." And, of course, many enter organized programs of therapy.

Thus we find that the prevalence of "mental illness" and the associated expenditures for mental health are propelled upward. For example, in the 20-year period between 1957 and 1977, the percentage of the U.S. population using professional mental health services increased from 14% to more than 25% of the population (Kulka, Veroff, & Douvan, 1979). When Chrysler Corporation insured its employees for mental health costs, the annual use of such services rose more than six times in 4 years ("Califano Speaks," 1984). Although mental health expenditures were minuscule during the first quarter of the century, by 1980 mental illness was the third most expensive category of health disorder in the United States, accounting for more than $20 billion annually (Mechanic, 1980). By 1983, the costs for mental illness, exclusive of alcoholism and drug abuse, were estimated to be almost $73 billion (Harwood, Napolitano, & Kristiansen, 1983). By 1981, 23% of all hospital days in the United States were accounted for by mental disorders (Kiesler & Sibulkin, 1987).

Phase 4: Vocabulary Expansion

The stage is now set for the final revolution in the cycle of progressive infirmity: Continued expansion in the vocabulary of deficit. As people increasingly construct their problems in the professional language, as they seek increasing help, and as the professional ranks expand in response to public demands, there are more individuals available to convert the common language into a professional language of deficit. There is no necessary requirement that such translation be conducted in terms of the existing categories of illness, and indeed there are distinct pressures on the professional for vocabulary expansion. In part, these pressures are generated from within the profession. To explore a new disorder within the mental health sciences is not unlike discovering a new star in astronomy: considerable honor may be granted to the explorer. In this sense "post-traumatic stress disorder," "identity crisis," and "midlife crisis," for example, are significant products of the "grand narrative" of scientific progress (Lyotard, 1984). They are self-proclaimed "discoveries" of the science of mental health. At the same time, new forms of disorder can be highly profitable for the practitioner, often garnering book royalties, workshop fees, corporate contracts, and/or a wealthier set of clients. In this respect such terms as *co-dependency*, *stress*, and *occupational burnout* have become able economic engines. The construction of Attention Deficit Disorder, and its steadily increasing application to populations of both children and adults, children has unleashed a virtual epidemic of deficit.

On a more subtle level, there are pressures toward expansion of the professional vocabulary produced by the client population itself. As the culture absorbs the emerging argot of the profession, the role of the professional is both strengthened and threatened. If the client has already "identified the problem" in the professional language, and is sophisticated (as in many cases) about therapeutic procedures, then the status of the professional is placed in jeopardy. The sacred language has become profane. (The worst-case scenario for the professional might be that people learn to diagnose and medicate themselves without professional help.) In this way, there is a constant pressure placed on the professional to "advance" understanding, to spawn "more sophisticated" terminology, and to generate new insights and forms of therapy. It is not that the shift in emphasis from classic psychoanalysis to cognitive-behavior therapy, is required by an increasingly sensitive understanding of mental dynamics. Indeed, each wave sets the stage for its own demise and replacement; as therapeutic vocabularies become commonly known the therapist is propelled into new modes of departure. The ever-shifting sea of therapeutic fads and fashions is no mere defect in the profession; rapid change is virtually demanded by a public whose discourse is increasingly "psychologized."

In this context, it is interesting to examine the expansion of deficit terminologies. Interestingly we find here a trajectory that is suspiciously similar to those encountered in the case of mental health professionals and mental health expenditures. The concept of neurosis did not originate until the mid-18th century. In 1769, William Cullen, a Scottish physician, elucidated four major classes of *morbi nervini*. These included the Comota (reduced voluntary movements, with drowsiness or loss of consciousness), the Adynamiae (diminished involuntary movements), Spasmi (abnormal movement of muscles), and Vesaniae (altered judgment without coma). Yet, even in 1840, with the first official attempt in the United States to tabulate mental disorders, categorization was crude. For some purposes it proved satisfactory, indeed, to use only a single category to separate the ill—including both the idiotic and insane—from the normal (Spitzer & Williams, 1985). In Germany both Kahlbaum and Kraepelin developed more extensive systems for classifying mental disease, but these were tied closely to a conception of organic origins.

With the emergence of the psychiatric profession during the early decades of the century, matters changed considerably. In particular, the attempt was made to distinguish between disturbances with a clear organic base (e.g., syphilis) and those with psychogenic origins. Thus, with the 1929 publication of Israel Wechsler's *The Neuroses*, a group of approximately a dozen psychological disorders were identified. With the 1938 publication of Aaron Rosanoff's *Manual of Psychiatry and Mental Hygiene,* some 40 psychogenic disturbances were recognized. Many of the categories remain familiar (e.g. hysteria, dementia praecox, paranoia). More interesting from the present perspective, many of these terms have since dropped from common usage (e.g., paresthetic hysteria, autonomic hysteria); and some now seem quaint or obviously prejudicial (e.g., moral deficiency, vagabondage, misanthropy, masturbation).

In 1952, with the American Psychiatric Association's publication of the first *Diagnostic and Statistical Manual of Mental Disorders* it became possible to identify some 50 to 60 different psychogenic disturbances. By 1987—only 20 years later—the manual had gone through three revisions. With the publication of *DSM-IIIR,* the line between organic and psychogenic disturbances had also been obscured. However, using the standards of the earlier decades, in the 350 year period since the publication of the first manual, the number of recognized illnesses more than tripled (hovering between 180–200, depending on choice of definitional boundaries). At the present time one may be classified as mentally ill by virtue of cocaine intoxication, caffeine intoxication, the use of hallucinogens, voyeurism, transvestism, sexual aversion, the inhibition of orgasm, gambling, academic problems, antisocial behavior, bereavement, and noncompliance with medical treatment. Numerous additions to the standardized nomenclature continuously appear in professional writings to the public. Consider, for example, seasonal affective disorder, stress, burnout, erotomania, the harlequin complex, and so on. Twenty years ago there was no category of illness termed *Attention Deficit Hyperactivity Disorder*. At present there are more than 500 authoritative books and 900,000 Web sites that describe, explain, and offer alleviation.

TOWARD INFINITE INFIRMITY

As I am proposing, when the culture is furnished a professionally rationalized language of mental deficit, and persons are increasingly understood in these ways, an expanded population of "patients" is created. This population, in turn, forces the profession to extend its vocabulary, and thus the array of mental deficit terms available for cultural use. More self-deficits are thus located within the culture, more help sought, and the deficit discourse again inflates. One can scarcely view this cycle as smooth and undisrupted. Some schools of therapy remain committed to a single vocabulary; others have little interest in disseminating their language; some professionals attempt to speak with clients only in the common language of the culture, and many popular concepts within both the culture and the profession lose currency over time (see, e.g., Hutschemaekers, 1990). Rather, we are speaking here of a general historical drift, but one without an obvious terminus.

It is also important to realize that in the past decade the upward spiraling of mental illness has been dramatically intensified. This intensification is due to the addition of two new parties to the process, the psychopharmacology industry and managed care programs. In the first instance, the pharmacology industry has been enormously successful in marketing drugs that promise to alleviate most forms of daily suffering (anxiety, social phobias, unhappiness, tension, distress). Putting aside the large percentage of people who experience little positive effects from such drugs, and the range of negative side effects, the public is invited by such marketing into a new utopia. All that is required is to seek psychiatric help. The result has been dramatic. Consider the major antidepressant, Prozac. According to a *Newsweek* (March 26, 1990) report, a year after the drug was introduced to the market sales reached $125 million. One year later (1989) the sales had almost tripled to $350 million. By 2002, Prozac was a $12 billion industry. At present there are more than 25 million prescriptions for Prozac (or its generic equivalent) in the United States. A similar number of prescriptions are written for Zoloft, a close cousin, and another 25 million for a combination of other competitors (*New York Times*, June 30, 2002). And, with the enormous profitability of such drugs, the pharmaceutical industry has launched myriad new initiatives for the future expansion of the market (see also Breggin, 1991).

The use of drugs to treat unhappiness has been additionally favored by the managed care movement in hospital administration. In an effort to reduce expenditures managed care has favored drugs over "talking cures" simply because it is more economical to dispense pills than pay for therapist time. By encouraging drug-centered treatment, managed care programs also send a message to therapeutic practitioners more generally: If you wish to sustain a practice supported by insurance programs, it is essentially to shift to drug-centered treatments. A case in point is the increase in the use of psychiatric drugs in treating children and teenagers. In less than a 10-year period in the United States, the use of psychotropic drugs tripled, and with scant research on their efficacy or side-effects (*Philadelphia Inquirer*, Jan. 14, 2003). The result has been that organizations such as the American Psychological Association, have mounted intense programs to license their therapists to prescribe "meds" for their "patients." Such programs are now achieving success, and within the next decade we can anticipate a dramatic increase in both the number of prescribing practitioners, and the percentage of the population dependent on drugs to "get them through the day."

There is an important sense in which the average citizen today faces a trap door into a land from which exit is difficult. There are at least three institutions of substantial size and means coordinating their efforts to effectively "seduce" people into mental illness. As day to day problems of living are progressively translated into the authoritative discourse of mental illness, and drugs are offered as a secure means to restoring happiness, the attraction of drug centered "cures" is obvious. In a broad sense one might say that pharmacology is now taking the place of religion as the favored means of achieving salvation on earth (see also Farber, 1999).

Ultimately my concern is not simply that the power of naming the defective self is increasingly lodged within a singular set of interlocking institutions. Nor is it only that the colonization process in this case leads to an exponential increase in mental illness. My concern extends as well to the slow eradication of alternative discourses of understanding the self, and the alternative forms of action that are invited by these discourses. We are losing, for example, the rich discourse of deficit provided by various religious traditions. The discourse of "guilt," "need for spiritual fulfillment," and "getting right with God," does not invite therapy and medication, but prayer, spiritual consultation, and good deeds. There are also many common vernaculars, or grass-roots terms, that can be enormously serviceable. Being "hung up on her," has entirely different implications than being "obsessed"; having a "case of the blues" is indeed an honorific term, in contrast to having a "depression." "Working too hard," having an "overly indulgent chocolate craving," or "loving sex too much," invites dialogue with friends, loved ones and colleagues, as opposed to entering an addiction program. As "quick to anger," "highly excitable," "fear of flying," "unrealistically suspicious," "too active," and "shy" are increasingly translated into a professional terminology so are the capacities of people in their locale surrounds to deal with the normal infelicities of life in a complex society. Much needed at this juncture are instigations to grass-roots resistance, movements not likely to kindle the interests of professional psychologists.

REFERENCES

Bakhtin, M. (1981). *The dialogic imagination*. Austin: University of Texas Press.

Beers, C. W. (1908). *The mind that found itself: An autobiography*. New York: Longmans, Green.

Breggin, P. (1991). *Toxic psychiatry*. New York: St. Martin's Press.

Bowker, G. C., & Star, S. L. (1999). *Sorting things out: Classification and its consequences*. Cambridge, MA: MIT Press.

Boyle, M. (1991). *Schizophrenia, a scientific delusion*. London: Routledge.

"Califano speaks on health care costs at Grace Square celebration." (1984). *Psychiatric News, 14.*

Derrida, J. (1976). *Of grammatology*. Baltimore: Johns Hopkins University Press.

Farber, S. (1999). *Unholy madness: The church's surrender to psychiatry*. Downers Grove, IL: Varsity Press.

Foucault, M. (1978). *The history of sexuality. Volume I: An introduction*. New York: Pantheon.

Foucault, M. (1979). *Discipline and punish: The birth of the prison*. New York: Random House.

Gallie, W. B. (1956). Essentially contested concepts. *Proceedings of the Aristotelian Society, 56,* 1956.

Graumann, C. F., & Gergen, K. J. (Eds.). (1996). *Historical dimensions of psychological discourse*. New York: Cambridge University Press.

Gordon, R. (1990). *Anorexia and bulimia*. Cambridge, MA: Basil Blackwell.

Harwood, H. J., Napolitano, D. M., & Kristiansen, P. L. (1983). *Economic costs to society of alcohol and drug abuse and mental illness*. Research Triangle, NC: Research Triangle Institute.

Izard, C. E. (1977). *Human emotions*. New York: Plenum.

Kiesler, C. A., & Sibulkin, A. (1987). *Mental hospitalization: Myths and facts about a national crisis*. Newbury Park, CA: Sage.

Kulka, R., Veroff, J., & Douvan, E. (1979). Social class and the use of professional help for personal problems: 1957–1976. *Journal of Health and Social Behavior, 26,* 2–17.

Laclau, E., & Mouffe, C. (1985). *Hegemony and socialist strategy*. London: Verso.

Lyotard, J. F. (1984). *The post-modern condition: A report on knowledge*. Minneapolis: University of Minnesota Press.

Mechanic, D. (1980). *Mental health and social policy*. Englewood Cliffs, NJ: Prentice-Hall.

Peeters, H. (1995). The historical vicissitudes of mental diseases, their character and treatment. In C. Grauman & K. Gergen (Eds.), *The historical context of psychological discourse.* (pp. 204–226). London: Sage.

Rose, N. (1990). *Governing the soul*. London: Routledge.

Rose, N. S. (1985). The psychological complex. London: Routledge and Kegan.

Sadler, J. Z. (2004). *Values and psychiatric diagnosis*. New York: Oxford University Press.

Sheff, T. J. (1966). *Being mentally ill: A sociological theory*. Chicago: Aldine.

Spitzer, R. L., & Williams, J. B. (1985). Classification of mental disorders. In H. L. Kaplan & B. J. Sadock (Eds.), *Comprehensive textbook of psychiatry* (pp. 580–602). Baltimore: Williams & Wilkins.

Tomkins, S. (1962). *Affect, imagery, and consciousness. Vol. 1*. New York: Springer.

Wiener, M. (1991). Schizophrenia: A defective, deficient, disrupted, disorganized concept. In W. F. Flack, Jr., D. R. Miller, & M. Wiener (Eds.). *What is schizophrenia?* (pp. 124–139) New York: Springer-Verlag.

Williams, R. (1980). *Problems in materialism and culture*. London: Verso.

Wittgenstein, L. (1953) *Philosophical investigations* (G. Anscombe, Trans.). New York: Macmillan.

8

The Self Between Philosophy and Psychology: The Case of Self-Deception

Thomas Sturm
Max Planck Institute for the History of Science, Germany

T he self has been a topic not only for psychology but also for its neighboring disciplines—one of them being philosophy—and it is embedded in human folk psychology as well. In all of these areas it is a contested topic, however, having been received with high interest sometimes, neglected or rejected at other times. Even in folk psychological thinking self-related notions and assumptions have had their ups and downs, if on a different, larger time frame than in the more rapid developments of scientific research and philosophical reflection. I shall ask how philosophy and psychology actually investigate, and how they could or even should investigate, questions concerning the self. This must be done with care, of course. It is a traditional privilege of my discipline, philosophy, to take a step back from current scientific research and to reflect upon certain conditions of such research. I am going to reflect upon certain ordinary and scientific understandings of the notion of the self and self-related phenomena, hoping that the reflections have some useful applications for psychology. The back side of this coin is that my goal is not to propose or defend any *theory* of the self. Talk of a distinctively philosophical theory of the self seems a bit presumptuous, especially in the sense of 'theory' in which a theory about X is supposed to systematize X-related phenomena and to do such things as to explain and predict them. But many psychologists as well tend to make too-general claims about the "self" or what "selves" are, instead of investing a sufficient amount of conceptual clarification. I should note that what I will say about current instances of philosophical reflection is not completely representative of philosophy as it is practiced nowadays, let alone as it has been practiced in the past. However, I think that these are important instances and have to be taken seriously. This is also true of the instances from psychology.

I start by discussing a number of ontological claims about the self in order to provide some conceptual framework to begin with. What are selves? In what sense may we say or deny that they exist? As will become clear, the ontological background itself does not allow one to evaluate quickly what to think of, say, certain statements made by members of different disciplines that selves do not exist, or that selves are merely societal artifacts. The clarification of ontological options primarily is supposed to show how careful we should be about talk about the self and how careless we oftentimes are. Also, I hope to make clear that psychologists commit themselves to certain ontological views, even if confused ones, and that attempts to neglect ontological disputes about the self are not helpful to achieve a well-reflected understanding of psychological research. At the same time, concentrating upon ontological debates is not sufficient either. As I will try to show in the first part of this chapter, a more productive approach can be developed if one focuses upon specific types of human thought, experience, and action in which reference to oneself is essential in order to compare how these are treated by philosophers and psychologists. One example, that of self-deception, must suffice to illustrate that approach here, and I shall especially try to explain the role of the self in self-deception in the second part of this paper. I close with a few metatheoretical remarks concerning the division of cognitive labor between philosophy and psychology.

I. ONTOLOGICAL MUDDLES ABOUT THE SELF

Ontological questions—such as "What is a self?" and "Do selves exist?"— are often discussed by philosophers, but they are by no means the only ones that are important to philosophical reflection about the self. Sometimes epistemological questions have been more central, and certain ontological views have (or have not) been developed from such epistemological questions. In the *Meditations*, Descartes (1644/1897–1910) inquires whether he can *know* anything at all with perfect certainty. He claims to find basic certainties in that it is his own self who doubts, or that he himself has doubts, and so on. From this, he infers that he as a doubting and hence thinking substance exists. He also claims—notoriously—that this thinking self cannot be a material substance, because the existence of all material substances can be doubted. More recently, philosophers have viewed ontological questions often against the background of semantical questions—for instance, What does a term such as 'I' refer to? How does it refer? Furthermore, they have asked whether certain cases of self-knowledge possess a special kind of epistemic authority, even if they cannot, as Descartes hoped they would, serve to justify our knowledge about the world (e.g., Cassam, 1994; see also Greve, 1996). Such epistemological and semantical questions do not necessarily commit oneself to specific ontological views about the self. One might claim that there is no need to start a discussion of how philosophy and psychology investigate, and how they could or should investigate, questions concerning the self in an ontological idiom. My reasons are purely pragmatic ones. The ontological issues are those that are best known within both disciplines. Starting here helps to understand how philosophers and psychologists have developed their inquiries about the self, and it helps to realize why it is misguided to distinguish approaches to the self in terms of customary disciplinary distinctions.

There are at least three main tendencies in the ontology of the self, deriving mostly from traditions of early modern philosophy as developed by Descartes and his various opponents. First, the self is often viewed as a particular, irreducible thing or mental subject. Second, there are eliminativist positions that argue that no such self really exists. Third, the self is viewed as reducible to or identical with some set of bodily or mental processes or states.

The first ontological view of the self has usefully been termed the "homunculus," or the "central headquarters," view (Dennett, 1991). One thinks of the self as a particular subject or bearer of thoughts, experiences, and actions, an internal mental observer or agent. It has often been pointed out—say, by Lichtenberg—that the assumption of such a self is due to practical needs (Lichtenberg, 1765–99, K 76). Moreover, this view is strengthened by the impression that the self seems to be an object of reference, of quantification and other procedures that lead to a reification of self-related thought and talk. It seems possible to count selves—only one self to a customer seems to be the rule, as Dennett (1991, pp. 419f.) wrote. When this rule is violated by human beings who seem to possess different selves, these selves might still be viewed as countable objects of reference. A self still would be like a homunculus within a human body, only some human beings have several of them.

This view of the self as a particular internal observer and agent leads to various well-known problems. For instance, there lurk regresses if one takes that concept as explanatory. It has often been pointed out that if such a homunculus is literally supposed to explain, for example, how we decide between different goals or how we initiate actions, then there must be another little man inside the little man making his decisions or beginning his actions, and yet another inside that one. Furthermore, the idea that there must be a central instance where our different experiences meet and where our actions begin suffers from a serious lack of empirical support: No such center of consciousness can be found (Churchland, 1995; Dennett, 1989; Dennett & Kinsbourne, 1992). This is so even if there are recent attempts to defend the notion of the self as a simple mental substance (McGinn, 1997; Strawson, 1997). Also, the connectedness of representations need not be due to a numerically identical subject or a simple mental substance. The Cartesian assumption that the self is a simple substance often leads to the expectation that there should be a central, unitary structure in the brain being the "seat of the soul" where our sensations meet and our actions are initiated. As Kant already pointed out—to some extent as a response to such early modern attempts to localize the seat of the soul (Hagner, 1997; McLaughlin, 1985)—the unity of consciousness might be the effect of an interaction of various substances or processes, much as we conceive of the movement of a body as resulting from the movement of its parts (Kant, 1781/1787, A 352f.; see also his earlier and later rejection of attempts to locate the self somewhere in the brain in Kant, 1900ff., Vol. II, p. 324f., Vol. XII, pp. 31–34).

Thus, self-related thought and talk have to be taken more carefully. Writers in the Wittgensteinian tradition often point out, plausibly, that the assumption that terms such as 'the self' or 'I' refer to a particular mental object may be the result of various cognitive and linguistic delusions. For instance, one misunderstands reflexive pronouns when one differentiates in a curious way between 'myself' and 'my Self' (Kenny, 1992). I can of course cut myself, but I cannot cut my Self; I can realize my goals, and these may be highly important to me; but I cannot literally realize my Self. The term 'I', in turn, hardly refers in the way a name such as "Donald Rumsfeld" does. This was pointed out already by Maimon (1800), in response to a problem raised by Kant in his *Anthropology* (Kant, 1900ff., Vol. VII, p. 127): When and how do children learn to use 'I' as opposed to their own name, and what significance has this development? 'I' is an indexical term like 'here' or 'now', the reference of which varies with the context of utterance or with the speaker (Ryle,

1949, p. 179f.; Tugendhat, 1979, pp. 74–81). The term 'I' may still refer to something, but to the human being who uses it, not to a presumed internal homunculus.

There are—secondly—eliminativist positions that argue that no such entity exists, or that what we call the "self" is an illusion due to bad philosophy, outdated folk psychology, or both at once. Such extreme views are rarely held among psychologists, but some philosophers and neuroscientists apply their eliminativism about the folk psychological idiom to self-related talk as well (e.g., Churchland, 1995). The idea that I might be the origin of my decisions and actions is taken to be as good an explanation as that the presence of a witch explains why certain cows give less milk than they normally do. There are many arguments against eliminativism, some of which also apply with regard to self-related talk, but it would lead too far afield to discuss them here (Greve, 1996; Newen & Vogeley, 2000; Pauen, 2001, pp. 97–106; Rager, Quitterer, & Rungaldier, 2002). Self-related thought and talk seems to be crucial to an appropriate understanding of human experience, thought, and action. It may be changing to some degree through history (Baumeister, 1987; Burkitt, 1994; Veney, 1969); however, the assumptions that the variations are so dramatic that no important interconnections can be found, and that we can therefore dispense with it, are at least premature.

Third, many prefer reductionist views, which identify the self with some set of bodily or mental processes or states. Some authors cannot easily be classified as either reductionistic or eliminativistic: for instance, Dennett views the self as a fictional entity, but an evolutionary useful one (Dennett, 1992; see also Roth, 2001). In any case, reductionist claims often build upon David Hume's famous "bundle" theory, according to which a self is simply the sum of our mental states ('perceptions' in Hume's terminology) held together by certain causal relations. Such an approach suffers not only from limitations of the current state of scientific knowledge, or from general problems of reductionism in the sciences, such as what criteria for the relevant reductive explanations are appropriate, or whether there are not always losses in reduction. What is important in the present context is this: Because reductionists assume that self-related talk refers to ordinary persons, what should be reduced are properties (or classes of particulars) shared by those to whom we ascribe a self. It is thus usually not "the self" but, for instance, the property of *self-representation* or *self-consciousness* that is taken as explanandum. Of course, we have representations of ourselves or are conscious in many ways of ourselves. We think we are good lovers or bad losers, we may esteem or criticize ourselves, and so on. But shifting explanatory interests to self-representation or self-consciousness leaves open an important question. To characterize oneself as a good lover or to criticize oneself for being a bad loser, or even to be aware of more simple feelings or perceptions, already presupposes that one ascribes these states to *oneself.* But how is it possible for a given set of mental representations to be *my* and not your representations? How should we explain this "mine-ness" of mental states without falling back to the idea that there must be an irreducible, isolated, "objective self" (Nagel, 1986, chap. 4)?

Starting from this problem of how various states can be self-ascribed, Robinson (1991) defends (a core part of) Descartes's substance theory of the self against Lockean and Humean arguments. Now, Robinson also thinks "that the 'sense of my bodily existence' is the referent whenever I refer to *my* sensations or perceptions or feelings" and that this is "not to challenge the substantialist thesis as much as to render it more precise ... there is nothing in the substance-theory that removes the Self from any and all commerce with the affairs of the body" (Robinson, 1991, p. 45). This hardly solves the difficulties, however. Robinson tries to show that although Descartes's arguments perhaps do not justify the claim that the self is a distinct mental substance, Locke and Hume have not shown that it might not be a substance after all. But although one should indeed distinguish between mentalistic and nonmentalistic substance theories, his own claim that talk of the self refers to the "sense of my bodily existence" is still puzzling. It can hardly lead to a convincing reductionism, because it already uses the term *my* in the explanans, and it also leaves open how we should understand this "sense of my bodily existence." The problem of "mine-ness" is still not solved.

Such are the muddles that one can be led into when one takes seriously William James's (1890) idea that "Metaphysics means nothing but an unusually obstinate effort to think clearly" (p. 145). At the beginning, it seems clear that each of us possesses a self (at least one of them), but when we try to explain what a self is we become torn between equally unacceptable theories. However we should react to this embarrassment, right now it is important to realize that the ontological disputes just outlined are pretty far removed from most psychological research on the self. Not being a psychologist, I should be careful in trying to express what psychologists have to say about the self nowadays. Some points are clear enough, however, showing not only how cautious psychologists try to be with regard to their ontological commitments but also how difficult it is to escape the predicament just outlined.

First, although the psychological literature nowadays often loosely speaks of "the self," or of a growing interest in the self within psychology during the latter half of the 20th century (Baumeister, 1987), or of an "inadvertent rediscovery of Self in social psychology" (Hales, 1985), most are aware of the dangers of a reintroduction of homunculi (cf.

Greve, 2000; W. Mischel, 1976; Sampson, 1985) or of a "monolithic self" (Markus & Wurf, 1987).

Second, to some extent at least, one can understand talk of a 'psychology of the self' as shorthand for a wide range of topics such as the development of self-consciousness and self-regard, the conditions and limitations of self-knowledge, the role of motives of self-consistency and self-enhancement, the mechanisms of self-control or self-image management, and so on. Sometimes it is claimed that this is all a psychology of the self can be, if one does not wish "to locate an elusive entity" (Toulmin, 1986, p. 41).

Yet, third, there are also attempts to explain what a self is in a more principled way. As is well known, James (1890) divided the self, so to speak, into three parts: its material, social, and spiritual (or introspective, thinking) parts. He furthermore distinguished between the self as knower and the self as known, the 'I' and the 'me.' The latter distinction is not one between various entities, as if we had two distinct selves in our bodies, but emphasizes the difference between the subject- and object-roles a numerically identical self can take in (James, 1890, Vol. I, chap. 10). The desire for a principled understanding of the self, its basic constituents and functions lives on, for instance, in recent cognitive and social cognitive theories, which try to develop a more comprehensive framework for dealing with such issues as the self-concept, its contents and processes, the discrepancy between real and ideal selves, the differences between interdependent and independent self-conceptions, and so on. Many reflected psychological conceptions are developed in order to see whether some law and order can be imposed upon the enormous range of research topics (Baumeister, 1999, pp. 1–21; Berkowitz, 1988, pp. 1–14; Greve, 2000, pp. 15–36; T. Mischel, 1977, pp. 3–28). But some have also taken up a stronger program.

To some extent, the history of psychology in this domain can also be told as a history of basic disputes about proper research programs. Not surprisingly, it is not rare that positions have changed with more the advent of new more general approaches within psychology. For instance, it has been argued (e.g., Calkins, 1908, 1915; Strunk, 1972) that psychology should be a science of the self in a quite emphatic manner: Its subject matter should be delineated around the idea of the self, its properties and functions. Others have claimed that this would clearly overstep the "normal bounds of scientific method" (Toulmin, 1986, p. 41; cf. T. Mischel, 1977, pp. 9–22). Again, this appeal to "normal bounds of scientific method" is taken by yet another party to be an indication that psychology should revise its understanding of what proper subject matter, methods, and goals are. This is claimed by the so-called "humanistic" approach (Rychlak, 1976) but also, if in a quite different way, by social constructivist views (Gergen, 1985b, 2007; Hales, 1985, 1986).

What are the ontological commitments of psychologists, especially when they discuss what an appropriate research program on the self should be like? There clearly are no defenders of eliminativism among them. In one case, something like a central headquarters view is defended in order to support a humanistic conception of psychology (Rychlak, 1976, vs. W. Mischel, 1976). This is done on grounds that are quite confused: Rychlak (1976) not only describes Kant as an introspectionist—already a historical distortion—but also views introspectionism as supporting a view of the self that does not identify selves with ordinary persons (p. 160). Already Hume pointed out that a self, understood as an internal object, cannot be found when one "looks inside oneself." This was a crucial starting point for his reductionistic bundle theory. There are further good reasons for denying the view that the self can be introspectively accessed (Pauen, 2001, p. 245f.; Shoemaker, 1986).

Given the rejection of eliminativism, on the one hand, and the explicit warnings against a reintroduction of homunculi or a monolithic self, on the other hand, one should expect that a sober reductionism would be favored among psychologists. It is somewhat surprisingly, however, that it is by no means clear that psychologists wish to explain the self or self-related phenomena in terms of something else, in the sense of 'explain' in which the explanans statements should not presuppose the explanandum statements. There is indeed a constant ambivalence between viewing the self as explanans or as explanandum of research. One of the reasons for the renewed interest in the self in psychology during recent decades is the recognition that, contrary to behavioristic orientations, we do not merely notice or remember our own behavior, but each of us "instead mediates and regulates this behavior. In this sense, the self-concept has been viewed as dynamic—as active, forceful, and capable of change." (Markus & Wurf, 1987, p. 299; cf. Greve, 2005). Our social and natural environments influence our actions to different degrees, and our actions, our very self-understandings or our personality, are also constantly reshaped by how we perceive environments. Now, the self-understandings of persons influence how they act, for instance, in psychological experiments: Experimental participants constantly try to protect or enhance their self-esteem in ways that make many areas of psychological experimentation quite difficult (Hales, 1985; Morawski, 2007). There is no reason to think, of course, that such self-image management does not equally occur outside of the psychological laboratory.

All this has led psychologists to think that we must view not merely individuals and what goes on inside of them but persons in social interaction and in their perception of social situations. Social constructivists go even further and commit themselves to a reductionistic view of the self when they claim that selves are *constituted* (or *constructed*, as some say) by social interactions. Still, one has to ask *who* is acting to protect his or her self-esteem. I therefore agree with a related criticism against social constructivism, namely, that the reductionism with which it often is combined does not sufficiently distinguish between different notions of the self, especially between the self-as-subject and the self-as-object. A similar distinction is accepted by Robinson and Harré, who otherwise disagree about the nature of the self (Robinson, 1991, p. 43; Harré, 1991, pp. 52, 55–58). In this light, Gergen (e.g., 2007) merely talks about the self-as-object. His view that the self is something that is, or can be, socially constructed refers at best to the *contents* of our personal identities: to the kinds of persons or characters we develop under the—undeniably strong—influence of society. On the one hand, we speak of *selves* in the sense of the kinds of persons we are—gentleman, feminists, narcissistic characters, and so on. On the other hand, we speak of the self in the sense of the identical (usually human) bearer or subject of different attributes (not only those meant in the first sense of self, although these typically play a central role). Ordinary language legitimizes both notions, but when theories of the self are presented it is not always clarified how they relate to such a distinction. A similar point holds for Morawski's (in press) assumption that psychologists in the early 20th century shaped their own selves and those of their experimental subjects through standardized procedures of research. It would be desirable if adherents of these claims would be conceptually more reflective in order to avoid misunderstandings between different disciplines. More to the point, philosophical problems about self-identity, self-reference, or self-control are hardly addressed by this social constructivism; neither is it plausible to assume that the self as the subject (not the object) of self-reference or self-control is socially constructed. Also, the basic question of whether the self figures as part of the explanans or the explanandum of psychological research is not taken up either by the social constructivists.

However, perhaps we should avoid using talk of the self in explanatory statements, for example, by simply saying that events of self-protection and self-image management occur, without being performed by a particular self? But if that is so, how could psychologists give advice as to how to protect or enhance one's self-esteem, how to develop one's own possibilities, or how to "manage" oneself (see also Heidelberger, 2007; Maasen, 2007)? Many people are familiar with Ryle's (1949) claim that we are capable of higher order actions, such as commenting, reflecting, or criticizing what others do, and of course such higher order actions can be directed at the person herself by herself. That removes one problem of the "systematic elusiveness of the 'I'": Much as a finger pointing at another finger cannot point at itself, I cannot, in criticizing my last action, thereby also criticize this particular act of self-criticism (Ryle, 1949, pp. 177–189). Ryle's point makes intelligible what it *means* to say that persons are able to manage or control themselves. Yet this does not solve the current problem: As long as one takes seriously the arguments in favor of the claim that we do mediate and regulate our own behavior, and that we can improve our self-understanding and self-control, the self (even if understood as a current dynamic self-image) figures not only in the explanandum but also in the explanans, and then we have failed to reductively explain the self.

Thus, ontological predicaments come up within psychological research and in applications of psychology themselves. They are not a mere fiction of the philosopher's imagination. At the same time, it seems hard to make psychologists aware of the predicaments. Clearly, this is largely due to the conceptual and methodological fragmentation between philosophical and psychological approaches to self-related thought, experience, and action (over and above the fragmentation within these disciplines themselves). Concepts, research interests, and methods differ often dramatically. But that is merely a remark on how things are, not they could or should be.

Can we clarify how the self figures in psychology? Yes, if we give up the *top-down approach* used until now, where the goal is to develop a general conception or theory of the self. It is more promising to try a *bottom-up approach*: We might begin by looking at a variety of phenomena of human thought, experience, and action where reference to or representation of oneself is (or at least appears to be) essential and where we may try to analyze the role of the self. Whether a unified theory of the self can ultimately achieved by this stepwise procedure is quite open, of course. But at least we can begin to better understand or relieve the conceptual and methodological fragmentation between philosophical and psychological talk about the self. This leads to the example of self-deception.

II. SELF-DECEPTION

There are distinctively philosophical and psychological literatures on self-deception, which have developed especially rapidly since the latter half of the 20th century. This does not mean that self-deception was discovered or, if you like, constructed only during the last decades. Plato used the concept, speaking of how discomforting it is if the deceiver is not even a step away from us and that self-deception must be taken to be the greatest evil (*Cratylos* 428d). Bishop Butler, Adam Smith, Kant, and others as well wrote about it. However, there are two new developments: First, in earlier centuries, philosophers treated self-deception mostly as an ethical problem. In recent decades, often in the mood of Wittensteinian puzzle-solving and ordinary language philosophy, philosophers have concentrated upon a theoretical problem, the "paradox of self-deception": How can someone deceive himself about a proposition *p*? If self-deception is understood along the model of interpersonal deception, then this seems to mean that one must deceive oneself into believing something one does not believe at the very same time. How is such inconsistency possible at all? Kant (1900ff., Vol. VI, p. 430) noted this puzzle, but a closer discussion of it began only in the 20th century. Second, psychologists have of course thought about self-deception earlier on, but what seems new during recent decades is the attempt to investigate it by empirical means. How could one show that there actually are cases of self-deception? What experiments could show that? Also, psychologists tried to explain anew mechanisms and functions of self-deception against the background of models of biased belief or its possible adaptive value.

To begin, how is it possible to solve the paradox of self-deception? There are many different proposals. Some argue that self-deception is possible because the conflicting beliefs are held "on different levels of awareness" (Demos, 1960): Whereas the belief a person is more motivated to accept and avow is transparent to the person, and while she denies to accept the contradictory belief, certain indices reveal that "deep" inside she believes otherwise. (When Demos [1960] uses the idea that a person may be unaware of her beliefs, this is not that of an autonomous subagent, or of the unconscious of psychoanalysis.) Fingarette (1969), in turn, claimed that talk of belief and of unconscious states should be abandoned here in favor of talking of different "engagements" we have in the world (including other persons), and which we are, in cases of self-deception, simply unable to spell out. That would solve the paradox, but probably at too high a price. Also, Fingarette does not argue against the conceptualization of self-deception through inconsistent and partially intransparent beliefs, and so it is unclear whether that is not simply old wine in new bottles. More moderate is a proposal such as that of Robert Audi (1982), who claims that one of the conflicting propositions is not really held as a belief but merely "avowed sincerely" (cf. Cohen, 1992). Donald Davidson (1986) in turn claims that self-deception is made possible by a division of our minds into independent sets of states and processes—independent in the sense that the usual logical and epistemic relations between them are broken down, although the states remain causally connected, such that the metaphor of several selves within one person can be avoided (see also Greve, 2000, p. 17).

These and other attempts are meant not as empirical hypotheses but as proposals for a correct conceptualization of the phenomenon. The criterion for correctness of such a conceptualization is usually simply that it helps to solve the puzzle of self-deception. Considering the variety of options, however, it seems that this criterion is not sufficient to find the most appropriate concept of self-deception, assuming that there is only one such concept. The value of a proposed conceptualization should also be seen in its usefulness for psychological research about domains, functions, and mechanisms of self-deception. For instance, which of the proposed conceptualization coheres with empirical theories on functions and mechanisms of self-deception? Which concepts of self-deception can be useful in empirical investigations on this difficult topic? Alfred Mele, whose work deals perhaps best with the current psychological literature, claims that the whole background model of interpersonal deception is misguided. We should rather think of self-deception as a species of *biased belief*, as Mele calls it, building upon certain strands of empirical research on so-called "cognitive illusions," or on heuristics and biases in judgment (e.g., Tversky & Kahneman, 1974; Nisbett & Ross, 1980). In this light, self-deception is brought about by mechanisms such as positive or negative misinterpretation of data, or selective evidence-gathering. Mele furthermore maintains that not all biased beliefs are beliefs about which one is self-deceived. In self-deception, the biasing—the selective focusing upon certain kinds of evidence only, or the misinterpretation of certain data—is *motivated*. Stated in ordinary terms, people believe things because they want to believe them, and so they look for appropriate premises that support the relevant belief (Mele, 1997, 2000).

Although Mele is in closer contact with current psychology than most other philosophers, his view is not unproblematic for purposes of psychological research. Is it convincing that self-deception is the motivated species of biased belief or reasoning? May we not be motivated in many of our biased beliefs without these being cases of self-deception (Kunda, 1990)? Also, could it not be that some cases of self-deception are unmotivated? Whichever answer one prefers to such questions, it is crucial to become clear about the meaning of *self* in *self-deception*. Furthermore, as will become clear, discussing the role of the self in self-deception will help to better distinguish between different and sometimes new research questions.

Before I turn to this, I wish to point out that, perhaps contrary to what folk psychology and many philosophical and psychological traditions assume, it is by no means beyond doubt that people really ever deceive themselves. Perhaps self-deception is merely ascribed to subjects by outside observers. Should we not more moderately interpret the relevant behaviors as expressing ambivalence or doubt? Often, this seems plausible. Also, the unclarity of the concept of self-deception will hardly help to reduce skepticism concerning the existence of the seemingly familiar phenomenon of self-deception. So it was justified when psychologists undertook attempts at a more serious experimental demonstration of self-deception. Of course, such empirical work has to be careful and reflective about which concept of self-deception to use. In an example, perhaps the first of such an investigation, Gur and Sackheim (1979; Sackheim & Gur, 1979) used Demos's (1960) idea that the inconsistent beliefs are held "on different levels of awareness." Part of the reason for this preference is that they find self-deception to be similar to perceptual defense, which also implies that people can often be unaware of their representations. People sometimes tend to avoid certain perceptions, but in order for a perceiver to avoid perceiving a stimulus, the stimulus must first be perceived. The solution is found by saying that it is erroneous to assume that perception must be subject to awareness. The concept of perceiving a stimulus equivocates on "being presented to one's sensory apparatus" and "being cognized with awareness." Gur and Sackheim listed the following criteria to be necessary and sufficient for ascribing self-deception to any given phenomenon:

1. The individual holds two contradictory beliefs (that p and not p).
2. These two contradictory beliefs are held simultaneously.
3. The individual is not aware of holding one of the beliefs.
4. The act that determines which belief is and which belief is not subject to awareness is a motivated act (Gur & Sackheim 1979, p. 149).

They then use voice-recognition experiments. In a typical experiment, participants are asked to recognize whether a taped voice is their own or that of another person; at the same time, while respondents report, behavioral indices—galvanic skin responses—are used to find out whether a contradictory belief is also held. People with negative attitudes about themselves, or with discrepant beliefs about what they believe themselves to be and what they should be, have been judged to find confrontation with themselves aversive. On the other hand, people who score low in such discrepancy have been said to not find self-confrontation aversive; on the contrary, they seek it. Gur and Sackheim (1979) indeed claimed that self-deception in this sense occurs.

It is problematic whether skin responses are really indicative of belief, and Sackheim (1988; Mele, 1987) granted this. It has also been pointed out that the task of recognizing one's own voice is not a good task for the ascription of self-deception, as similar results were achieved for participants' recognition of voices of their acquaintances (Douglas & Gibbins, 1983). Similar points can be made against Quattrone and Tversky (1986), who adopted Gur and Sackheim's notion of self-deception to explain why people often seem to confuse *causal* with *diagnostic* contingencies in their actions (for criticism, see Mele, 1997, p. 96f.) Still, it would be premature to conclude that the occurrence of self-deception cannot be shown at all, as some have claimed (e.g., Gergen, 1985a). It is an open question demanding at least more empirical studies testing out, so to speak, all the various proposed concepts of self-deception. I do not wish to evaluate such a debate the way psychologists might. What is conceptually important is that a specific notion of self-deception has been used here. If you think, for instance, that self-deception demands a deeper division of the self than a difference in levels of awareness, or that it involves intention, you will certainly not be satisfied by the whole approach.

This brings me back to the role of the self in self-deception. What is that role? The basic options here are the following: The self may be the author of the deception, or it may be the subject matter of the deception (or both). A person may be deceived *by* herself, or she may be deceived *about* herself. This reminds one of Kant's distinction between the self-as-subject and the self-as-object (Kant, 1781/1787, B407–409; 1900ff., Vol. VII, p. 134n.), or James's (1890) already-mentioned distinction between the self as knower and the self as known, the 'I' and the 'me'. (Kant, 1781/1787, B407-409; 1900ff., Vol. VII, p. 134n.)

To avoid misunderstandings, it should be said that it is not adequate, as James (1890) did (and, e.g., Mead, 1934), to associate the distinction between the self-as-knower and the self-as-known too closely to the *linguistic* distinction between the personal pronoun 'I' on the one hand, and reflexive or possessive pronouns like 'me', 'myself', and so on, on the other. Consider various statements such as: (1) "There is a dot on my forehead," (2) "I know the car keys are here," (3) "I think I have mislaid the car keys," (4) "I still have the same job I had a year ago," and (5) "It is my claim that sheep don't grow on trees." Statements 1 and 2 fit into James's scheme. But in Statement 3, the second instance of 'I' is used to refer to oneself as an object, and in Statement 4 even both instances of *I* seem to play that role. In Statement 5, on the other hand, 'my claim' plays the same role as 'I know' in Statement 2. Although language is an important ingredient in the development of certain forms of self-consciousness, neither the self-as-subject nor the self-as-object is tied to specific linguistic categories.

Kant's basic point is not a linguistic one. Instead, he makes clear that sometimes we use talk of the self not to *describe* ourselves in some way

or other, as when we speak of our height or hair color, our beliefs or desires, or our personality; instead, sometimes locutions such as 'I' are
used to express that we *do* certain things. Relating to the first, descriptive usages of self-talk, Kant speaks of the "I as object of thought"; he
calls the second, nondescriptive usages of the expression 'I', he calls the
"I as subject" of thought. This is not a distinction between two different
objects; it is the human being that is the common reference point of the
different notions (Kant, 1900ff., Vol. XXV, p. 245; Vol. VII, p. 134n.). The
self-as-subject is not an independently existing entity but a built-in part
of certain mental acts. Kant's main examples of mental acts that essentially refer to a self-as-subject are epistemic ones, as when we make
knowledge claims or think critically about them. Here, the role of the
self-as-subject is made possible by the possession of certain capacities,
especially the understanding (*Verstand* in German; Kant, 1900ff., Vol.
VII, p. 127). Kant's claims are not intended to constitute a theory about
the self. He states certain points about the notion of the self-as-subject to
support certain transcendental claims about the conditions for the possibility of knowledge. He does not exclude that such theories or explanation of self-related phenomena might be developed, despite his
famous criticism of rational psychology. Accordingly, he applied his distinction between self-as-subject and self-as-object in his *Anthropology*,
his own empirical investigation of human thought and action (Kant,
1900ff., Vol. VII, p. 134; Vol. XXV, pp. 859, 1215f., 1438).

There are other examples of such a first-person point of view in
thought and action, such as certain cases of verbal action, as John Austin
(1953/1962) pointed out in his analysis of the so-called explicit
performative utterances: "I will" (uttered by the groom), "I shall be
there" (used to express a promise), or "I promise to hold on to the principles of constitution" (p. 60f.). Austin himself characterizes Kant as the
pioneer in questioning that all statements must be understood descrip-
tively (Austin, 1953/1962, p. 2f.).

Now we can return to the topic of self-deception. Can it be that the
role of the self in self-deception is merely that of an object, such that the
idea that it is caused by oneself is left out? An alternative way to raise
such a question is this: Where do conceptualizations of self-deception
locate the controlling (independent) variables of self-deception? Can
we not assume that explanations of self-deception leave out what goes
on "inside" the person? Some instances of self-deception point in this
direction, for example, when we say that people are deceived about
their own talents or character traits. It has been claimed that the concept
of self-deception sometimes meant merely this (Holton, 2000–2001). A
behavioristic approach that locates the controlling (independent) variables of self-deception outside the deceived person comes close to such

a view as well. Self-deception is then construed as the absence of self-knowledge: as a lack of knowledge what oneself is doing, established perhaps through negatively reinforcing consequences (Day, 1977; Skinner, 1953, chap. 18). How much such a concept differs from others can be made clear if one realizes that an experimental demonstration of the type pursued by Gur and Sackheim (1979) would be unnecessary, because no inconsistent believing is assumed here. In any case, such a conception of self-deception ignores, first, the difference between stronger cases of self-deception and cases of mere ignorance or error about oneself. Second, not all cases of self-deception must be about oneself: I may be self-deceived about my spouse's actions, or about my children's talents and character.

Even historically, the concept of self-deception has been quite stable in meaning the following: It is a kind of deception brought about by oneself, and then it may, or may not, be about oneself. This is Plato's usage of the term, and it is at least indicated in Smith (1759, iii. 4); it is on Kant's mind and on that of Karl Philipp Moritz (1789). Variation in the concept seems more likely with regard to whether self-deception is motivated, intentional, a result of unconscious activities, whether it involves multiple selves within one person, whether it occurs only with regard to beliefs or not, and so on.

One may still wish to legislate that the concept of self-deception should be understood as deception about oneself and merely that. Terminology is to some extent a matter of decision, but one should be aware what concept is used within an empirical study, even outside of studies attempting to experimentally demonstrate the existence of self-deception. Many studies, for instance, concern the question of what adaptive advantages self-deception might have (Lockard & Paulus, 1988; Welles, 1986). Consider the relation among deception, self-deception, and social dominance in tennis (Whittaker-Bleuler, 1988). By being deceived about her ability level, the situation of the match, and so on, a tennis player might be able to hide her insecurity better from the opponent. She might be able to keep her head up in a more natural fashion and to avoid acts like shaking her head horizontally or going through a stroke motion without a ball. One assumption here is that the degree of self-deception must be high when the player has lost the majority of previous points, and also the current point, and still behaves dominantly by showing, for example, coolness (Pete Sampras almost never showed any strong emotions, no matter whether it was going well for him or not). In such cases one need not be the author of the deception. Nick Bollitieri might have caused that great self-confidence in young Sampras in his tennis camp. He might not take the evidence of previous and current points to be as important as the belief in his bodily fitness, his excellent technique, or his ability to concentrate upon the next point only. No inconsistent believing is involved here.

Perhaps we should not even call Sampras's behavior a case of self-deception. Maybe this is just overconfidence in oneself, although claiming such a thing would be odd in the case of Sampras, who won more Grand Slam tournaments than Rod Laver. We should at least admit that there is not just one right notion of self-deception and that it is a continuous task of theorizing in empirical psychology to reflect on this. In any case, we can now say how the stronger cases of self-deception, where one is the author of the deception, differ from other reflexive types of experience, thought, and action. In self-knowledge, the object of reference is always oneself, and so it is part of the content of the known proposition; similarly in self-evaluation or self-control, where reference to oneself has to be a part of the content of the evaluative or prescriptive propositions in question. In self-deception, by contrast, reference to oneself need not be part of the content of the relevant belief. I may be self-deceived in that a certain person is not a cheater or that there will be no further war in the Middle East this year. One might reply that there is a hidden relation to oneself in at least the first of these familiar examples. Self-deception often relates to one's friends or spouses, so it concerns one's personal relationship to them and, thereby, one's own self-esteem. However, the relevant propositions need not contain reference to oneself as the object of deception. Even when they are often derived from self-regarding motives, they need not always be. I might deceive myself about the prospects for another war because of other-regarding, altruistic motives.

What about the idea that the role of the self in self-deception is that of the self-as-subject? Philosophers differ over how this can be meant. In interpersonal deception a person's deceiving another person happens *deliberately* or *intentionally*: For instance, Donald Rumsfeld might intend to make Colin Powell believe the opposite of what Rumsfeld takes to be the case, and attempts to bring this about by various intentional actions. If we understand self-deception against the background of this model, however, this not only implies the odd idea that one must lie to oneself (whether through verbal or nonverbal actions) but also comes close to the introduction of an additional internal agent doing the deceiving within the self-deceived person. What was called *self-deception* becomes actually a case of interpersonal deception, except the different agents happen to be within one human being. That is not the concept used by Demos (1960) or Gur and Sackheim (1979), and others as well, and it comes perhaps too close to cases of deeper mental pathologies to be called self-deception. So, viewing the author-self as an intentional deceiver of himself should be rejected, at least if one does not wish to abandon the condition of simultaneity, which holds in standard interpersonal deception.

Somewhat surprisingly, Sackheim (1988) more recently accepted that self-deception may be intentional: "For instance, setting our watches ahead to fool ourselves about the time is a likely exception to the statement" (p. 156). This is at best a case of a mediated intentional action that brings about self-deception, perhaps also a bad example. I tried to fool myself this way because I tended to be 3 to 5 minutes late in meetings. It was not long until I realized that my clocks were ahead; still, the clock-setting trick seemed to do work. But it was not that I was in self-deception then. Either I firmly believed in my clocks and had no belief inconsistent with that one, but got on my way a bit earlier, or I realized that I had a few minutes more time but did not at the same time believe that my clocks and watches were showing the right time. Tricking oneself is not necessarily deceiving oneself; instead, it can be training oneself. There are also other attempts to defend intentionalism about self-deception (e.g., Bermudez, 2000), but they frequently do not note that standard interpersonal deception shows an immediacy or simultaneity of deceiving and being deceived, as opposed to the obliqueness or nonsimultaneity characteristic of self-deception.

So, the role of the self-as-subject in self-deception has to be a moderate one. We think that the person herself might in principle be able to overcome the deception (e.g., by focusing attention upon relevant evidence in the right way). That involves some assumptions about human beings being rational, but only quite moderate assumptions. Because the boundary between conscious and subconscious processes, or between intentional and subintentional states, is permeable (Brandtstädter, 2007), people can become aware of what has been unaware to them. They can, moreover, reflect their beliefs and desires critically because of our ability to develop second-order beliefs and desires, and so on (Frankfurt, 1988). That is a weak role of the self-as-subject in a self-related phenomenon, but it should hardly surprise us that this is so in the present case. Davidson (1980) wrote in a related context: "The point isn't that desires and beliefs aren't ever in an agent's control, but rather that coming to have them isn't something an agent does" (p. 73). If coming to have certain beliefs and desires is not (or, in some cases, cannot) be something an agent does, and if this holds also for, say, self-knowledge or self-determination, we should hardly be surprised that it is also true in self-deception. On the other hand, this does not exclude that we can view ourselves as being able to gain control over the relevant beliefs and desires.

III. CONCLUSION: THE DIVISION OF LABOR BETWEEN PHILOSOPHY AND PSYCHOLOGY

If one goes through a list of concepts of self-related thought and talk (e.g., self-knowledge, self-control, or self-realization), we should by no means expect the role and constitution of the self to be always the same. That is not a fashionable plea for a fragmentation of the "modern self" or the like but rather a methodological remark on the philosophy and psychology of the self. Whether the approach used here will ultimately lead to something deserving the title of a coherent theory of "the self" can be left open here. Piecemeal engineering in order to deal with conceptual and methodological fragmentation between the disciplines will suffice. Sometimes improvements will be achieved by translation. At other points, even firmly held beliefs may have to be revised, which is why I emphasized that we should take seriously the question of whether self-deception really occurs. This should be treated strictly as an empirical matter, although it depends on reasonable prior conceptualizations of the phenomena.

Much current conceptual work in philosophy, while being shrewd and careful, tends to be too distanced from empirical research. It would be profitable if philosophers would engage more in thinking about how their concept-chopping is relevant to questions that can be pursued empirically (Brandtstädter & Sturm, 2004). For instance, if self-deception in the sense outlined earlier occurs, then more about what is involved in self-deception can be said on the basis of richer psychological investigations: How do people differ in their inclination towards such self-deception? What circumstances or contexts may induce self-deception? How does self-deception affect the self-image and self-esteem of persons, their motives of self-consistency and self-enhancement? What functions does self-deception have? And—a question that we should not avoid—how should we evaluate self-deception? Particularly with regard to the last question, we should expect further ground for discussion between philosophers and psychologists. Philosophers often think of self-deception as an irrational phenomenon because of its tendency toward inconsistent believing. In current psychological research, self-deception is not seen as necessarily irrational: It can be an adaptive strategy, or it may be profitable if viewed in broader contexts such as self-defense or self-image management. Behind different approaches to self-deception there may not only be different broader research agendas and methods but also different evaluations of the phenomenon. Again, however, different evaluations of self-deception may also have to do with that one does not really talk about sufficiently similar kinds of self-deception.

Thus, basic understandings of self-related concepts are influenced by the basic research agendas and practices of the disciplines of philosophy and psychology and vice versa. But it does not always follow that philosophers and psychologists are talking past one another on this question. There is a common ground of folk psychology, of typical instances of the phenomenon, and of a shared (if only partially overlapping) history of research and reflection. This is not so in many other areas of self-related phenomena, because philosophers do not address the whole variety of topics psychologists are interested in. But things may change.

REFERENCES

Audi, R. (1982). Self-deception, action, and will. *Erkenntnis, 18*, 133–158.

Austin, J. (1962). *How to do things with words* (2nd ed., J. O. Urmson, Ed.). Cambridge, MA: Harvard University Press. (Original work published 1953)

Baumeister, R. (1987). How the self became a problem: A psychological review of historical research. *Journal of Personality and Social Psychology, 52*, 163–176.

Baumeister, R. (Ed.). (1999). *The self in social psychology*. Ann Arbor, MI: Taylor & Francis.

Berkowitz, L. (Ed.). (1988). *Social psychological studies of the self.* In *Advances in experimental social psychology* (Vol. 21). New York: Academic.

Bermudez, J. L. (2000). Self-deception, intentions and contradictory beliefs. *Analysis, 60*, 309–319.

Brandtstädter, J. (2007). Causality, intentionality, and the causation of intentions: The problematic boundary. In M. G. Ash & T. Sturm (Eds.), *Psychology's territories: Historical and contemporary perspectives from different disciplines*. Mahwah, NJ: Lawrence Erlbaum Associates.

Brandtstädter, J., & Sturm, T. (2004): Apriorität, Erfahrung und das Projekt der Psychologie [Apriority, experience, and the project of psychology]. *Zeitschrift für Sozialpsychologie, 35*, 15–32.

Burkitt, I. (1994). The shifting concept of the self. *History of the Human Sciences, 7*, 7–28.

Calkins, M. W. (1908). Psychology as science of self. *Journal of Philosophy, Psychology and Scientific Methods, 5*, 12–20, 64–68, 113–122.

Calkins, M. W. (1915). The self in scientific psychology. *American Journal of Psychology, 26*, 495–524.

Cassam, Q. (Ed.). (1994). *Self-knowledge*. Oxford, England: Oxford University Press.

Churchland, P. (1995). *The engine of reason, the seat of the soul*. Cambridge, MA: MIT Press.

Cohen, L. J. (1992). *An essay on belief and acceptance*. Oxford, England: Oxford University Press.

Davidson, D. (1980). *Essays on actions and events*. Oxford, England: Clarendon.

Davidson, D. (1986). Deception and division. In J. Elster (Ed.), *The multiple self* (pp. 79–82). Cambridge, England: Cambridge University Press.

Day, W. (1977). On the behavioral analysis of self-deception and self-development. In T. Mischel (Ed.), *The self: Philosophical and psychological issues* (pp. 224–249). Oxford, England: Blackwell.

Demos, R. (1960). Lying to oneself. *Journal of Philosophy, 57,* 588–595.

Dennett, D. (1989). The origin of selves. *Cogito, 3,* 163–173.

Dennett, D. (1991). *Consciousness explained.* Boston: Little, Brown.

Dennett, D. (1992). The self as a center of narrative gravity. In F. Kessel, P. Cole, & D. Johnson (Eds.), *Self and consciousness* (pp. 103–115). New York, NY: Macmillan.

Dennett, D., & Kinsbourne, M. (1992). Time and the observer: The where and when of consciousness in the brain. *Behavioral and Brain Sciences, 15,* 183–247.

Descartes, R. (1897–1910). Meditations. In C. Adam & P. Tannery (Eds.), *Œuvres de Descartes* (Vol. 7). Paris: Vrin. (Original work published 1644)

Douglas, W., & Gibbins, K. (1983). Inadequacy of voice recognition as a demonstration of self-deception. *Journal of Personality and Social Psychology, 44,* 589–592.

Fingarette, H. (1969). *Self-deception.* London: Routledge & Kegan Paul.

Frankfurt, H. (1988). Freedom of the will and the concept of a person. In *The importance of what we care about* (pp. 11–25). Cambridge, England: Cambridge University Press.

Gergen, K. J. (1985a). The ethnopsychology of self-deception. In M. W. Martin (Ed.), *Self-deception and self-understanding* (pp. 228–243). Lawrence: University of Kansas Press.

Gergen, K. J. (1985b). The social constructionist movement in modern psychology. *American Psychologist, 40,* 266–275.

Gergen, K. J. (2007). The self: Colonization in psychology and society. In M. G. Ash & T. Sturm (Eds.), *Psychology's territories: Historical and contemporary perspectives from different disciplines.* Mahwah, NJ: Lawrence Erlbaum Associates.

Greve, W. (1996). Erkenne Dich Selbst? Argumente zur Bedeutung der "Perspektive der ersten Person" [Know Thyself? Considerations concerning the "First-Person-Perspective"]. *Sprache und Kognition, 15,* 104–119.

Greve, W. (Ed.). (2000). *Psychologie des Selbst.* [Psychology of the self]. Weinheim, Germany: Beltz.

Greve, W. (2005). Die Entwicklung von Selbst und Persönlichkeit im Erwachsenenalter [The development of self and personality in adulthood]. In S.-H. Filipp & U. Staudinger (Eds.), *Entwicklungspsychologie im Erwachsenenalter (Enzyklopädie der Psychologie,* C/V/6, pp. 343–376). Göttingen, Germany: Hogrefe.

Gur, R. C., & Sackheim, H. A. (1979). Self-deception: A concept in search of a phenomenon. *Journal of Personality and Social Psychology, 37,* 147–169.

Hagner, M. (1997). *Homo cerebralis: Der Wandel vom Seelenorgan zum Gehirn.* [Homo cerebralis: The transition from the organ of the soul to the brain]. Berlin, Germany: Berlin Verlag.

Hales, S. (1985). The inadvertent rediscovery of the self in social psychology. *Journal for the Theory of Social Behaviour, 15,* 237–282.

Hales, S. (1986). Epilogue: Rethinking the business of psychology. *Journal for the Theory of Social Behaviour, 16,* 57–76.

Harré, R. (1991). The discursive production of selves. *Theory & Psychology, 1*, 51–63.

Heidelberger, M. (2007). Freedom AND science! The presumptuous metaphysics of free will disclaimers. In M. G. Ash & T. Sturm (Eds.), *Psychology's territories: Historical and contemporary perspectives from different disciplines*. Mahwah, NJ: Lawrence Erlbaum Associates.

Holton, R. (2000–2001). What is the role of the self in self-deception? *Proceedings of the Aristotelian Society, 101*, 53–69.

James, W. (1890). *Principles of psychology*. New York: Dover.

Kant, I. (1900ff.). *Gesammelte Schriften* [Collected writings]. (Academy ed.). Berlin, Germany: De Gruyter.

Kant, I. (1996). *Kritik der reinen Vernunft*. [Critique of pure reason]. (J. Timmermann, Ed.). Hamburg, Germany: Meiner. (Original work published 1781/1787)

Kenny, A. (1992). *The metaphysics of mind*. Oxford, England: Oxford University Press.

Kunda, Z. (1990). The case for motivated reasoning. *Psychological Bulletin, 108*, 480–498.

Lichtenberg, G. C. (1765–99). Sudelbücher. In W. Promies (Ed.), (1968ff.), *G.C. Lichtenberg: Schriften und Briefe* (5 Vols), Vol. 1–2. Munich, Germany: Carl Hanser.

Lockard, J. S., & Paulus, D. L. (Eds.). (1988). *Self-deception: An adaptive mechanism?* Englewood Cliffs, NJ: Prentice Hall.

Maasen, S. (2007). Governing by will: The shaping of the will in self-help manuals. In M. G. Ash & T. Sturm (Eds.), *Psychology's territories: Historical and contemporary perspectives from different disciplines*. Mahwah, NJ: Lawrence Erlbaum Associates.

Maimon, S. (1800). Erklärung einer allgemeinbekannten merkwürdigen anthropologischen Erscheinung [An explanation for a generally known notable anthropological phenomenon]. *Neue Berlinische Monatsschrift, 3*, 61–72.

Markus, H., & Wurf, E. (1987). The dynamic self-concept: A social psychological perspective. *Annual Review of Social Psychology, 38*, 299–337.

McGinn, C. (1997). *The character of mind*. Oxford, England: Oxford University Press.

McLaughlin, P. (1985). Soemmerring und Kant: Über das Organ der Seele und den Streit der Fakultäten [Soemmerring and Kant: On the organ of the soul and the contest of the faculties]. In G. Mann & F. Dumont (Eds.), *Samuel Thomas Soemmerring und die Gelehrten der Goethezeit* (pp. 191–201). Stuttgart, Germany: Schwabe.

Mead, G. H. (1934). *Mind, self, and society*. Chicago: University of Chicago Press.

Mele, A. (1987). Recent work on self-deception. *American Philosophical Quarterly, 24*, 1–17.

Mele, A. (1997). Real self-deception. *Behavioral and Brain Sciences, 20*, 91–136.

Mele, A. (2000). *Self-deception unmasked*. Princeton, NJ: Princeton University Press.

Mischel, T. (Ed.). (1977). *The self: Philosophical and psychological issues*. Oxford, England: Blackwell.

Mischel, W. (1976). The self as the person: A cognitive social learning view. In A. Wandersman, P. J. Poppen, & D. F. Ricks (Eds.), *Humanism and behaviorism: Dialogue and growth* (pp. 145–156). New York: Pergamon.

Morawski, J. (2007). Scientific selves: Discerning the subject and experimenter in experimental psychology in the U.S., 1900–1935. In M. G. Ash & T. Sturm (Eds.), *Psychology's territories: Historical and contemporary perspectives from different disciplines*. Mahwah, NJ: Lawrence Erlbaum Associates.

Moritz, K. P. (1789). Über Selbsttäuschung. [On self-deception]. *Gnothi sauton oder Magazin zur Erfahrungsseelenkunde, 3,* 45–47.

Nagel, T. (1986). *The view from nowhere*. Oxford, England: Oxford University Press.

Newen, A., & Vogeley, K. (Eds.). (2000). *Selbst und Gehirn*. [Self and brain]. Paderborn, Germany: Mentis.

Nisbett, R. E., & Ross, L. (1980). *Human inference: Strategies and shortcomings of social judgment*. Englewood Cliffs, NJ: Prentice Hall.

Pauen, M. (2001). *Grundprobleme der Philosophie des Geistes*. [Basic problems of the philosophy of mind]. Frankfurt, Germany: Fischer Taschenbuchverlag.

Quattrone, G. A., & Tversky, A. (1986). Self-deception and the voter's illusion. In J. Elster (Ed.), *The multiple self* (pp. 35–58). Cambridge, England: Cambridge University Press.

Rager, G., Quitterer, J., & Rungaldier, E. (2002). *Unser Selbst. Identität im Wandel der neuronalen Prozesse*. [Our self. Identity under changing neuronal processes]. Paderborn, Germany: Ferdinand Schöningh.

Robinson, D. N. (1991). The discursive production of selves. *Theory & Psychology, 1,* 51–63.

Roth, G. (2001). *Fühlen, Denken, Handeln. Wie das Gehirn unser Verhalten steuert*. Frankfurt, Germany: Suhrkamp.

Rychlak, J. F. (1976). Is a concept of "self" necessary in psychological theory, and if so why? A humanistic perspective. In A. Wandersman, P. J. Poppen, & D. F. Ricks (Eds.), *Humanism and behaviorism: Dialogue and growth* (pp. 121–143). New York: Pergamon.

Ryle, G. (1949). *The concept of mind*. London: Hutchison.

Sackheim, H. A. (1988). Self-deception: A synthesis. In J. S. Lockard & D. L. Paulhus (Eds.), *Self-deception: An adaptive mechanism?* (pp. 146–165). Englewood Cliffs, NJ: Prentice Hall.

Sackheim, H. A., & Gur, R. C. (1979). Self-deception, other-deception and self-reported psychopathology. *Journal of Consulting and Clinical Psychology, 47,* 213–215.

Sampson, E. E. (1985). What has been inadvertently rediscovered? *Journal for the Theory of Social Behaviour, 16,* 33–40.

Shoemaker, S. (1986). Introspection and the self. In P. A. French, T. E. Vehling, & H. K. Wettstein (Eds.), *Studies in the philosophy of mind* (Vol. 10, pp. 101–120). Minneapolis: University of Minnesota Press.

Skinner, B. F. (1953). *Science and human behavior*. New York: Macmillan.

Smith, A. (1759). A Theory of Moral Sentiments. London, UK: A. Millar.

Strawson, G. (1997). The self. *Journal of Consciousness Studies, 5/6,* 405–428.

Strunk, O. (1972). The self-psychology of Mary Whiton Calkins. *Journal of the History of the Behavioral Sciences, 8,* 196–203.

Toulmin, S. (1986). The ambiguities of self-understanding. *Journal for the Theory of Social Behaviour, 16,* 41–55.

Tugendhat, E. (1986). *Selbstbewusstsein und Selbstbestimmung.* [Self-consciousness and self-determination] (P. Stern, Trans.). Cambridge, MA: MIT Press. (Original work published 1979)

Tversky, A., & Kahneman, D. (September 27, 1974). Judgment under uncertainty: Heuristics and biases. *Science, 185,* 1124–1131.

Veney, L. (1969). The self: The history of a concept. *Journal of the History of the Behavioral Sciences, 5,* 349–359.

Welles, J. F. (1986). Self-deception as a positive feedback mechanism. *American Psychologist, 41,* 325–326.

Whittaker-Bleuler, S. (1988). Deception and self-deception: A dominance strategy in competitive sport. In J. S. Lockard & D. L. Paulhus (Eds.), *Self-deception: An adaptive mechanism?* (pp. 212–228). Englewood Cliffs, NJ: Prentice Hall.

Part II

Roles of Instruments
in Psychological Research

⇥ ⇤

9

What is a Psychological Instrument?

Horst Gundlach
University of Passau, Germany

Countless instruments have been used in the science of psychology—in research, for demonstrations and teaching purposes, and in psychological practice. These implements have come to be known as psychological instruments. Before investigating what the term *psychological instrument* designates, a few remarks on the phrase itself are in order. The term is not often used, and we rarely encounter it even in studies on scientific instruments or on the history of such instruments. Yet the term is not introduced here ad hoc. It has a past of its own.

THE TERM "PSYCHOLOGICAL INSTRUMENT"

No one knows exactly when the expression "psychological instrument" or a synonymous phrase was first used, but the term does surface regularly toward the end of the 19th century. That makes it younger than some of the more familiar terms in the history of science, such as "philosophical instrument", "physical instrument", or "physiological instrument." This results from the development of psychology as a science and as a discipline. Whereas psychological topics have been investigated scientifically for centuries, and such investigations have involved experiments using instruments for much of that time, the discipline of psychology itself has been established only comparatively recently.

A key event for the history of psychology is Wilhelm Wundt's establishment of an institute and laboratory for psychology at the University of Leipzig in 1879. Perhaps he was also the first investigator to coin the term "psychological apparatus." A note on terminology seems appropriate here. The German term "Apparat" denotes quite often something that would be named "instrument" in English. Whereas the German usage "Instrument-plus-Apparat" is coextensive with the English usage

M. Matsumoto
Oct 1898
Leipzig

Liste XV, 1897.

Psychologische und physiologische

Apparate.

E. ZIMMERMANN,

Präcisionsmechaniker,

Leipzig,
Emilienstrasse 21.

Silberne Medaille
Rom 1894.
Ausstellg. d. XI. internat. med. Congresses.
Gegr. 1887.

Königl. Sächs. Staatsmedaille
Leipzig 1897.

Figure 9–1.   Zimmermann (List XV, 1897).

"instrument-plus-apparatus," the domain of the word "Apparat" seems at present to be larger than of "apparatus." Therefore, it is often appropriate to render the German word "Apparat" with the English "instrument." This should not constitute a severe problem because Warner (1990, p. 83), talking about the past without being specific about dates, stated that the words "instruments" and "apparatus" were also used interchangeably in the English-speaking world.

In 1893, Wundt published the brief *Note on Psychological Instruments*, advising his readers where to procure psychological instruments of the kind he used for his own research. As he wrote, he did this because "from time to time I still receive letters asking where to purchase the instruments needed for experimental psychological research and lecture demonstrations. My institute commissions Mr. C. Krille, a local mechanic, to make most of our instrumental devices." (1893, p. 649). Once this note was published, use of the expression "psychological apparatus" spread, particularly in sales catalogues distributed by manufacturers.[1] As psychological laboratories modeled after Wundt's sprang up all over the world, there also arose a market for psychological instruments. Wundt's own supply situation changed within months of his suggestion, for C. Krille died in 1893. Wundt now patronized precision mechanic Ernst Zimmermann, who soon became the preferred supplier for the Leipzig laboratory and one of the leading manufacturers of psychological instruments on the market. Zimmermann issued a large number of trade catalogues, many of which he titled *Psychologische Apparate*, or *Psychological Instruments*.

Zimmermann, however, did not remain the sole pertinent manufacturer. New suppliers, such as the Heinrich Diel Company in Leipzig, established in 1905, joined the market. In Göttingen, Carl Diederichs designed psychological instruments for Georg Elias Müller and made use of catalogue advertising. In 1898, Spindler and Hoyer took over this position. In America, Wundt's pupil Edward Bradford Titchener cooperated with the Chicago Laboratory Supply and Scale Company, later known as the C. H. Stoelting Company. In his *Experimental Psychology*, Titchener (1901, 1905) listed 46 companies that furnish psychological laboratories, found around the world. Most produced mechanical, chemical, physiological, and medical devices in general, as the market

---

[1]Davis and Dreyfuss (1986) produced a bibliography of sales catalogues for scientific instruments in scholarly libraries. One finds there some trade catalogues for psychological instruments but can also register how scarce the holdings of these libraries are and how poorly they esteem this material. Its value as a source for the history of science was shown by Brenni (1989). Very useful for our topic is the trade catalogue collection in the Internet site launched by the Berlin Max Planck Institute for the History of Sciences (http://vlp.mpiwg-berlin.mpg.de/library/tradecatalogues.html).

was still too small for companies to specialize exclusively in manufacturing psychological instruments.

The term "psychological instrument," consequently, is not an ad hoc invention but has been current for more than 100 years. A new market had arisen, in which the demands of specific customers were catered to by various instrument producers and dealers, and a new name had to be found for this novel kind of commodity. Although trade catalogues contributed to making the term popular, not all of the instruments in use were designed by commercial manufacturers. Some psychologists built their instruments themselves, and some laboratories hired technicians specifically for the purpose. As I will show, there also exist varieties of psychological instruments that were not built by mechanics or electronics engineers.

The term "psychological instrument" may be slightly more than 100 years old, but this does not permit us to deduce that the objects it designates are of the same age. As stated above, psychological instruments existed long before the late 19th century (Sturm & Ash, 2005, p. 9f.). It is therefore necessary to ask whether it is possible to develop a definition of the term "psychological instrument" that is not limited to the recent period.

THE CONCEPT OF *PSYCHOLOGICAL INSTRUMENT*: PURPOSE- AND KNOWLEDGE-SPECIFIC DEFINITIONS

Let us now examine what the term designates. Just what is a psychological instrument? The answer seems simple enough: Any scientific instrument used in or resulting from psychological research, demonstrations and teaching purposes, or in psychological practice. Alternatively, we could define the domain of the concept *psychological instrument* as the set of all scientific instruments used in or resulting from psychological research, demonstration and teaching, or practice.

The entirety of all scientific instruments, however, does not form classes that can be grouped exhaustively according to *genus proximum* and *differentia specifica*. The word "psychological" therefore does not designate a special kind of scientific instrument, one that differs essentially from other kinds of instruments. Instead, it designates the functional context in which a given instrument is used. Psychological instruments have always been used in a variety of other scientific endeavors, and this will not change. They are not psychological as such beyond all context; they become psychological instruments only by fulfilling certain functions. A. J. Turner (1993) noted that "from the beginning, students of the history of scientific instruments have been aware that the scientific purposes that an instrument was to serve, and the scientific context from which it came should be an integral part of that instrument's story" (p. 19). Add to this the fact that some instruments have been used in unscientific and pseudoscientific contexts as well, and a potential further line of research becomes visible. Unfortunately, there has not been much work done on instruments in pseudo-psychological contexts, although there is plenty of material, for example, Wilhelm Reich's orgon accumulator or Zachar Bissky's diagnoscopy apparatus, with which he presumed to provide a thorough personality analysis (Bissky, 1925; Giese, 1926; Sommer, 1928; Walter, 1927).

Before we delineate what constitutes the set of all scientific instruments used in psychological research, demonstrations and teaching, or practice, we must settle two questions: (a) just what constitutes a scientific instrument and (b) what we mean by psychology.

The Science Museum in London and the Smithsonian Institute in Washington, DC, published an encyclopedia entitled *Instruments of Science* (Bud & Warner, 1998). In the introduction, the authors ask straightforwardly "What is a scientific instrument?" without, however, giving us anything remotely near an answer (Bud, Warner, & Johnson, 1988). This may be prudent. Nonetheless, other authors have attempted definitions. Rather infelicitous is the explication given by Van Helden and Hankins (1994): "Perhaps it is best to say that instruments are the technology of science" (p. 5). Not only do they follow the inaccurate American custom of mixing up the words "technology" and "technique", technology being the science of techniques, but even if one accepts the interpretation "that instruments are the techniques of science," this seems far too vague to be helpful here. Turner (1993) was more helpful when he wrote: "a scientific instrument is a device which represents or adapts for a specific purpose a part of the rational knowledge of a particular society at a particular time" (p. 22). Similar in content, but slightly different in wording, is Turner's other formulation: "We may reasonably describe as scientific any device which represents, displays, or adapts for a specific purpose some part of the organized, rational, often—but not necessarily—mathematically expressed, established body of learning of a given society" (p. 20).

Going by these formulations, and by specifying the purpose more concretely, we may attempt an answer to our question with a purpose-specific (Ps) definition:

DPs — A psychological instrument is a device that represents or adapts for psychological research, or for teaching in psychology, or for psychological practice, a part of the rational knowledge of a particular society at a particular time.

This definition adds a few parameters to the simple delineation with which we started.

Assuming that the concept of *scientific instrument* as explicated by Turner (1993) is sufficiently clear for our aims, we must now agree upon just what we mean by psychological research, by teaching in psychology, and by psychological practice. This is crucial, because nowadays the word "psychology" carries (at least) two different meanings. These meanings do not coincide today and did not do so at any time in the history of psychology. On the one hand, the word "psychology" denotes a field of scientific research. Interest in it started in antiquity, although it was not called psychology then. On the other hand, psychology can be understood as a discipline, that is, a social institution combining specific instruction, education, and examinations, and including teachers, trainees, and trained persons who—once they have completed their qualification—become members of a particular and acknowledged social grouping.

The academic discipline we call psychology is much younger than the scientific field of psychological research (cf. Gundlach, 2004). The first step toward establishing the academic discipline was taken in Prussia in 1824, when university students aspiring for teacher positions at secondary schools were required to take examinations in psychology. It therefore became necessary to provide regular university courses in psychology. This, however, did not imply that academic chairs were established especially for psychology. It was considered sufficient that professors of philosophy teach the subject and execute the relevant examinations. The objective was not to train psychologists but to have teachers in secondary level education who had enjoyed a smattering of training and been certified in psychology. The founding of psychological laboratories mentioned earlier and the resulting dissemination of the term "psychological instruments" occurred during a period of transition, when German states considered psychology an auxiliary discipline to philosophy, not yet an autonomous discipline training psychologists. It is within that auxiliary discipline that we find the first attempts at scientifically founded psychological practices and the development of instruments of applied psychology, which paved the way for an autonomous discipline of psychology training professional psychologists.

Not until the 20th century did psychology become an entirely independent discipline, possessing specific academic chairs training specialists who in turn elicited a wide range of psychological study and applications, for which they needed the most diverse instruments. As a result, the distinction between psychologists and amateurs became pronounced. There were and still are also dabblers who call their activities psychology. That sort of lay understanding of the term is naturally irrelevant here.

We must note the distinction between these two meanings of the word "psychology," because the second usage discussed earlier perhaps suggests that psychological instruments are only those used by persons associated with the discipline of psychology. Here I recommend following the first usage, and taking the science rather than the discipline of psychology as our point of reference, because otherwise we would face anachronistic and distracting questions such as whether or not Wilhelm Wundt counts as a psychologist, and if so, from which point onward, and to what extent, and so on.

If we can agree on the two meanings of the word "psychology" and accept the one used here exclusively, we can now turn our attention to definition DPs and ask whether an assignment to the category of psychological instruments should be based on specifying the purpose the instruments are used to alone or whether we must rather specify which sort of knowledge is represented or adapted when creating such an instrument.

If we ask for that kind of specification, the definition we get is going to be knowledge specific (Ks):

DKs — A psychological instrument is a device that represents or adapts for a specific purpose a part of the rational psychological knowledge of a certain society at a particular time.

We might even consider answering with a double specification and thus derive a purpose- and knowledge-specific (PsKs) definition:

DPsKs — A psychological instrument is a device that represents or adapts for psychological research, or for teaching in psychology, or for psychological practice, part of the rational psychological knowledge of a certain society at a particular time.

Reflecting on Our Definitions

The result of our attempt to understand what is meant by the concept of *psychological instrument* is certainly not final, but it seems worthy of closer examination. We arrived at both a purpose-specific and a knowledge-specific interpretation of the concept: DPs reflecting the fact that the instruments are used in psychological research, teaching, or practice; DKs reflecting the fact that the devices are used to represent or adapt rational psychological knowledge of a particular society at a particular time.

DPS has (at least) one drawback: Any common instrument found in many sciences would have to be considered a psychological instrument as soon as it were used in psychological research, teaching, or practice. The definition would thus apply, for example, to batteries, voltmeters, thermometers, tape recorders, slide rules, or computers. Even common mathematical procedures, such as statistically processing data, or operations of logical thought, could then be considered psychological instruments. Naturally, the student or the historian of science must know and account for which types of tools and instruments are used in psychological research, teaching, and practice, but the fact that an instrument is being used in such contexts may not always suffice to consider the object in question a psychological instrument. DPS seems to permit to stretch the meaning of the concept to such a degree that it becomes useless.

DKS likewise has (at least) one considerable drawback: Instruments that play or have played an important role in psychological research and therefore are considered psychological instruments would be excluded from this set. Take, for example, the chronoscope, a millisecond chronometer. We cannot claim that psychological knowledge had any part in its development. Nevertheless, its role in the evolution of psychology is undisputed. So there must be a place for the set DPS minus DKS.

The third interpretation, DPsKs, represents the intersection of DPS and DKS. It may be concise, but it is definitely too narrow, as there are psychological instruments in the set DPS minus DKS, as well as in the set DKS minus DPS. We could also try the union of DPS and DKS. This would amend the default we found in DKS but keep the unwelcome aspect of DPS of being too broad.

The definitions suggested here delimit different sets of instruments. None of them corresponds exactly to any intuitively and inductively acquired concept that may have grown out of research in psychological instruments and their history, or from studying catalogues advertising scientific instruments. The set of all scientific instruments used in psychological research, teaching, and practice, DPS, seems to be a particularly fuzzy set, and therefore the union of DPS and DKS is also a fuzzy set.

INDUCTIVE CONCEPT FORMATION

Aiming for a *nominal* definition of psychology and scientific instruments is not the only possible way to arrive at an understanding of what psychological instruments are. Perhaps an inductive approach, working with the unavoidably vague relation of similarity, will get us further. Let us take a look at a number of different psychological instruments, examining preferably older specimens, because these are basically simpler to understand than more contemporary equipment. Because space is limited, only a small number of instruments can be shown. Plenty of illustrations are to be found in publications on local holdings of historical instruments of various psychological institutes, at Belgrade (Kostic & Todorovic, 1997); Florence (Gori-Savellini, 1986; Bertini, 1989); Graz (Huber, Dorfer, & Hohenester, 1994); Groningen (Draaisma, 1992); Heidelberg, (Gundlach, 1986); Copenhagen (Funch, 1986); Ljubljana (Pecjak, 2002), Prague (Hoskovec & Stikar, 1984), Siena (Terenna & Vannozzi, 1998), Sydney (Turtle, 1981), and Zürich (Lauber & Bründler, 1981). Harteveld (1989) produced an illustrated register of holdings in the Netherlands. A large number of historical instruments may be examined at the Institute for the History of Psychology at the University of Passau, Germany.

Weights and Balances

Let us begin with something relatively simple: mechanical pressure. Not only was the science of mechanics the vanguard and model for modern science in general, but throughout the history of psychology, the study of mechanical pressure and its effect on sensors and central nervous processes was one of the conspicuous paradigms.

Many biological systems, including humans, can distinguish variations in pressure. In the early 19th century, science began investigating just how and with how much precision this can be done. The most obvious method is to use gravity to create pressure stimuli on the surface of the skin. Little pieces of metal having certain weights and also called "weights" were used. Put simply, researchers asked: Which weights can be distinguished, and which are the smallest differences among weights that can be noticed? It was necessary to know the exact weight of the individual pieces, and thus balances became an important item in psychological laboratories.

However, there arises a difficulty in distinguishing various weights that is not given in using balances. Participants who are asked to report their pressure sensations normally also have optical information at their disposal, and visual and tactile information are not always easy to keep apart. To neutralize visual input, scientists created deceptive weights. They were meant not to deceive the sense of touch but to equalize the visual impression by all looking alike, and by being the same volume. You will probably find this kind of weight only in psychological laboratories. The Bureau of Standards and your local farmer's market have no need of them.

Figure 9–2. Balance (a), apothecary weights (b), deceptive weights (c).

In investigating the sensation of pressure the main issue was initially a question of general psychology, because researchers were looking for general regularities, or even laws. However, other research perspectives also became significant: the differential, the social, the developmental, the pathological, and the comparative perspectives. If necessary, instruments were modified according to the specific inquiries being undertaken.

Balances, whether we find them in the pharmacy or in a psychological laboratory, have to be examined not only for their precision but also for their *sensitivity*. Bureaus of standards test whether a particular balance can distinguish standard weights, for example, of 1100 mg from 1200 mg. Since the time of Albrecht von Haller, in the 18th century, sensitivity is the criterion that distinguishes living beings from nonliving matter. So it is surprising to find sensitivity attributed to mechanical balances. Notice the swing in analogy: The human being has become the model for the instrument, the balance, and the balance is attributed sensitivity. Methods spring up for determining the balance's sensitivity. In turn, investigating the balance becomes a paradigm for investigating sensation—principles used to determine the sensitivity of an inanimate instrument of measurement begin to be used to investigate the sensitivity of living beings.

This swing in analogies back and forth between instruments and living beings may give rise to a suspicion that psychology began to consider human beings or animals themselves as instruments. So we must keep in mind that these are foremost *objects* of psychological research, and not *implements*. But it is certainly correct to say that some psychological research does use humans as *means*. Of course, that does not basically distinguish psychological research from other forms of research. For the sake of brevity, I suggest that we (admittedly arbitrarily) confine our present discussion to inorganic instruments.

In terms of studying sensitivity, the analogy between humans and balances helps us to formulate a general finding: We are no longer surprised to discover that the same instruments turn up in physical and in psychological contexts. The attributes *physical* or *psychological* characterize the context, not the individual instrument.

Excursus: Instruments of Modern Science and Repercussions in Psychology

This provides an insight of importance for understanding the history of psychology and how the science of psychology relates to the development of scientific instruments. I have discussed this connection elsewhere (cf. Gundlach, 1997), so a brief summary may suffice for our present purposes.

The more scientific instruments, telescopes, microscopes, barometers, and so on, came to be recognized as legitimate means to knowledge in modern science, the more refined and precise they became and the better their functions were understood, the more it became clear that we must question just how precisely our own unaided organs of perception work. Thus, exploring the function of perceptual organs, and doing so—as we have seen in the case of baraesthesia—in analogy to investigating how manmade instruments work, interested both physicists and physiologists alike. This pushed work in sensory psychology forward, particularly after 1800.

Carrying this point to an extreme, we could say that the shape psychology acquired over the course of the 19th century was an unintended by-product of the widespread introduction and refinement of instruments into modern science.

Aesthesiometers

Besides the study of pressure stimuli on skin surfaces, it is also interesting to note how pointed pressure stimuli were explored. In order to generate punctiform pressure, special instruments, called *aesthesiometers*, had to be invented. Instrument manufacturers offered a variety of models, for instance, the hair aesthesiometer (see Fig. 9–3a) developed by Max von Frey.

Now, some may object that Max von Frey (1852–1932) was a professor for *physiology* and head of an institute for that field in Würzburg,

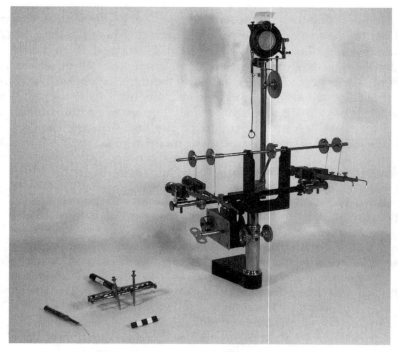

Figure 9–3. Aesthesiometers (a + b) and stimulus lever apparatus (c).

where there also existed an institute for psychology. So why should we consider one of his instruments a psychological instrument? Viewing our subject from the standpoint of one particular discipline does not mean that the subject matter as such can be easily divided among disciplines. Clearly, questions of psychology were also studied in laboratories for physiology, without anyone finding that improper. What counts again is the research context: When the aesthesiometer was used to locate sensitive nerve endings and pressure spots on the skin, it was not considered a psychological instrument; when it was used to study the subjective phenomena of central nervous system processes, it became a psychological instrument, regardless of where the investigation took place.

Stimulus Lever Apparatus

Let us continue with instruments for tactile stimulation. Some of them were important for studying questions of greater scope than merely the sense of touch. Richard Pauli (1886–1951), for example, who incidentally had worked as a voluntary assistant at von Frey's institute for physiology (Traxel, 1995, p. 53), designed an instrument for investigating the narrowness of consciousness. He called it a *stimulus lever apparatus, Reizhebelapparat* in German (see Fig. 9–3c).

Originally, we find the concept of the narrowness of consciousness in John Locke's (1690/1975) *Essay Concerning Human Understanding*: "The narrow Mind of Man, not being able of having many *Ideas* under View and Consideration at once" (p. 150, chap. II, x, 2). This means that the number of contents simultaneously present in consciousness is limited. Pauli (1930) explored the quantitative relationships of that limitedness by presenting several impressions of brief duration. His stimulus lever apparatus creates tactile and visual impressions. A person rests his hands on hand supports (not shown here) on the left and the right, just below the ivory pointers that create tactile stimuli on the hand. Visual stimuli are produced by the shutter, a kind of tachistoscope positioned at the top of the instrument. On the tactile level, the test person is asked to distinguish which of the two stimuli is stronger. The visual stimuli may consist of two semicircles of varying intensities of gray. The person has to ascertain which side is darker. These experiments are meant to show how many items may be present in consciousness simultaneously. The answer is very few indeed, as Locke suspected, but he had no means of measuring it.

Of course, the tactile sense is only one of the skin's senses, and those senses themselves constitute only a small topic within the realm of the psychology of perception, which in turn is only one area of psychology as a whole. And yet even for this minor topic we find a wealth of instruments, of which our examples represent only a tiny selection. Multiply the abundance of instruments we find for the tactile sense alone by the number of areas in all of psychology and you will begin to get an idea of the variety of instruments that has evolved.

Sound Variation

Mechanical pressure and its effects on living beings are not restricted to tactile stimuli. Evolution created a special organ for detecting air pressure variations: the ear. It can distinguish various dimensions of acoustic pressure, such as force or volume and frequency or pitch. Again, we can start with the question of sensitivity. Psychologists developed various instruments to vary the volume of sound. These were usually designed as drop devices—an object, for instance, a steel ball, was dropped from varying heights.

Even more instruments were designed to vary pitch. The tuning fork was invented in 1711 by lute player John Shore—for musical purposes,

Figure 9–4.   Tuning fork (a) and tone variators (b, c).

of course (Brenni, 1998). Nineteenth-century research in acoustics discovered the usefulness of this instrument for scientific purposes, and it
found its way into laboratories, where it was used to create constant pitch
stimuli and for other purposes, such as short time measurements. Louis
William Stern (1897, 1902) invented the tone variator (see Fig. 9–4b, c)
for generating continuous variations of pitch. It works similarly to an organ pipe, but the volume of the cylinder and thus the pitch generated can
be continuously altered by moving a piston inside the cylinder.

Of particular interest is the transmission of the angular rotation of the
graduating disc to the piston, which is done by the variator in the stricter
sense, a metal disc cut to a logarithmic shape. It makes equal angular ro-
tations produce equal changes of tone and is actually a reified, mechanical version of the law that states that multiplicative changes in vibration
frequency result in additive changes in pitch intervals. Fechner s(1860,
1966) stated a general version of this relation in his basic law of psychophysics; the tone variator is—as it were—a metal embodiment of that
law. This demonstrates how psychological theory and knowledge can
influence the design of instruments. By our definition Dps, the tuning
fork is a psychological instrument; the tone variator is one also by Dpsks.

And it was also used in a different context, in an aurist's practice, which context would make it fit Dᴋs.

Color Mixer

Besides mechanical vibration, we also have electromagnetic oscillation that underlies optical phenomena. The eye can distinguish various dimensions of light, for example, brightness and color. Here also we can start with the question of sensitivity.

Since antiquity, there was an interest in color mixture. Rotating discs for additive color mixing (see Fig. 9–5a) became popular when Pieter van Musschenbroek introduced them in the 18th century (Muncke, 1827, p. 137). There, the color proportions cannot be changed in the course of rotation. To alter proportions, you must first stop the instrument. Wundt's pupil Karl Marbe (1894) found it necessary to design an instrument that allowed for altering the size of color segments without interrupting rotation: The result was the color mixer (see Fig. 9–5b). This instrument can be used convincingly for demonstration purposes, but it has, like Musschenbroeck's discs, one flaw: It does not mix spectrally pure light but works with the segments of daylight reflected by the color pigments on the disks, which are rarely spectrally pure light. This obstructs its usefulness for serious research in color perception. Such research required

Figure 9–5.   Rotating disc (a), color mixer (b).

an instrument that could mix spectral colors. Hermann Helmholtz designed the first practical instrument to achieve that. It was made by the firm Schmidt & Haensch in Berlin, presented to the public in 1879, but too expensive for the psychological laboratories of the time.

Once again, some may object that tone variators and color mixers were instruments for physics, namely, for acoustics and optics. In the 18th century it would in fact have been correct to call them physical instruments used for physics. However, that does not exclude them from being psychological instruments used for psychological research. Only during the 19th century did the consensus arise that organisms and subjective phenomena are not the proper subject of physics, and the corresponding scientific questions moved into the fields of physiology, psychology, and biology.

Yet, questions in physics and in psychology can be meaningfully posed by one and the same researcher. Gustav Theodor Fechner, founder of psychophysics and one of the greatest inspirations for 19th-century experimental psychology, was a professor of physics. Hermann Helmholtz, professor for physiology and later professor of physics, produced two comprehensive classic works on the psychology of the senses. His *On the Sensations of Tone as a Physiological Basis for the Theory of Music* was published in 1863. Tones and other sensations are undoubtedly topics for psychology. His *Treatise on Physiological Optics* was published in 1867 as Volume IX of the *General Encyclopedia of Physics*. Its three sections deal with the *Dioptrics of the Eye*, with *Visual Sensations* and *Visual Perceptions,* the last two clearly being topics of psychology.

There simply is no clear line dividing physical from psychological instruments; for both cases the context is crucial and not the disciplinary but the thematic context. Also, we must keep in mind that over the course of modern science, the borders of physics were drawn differently at different times.

The instruments shown, once again, represent only a minute sampling from the psychology of perception, which, again, is only one of many fields in psychology. And within the scope of this chapter I can merely hint at the enormous number of instruments designed for use in psychological research, teaching, and practice.

The Chronoscope and Reaction Time Measurement

One of the earliest topics for psychologists working with instruments was the measuring of reaction time and thereby the time mental processes take. In Wundt's laboratory this became an outstanding field of investigation, and up to this day measuring reaction times is a central task in

Figure 9–6.   Chronoscope (a), card changer (b), voice key (c).

psychological research. The most important instrument in the pioneering days was the chronoscope (see Fig. 9–6a; cf. Schmidgen, 2005).

To measure reaction times, researchers needed instruments that presented stimuli, were connected to the chronoscope, and allowed a precise fixation of the time of stimulus presentation; for example, a card changer (see Fig. 9–6b) as used in association studies. Another instrument was used to register the subject's reactions, for example a voice key (see Fig. 9–6c), an acoustic switch. Around 1900, knowing how to use the chronoscope, how to continually control the processes and how to set up all the peripheral equipment properly was expert knowledge that distinguished experimental psychologists from many other scientists.

Today, most instruments for measuring reaction times have been substituted by the PC, our universal instrument with an inbuilt clock (not always reliable), a monitor screen for presenting stimuli, and microphones or keyboards for recording reactions.

Artificial Environments

Although we sometimes get the impression that psychology is only about humans, animals have always been part of the picture. As animals

Figure 9–7.   Skinner boxes.

are not subjects interested in focusing their attention on the parameters important for research, one has to build artificial, totally controlled environments that permit the directing of their attentional processes. Its most famous, but of course not its only, research instrument is the Skinner box, originally named the *experimental* or the *problem box* (see Fig. 9–7) (Skinner, 1938, p. 48f), also known as an *operant conditioning chamber*.

These cages draw to our attention the fact that occasionally it is important not to simply add individual instruments to the surroundings of the being we are exploring but to arrange the entire environment such that it supports the demands of the study. Such total instruments may be advisable in studying certain questions of human psychology as well. A celebrated example is the anechoic chamber, *camera silens*.

Psychological Tests, Inventories, Questionnaires, Rating Scales, Inventories, Standardized Interviews, Observation Systems, and So On

There is yet another group of psychological instruments that we should not overlook. Up to this point, we have been concerned mainly with questions of general psychology. Throughout the 20th century, however, perspectives in differential psychology led to the development of a number of instruments of a very special kind: psychological tests. They are used in psychological research and, certainly to an even larger degree, in psychological practice. To some, it may seem unusual to think of tests as instruments, but it has become such a common designation that *Instruments of Science* (Bud & Warner, 1998) includes articles on intelligence tests (Sokal, 1998) and vocational aptitude tests (Gundlach, 1998).

Figure 9–8.   Intelligence tests.

Figure 9–9.   Berlin Tram aptitude test.

Psychological tests are methodically prepared, standardized situations in which a person shows behavior that is considered exemplary of a larger amount of behavior, of an aptitude, or of a personality characteristic, and that is used to draw conclusions about future behavior in other situations. Tests measure the degree to which an individual exhibits a certain attribute. *Measuring* in this case means finding where this degree and thus this individual fit into the distribution of that attribute across a defined population.

Psychological tests are definitely measuring instruments, and in order to be classified rightly as such, they must meet certain quality standards of objectivity, reliability, and validity (see chap. 10, this volume, Strack & Schwarz, 2007). Their sensitivity is also a matter of investigation.

An enormous number of test procedures have been developed. One pragmatic classification method distinguished tests performed with pencil and paper from those involving behavior samples in other situations. This classification became obsolete with the advent of the PC and the development of computer-aided diagnostics.

One example of studying behavior in complex artificial situations and environments is the aptitude testing procedure (see Fig. 9–9), developed in 1919 for the Berlin Streetcar Society to find suitable candidates for the job of conductor (Tramm, 1919). The similarity to the Skinner box is scarcely accidental.

Psychological tests are much less material than telescopes, microscopes, and air pumps. They may involve materials such as paper, metal, wood—and plenty of it, as Figure 9–8 shows—but that is not essential to them, as computer-aided diagnostics demonstrate. The essential part of the test is not the material of which it is made but the rule that governs the chain of events it generates and the way reactions or spontaneous actions get recorded, independent of how that rule is stored and transmitted. This is also true of other types of psychological instruments that we must also mention, namely, inventories, questionnaires, rating scales, inventories, standardized interviews, observation systems, and so on. These types of *assessment tools* have been designed in such great numbers that I must refer the reader to available literature for more information (Groth-Marnath, 2003; Newmark, 1996).

These tools, too, are not primarily material objects but rather rules for generating defined chains of events and measuring the reactions to those events. Incidentally, today most professional psychologists first think of this variety of tools when they hear the term "psychological instrument." They constitute a set of instruments that undoubtedly are implements of psychology, even if similar tools are used in neighboring disciplines, such as sociology and education. Certainly, psychological insights were used in developing them. They correspond fairly well to our definition D$_{PSKS}$, in contrast to the chronoscope, which only matches definition D$_{PS}$.

Instruments Incorporating Psychological Knowledge Unrelated to Purposes of Psychological Research, Teaching, or Practice

We need at least one distinct instance of a psychological instrument that fits the definition D$_{KS}$ minus D$_{PS}$ where psychological knowledge is adapted and used for a specific purpose that is not in itself psychological research, teaching, or practice. There are many to be found as products of applied psychology.

Our example is the red and orange retroreflecting rear marking plates (see Fig. 9–10) developed by Erke (1977) and described by Rogers (1984). These plates can be seen at the rear end of all U.S. Army vehicles, of Bundeswehr motortrucks, of all Australian trucks, and in some other places. They became internationally visible during the 2003 invasion of Iraq when embedded U.S. television often showed vehicles advancing head on against the enemy. The plates have a purpose, but it is not psychological in the sense that a scientific aim, be it research or practice, is contemplated. Their purpose is psychical or, to avert this equivocal word, perceptual and behavioral, namely, to reduce the main risk of driving in convoys: rear-end collisions. The plates resulted from sophis-

Figure 9–10.   Retroreflecting rear marking plates.

ticated experiments on distance perception and sensitivity for distance alteration cues, and they incorporate what Baird (2004) called "thing knowledge," in this case, psychological thing knowledge. Our present-day man-made environment is full of such products of applied psychological research, and it is deliberate that they usually are not recognized as such.

AN IMPROVED DEFINITION OF THE CONCEPT
OF *PSYCHOLOGICAL INSTRUMENT*

This concludes my attempt to induce in the reader the inductive emergence of an intuitive concept of *psychological instrument*. Our journey consisted of two phases. First, I tried out various abstract definitions of *psychological instrument*, second, I surveyed individual specimens from the class of psychological instruments. I hope that the results of two phases elucidate and lend support to each other.

We started with the assumption that the attributes *physical* or *psychological* characterize the context, not the individual instrument, that an instrument is psychological by the context in which it appears, not by its nature.

We also learned that it may not be helpful for understanding the historical roles of instruments in psychological research to use the word "psychological" in a way that confines us to the discipline. Here, I prefer to use it as denoting the field of scientific research and practice.

On the way, we saw that the rise of scientific instruments in modern science played a key role in the development of modern psychology as an area of scientific research and practice.

Did the intuitive concepts developed inductively provide us with generalizations that help us define the character of psychological instruments more closely than has been possible so far with abstract definitions?

We have learned a lesson not to be found in the literature on scientific instruments, to my knowledge. Remember that the objects of psychological research are processes. We can then say that the purpose of psychological instruments is to reliably and repeatedly elicit interesting processes under controlled circumstances and to carefully record their spatial, temporal, and other characteristics. We can distinguish three groups of such processes: (a) those happening in the being's surroundings; (b) those occurring within the being; and (c) finally, those that the being brings about. We can also use the terms—common in psychology—of *stimulus, reaction*, and *spontaneous vegetative and motor impulses*.

This identification of the general purpose of psychological instruments corresponds to definition Dps. This means that even simple material objects such as apothecary weights can be considered psychological instruments, because they are used to generate specific processes. The production of the processes in question must be defined by procedural rules, and these processes are only contingently related to the weights as there are other ways of producing just those processes. In other contexts we do not mean material objects, but the rules themselves when we say "instruments." Psychological tests are a prominent example here, and usually Dpsks as subset of Dps is appropriate for those cases. Dks finally encompasses all the results of psychological research that are used to influence experience and conduct of behavior, and they might be process-inducing material things or procedural rules.

If we substitute the general concept of *information* for *procedural rules*, our concept of *psychological instrument* begins to oscillate back and forth between the categories of material object and information (There is no room to consider Wittgenstein here; see Hunter, 1990). Information must take on some material form, but often a great variety of forms can serve the same purpose. An intelligence test or a personality questionnaire may materialize on paper, but they can just as well be on an electronic file or carved in stone.

Matter without information may look like an instrument, but cannot be instrumental. Some of the objects in the collections at the Institute for the History of Psychology at the University of Passau emphasize precisely that point; although they stem from stocks of old psychological research institutions, today we can no longer determine what purpose they served because the pertinent rules of application are lost. Thus, the lesson is on the ontological status of an instrument (Gundlach, 2006), namely, that it is a combination of material and information that makes an instrument, whether it is a psychological instrument or not. Learned by studying psychological instruments, this is a lesson for research of scientific instruments in general, which often leaves the deceptive impression that the material object should be decisive for how we define instruments.

We may therefore venture a general definition, DG, of a psychological instrument, the union of Dps and Dks, provided with a sharper ontological specification:

DG — A psychological instrument is an association of some material object and a process-generating rule, or a somehow materialized procedural rule, which for psychological research, teaching, or practice, represents or adapts a part of the rational knowledge of a particular society at a particular time, that knowledge possibly but not necessarily being psychological.

Again, we should keep in mind that we are dealing with a fuzzy set. Future reflection might help reduce the fuzziness.

HOW PSYCHOLOGICAL INSTRUMENTS CREATED THE DISCIPLINE OF PSYCHOLOGY

In closing, a few remarks are in order about the role of instruments in the institutionalization of psychology as a discipline. As we have seen, instruments for psychological research arose in varied contexts during the modern era, for example, in investigations of sensory functions or the functioning of the nervous system; but a significant proportion of this research took place without any explicit connection with the academic field called psychology. Indeed, during the first two thirds of the 19th century, at least in German-speaking lands, psychology was institutionalized in a context in which research using instruments played almost no role at all, that is, as part of the newly reorganized Philosophical Faculty, the primary task of which was to train elite secondary school (gymnasium) teachers. Because university policymakers in the ministries of the German states understood that such teachers should not only have a good grasp of their subject matter but also understand something about how to deal with young people, they introduced pedagogy as a required examination subject, combined it with psychology, because this field had the reputation of being foundational for pedagogy, pasted all of this into philosophy, and created combined chairs of philosophy, psychology, and pedagogy (for further discussion, see Gundlach, 2004). One result of this was a large amount of paper productivity for the psychology of the 19th century—theoretical works and textbooks of variable depth and quality, but little or no empirical, let alone experimental or apparatus-driven, research.

All this changed with the founding of the first psychological laboratory in a Philosophical Faculty by Wilhelm Wundt in the 1870s. Part of the context of this development was the relocating of the study of sensory phenomena out of physics early in the 19th century. This topic was taken up by physiology, which transformed itself in the same period into an experimental discipline and received its own laboratories in the process (see the relevant chapters in Coleman & Holmes, 1988). Wundt's laboratory was a by-product of this transformed physiology, founded by a physiologist who was frustrated in his own efforts to establish himself in that discipline and had to move from the medical to the Philosophical Faculty. His example was then followed within that part of philosophy that had dedicated itself to psychological questions.

Chairs of philosophy with attached psychological laboratories were suddenly not available for most philosophers, and that caused unhappiness. As one of the leading neo-Kantian philosophers, Wilhelm Windelband, remarked in a lecture in Frankfurt am Main in 1908:

> For a time in Germany it was almost so, that one had already proven himself capable of ascending a philosophical chair when he had learned to type methodically on electrical keys and could show statistically in long experimental series carefully ordered in tables that something occurs to some people more slowly than it does to others. That was not a very pleasant page in the history of German philosophy. (Windelband 1909, p. 92)

In 1912, the patience of these philosophers clearly came to an end. On the initiative of the leading neo-Kantians, more than 100 teachers of philosophy at German higher education institutions signed a declaration calling for the creation of separate chairs for experimental psychology and demanding that chairs of philosophy no longer by awarded to scholars in that field. The petition was published in all of the philosophical journals and sent to the relevant education ministries in all of the German states (for further discussion, see Ash, 1995, chap. 3, and the literature cited there).

Of course, "experimental psychology" meant psychological research conducted with apparatus in laboratories, the techniques of which had been learned by only a minority of academic philosophers. The opponents of this collective exclusionary action—not all of whom were experimenting psychologists—knew well that the pleasant-sounding call for new chairs in experimental psychology was unlikely to be heard and that the demand for the return of professorships from experimental psychology to "pure" philosophy was likely to inhibit the development of psychology. In fact, the philosophers' petition had little effect at all at the time, in part because state officials responsible for new positions remained unpersuaded that psychology had any clear link to professional or civil service training other than the one already established with the training of Gymnasium teachers in the 19th century. The result was that for decades afterward experimental psychologists in Germany generally continued to compete for chairs in philosophy (Ash, 2003, p. 257).

As far as the content of the science is concerned, it can be said that the emergence of a research field in which laboratories filled with instruments took on a central role had a significant negative impact on all fields of psychology that did not then use experimental methods, such as social psychology (Ash, 2003, p. 261). New groups arose with new research norms and new rules for inclusion and exclusion; competing groups were kept out. Danger from without only strengthens group cohesion; as a result, the philosophers' protest narrowed the research agenda of experimental psychology still further. One result was that the number of psychologists from the Medical Faculty in the Society for Experimental Psychology (later renamed the German Society for Psychology) decreased. It was from the new social group of academic teachers and researchers in the field of psychology located in the Philosophical Faculty that the nonuniversity profession of practical or applied psychology arose during and after the first world war (Gundlach, 2004).

In this field, too, it was clear from the outset that one of the decisive criteria of inclusion in the new social group of applied psychologists was the ability to work with instruments and apparatus. This was true everywhere, but one important difference between developments in Germany and the United States should be noted: Whereas in Germany, apparatus from academic laboratories was imported into practical contexts at considerable, perhaps exaggerated, effort and expense, and the chronoscope acquired emblematic character in the field (Gundlach, 1996), in the United States another sort of instrument, the paper test, became the leading symbol of the new profession.

Instruments thus became catalysts for the emergence of the discipline now called psychology in two steps: first through the appearance of a new community of scientists doing research in experimental psychology and then in the emergence of the new profession of applied psychologists outside the universities, the training for which was provided by the university psychologists.

ACKNOWLEDGMENTS

Translated by Cynthia Klohr and Mitchell Ash, with editorial revisions by the author and volume editors.

REFERENCES

Ash, M. G. (1995). *Gestalt psychology in German culture 1890–1967: Holism and the quest for objectivity*. New York: Cambridge University Press.

Ash, M. G. (2003). Psychology. In D. Ross & T. Porter (Eds.), *Cambridge history of science: Vol. 7. The modern social sciences* (pp. 251–274). New York: Cambridge University Press.

Baird, D. (2004). *Thing knowledge: A philosophy of scientific instruments*. Berkeley: University of California Press.

Bertini, S. (1989). Instruments of the Florentine psychology laboratory between 1800 and 1900. In C. Blondel, F. Parot, A. Turner, & M. Williams (Eds.), *Studies in the history of scientific instruments: Papers presented at the 7th Symposium of the Scientific Instruments Commission* (pp. 265–270). London and Paris: Roger Turner Books and Centre de Recherche en Histoire des Sciences et des Techniques de la Cité des Sciences et de l'Industrie.

Bissky, Z. (1925). Die Diagnoskopie Z. [The diagnoscopy Z. Bissky]. Bissky. In Bios-Institut für praktische Menschenkunde (Ed.), *Die Diagnoskopie Z. Bissky*.

Eine neue Methode zur medizinischen, psychologischen und forensischen Diagnostik [The diagnoscopy Z. Bissky. A new method for medical, psychological and forensic diagnostics.] (pp. 15–34, 41–47). Karlsruhe, Germany: Bios-Institut für praktische Menschenkunde.

Brenni, P. (1989). The illustrated catalogues of scientific instrument makers. In C. Blondel, F. Parot, A. Turner, & M. Williams (Eds.), *Studies in the history of scientific instruments: Papers presented at the 7th Symposium of the Scientific Instruments Commission* (pp. 169–178). London and Paris: Roger Turner Books and Centre de Recherche en Histoire des Sciences et des Techniques de la Cité des Sciences et de l'Industrie.

Brenni, P. (1998). Tuning fork. In R. Bud & D. J. Warner (Eds.), *Instruments of science: An historical encyclopedia* (pp. 635–637). New York: Garland.

Bud, R., & Warner, D. J. (Eds.). (1998). *Instruments of science: An historical encyclopedia*. New York: Garland.

Bud, R., Warner, D. J., & Johnston, S. (1998). Introduction. In R. Bud & D. J. Warner (Eds.), *Instruments of science: An historical encyclopedia* (pp. ix–xi). New York: Garland.

Coleman, W., & Holmes, F. L. (Eds.). (1988). *The investigative enterprise: Experimental physiology in nineteenth-century medicine*. Berkeley: University of California Press.

Davis, A. B., & Dreyfuss, M. S. (1986). *The finest instruments ever made: A bibliography of medical, dental, optical, and pharmaceutical company trade literature 1700–1939*. Arlington, MA: Medical History Publishing Associates I.

Draaisma, D. (Ed.). (1992). *Een laboratorium voor de ziel: Gerard Heymans en het begin van de experimentele psychologie.* [A laboratory for the soul: Gerard Heymans and the beginning of experimental psychology]. Groningen, Germany: Historische Uitgeverij/Universiteitsmuseum.

Erke, H. (1977). Ein Konzept zur zusätzlichen Sicherung von LKW-Hecks. [A new concept for the additional securing of tail-ends of trucks]. Braunschweig, Germany: Technische Universität.

Fechner, G. T. (1860). *Elemente der Psychophysik* [Elements of Psychophysics] (2 Vols.). Leipzig: Breitkopf und Härtel.

Fechner, G. T. (1966). *Elements of Psychophysics* (Transl. by H. E. Adler) (Vol. 1). New York, NY: Holt, Rinehart and Winston.

Funch, B. S. (1986). *Alfred Lehmanns psykofysiske laboratorium 1996–1921.* [Alfred Lehmann's psychophysical laboratory 1996-1921]. Copenhagen, Denmark: Psykologisk Laboratorium.

Giese, F. (1926). Elektrodiagnostik des Charakters. [Electrodiagnostics of personality traits]. In K. Bühler (Ed.), *Bericht über den IX. Kongress für experimentelle Psychologie in München vom 21–25.* April 1925 [Report on the ninth Congress for experimental psychology in Munich on 21st–25th April 1925]. (pp. 162–164). Jena, Germany: Gustav Fischer.

Gori-Savellini, S. (1986). La misura del tempo nel laboratorio di psicologia sperimentale [Time measurement in the laboratory of experimental psychology]. In G. Barsanti, S. Gori-Savellini, P. Guarnieri, & C. Pogliano, (Eds.), *Misura d'uomo. Strumenti, teorie e pratiche dell'antropometria e della psicologia sperimentale tra '800 e '900* [Measurement of man: Instruments, theories and

222 GUNDLACH

practices in anthropometry and experimental psychology in the 19th and 20th
century] (pp. 85–118). Florence, Italy: Istituto e Museo di Storia della Scienza.
Groth-Marnath, G. (2003). *Handbook of psychological assessment* (4th ed.). New
York: Wiley.
Gundlach, H. (1986). *Inventarium der älteren Experimentalapparate im Psychologischen Institut Heidelberg* (2nd ed.). [Inventory of the older experimental instruments in the Psychological Institute Heidelberg]. Heidelberg, Germany: Psychologisches Institut der Universität Heidelberg.
Gundlach, H. (1996). The Hipp chronoscope as totem pole and the formation of a new tribe—Applied psychology, psychotechnics and rationality. *Teorie & Modelli, 1,* 65–85.
Gundlach, H. (1997). Sinne, Apparate und Erkenntnis—Gibt es besondere Gründe, weshalb die neue Psychologie apparativ wurde? [Senses, instruments and knowledge-are there specific reasons for the new psychology to apply research instruments]. In D. Albert & H. Gundlach (Eds.), *Apparative Psychologie: Geschichtliche Entwicklung und gegenwärtige Bedeutung* [Instrumental psychology: Historical development and present significance] (pp. 35–50). Lengerich, Germany: Pabst Science.
Gundlach, H. (1998). Vocational aptitude tests (psychotechniques). In R. Bud & D. J. Warner (Eds.), *Instruments of science. An historical encyclopedia* (pp. 648–650). New York: Garland.
Gundlach, H. (2004). Reine Psychologie, Angewandte Psychologie und die Institutionalisierung der Psychologie [Pure psychology, applied psychology, and the institutionalization of psychology]. *Zeitschrift für Psychologie, 212,* 183–199.
Gundlach, H. (2006). Was ist ein psychologisches Instrument? [What is a psychological instrument?] In Berlin- Brandenburgische Akademie der Wissenschaften (Ed.), *Berichte und Abhandlungen, 11.*
Harteveld, M. A. (1989). *Catalogus van historische psychologische apparaten in Nederland. Een registratie van historische psychologische apparatuur aanwezig bij universiteiten, musea, bedrijven en instellingen.* [Catalogue of historical psychological apparatus in the Netherlands. A register of historical psychological apparatus in universities, museums, corporations and institutions]. Groningen, Germany: Werkgroep historische materialien psychologie.
Helmholtz, H. (1863). *Die Lehre von den Tonempfindungen als physiologische Grundlage für die Theorie der Musik.* [The sensations of tone as a physiological basis for the theory of music]. Braunschweig, Germany: Friedrich Vieweg und Sohn.
Helmholtz, H. (1867). *Handbuch der physiologischen Optik.* [Handbook of physiological optics]. Leipzig, Germany: Leopold Voss.
Hoskovec, J., & Stikar, J. (1984). Historické pristroje v experimentální a pracovní psychologii. [Historical experimental apparatus of psychology in Prague]. *Psychologie v ekonomické praxi, 19,* 63–70.
Huber, H. P., Dorfer, A. J., & Hohenester, A. (1994). *Das erste "Experimental psychologische Labor" in Österreich—die Anfänge der apparativen Psychologie."* [The first laboratory for experimental psychology in Austria-the beginning of apparative psychology]. Graz, Austria: No publisher.
Hunter, J. F. M. (1990). *Wittengenstein on words as instruments. Lessons in philosophical psychology.* Edinburgh, Scotland: Edinburgh University Press.

Kostic, A., & Todorovic, D. (1997). *Sense, mind and measure: Collection of old scientific instruments from the Laboratory for Experimental Psychology, University of Belgrade.* Belgrade, Yugoslavia: Museum of Science and Technology.

Lauber, B., & Bründler, P. (1981). *Geraete und Apparate aus den Anfaengen der experimentellen Psychologie.* [Instruments and apparatus from the beginnings of experimental psychology]. Zürich, Switzerland: Psychologisches Institut der Universität Zürich.

Locke, J. (1975). *An essay on human understanding* (P. H. Nidditch, Ed.). Oxford, England: Clarendon. (Original work published 1690)

Marbe, K. (1894). Vorrichtung zur successiven Variirung der Sectoren rotirender Scheiben und zur Ablesung der Sectorenverhältnisse während der Rotation [Device for the successive variation of the sectors of rotating discs and for the reading of the proportions of the sectors during rotation]. *Centralblatt für Physiologie, 7,* 811–813.

Muncke, G. W. (1827). Farbenspindel. In H. W. Brandes, L. Gmelin, J. C. Horner, G. W. Muncke, & C. H. Pfaff (Eds.), *Johann Samuel Traugott Gehler's Physikalisches Wörterbuch, neu bearbeitet* [Johann Samuel Traugott Gehler's dictionary of physics] (Vol. 4, 1; pp. 136–141). Leipzig, Germany: Schwickert.

Newmark, C. S. (Ed.). (1996). *Major psychological assessment instruments* (2nd ed.). Boston: Allyn & Bacon.

Pauli, R. (1930). Die Enge des Bewusstseins und ihre experimentelle Untersuchung [Narrowness of consciousness and its experimental investigation]. *Archiv für die gesamte Psychologie, 74,* 201–257.

Pecjak, V. (2002). *Vodic po muzejski zbirki oddelka za psihologijo.* [Guide to the museum collection of the psychology department]. Ljubljana, Slovenia: Filozofska fakulteta. Oddelek za psihologijo.

Rogers, W. C. (1984). *Retroreflectorization of the U.S. Army's line haul carrier in Germany.* Proceedings of at the 28th annual conference of the American Association for Automotive Medicine. Arlington Heigts, IL: American Association for Automotive Medicine.

Schmidgen, H. (2005). Physics, ballistics, and psychology: A history of the chronoscope in/as context. *History of Psychology, 8,* 46–78.

Skinner, B. F. (1938). *The behavior of organisms: An experimental analysis.* New York: Appleton-Century.

Sokal, M. M. (1998). Intelligence test. In R. Bud & D. J. Warner (Eds.), *Instruments of science: An historical encyclopedia* (pp. 336–339). New York: Garland.

Sommer, R. (1928). Nachprüfung der elektrodiagnostischen Methoden von Dr. Rahner und Dr. Bisski [Examination of the electrodiagnostic methods of Dr. Rahner and Dr. Bisski]. In E. Becher (Ed.), *Bericht über den X. Kongress für experimentelle Psychologie in Bonn vom 20–23, April 1927* [Report on the X congress on experimental psychology in Bonn, 20-23 April, 1927] (pp. 167–169). Jena, Germany: Gustav Fischer.

Stern, L. W. (1897). Demonstration eines Apparates zur continuirlichen und gleichmässigen Veränderung der Tonhöhe [Demonstration of an instrument for the continual and uniform variation of pitch]. *Verhandlungen der Physikalischen Gesellschaft zu Berlin im Jahre 1897, 16,* 42–48.

Stern, L. W. (1902). Der Tonvariator [The tone variator]. *Zeitschrift für Psychologie und Physiologie der Sinnesorgane, 30,* 422–432.

Strack, F., & Schwarz, N. (2007). Asking questions: Measurement in the social sciences. In M. G. Ash & T. Sturm (Eds.), *Psychology's territories: Historical and contemporary perspectives from different disciplines.* Mahwah, NJ: Lawrence Erlbaum Associates.

Sturm, T., & Ash, M. G. (2005). Roles of instruments in psychological research. *History of Psychology, 8,* 3–34.

Terenna, G., & Vannozzi, F. (1998). *La collezione degli strumenti di psicologia.* Siena: Nuova Immagine Editrice.

Titchener, E. B. (1901). *Experimental psychology: A manual of laboratory practice* (Vols. I/II). New York: Macmillan.

Titchener, E. B. (1905). *Experimental psychology: A manual of laboratory practice* (Vols. I/II). New York: Macmillan.

Tramm, K. A. (1919). Die Auswahl und Ausbildung des Fahrpersonals auf psychotechnischer Grundlage [The selection and training of driving personell on a psychotechnical basis]. *Verkehrstechnik, 50,* 25–28.

Traxel, W. (1995). Richard Pauli (1886–1951). Ein Klassiker der Experimentellen Psychologie seiner Zeit [Richard Pauli (1886–1951). A classical experimental psychologist in his time]. In *Geschichte für die Gegenwart II. Vorträge und Aufsätze zur Psychologiegeschichte* [History for the present II. Talks and papers on the history of psychology] (pp. 52–86). Passau, Germany: Passavia Universitätsverlag.

Turner, A. J. (1993). Interpreting the history of scientific instruments. In R. G. W. Anderson, J. A. Bennett, & W. F. Ryan (Eds.), *Making instruments count: Essays on historical scientific instruments presented to Gerard L'Estrange Turner* (pp. 17–26). Aldershot, England: Variorum.

Turtle, A. M. (1981, May). The psychology museum at the University of Sydney. *D.C.P. Bulletin,* 32–37.

Van Helden, A., & Hankins, T. L. (1994). Introduction: Instruments in the history of science. In A. Van Helden & T. L. Hankins (Eds.), *Instruments* (pp. 1–6). Chicago: University of Chicago Press.

Walter, F. K. (1927). Über die Elektrodiagnose seelischer Eigenschaften (»Diagnoskopie«) nach Bissky. Eine kritische Besprechung [On the electrodiagnosis of mental properties ("Diagnoscopy") according to Bissky. A critical review]. *Jahrbuch der Charakterologie, 4,* 299–324.

Warner, D. (1990). Essay review: What is a scientific instrument, when did it become one, and why? *British Journal for the History of Science, 23,* 83–93.

Windelband, W. (1909). *Die Philosophie im deutschen Geistesleben des neunzehnten Jahrhunderts: Fünf Vorlesungen.* [Philosophy in German intellectual life of the nineteenth century. Five lectures]. Tübingen, Germany: Mohr.

Wundt, W. (1893). Notiz über psychologische Apparate [Note on psychological instruments]. *Philosophische Studien, 8,* 655–656.

Zimmermann, E. (1897). *Liste XV. Psychologische und physiologische Apparate.* [Psychological and physiological apparatus]. Leipzig, Germany: No publisher.

10

Asking Questions: Measurement in the Social Sciences

Fritz Strack
University of Würzburg, Germany

Norbert Schwarz
University of Michigan

P sychology is an empirical science. This implies that its validity is rooted in reality, and that reality must have a chance to influence our conceptualizations (e.g., Rosenthal & Rosnow, 1984). In the natural sciences, the link between theory and reality is systematic observation. Often, however, manifestations of reality need to be translated in order to be perceived by our senses. Moreover, to communicate what is perceived, we need a shared reference point, at best, a meter. In this case, measurement affords objectivity in that it does not hinge on subjective experience of the observer (e.g., Wilson, 1992).

The diagnosticity of a datum, however, depends not only on reality but also on the theory on which the measurement is based. If we measure the acidity of a fluid by scaling the color of a litmus paper on a red–blue dimension, the recorded color reflects the acidity to the extent that the theory linking the acidity of the fluid to the color of the litmus paper is correct (e.g., Sydenham & Thorn, 1996).

Observation and measurement have their place in the social sciences, where the reality consists of people and their behavior, as well (see Rosenthal & Rosnow, 1984). Some features of persons can be directly perceived (e.g., gender, mother tongue, race, age), whereas other characteristics are not directly observable, such as traits, attitudes, or motives. For them, a special instrument of measurement is needed to assign numbers to objects.

However, the social sciences seem to have an alternative way of accessing human characteristics: asking questions. Because people are capable of answering questions, their responses serve as data of measurement (Sudman & Bradburn, 1982). As for the natural sciences, however, the validity of the theories that mediate between response and the target of measurement determines the diagnosticity of the assessment. Interestingly, the social sciences have more than one theory linking responses to underlying characteristics. Although these theories are not always explicitly stated, they share a similar terminology but reflect entirely different substantive orientations.

MEASUREMENT BY ASKING QUESTIONS

1. Psychometrics: The Behaviorist Model

One of the most widespread models of measurement-by-asking-questions is that of psychometric testing. It is based on the behaviorist assumption that the answer to a question is simply a response elicited by a stimulus, in this case, the question (for a more complete account of psychometric test theory, see Lord & Novick, 1974). The response consists of two components: (a) a *true-value* component and (b) an *error* component. Psychometric test theory further assumes that the error is randomly determined and that its dispersion around the true value will approximate a normal distribution with increasing number of questions. Because the error (i.e., the deviation from the true value that is associated with one particular question) is considered to be random, psychometricians do not focus on the content or the wording of a particular question. Multiple measurement, many questions tapping the same phenomenon, is the route on which the psychometrician approaches the true value. The validity hinges not on one single question but solely on the covariations of the responses with other behaviors, that is, response behaviors under standardized conditions (for a related discussion, see Abelson, 1984).

Moreover, the respondents do not even have to know their "true value." For example, if a psychometrician wants to find out whether a respondent is extraverted or a type A person, it is not necessary that the respondent has any idea what this concept refers to or where he or she would be located on that dimension. Of interest is primarily the relationship between the responses, usually in form of a summary score, and a criterion variable. Accordingly, psychometricians show little interest in how a question is understood and how an answer is generated.

2. Survey Research: The Introspective Model

A rather different metatheory underlies standardized questioning in survey situations. Although survey researchers use a similar terminology (e.g., the terms *true value* and *error*; see Lessler, 1984), their approach to measurement is quite different. On the surface, this is reflected in the fact that, unlike psychometricians, survey researchers often use one single question to address a particular phenomenon and do care extensively about the content of the question as well as its wording and comprehension (e.g., Belson, 1981; Payne, 1951; Schuman & Presser, 1981; Sudman & Bradburn, 1982). Still, as for psychometricians, it is their goal to capture respondents true values. How is that possible without multiple measurements? What is the rationale behind this logic?

Table 10–1 summarizes the classic meta-theory of survey responding, which dominated survey research through the 1980s. (The characterization of the metatheory of survey responding is based on various parts of the handbook edited by Turner & Martin [1984].) In subsequent years, this metatheory changed in ways we address in the next section. In its classic version, the metatheory of survey responding has four components that refer to features of the respondent, to a psychological process that guarantees validity, and to a possible source of error. We discuss each of them in turn.

The starting point is the assumption that respondents possess certain features. These features are either *objective*, such as a specific age and gender, or *subjective*, such as a certain attitude and belief. The only difference between the two classes is the existence of external criteria for the objective features and the absence of external criteria for the subjective ones. Thus, the true value of respondents age can be checked by inspecting their birth certificates, whereas the true value of a specific attitude cannot be examined by such means.

Such objective validation, however, is not a necessary criterion for survey measurement because its internal validity is guaranteed by the method of accessing the true value. It is assumed that independent of whether external criteria exist (i.e., whether the features are objective or subjective), respondents have immediate access to their true value. Quite succinctly, Martin (1984) summarized this position as follows:

TABLE 10–1
The Introspection Theory of Standardized Question Situations

Assumption

Features of respondent

(a) Objective (age, gender, income …)—objective criterion

(b) Subjective (beliefs, attitudes, evaluations …)—*no* objective criterion

Claim

Immediate access to true value of features

Method of access

Introspection

Source of error

Respondents lie if goal of reporting true value is less desirable than other goals (e.g., making a good impression)

"There is a fundamental assumption in survey research that respondents can give valid reports of their own subjective states" (p. 298). Just as respondents can report their true age, they can describe their true attitude with candor and accuracy (Campbell, 1981, p. 23).

What is the psychological mechanism that guarantees such a privileged, immediate, and unbiased access to one's own subjective features? It is the method of introspection. (For a recent general discussion of the literature on introspection, see Lyons, 1986; for a more empirically oriented treatment of the topic, see Nisbett & Wilson, 1977, and Ericsson & Simon, 1980.) As Martin (1984) put it: "It might be assumed … that respondents base their report on introspective self-examination" (p. 298) Given the assumption that respondents *can* access the true values of their subjective features, errors are possible in this conceptualization only if respondents do not *want* to communicate their true values if they do not tell the truth (although they know it); that is, if they lie. Thus, if the respondents' *competence* is ruled out as a determinant of error, then it is their *motivation* that must be held responsible for deviations from the truth. Almost exclusively, the influence that affects respondents' motivation not to communicate their true values is assumed to be *social desirability*—that is, the desire to make a positive impression, or at least to avoid a negative one (see DeMaio, 1984).

In this metatheory, the key issue in the collaboration of respondent and researcher is a motivational one: Does the respondent comply with what the questioner wants her to do; that is, does she tell the truth? Although this is an important insight, this introspective theory limits theorizing in survey methodology to addressing only one aspect of collaboration. This shortcoming makes it difficult for the metatheory of survey research to explain a substantial body of findings bearing on the impact of question wording and question context (e.g., Schuman & Presser, 1981). Specifically, survey researchers found that rather innocuous variations, such as changes in the order in which questions are asked, may have enormous effects on respondents answers (for research examples, see Belson, 1981; Payne, 1951; Schuman & Presser, 1981; Schwarz & Sudman, 1992). In explaining these so-called *response effects*, survey methodologists realized the limits of their metatheory; it proved rather implausible to invoke changes in respondents' motivation to collaborate and tell the truth as the major variable underlying the impact of question wording and question context (see Hippler & Schwarz, 1987; Strack & Martin, 1987).

3. Measurement as Cooperative Communication

Given these limitations, an alternative conceptual framework for response processes seemed warranted and has found increasing acceptance in survey research. This conceptualization recognizes that asking and answering questions is a type of conversation and has properties of a natural discourse in which two (or more) people engage in a purposeful verbal interaction. As Paul Grice (1975), a philosopher of language, put it: "Our talk exchanges do not normally consist of a succession of disconnected remarks, and would not be rational if they did. They are … cooperative efforts; and each participant recognizes in them … a common purpose or set of purposes, or at least a mutually accepted direction" (p. 45).

The conversational nature of measurement-by-asking-questions tends to be overlooked because contributions are typically restrained by the standardized format in which questions are asked and answers are to be provided (Schwarz, 1994, 1996; Strack, 1994; Strack & Schwarz, 1992; see also Clark & Schober, 1992). Examples of standardized question situations include attitude surveys (see Schwarz & Strack, 1991) and experiments in the social and psychological sciences (see Bless, Strack, & Schwarz, 1993), which share the standardization of the researcher contributions (e.g., questions, instructions) and constrain the respondent' answers to a specified format. Because of these restrictions, standardized questioning in the social sciences is often considered equivalent to standardized measurement in the natural sciences.

However, to understand response processes it is useful to recognize the conversational nature of interactions in research situations (Schwarz, 1996; Strack, 1994). As indicated before, communications in natural settings give participants a large degree of freedom to generate messages in a format of their choosing. In most situations, questioners and respondents can decide to be more or less specific, to be elliptical or redundant, or to ask for feedback about an earlier comment. This lack of restriction serves an important function in the conversation process (see Clark & Clark, 1977). Specifically, it has become apparent that to identify the intended meaning of a communication, a collaborative interaction between conversants plays a crucial role.

Quite some time ago, Krauss and Weinheimer (1964, 1966) found that in the course of an interaction, respondents became more accurate and efficient in identifying ambiguous objects that the questioner had selected if the respondent received feedback from the questioner. On the basis of these observations, Clark and his collaborators (e.g., Clark & Wilkes-Gibbs, 1986) developed a collaborative theory of reference (Schober & Clark, 1989) to explain the process of understanding in natural discourse. In this collaborative perspective, speakers and listeners give each other feedback to ensure that a communication' intended meaning is understood. The studies conducted within this perspective (Garrod & Anderson, 1987) have convincingly demonstrated that, to understand what is meant, deciphering the semantic meaning of a particular word or sentence is not sufficient. Instead, the respondent must go beyond the linguistic units to identify the intended meaning of an utterance (i.e., the questioner' communicative intention). In the endeavor, the unrestricted interaction between participants plays a crucial role.

Obviously, standardized questioning lacks this type of unconstrained exchange. Respondents typically do not receive feedback if their interpretation of a question corresponds to what the questioner had in mind. Furthermore, the questioner has no indication of whether a response that is provided in a given format is based on the intended meaning of the question. In such situations, the standardized context of questions and answers may serve as a substitute for the unrestricted feedback that occurs in natural situations. Specifically, respondents are likely to rely on contextual features to a greater degree than participants in natural settings (Bless et al., 1993).

At this point, another difference between natural discourses and standardized situations becomes apparent. In natural communications, the communicative intentions of both the questioner and the respondent are often ambiguous; that is, a person who asks a question may not necessarily request information in natural settings. Instead, questions may represent indirect speech acts (Searle, 1975, 1976) that express or imply behavioral requests (e.g., "Can you open a window?"), threats (e.g., "Do you want me to lock away your bicycle again?"), assertions (e.g., "Don't you think the play was awful?"), and other actions. Similarly, in natural discourses responses may not be intended merely to inform the questioner. However, in standardized situations respondents can (or at least should) assume that questioners want information. (Of course, in a psychological experiment, a question may be asked to influence cognitive processes; however, it is important that this intention is not recognized by the respondent; see Bless et al., 1993.) This intention can be conveyed by a direct request or a question. In turn, respondents in standardized situations most likely will try to obey this request and provide the desired information. To be sure, in specific situations, respondents may strive for alternative goals, particularly the goal to make a good impression. However, as mentioned before, this goal will be activated only under very specific circumstances. Thus, it can be assumed that respondents can recognize the questioner intention and are motivated to cooperate.

The Cooperative Principle.   Determination of the motivation to cooperate is necessary, but not sufficient, to understand response effects. One must also identify the mechanisms of cooperation once the motivation is established. The principles best known and studied as rules for communicating in natural situations are those identified by Grice (1975), whose central postulates were subsumed under a general *cooperative principle*. This principle is composed of four maxims.

A *Maxim of Quantity* requires participants in a discourse to provide the right amount of information; that is, a contribution should convey not more and not less information than is necessary to understand what is meant. A Maxim of Quality demands that the conversants tell the truth, whereas a *Maxim of Relevance* requests that contributions should relate to one another. Finally, a *Maxim of Manner* requires the contributions to be clear and without obscurity (for a more detailed discussion of the Gricean principles, see Levinson, 1983). The assumption that speakers adhere to these rules (Higgins, 1981; McCann & Higgins, 1992) is important for the listener to both infer the intended meaning of an utterance and generate a response that meets the expectations of the speaker.

However, the implementation of these rules can require additional information from the speaker. An example is the application of the Maxim of Quantity. To determine the appropriate amount of information, a respondent may ask the questioner for further specification. Thus, the question "Where do you live?" could be countered with whether the request for information refers to the country, the city, or the neighborhood. Instead of bothering the questioner, however, the respondent may infer what would be new information to the questioner and what would not. Such an inference may be based on the larger context in which the question is posed. Thus, if the information is requested by a foreign colleague, the response "lower East side" would violate the Maxim of Quantity, whereas "New York" would be appropriate. The reverse would be true if the same question were asked by a colleague at a New York university. Who asks a question and under what circumstances allows inferences about the state of knowledge and what would be new to the questioner. This *given-new contract* (Clark, 1985; Clark & Haviland, 1977), according to which participants in a discourse add information to what they assume the partner already knows, must also be realized by monitoring the course of a conversation. That is, an answer should go beyond the information that already has been provided.

Cooperation Under Natural and Standardized Conditions. In natural situations, it is the context at large that helps to interpret people's communicative intentions. For example, the question "Can you open a window?" will be interpreted as a request for information only if the respondent's pertinent capability is, in fact, questionable and the Maxim of Quantity is observed. If it is not, the respondent will take it as a request for action. Thus, a child may cooperate by answering "Yes, I can," whereas a cooperative adult may respond with "Just a second."

Although such indirect speech acts rarely occur in standardized situations, this example shows how pragmatic characteristics that are external to the question proper determine the response under natural conditions. In standardized situations, the respondent cannot expect the questioner to take his or her specific situation (e.g., his or her capability) into account. Therefore, contextual cues that help determine the communicative intention of the questioner are sought. The particular response format, the order in which questions are asked, and the wording of questions can provide these cues.

In the following paragraphs, we describe how research participants use different aspects of standardized question situations to determine the intended meaning of a question: What is the information that the researcher wants them to provide?

IMPLICATIONS FOR SOCIAL SCIENCE MEASUREMENT

The literature on response effects in survey measurement offers many examples of the pervasive influence of minor changes in question wording, format and order. Although these observations were long treated as surprising oddities, they are to be expected from a conversational perspective. Specifically, respondents bring the tacit assumptions that govern the conduct of conversation in daily life to the research situation and assume that the researchers are cooperative communicators, whose contributions to the research conversation come with a "guarantee of relevance" (Sperber & Wilson, 1986). What is often overlooked is that these contributions include apparently formal features of the research instrument, which the researcher may have chosen for reasons of technical convenience. Respondents, however, draw on these features to determine the pragmatic meaning of the question asked.

We first address the supposedly most "formal" aspect of questionnaires, namely, the nature of response alternatives. Next, we turn to issues of question wording and, finally, we consider the context in which a question is presented, including the preceding questions, introductions to a study, and the researcher affiliation.

1. Response Formats

Open Versus Closed Response Formats.   Suppose that respondents are asked in an open response format, "What have you done today?" To give a meaningful answer, respondents have to determine which activities may be of interest to the researcher. In an attempt to be informative, respondents are likely to omit activities of which the researcher is obviously aware (e.g., "gave a survey interview") or may take for granted anyway (e.g., "took a shower"), thus observing the Maxim of Quantity. If respondents were given a list of activities that included giving an interview and taking a shower, most respondents would endorse them. At the same time, however, such a list would reduce the likelihood that respondents report activities that are not represented on the list (see Schuman & Presser, 1981; Schwarz & Hippler, 1991, for a review of relevant studies). Both of these question form effects reflect that response alternatives can clarify the intended meaning of a question, in the present example by specifying the activities in which the researcher is interested. In addition, response alternatives may remind respondents of material that they may otherwise not consider.

In combination, these processes can result in pronounced and systematic differences between open and closed question formats, as a study on parental values illustrates. When asked what they consider "the most important thing for children to prepare them for life," 61.5% of the respondents picked "to think for themselves" when this alternative was offered as part of a list. Yet only 4.6% provided an answer that could be assigned to this category in an open response format (Schuman & Presser, 1981, pp. 105–107). Obviously, we would draw very different conclusions about parental values depending on the question format used.

Frequency Scales and Reference Periods. Suppose that respondents are asked how frequently they felt "really irritated" recently. To provide an informative answer, respondents have to determine what the researcher means by *really irritated*. Does this term refer to major or to minor annoyances? To identify the intended meaning of the question, they may consult the response alternatives provided by the researcher. If the response alternatives present low-frequency categories, for example, ranging from "less than once a year" to "more than once a month," they may conclude that the researcher has relatively rare events in mind. Hence, the question cannot refer to minor irritations, which are likely to occur more often, so the researcher is probably interested in more severe episodes of irritation. In line with this assumption, Schwarz, Strack, Müller, and Chassein (1988; see also Gaskell, O'Muircheartaigh, & Wright, 1994) observed that respondents who had to report the frequency of irritating experiences on a low-frequency scale assumed that the question referred to major annoyances, whereas respondents who had to give their report on a high-frequency scale assumed that the question referred to minor annoyances. Thus, respondents identified different experiences as the target of the question, depending on the frequency range of the response alternatives provided to them.

Similarly, Winkielman, Knäuper, and Schwarz (1998) observed that the length of the reference period can profoundly affect question interpretation. In their studies, respondents were either asked how frequently they had been angry "last week" or "last year." Again, they inferred that the researcher was interested in more frequent and less severe episodes of anger when the question pertained to 1 week rather than 1 year, and their examples reflected this differential question interpretation.

These findings have important implications for the interpretation of commonly observed differences in concurrent and retrospective reports of behaviors and emotions. Empirically, individuals report more intense emotions (e.g., Parkinson, Briner, Reynolds, & Totterdell, 1995; Thomas & Diener, 1990), and more severe marital disagreements (e.g., McGonagle, Kessler, & Schilling, 1992), in retrospective than in concurrent reports. Whereas findings of this type are typically attributed to the higher memorability of intense experiences, Winkielman et al.'s (1998) results suggest that discrepancies between concurrent and retrospective reports may in part be due to differential question interpretation: Concurrent reports necessarily pertain to a short reference period, with

1 day typically being the upper limit, whereas retrospective reports cover more extended periods. Hence, the concurrent and retrospective nature of the report is inherently confounded with the length of the reference period. Accordingly, participants who provide a concurrent report may infer from the short reference period used that the researcher is interested in frequent events, whereas the long reference period used under retrospective conditions may suggest an interest in infrequent events. Accordingly, respondents may deliberately report on different experiences, rendering their reports noncomparable.

On theoretical grounds, we may further expect that formal features, such as the values of a frequency scale or the length of a reference period, seem more relevant when they are unique to the question asked rather than shared by many heterogeneous questions. In the latter case, respondents may conclude that this is the format used for all questions, rendering it less informative for the intended meaning of any given one. Empirically, this is the case. In a replication of Winkielman et al.'s (1998) study, Igou, Bless, and Schwarz (2002) observed that using the same reference period for several substantively unrelated questions attenuated or eliminated its influence on respondents' interpretation of the anger question relative to a condition in which each question was associated with a unique reference period.

Numeric Values of Rating Scales. Similar considerations apply to psychologists' favorite question format, the rating scale. Suppose respondents are asked, "How successful would you say you have been in life? ," accompanied by a rating scale that ranges from *not at all successful* to *extremely successful*. To answer this question, respondents have to determine what the researcher means by *not at all successful*: Does this term refer to the absence of outstanding achievements or to the presence of explicit failures? To do so, they may draw on what is supposedly a purely formal feature of the rating scale, namely, its numeric values. Specifically, Schwarz, Knäuper, Hippler, Noelle-Neumann, and Clark (1991) presented the success-in-life question with an 11-point rating scale that ranged either from 0 (*not at all successful*) to 10 (*extremely successful*), or from –5 (*not at all successful*) to +5 (*extremely successful*). The results showed a dramatic impact of the numeric values presented to respondents. Whereas 34% of the respondents endorsed a value between 0 and 5 on the 0-to-10 scale, only 13% endorsed one of the formally equivalent values between and 0 on the –5-to-+5 scale.

Subsequent experiments indicated that this difference reflects differential interpretations of the term *not at all successful*. When this label was combined with the numeric value, respondents interpreted it to reflect the absence of outstanding achievements. However, when the same label was combined with the numeric value 5 and the scale offered 0 as the midpoint, they interpreted it to reflect the presence of explicit failures (see also Schwarz, Grayson, & Knäuper, 1998; Schwarz & Hippler, 1995). In general, a format that ranges from negative to positive numbers conveys that the researcher has a bipolar dimension in mind, where the two poles refer to the presence of opposite attributes. In contrast, a format that uses only positive numbers conveys that the researcher has unipolar dimension in mind, referring to different degrees of the same attribute.

Unfortunately, researchers are typically not aware of the informative functions of formal characteristics of their research instruments and choose them mostly on the basis of technical convenience, as the case of rating scales illustrates. (Our summary is based on a conversation with Charles Cannell, who headed the field department of the Survey Research Center at the University of Michigan during those decades.) Rensis Likert (1932) introduced rating scales with a graphic response format, shown in the first row of Table 10–2. With the introduction of punch cards this format was changed to the numeric format shown in the second row to reduce transcription errors at the data entry stage. This format, however, still required two keystrokes for each entry and was hence changed to the format shown in the third row, thus cutting data entry cost. Along the way, a clearly bipolar presentation format changed into the now-familiar unipolar one—even for questions that are intended to present a bipolar response dimension, which is now merely indicated by the verbal end anchors. Of course, these technical changes were not assumed to affect question interpretation. In light of the above findings, however, one may wonder the extent to which they contaminated time series of attitude data by confounding attitude change over time with changes in the response format.

Range of Targets. Respondents' goal of identifying the intended meaning of a question and its accompanying rating scale can also be reached in other ways. When several stimuli have to be judged along the same response scale, the range of stimuli presented may serve as a conversational cue. Assume, for example, that respondents have to rate how pricy a restaurant is. In one condition, the restaurants to be as-

TABLE 10–2
Different Formats of Rating Scales

– – –	– –	–	+	+ +	+ + +
– 3	– 2	– 1	+ 1	+ 2	+ 3
1	2	3	4	5	6

sessed include Joe' Pizza Parlor and The Golden Goose, a restaurant that has been awarded a Michelin star. In another condition, the targets are confined to restaurants that have the Michelin distinction. The first condition suggests that the questioner refers to restaurants in general; the second condition allows the inference that gourmet restaurants are the topic of discourse. As a consequence, the same target is rated as more expensive in the first case than in the second.

This prediction corresponds to explanations that construe the response scale as a flexible rubber band (Postman & Miller, 1945; Volkmann, 1951), rather than a rigid yardstick. In this view, the respondent anchors the scale so that its endpoint corresponds to the most extreme stimulus in the range. In the restaurant example, the lower anchor would be 'Joe,' and all the gourmet restaurants would be assembled at the upper end of the scale. Therefore, the latter restaurants would be rated as more expensive along the scale than they would if Joe' were not among the set of those considered. In other words, the introduction of the pizza parlor as an anchor would produce a contrast effect on ratings of the other stimuli.

Technically, the rubber-band notion does not imply an identification of the topic of discourse. It merely requires that the most extreme values be identified for use in anchoring the scale. However, this presupposes that all stimuli are simultaneously available at the time of judgment. This is not always the case; that is, the targets are often presented sequentially and have to be assessed in a consecutive manner. Thus, judges have to infer the possible range of the stimuli. Of course, such an inference can be drawn if the topic of discourse is identified. When a scale applies to attitudinal judgments, one stimulus that might be considered in construing the range of values to which the scale is relevant is one's own position (Upshaw, 1965). For example, suppose several persons attitudes toward the legalization of drugs have to be rated on a scale ranging from *liberal* to *conservative*. If the judge favors the legalization of heroin and all of the attitude statements considered are less extreme than this position, then the judge's attitude might be used to anchor the scale. Thus, a statement advocating the legalization of marijuana would be judged as more conservative than it would if the judge's attitude were moderate (i.e., within the range of alternatives considered). In other words, the judge's attitude has a contrast effect on the ratings of others' attitudes. More generally, if a respondent's perspective (Upshaw, 1965; Upshaw & Ostrom, 1984) changes as a function of one's own attitude on an issue, one's judgments of other stimuli on the relevant dimension change as well.

The fact that people include their own attitudes into the range of stimuli has consequences for communication. For example, the way a friend who is extremely conservative will be described to a third person will depend on the recipient's own political stand. That is, if the recipient is liberal, a description implying a higher degree of conservatism (e.g., very conservative) will be provided than if the recipient leans toward conservatism (e.g., rather conservative). At the expense of being inconsistent by using different categories to describe the same stimulus, respondents are more informative if they take the presumed interpretation of the receivers into account, which is determined by their stand on the issue.

Summary.   In combination, the reviewed examples highlight that respondents draw on apparently formal features of the questionnaire as a source of relevant information in determining the pragmatic meaning of the question asked. Little do they know how haphazardly those features may have been chosen, as the example of numeric values of rating scales illustrates. When respondents become aware that the feature may be of questionable relevance to the specific question at hand—for example, because it is used for several heterogeneous questions—they no longer rely on it, eliminating its otherwise observed influence. Throughout, these question form effects undermine the comparability of answers to highly similar questions, only differ only in their presumably "formal" features.

2. Question Wording

It is not surprising that the way a question is worded influences its interpretation. The semantic meaning can obviously vary as a function of the words used and thus influence responses. However, different question wordings may influence responses even under conditions in which the wordings seem semantically equivalent.

For example, semantically, to *forbid* and to *allow* are antonyms, and *not allow* seems equivalent to *forbid*. However, the proportion of survey respondents who answered "yes" when asked if an activity (e.g., smoking marijuana) should be "forbidden" was consistently lower than the proportion who answered "no" when asked if this same activity should be "allowed" (Rugg & Cantril, 1944; Schuman & Presser, 1981). This asymmetry suggested that *not forbidding* was not *allowing*. As Hippler and Schwarz (1986) demonstrated, many respondents considered the possibility that they would not actively oppose the activity but would not support it either. Those respondents answered "no" to the "allow" as well as the "forbid" form of the question, resulting in the observed asymmetry.

The *type* of article is another example of how the wording of a question can affect responses. Most prominently, consequences of the use of the definite versus indefinite article were investigated by Loftus (1975) in the context of eyewitness testimony. Participants in her studies saw a videotape of a car accident. Some were subsequently asked if they had seen "*the* broken headlight," whereas others were asked if they had seen "*a* broken headlight." This manipulation typically resulted in more affirmative responses when the definite article was used.

The explanation of this phenomenon has been primarily memorial in nature. It is assumed that the presupposition semantically implied by the use of the definite article (i.e., "there *was* a broken headlight") distorted the memory representation of the event, which in turn caused erroneous recall. Despite some dissenting opinions (Lindsay & Johnson, 1989; McCloskey & Zaragoza, 1985; Tversky & Tuchin, 1989), memory mechanisms are still widely held responsible for the phenomenon (Loftus & Hoffman, 1989). However, there is evidence that the wording of the question per se is not sufficient to produce the effect (e.g., Dodd & Bradshaw, 1980; Smith & Ellsworth, 1987). Instead, listeners draw on the information provided by the definitive article only when they can assume that the speaker is a cooperative communicator (the default assumption in psychological experiments), but not otherwise. Hence, the wording has little influence when it is introduced by a defendant lawyer, who is assumed to follow a self-serving agenda (e.g., Dodd & Bradshaw, 1980).

Moreover, Strack and Bless (1994) found that the presupposition implied by the use of the definite article was used as a basis of inference only when other strategies were not applicable. In some of their experimental conditions, participants could base their answers to the question of whether they had previously seen a certain object both on the conversationally conveyed presupposition that the object had been presented ("Did you see *the* screwdriver?" and on their own metacognitive knowledge (i.e., the belief that they *would* have remembered the particular object had it been presented). The applicability of this metacognitive strategy was manipulated by varying the salience of the items in the recognition set. The differential use of judgmental strategies was observed when participants were asked if they had seen an item that had not been presented. Then, the use of the direct versus the indirect article only increased false alarms if the object was not salient. If the object was salient, almost all participants correctly rejected the item as not seen before. These findings suggest that, in the absence of a memory trace, judgmental strategies may come into play, and judges may prefer one strategy over the other. These findings also suggest that the surface structure of a task does not fix the mental mechanisms used to solve it. Thus, a memory task may be solved by inferential strategies that are applicable in a given situation. In this perspective, leading questions influence responses not by altering what has been encoded about the target but by allowing the respondent to infer what was probably the case. If better alternatives are not available, respondents may use those cues to generate a required response.

3. Preceding Questions

In natural conversations, listeners are expected to draw on the context of an utterance in determining its meaning, and not doing so may be interpreted as a lack of attention or interest. In contrast, researchers often hope that each question is considered in isolation and deplore the emergence of context effects in question comprehension. These context effects take two forms. First, respondents may deliberately draw on the content of preceding questions to determine the meaning of subsequent ones. Second, the answers to preceding questions become part of the common ground, and respondents avoid reiterating information that they have already provided earlier, consistent with the Maxim of Quantity. We address both in turn.

Contextual Information and the Resolution of Ambiguity.   As an extreme case, consider research in which respondents are asked to report their opinion about a highly obscure, or even completely fictitious, issue, such as the Agricultural Trade Act of 1978 (e.g., Bishop, Oldendick, & Tuchfarber, 1983; Schuman & Presser, 1981). Public opinion researchers introduced such questions to explore the extent to which respondents are willing to report an opinion in the absence of any knowledge about the topic. In fact, about 30% of any representative sample do offer an opinion on fictitious issues. Yet their answers may be less meaningful than has typically been assumed.

From a conversational point of view, the sheer fact that a question about some issue is asked presupposes that this issue exists—or else asking a question about it would violate every norm of conversational conduct. However, respondents have no reason to assume that the researcher would ask a meaningless question and will hence try to make sense of it. To do so, they are likely to turn to the context of the ambiguous question, much as they would be expected to do in any other conversation. Once they have assigned a particular meaning to the issue, thus transforming the fictitious issue into a subjectively better defined one that makes sense in the context of the questionnaire, they may have no difficulty reporting a subjectively meaningful opinion. Even if they have not given the particular issue much thought, they may identify the broader set of issues to which this particular one apparently belongs, allowing them to derive a meaningful answer.

Supporting this assumption, Strack, Schwarz, and Wänke (1991, Experiment 1) observed that German university students reported different attitudes toward the introduction of a fictitious "educational contribution," depending on the nature of a preceding question. Specifically, some students were asked to estimate the average tuition fees that students have to pay at U.S. universities (in contrast to Germany, where university education is free), whereas others had to estimate the amount of money that the Swedish government pays every student as financial support. As expected, respondents inferred that the fictitious educational contribution pertained to students having to pay money when it followed the tuition question, but when it followed the financial support question they inferred that it pertained to students receiving money. Reflecting this differential interpretation, they reported a more favorable attitude toward the introduction of an educational contribution in the latter than in the former case—hardly a meaningless response.

Common Ground and Redundancy Avoidance.   Questions that were previously asked and answered provide information about the questioner's current state of knowledge. This information is important, because it allows the respondent to obey the Maxim of Quantity by making his or her answer as informative as required. This is the case if an answer adds to what the recipient already knows. However, the respondent's knowledge changes as a function of the ongoing discourse. As a consequence, the informativeness of a statement depends on communications that have preceded it in the conversation. In other words, a contribution should build on the "common ground" (Clark, 1985) that has been established between participants of the discourse. Syntactically, switching from the indirect to the direct article symbolizes that a target has become a given and allows for new information to be added. Clark and Haviland (1977) described this application of Grice's (1975) Maxim of Quantity to a natural discourse as the *given-new contract*.

The fact that the new value of a contribution is determined by one previous contributions requires participants in a discourse to keep track of what one has said before. In a natural situation, this type of monitoring occurs automatically; a conversant would normally not repeat a previous contribution unless there were reason to assume that the recipient has not understood its content. For example, suppose a person is first asked the question "How is your wife?" followed by "And how is your family?" He is unlikely to take his wife's well-being into consideration in answering the second question, because of his previous answer it would not be informative. Note that this is not the case if the questions had been asked in the reverse order.

The given-new contract should be obeyed in standardized situations when two questions overlap in their content. This is the case if a general question follows a more specific one and their contents are in a subset–superset relation or if their content intersects. In addition, the two (or more) questions must be related to each other. In natural contexts, the speaker guarantees that the rule of relation is observed. In standardized situations, however, this rule is not always obeyed. On the contrary, such a perception is actively avoided by placing related questions at different positions in a questionnaire, separating them by several filler items. Thus, a respondent may or may not see a series of questions as belonging together. More generally, a respondent application of the Maxim of Quantity depends on his or her perception of the relatedness of the items involved (Strack, 1992).

This hypothesis was tested in a study by Strack, Martin, and Schwarz (1988; cf. Tourangeau, Rasinski, & Bradburn, 1991), in which the conversational context was manipulated experimentally. Participants were given a questionnaire that included two questions whose content stood in a subset–superset relationship. The more specific question addressed respondents' happiness with their dating, whereas the more general one concerned their happiness with life as a whole. If the two questions are perceived to belong to the same context of discourse, then the given-new contract should be applied, and the respondents should avoid being redundant. In analogy to the previous example, they should not base the judgments of happiness with life in general on their happiness with dating if they have already reported their dating happiness. However, if the questions are not perceived to belong together, then answering the specific question should render the relevant content more accessible and should increase the probability that the answer to the general question is based on the content of the specific one (see Higgins, Rholes, & Jones, 1977; Srull & Wyer, 1979, 1980). Thus, correlations between the answers should be high in the specific–general order if no conversational context is established. However, under the conversational-context condition, the correlation should be reduced, because the same contents should not be communicated twice.

To establish the conversational context, the two questions were introduced with the following statement: "We are now asking two questions about your life, a) happiness with dating, b) happiness with life in general." No such introduction was used in the no-context condition. Moreover, to further avoid the perception of relatedness, the questions in the latter condition were printed on different pages of the questionnaire. The pattern of correlations corresponded to the predictions. Compared with the control conditions, in which the general question preceded the specific one, the correlation decreased when a conversational context was introduced ($r = .16$) but increased when it was not ($r = .55$).

The assumption that the decreased correlation under the latter condition was caused by an exclusion of the activated content requires a more diagnostic test. Therefore, a conceptual replication was conducted by Schwarz, Strack, and Mai (1991). German adults who had either a spouse or a partner were asked how satisfied they were with both their current relationship and their lives. Both the order of the questions and the conversational context were varied. Two new conditions were added, in which respondents were explicitly instructed either to include or exclude the redundant content of the specific question when they rated their satisfaction with their lives in general.

The previous pattern of correlation coefficients clearly was replicated; that is, the correlation between the answers decreased if the conversational context was introduced. Moreover, the correlations under conditions where respondents were explicitly instructed to include or exclude the specific content matched exactly the conditions under which the given-new contract was expected to implicitly require respondents to consider the specific information or not. Taken together, this set of findings suggests that respondents in standardized situations comply with the Gricean Maxim of Quantity when they answer questions whose content is related in a part–whole fashion.

In an extension of this logic, Strack et al. (1991) applied the same procedure to questions whose contents were semantically similar. Specifically, they asked participants how happy and satisfied they were with their lives. It was assumed that respondents who observed the given-new contract would be more likely to differentiate between the similar concepts of happiness and satisfaction than would respondents who where not concerned about avoiding redundancy. To foster the perception of relatedness, a box was drawn around the questions "Here are two questions about your life." To prevent such a perception, the two questions were presented as being part of two different questionnaires that used different scales, colors, and typefaces and were described as serving different purposes. "Happiness" was the last item of Survey 1, and "satisfaction" was the opening question of the second questionnaire.

In contrast to many cognitive theories (e.g., Wyer & Srull, 1989), the conversational logic predicted that the correlation between the two answers would be higher if the questions were separated and lower if they were presented as conversationally related. These predictions were borne out by the data. The correlation between the similar dimensions of subjective well-being was almost perfect ($r = .96$) if the questions belonged to different surveys. In contrast, if they were perceived as related, the correlation of the answers dropped dramatically ($r = .65$).

These results provide further evidence that conversational principles are often relevant in standardized question situations. However, this is true only if the standardized exchange has features of natural discourse; that is, the questions must represent an ongoing dialogue in which both the questions and answers to them are perceived as part of the same exchange. This is often ambiguous, however, in standardized situations.

It is not necessary to establish a conversational context explicitly. The immediate sequence of questions may be sufficient to elicit such a perception. This was the case in a study conducted by Ottati, Riggle, Wyer, Schwarz, and Kuklinski (1989); they found that respondents expressed a more positive attitude toward the general topic of free speech if a preceding question about the same issue referred to a specific group that was positively evaluated (e.g., the American Civil Liberties Union) than if it referred to a group that was negatively evaluated (e.g., the American Nazi Party). However, this assimilation effect was found only when the two questions were separated in the questionnaire. If the specific question immediately preceded the general one, a contrast effect was found such that the positive content produced a more negative attitude and vice versa.

Another aspect of informativeness concerns the required accuracy of a response. Respondents are often uncertain as to how exact their answer has to be. This is particularly relevant if they are requested to report past occurrences and their frequencies. For example, suppose participants are asked to report whether or how often they went to see a movie or a doctor during the last 6 months. They may not interpret the interviewer's request as a demand to engage in an exhaustive memory search. Instead, they may infer that their communication goal will be attained by providing an estimate that is only approximate. Given the constraints of most question situations, such an interpretation seems to comply with the cooperative principle.

To make such frequency estimates, participants may first recall the number of instances that occurred during a shorter period of time and extrapolate. Thus, in the previous example, they might recall the number of movies they have seen during the last month and extrapolate from that database to the requested time period (Bradburn, Rips, & Shevell, 1987). This strategy could result in over- or underestimations of the actual frequency.

To induce respondents to provide a more precise answer, Loftus, Klinger, Smith, and Fiedler (1990) suggested a "two-time frame questioning procedure." Specifically, these authors recommended asking for the frequency of the same behavior in different time periods. For example, to increase the accuracy of participants' estimates of how often they had had a physical examination within the last 2 months, they first might be asked to indicate the number of physicals they had during a different period (e.g., the last 6 months). Loftus et al. compared respondents' medical records with their reports of doctor visits and found more accurate responses under such conditions than under conditions in which the initial question had not been asked.

The effectiveness of this procedure apparently results from an inference that respondents draw about the level of accuracy they are expected to attain; that is, the fact that two questions are asked pertaining to the same content in slightly different temporal frames suggests to respondents that the questioner has a specific interest in possibly different frequencies of occurrence of the event at different points in time, and therefore they make a greater effort to compute the frequency accurately. Thus, as in experimental situations where repeated measures draw participants' attention to what the experimenter wants to know (see Bless et al., 1993), the repeated posing of similar survey questions can be used to communicate this interest (see also Strack et al., 1988).

4. Researcher Affiliation

So far, our discussion focused on the information provided by questions and their context in the questionnaire. Note, however, that additional relevant context information is already provided in the cover letter that accompanies written questionnaires or the opening lines of interviews. One such piece of information is the researcher's affiliation, which respondents consider in determining the researcher's epistemic interest. For example, Norenzayan and Schwarz (1999) presented respondents with newspaper accounts of mass murders and asked them to explain why the mass murder occurred. In one condition, the questionnaire was printed on the letterhead of an alleged "Institute for Personality Research," whereas in the other condition it was printed on the letterhead of an "Institute for Social Research." As expected, respondents' explanations showed more attention to personality variables or to social–contextual variables, depending on whether they thought the researcher was a personality psychologist or a social scientist. Apparently, they took the researcher's affiliation into account in determining the kind of information that would be most informative, given the researcher's likely epistemic interest.

CONCLUSIONS

The program of research that has been outlined in this chapter describes the psychological mechanisms of answering questions in both natural and standardized situations. Moreover, it identifies some crucial influences researchers need to know if they are asking questions to collect data in the social domain. We emphasize context and conversation as the perhaps most important influences.

In detail, we have contended in this chapter that answers are always generated in a social context. Even without specific evidence, it is safe to assume that answering a question is always influenced by the "actual, imagined or implied presence of others" (Allport, 1954), in this case, the presence of the questioner. This true not only for personal or telephone interviews but also for self-administered questionnaires. If recipients of the response are not present, they are always implied. In particular, it is the questioner's anticipated expectation that determines the generation of the response. To understand the specific influences, it is necessary to understand the rules of natural conversation. As we have demonstrated in this chapter, the Gricean (1975) maxims of conversational cooperation have proved exceptionally useful to understand and predict how various aspects of survey questions affect the generation of responses. Thus, the psychological processes that operate in natural communications may be fruitfully transferred to standardized settings. As a result, asking questions for the purpose of social measurement will become less of an art (Sudman & Bradburn, 1982) and more of a methodological practice that is guided by principles rooted in psychological evidence.

REFERENCES

Abelson, R. P. (1984). Psychological measurement: An introduction to the subjective domain. In C. F. Turner & E. M. Martin (Eds.), *Surveying subjective phenomena* (Vol. 1, pp. 117–125). New York: Russell Sage Foundation.

Allport, G. W. (1954). *The nature of prejudice*. Reading, MA: Addison-Wesley.

Belson, W. A. (1981). *The design and understanding of survey questions*. Aldershot, England: Gower.

Bishop, G. F., Oldendick, R. W., & Tuchfarber, A. J. (1983). Effects of filter questions in public opinion surveys. *Public Opinion Quarterly, 47*, 528–546.

Bless, H., Strack, F., & Schwarz, N. (1993). The informative functions of research procedures: Bias and the logic of conversation. *European Journal of Social Psychology, 23*, 149–165.

Bradburn, N. M., Rips, L. J., & Shevell, S. K. (1987, April 10). Answering autobiographical questions: The impact of memory and inference on surveys. *Science, 236*, 157–161.

Campbell, A. (1981). *The sense of well-being in America*. New York: Russell Sage Foundation.

Clark, H. H. (1985). Language and language users. In G. Lindzey & E. Aronson (Eds.), *Handbook of social psychology* (Vol. 2, pp. 179–232). New York: Random House.

Clark, H. H., & Clark, E. V. (1977). *Psychology and language: An introduction to psycholinguistics*. New York: Harcourt Brace Jovanovich.

Clark, H. H., & Haviland, S. E. (1977). Comprehension and the given-new contract. In R. O. Freedl (Ed.), *Discourse production and comprehension* (pp. 1–40). Hillsdale, NJ: Lawrence Erlbaum Associates.

Clark, H. H., & Schober, M. F. (1992). Asking questions and influencing answers. In J. M. Tanur (Ed.), *Questions about questions. Inquiries into the cognitive bases of surveys* (pp. 15–47). New York: Russell Sage Foundation.

Clark, H. H., & Wilkes-Gibbs, D. (1986). Referring as a collaborative process. *Cognition, 22,* 1–39.

DeMaio, T. J. (1984). Social desirability and survey measurement: A review. In C. F. Turner & E. Martin (Eds.), *Surveying subjective phenomena* (Vol. 2, pp. 257–282). New York: Russell Sage Foundation.

Dodd, D. H., & Bradshaw, J. M. (1980). Leading questions and memory: Pragmatic constraints. *Journal of Verbal Learning and Verbal Behavior, 19,* 695–704.

Ericsson, K. A., & Simon, H. A. (1980). Verbal reports as data. *Psychological Review, 87,* 215–225.

Garrod, S., & Anderson, A. (1987). Saying what you mean in a dialogue: A study in conceptual and semantic co-ordination. *Cognition, 27,* 181–218.

Gaskell, G. D., O'Muircheartaigh, C. A., & Wright, D. B. (1994). Survey questions about the frequency of vaguely defined events. *Public Opinion Quarterly, 58,* 241–254.

Grice, H. P. (1975). Logic and conservation. In P. Cole & J. L. Morgan (Eds.), *Syntax and semantics 3: Speech acts* (pp. 41–58). New York: Academic.

Higgins, E. T. (1981). The "communication game": Implications for social cognition and persuasion. In E. T. Higgins, C. P. Herman, & M. P. Zanna (Eds.), *Social cognition: The Ontario Symposium* (Vol. 1, pp. 343–392). Hillsdale, NJ: Lawrence Erlbaum Associates.

Higgins, E. T., Rholes, W. S., & Jones, C. R. (1977). Category accessibility and impression formation. *Journal of Experimental Social Psychology, 13,* 141–154.

Hippler, H. J., & Schwarz, N. (1986). Not forbidding isn't allowing: The cognitive basis of the forbid-allow asymmetry. *Public Opinion Quarterly, 50,* 87–96.

Hippler, H. J., & Schwarz, N. (1987). Response effects in surveys. In H. J. Hippler, N. Schwarz, & S. Sudman (Eds.), *Social information processing and survey methodology* (pp. 102–122). New York: Springer.

Igou, E. R., Bless, H., & Schwarz, N. (2002). Making sense of standardized survey questions: The influence of reference periods and their repetition. *Communication Monographs, 69,* 179–187.

Krauss, R. M., & Weinheimer, S. (1964). Changes in reference phrases as a function of frequency of usage in social interaction: A preliminary study. *Psychonomic Science, 1,* 113–114.

Krauss, R. M., & Weinheimer, S. (1966). Concurrent feedback, confirmation, and the encoding of referents in verbal communication. *Journal of Personality and Social Psychology, 4,* 343–346.

Lessler, J. T. (1984). Measurement error in surveys. In C. F. Turner & E. M. Martin (Eds.), *Surveying subjective phenomena* (Vol. 2, pp. 405–440). New York: Russell Sage Foundation.

Levinson, S. (1983). *Pragmatics.* Cambridge, England: Cambridge University Press.

Likert, R. A. (1932). A technique for the measurement of attitudes. *Archives of Psychology, 140,* 1–55.

Lindsay, D. S., & Johnson, M. K. (1989). The eyewitness suggestibility effect and memory for source. *Memory & Cognition, 17*, 349–358.

Loftus, E. F. (1975). Leading questions and the eyewitness report. *Cognitive Psychology, 7*, 560–572.

Loftus, E. F., & Hoffman, H. G. (1989). Misinformation and memory: The creation of new memories. *Journal of Experimental Psychology: General, 118*, 100–104.

Loftus, E. F., Klinger, M. R., Smith, K. F., & Fiedler, J. (1990). A tale of two questions: Benefits of asking more than one question. *Public Opinion Quarterly, 54*, 330–345.

Lord, F. M., & Novick, M. R. (1974). *Statistical theories of mental test scores.* Reading, MA: Addison-Wesley.

Lyons, W. (1986). *The disappearance of introspection.* Cambridge, MA: MIT Press.

Martin, E. (1984). The tasks posed by survey questions. In C. F. Turner & E. Martin (Eds.), *Surveying subjective phenomena* (Vol. 1, pp. 295–300). New York: Russell Sage Foundation.

McCann, C. D., & Higgins, E. T. (1992). Personal and contextual factors in communication: A review of the "communication game." In G. R. Semin & K. Fiedler (Eds.), *Language, interaction and social cognition* (pp. 144–172). London: Sage.

McCloskey, M., & Zaragoza, M. (1985). Misleading postevent information and memory for events: Arguments and evidence against the memory impairment hypothesis. *Journal of Experimental Psychology: General, 114*, 1–16.

McGonagle, K. A., Kessler, R. C., & Schilling, E. A. (1992). The frequency and determinants of marital disagreements in a community sample. *Journal of Social and Personal Relationships, 9*, 507–524.

Nisbett, R. E., & Wilson, T. D. (1977). Telling more than we can know: Verbal reports on mental processes. *Psychological Review, 84*, 231–259.

Norenzayan, A., & Schwarz, N. (1999). Telling what they want to know: Participants tailor causal attributions to researchers interests. *European Journal of Social Psychology, 29*, 1011–1020.

Ottati, V. C., Riggle, E., Wyer, R. S., Schwarz, N., & Kuklinski, J. (1989). Cognitive and affective bases of opinion survey responses. *Journal of Personality and Social Psychology, 57*, 404–415.

Parkinson, B., Briner, R. B., Reynolds, S., & Totterdell, P. (1995). Time frames for mood: Relations between momentary and generalized ratings of affect. *Personality and Social Psychology Bulletin, 21*, 331–339.

Payne, S. L. (1951). *The art of asking questions.* Princeton, NJ: Princeton University Press.

Postman, L., & Miller, G. A. (1945). Anchoring of temporal judgments. *American Journal of Psychology, 58*, 43–53.

Rosenthal, R., & Rosnow, R. L. (1984). *Essentials of behavioral research: Methods and data analysis.* New York: McGraw-Hill.

Rugg, D., & Cantril, H. (1944). The wording of questions. In H. Cantril (Ed.), *Gauging public opinion* (pp. 23–50). Princeton, NJ: Princeton University Press.

Schober, M. F., & Clark, H. H. (1989). Understanding by addresses and overhearers. *Cognitive Psychology, 21*, 211–232.

Schuman, H., & Presser, S. (1981). *Questions and answers in attitude surveys.* Orlando, FL: Academic.

Schwarz, N. (1994). Judgment in a social context: Biases, shortcomings, and the logic of conversation. In M. Zanna (Ed.), *Advances in experimental social psychology* (Vol. 26, pp. 123–162). New York: Academic.

Schwarz, N. (1996). *Cognition and communication: Judgmental biases, research methods, and the logic of conversation.* Hillsdale, NJ: Lawrence Erlbaum Associates.

Schwarz, N., Grayson, C. E., & Knäuper, B. (1998). Formal features of rating scales and the interpretation of question meaning. *International Journal of Public Opinion Research, 10*, 177–183.

Schwarz, N., & Hippler, H. J. (1991). Response alternatives: The impact of their choice and ordering. In P. Biemer, R. Groves, N. Mathiowetz, & S. Sudman (Eds.), *Measurement error in surveys* (pp. 41–56). Chichester, England: Wiley.

Schwarz, N., & Hippler, H. J. (1995). The numeric values of rating scales: A comparison of their impact in mail surveys and telephone interviews. *International Journal of Public Opinion Research, 7*, 72–54.

Schwarz, N., Knäuper, B., Hippler, H. J., Noelle-Neumann, E., & Clark, L. (1991). Rating scales: Numeric values may change the meaning of scale labels. *Public Opinion Quarterly, 55*, 570–582.

Schwarz, N., & Strack, F. (1991). Context effects in attitude surveys: Applying cognitive theory to social research. In W. Stroebe & M. Hewstone (Eds.), *European review of social psychology* (Vol. 2, pp. 31–50). Chichester, England: Wiley.

Schwarz, N., Strack, F., & Mai, H. P. (1991). Assimilation and contrast effects in part–whole question sequences: A conversational-logic analysis. *Public Opinion Quarterly, 55*, 3–23.

Schwarz, N., Strack, F., Müller, G., & Chassein, B. (1988). The range of response alternatives may determine the meaning of the question: Further evidence on informative functions of response alternatives. *Social Cognition, 6*, 107–117.

Schwarz, N., & Sudman, S. (Eds.). (1992). *Context effects in social and psychological research.* New York: Springer-Verlag.

Searle, J. R. (1975). Indirect speech acts. In P. Cole & J. L. Morgan (Eds.), *Syntax and semantics: Vol. 3. Speech acts* (pp. 59–82). New York: Seminar.

Searle, J. R. (1976). The classification of illocutionary acts. *Language in Society, 5*, 1–24.

Smith, V. L., & Ellsworth, P. C. (1987). The social psychology of eyewitness accuracy: Misleading questions and communicator expertise. *Journal of Applied Psychology, 72*, 294–300.

Sperber, D., & Wilson, D. (1986). *Relevance: Communication and cognition.* Cambridge, MA: Cambridge University Press.

Srull, T. K., & Wyer, R. S. (1979). The role of category accessibility in the interpretation of information about persons: Some determinants and implications. *Journal of Personality and Social Psychology, 37*, 1660–1672.

Srull, T. K., & Wyer, R. S. (1980). Category accessibility and social perception: Some implications for the study of person memory and interpersonal judgments. *Journal of Personality and Social Psychology, 38*, 841–856.

Strack, F. (1992). "Order" effects in survey research: Activative and informative functions of preceding questions. In N. Schwarz & S. Sudman (Eds.), *Order effects in survey research* (pp. 23–34). New York: Springer.

Strack, F. (1994). *Kognitive und kommunikative Einflüsse in standardisierten Befragungssituationen.* [Cognitive and communicative influences in standardized question situations]. Heidelberg, Germany: Springer.

Strack, F., & Bless, H. (1994). Memory for non-occurrences: Metacognitive and presuppositional strategies. *Journal of Memory and Language, 33,* 203–217.

Strack, F., & Martin, L. L. (1987). Thinking, judging, and communicating: A process account of context effects in attitude surveys. In H. J. Hippler, N. Schwarz, & S. Sudman (Eds.), *Social information processing and survey methodology* (pp. 123–148). New York: Springer.

Strack, F., Martin, L. L., & Schwarz, N. (1988). Priming and communication: Social determinants of information use in judgments of life satisfaction. *European Journal of Social Psychology, 18,* 429–442.

Strack, F., & Schwarz, N. (1992). Communicative influences in standardized question situations: The case of implicit collaboration. In G. Semin & K. Fiedler (Eds.), *Language and social cognition* (pp. 173–193). London: Sage.

Strack, F., Schwarz, N., & Wänke, M. (1991). Semantic and pragmatic aspects of context effects in social and psychological research. *Social Cognition, 9,* 111–125.

Sudman, S., & Bradburn, N. M. (1982). *Asking questions. A practical guide to questionnaire design.* San Francisco: Jossey-Bass.

Sydenham, P. H., & Thorn, R. (1996). *Handbook of measurement science: Vol. 1. Theoretical fundamentals.* New York: Wiley.

Thomas, D. L., & Diener, E. (1990). Memory accuracy in the recall of emotions. *Journal of Personality and Social Psychology, 59,* 291–297.

Tourangeau, R., Rasinski, K. A., & Bradburn, N. (1991). Measuring happiness in surveys: A test of the subtraction hypothesis. *Public Opinion Quarterly, 55,* 255–266.

Turner, C. F., & Martin, E. (Eds.). (1984). *Surveying subjective phenomena* (Vols. 1 and 2). New York: Russell Sage Foundation.

Tversky, B., & Tuchin, M. (1989). A reconciliation of the evidence on eyewitness testimony: Comments on McCloskey and Zaragoza (1985). *Journal of Experimental Psychology: General, 118,* 86–91.

Upshaw, H. S. (1965). The effect of variable perspectives on judgments of opinion statements for Thurstone scales: Equal-appearing intervals. *Journal of Personality and Social Psychology, 2,* 60–69.

Upshaw, H. S., & Ostrom, T. M. (1984). Psychological perspective in attitude research. In J. R. Eiser (Ed.), *Attitudinal judgment* (pp. 23–41). New York: Springer.

Volkmann, J. (1951). Scales of judgment and their implications for social psychology. In J. H. Rohrer & M. Sherif (Eds.), *Social psychology at the crossroads* (pp. 273–294). New York: Harper.

Wilson, M. (Ed.). (1992). *Objective measurement: Theory into practice* (Vol. 1). Norwood, NJ: Ablex.

Winkielman, P., Knäuper, B., & Schwarz, N. (1998). Looking back at anger: Reference periods change the interpretation of (emotion) frequency questions. *Journal of Personality and Social Psychology, 75,* 719–728.

Wyer, R. S., & Srull, T. K. (1989). *Memory and cognition in its social context.* Hillsdale, NJ: Lawrence Erlbaum Associates.

11

Can the Psyche be Visualized by the Neurosciences?

Gerhard Roth
University of Bremen, Germany

Thomas F. Münte and Hans-Jochen Heinze
Otto von Guericke University of Magdeburg, Germany

The link between perception, cognition, and motor processes on the one hand and brain processes on the other has been known since antiquity. Knowledge about this correspondence stemmed mainly from the study of brain lesions and has been strengthened over the last decades by neuroanatomical and neurophysiological methods in animals. In the past few years, neuroimaging methods, such as positron emission tomography (PET), functional magnetic resonance imaging (fMRI), event-related brain potentials derived from electroencephalography, and magnetoencephalography (MEG) have corroborated this link for the human brain, which cannot be studied by invasive techniques.

Although the examination of perception and cognition has been a success study, affective–emotional states have been investigated to a much lesser extent. Until the 20th century, these states were not studied in conjunction with the brain at all; instead, they were located in the intestines or in the nerve ganglia of the abdomen. Sigmund Freud—a talented neuroscientist in his earlier years—searched for them in the lower brain stem. It was only several decades later that the limbic system was identified as the origin and control center for affective–emotional states. Which brain regions exactly constitute the limbic system has been a matter of long and intense discussions. Only recently a certain consensus has been reached (cf. McDonald, 2003; Roth & Dicke, 2005).

A parallel discussion within psychology concerned the nature of *psychic*, that is, affective and emotional, states: How many basic emotions exist? What is their function? How can they be separated from cognitive processes? Most neuroscientists agree with the leading experts in emotion, such as Ekman (1999), that there are only a limited number of basic emotions, such as happiness, surprise, fear, disgust, sadness, and anger. Moreover, differential patterns of activity within the limbic system appear to correspond to these basic emotions (Panksepp, 1998). In the following pages, we will be concerned mostly with one basic emotion, fear, which has been studied most extensively at a behavioral and neurobiological level. Moreover, we will discuss a psychological condition, posttraumatic stress disorder (PTSD) due to psychological trauma, which has been viewed by many experts as a disorder of the fear system. This is our test case for the question regarding the extent to which animal experiments can be corroborated by neuroimaging methods.

NEUROBIOLOGICAL FOUNDATIONS OF COGNITION AND EMOTION

There has been a long-standing tradition in psychology and neurobiology to strictly separate cognitive and affective–emotional processes. This has been replaced by the insight that this separation holds only for certain areas of the brain and that there are other areas for which there is an intense interaction of cognitive and affective emotional processes. This is especially true for areas that are concerned with evaluation (including that of one's own actions), with memory processes, and with the anticipation and preparation of actions. These functions have also been subsumed under the heading of *executive functions.*

In spite of this interaction of cognition and emotion, we can point to areas of the human (and animal) brain that deal primarily with perceptual and cognitive processing and to other regions that support emotional and executive processes. The site of perceptual and cognitive functions is mainly the cerebral cortex in its narrow sense, that is, the six-layered *neo-* or *isocortex* (see Figs. 11–1a & 11–1b). The neocortex

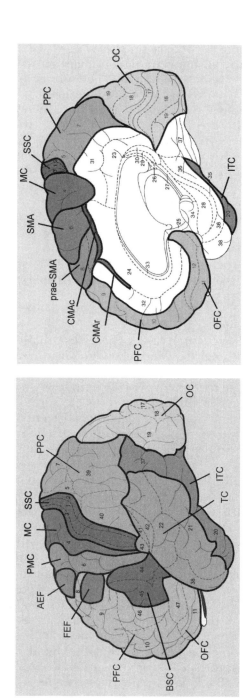

Figure 11–1.   (a): Functional anatomical division of the lateral surface of the cerebral cortex. The numbers refer to the cytoarchitectonic areas defined by K. Brodmann. AEF = anterior eye field; BSC = Broca speech center; FEF = frontal eye field; ITC = inferior temporal cortex; MC = motor cortex; OC = occipital cortex; OFC = orbitofrontal cortex; PFC = prefrontal cortex; PMC = dorsolateral premotor cortex; PPC = posterior parietal cortex; SSC = somatosensory cortex; TC = temporal cortex. (after Nieuwenhuys, Voogd, & van Huijzen, 1991).
(b) Mesial surface of the cerebral cortex. Abbreviations: CMAc = caudal cingulate motor area; CMAr = rostral cingulate motor area; ITC = inferior temporal cortex; MC = motor cortex; OC = occipital cortex; OFC = orbitofrontal cortex; pre-SMA = pre-supplementary motor area; PFC = prefrontal cortex; PPC = posterior parietal cortex; SMA = supplementary motor area; SSC = somatosensory cortex. Adapted from Roth, G. (2003). Fühlen, Denken, Handeln [Feeling, Thinking, Acting], pp. 100–101.

can be divided into primary and secondary sensory (i.e., visual, auditory, somatosensory, vestibular, gustatory) areas, primary motor and premotor areas, and so-called "associative" areas. The latter comprise mainly the parietal, temporal, and frontal association cortices.

The *parietal association cortex* (also known as the *posterior parietal cortex* [PPC]) comprises Brodmann areas BA 5, 7a, and 7b and the inferior parietal cortex (angular gyrus, BA 39; supramarginal gyrus, BA 40). The PPC is concerned with spatial perception, spatial orienting, and spatial imagery. This requires the construction of a three-dimensional representation of the environment as well as the localization of sensory stimuli and of one's own body and its movements within the environment. The PPC further is involved in the preparation of goal-directed movements and the handling of abstract spatial concepts, including the perception, interpretation, and use of maps and pictorial representations. Additional functions supported by the PPC include reading, mental arithmetic, and the perception and use of symbols in a more general sense.

The *temporal association cortex* comprises parts of the superior (BA 22), medial (BA 37, 38), and inferior temporal cortex (BA 20, 21). The superior and medial temporal association cortex processes complex auditory and language-related information. Wernicke's language area (approximately BA 22 for most people in the left hemisphere) is located here, which deals with language processing with an emphasis on comprehension. The temporal pole (BA 38) has been shown to support autobiographical memory. In the inferior temporal cortex adjacent to the occipital lobe complex visual information is processed, such as the identification of faces and facial expressions (mainly in the right hemisphere) and the analysis of visual scenes. The mesial aspect of the temporal lobe also hosts the amygdala and the hippocampal formation.

The *frontal association cortex*, often called *prefrontal cortex* (PFC), includes areas BA 9, 10, and 46 constituting the *dorsolateral* PFC and areas BA 11, 13, 14, and 47, which are subsumed under the term *orbitofrontal* PFC. The dorsolateral PFC is concerned with the temporo–spatial structuring of perceptual events and actions, with the planning of context-appropriate actions (including speech) and with the development of action goals (Davidson & Irwin, 1999; Petrides, 2000; Petrides & Pandya, 1999). Lesions of this area lead to deficits in these functions, in particular to the inability to evaluate the relevance of external events and to an impairment of working memory. Lesions of the orbitofrontal and ventromedial cortex, on the other hand, cause a deficit in the ability to process the social–communicative context. Patients with such lesions are unable to anticipate long-term negative or positive consequences of their actions, even though immediate reward or punishment has an influence on their behavior (Davidson & Irwin, 1999). These patients often show extremely risky behavior in spite of being aware of these risks at a cognitive level (Anderson, Bechara, Damasio, Tranel, & Damasio, 1999).

Affect and emotion as experienced by a subject are the conscious representation of the actions of the limbic system, which mainly works outside of consciousness. This system is distributed across the entire brain (Akert, 1994; Nieuwenhuys et al., 1991; Panksepp, 1998) and features (1) parts of the cerebral cortex (cytoarchitectonically: pro-isocortex and periallocortex), such as the orbitofrontal, cingulate, insular, parahippocampal, and perirhinal cortex (including the entorhinal cortex); (2) allo- and subcortical centers of the telencephalon, that is, the hippocampal formation, the amygdala, the septum and basal forebrain, and the ventral striatum/nucleus accumbens; (3) parts of the diencephalon, such as the hypothalamus/preoptic region, the mammillary bodies, and anterior–lateral, medial, and intralaminar nuclei of the thalamus, (4) the ventral tegmental area, the substantia nigra (pars compacta), and nuclei of the tegmental grey in the midbrain; and (5) the nuclei of the reticular formation in the midbrain and brain stem, such as the locus coeruleus and the raphe nuclei (see Fig. 11–2). We restrict the following discussion to the most important parts of the limbic system.

The *amygdala* (corpus amygdaloideum) has a central role in the generation and control of emotions, both anatomically and functionally (Aggleton, 2000; LeDoux, 2000; Zald, 2003). It features a corticomedial group of nuclei, which is primarily involved in the processing of olfactory information (e.g., pheromones), and a basolateral group, which is concerned with emotional conditioning and evaluation with respect to emotions, predominantly those with negative valence. Finally, the central nucleus of the amygdala is involved in the generation of visceral and automatic reactions in the context of stress and fear (see Fig. 11–3). The amygdala has feedback projections to the associative isocortex, in particular to the visual and auditory associative cortex, as well as the orbitofrontal, insular, cingulate, parahippocampal, perirhinal, and entorhinal cortex. In general, the pathways from the amygdala to the cortex are more strongly evolved than vice versa. In nonhuman mammals the function of the amygdala seems to be restricted to the generation and regulation of inborn and acquired fear responses (Aggleton, 2000). In humans, the amygdala appears to be also involved in non-fear-related and even strongly positive or surprising emotions, and in the modulation of learning and memory (Cahill & McGaugh, 1998; Cardinal, Parkinson, Hall, & Everitt, 2003; Robbins & Everitt, 1995; Rolls, 1999; Zald, 2003).

The hippocampus, together with its surrounding cortical areas, can be viewed as the organizer of conscious, *declarative* memory. Adjacent

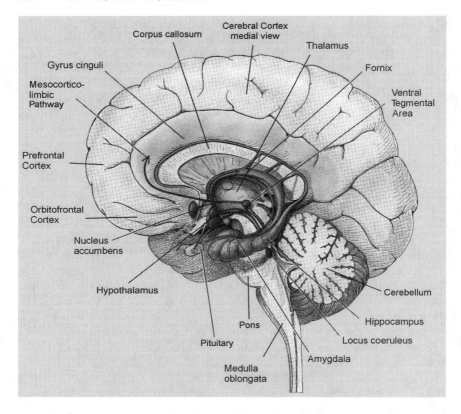

Figure 11–2. Longitudinal section through the human brain with the most important limbic centers. These can be divided into areas responsible for the processing of positive (nucleus accumbens, ventral tegmental area) and negative affects (amygdala), for the organization of memory (hippocampus), for the control of attention and conscious processing (basal forebrain, locus coeruleus, thalamus), and for the control of vegetatite functions (hypothalamus). Adapted from *Fühlen, Denken, Handeln* [Feeling, thinking, Acting] (p. 257), by G. Roth, 2003. Copyright 2003 by G. Roth.

to the hippocampus is the entorhinal cortex, which in turn has the perirhinal and parahippocampal cortex (together, *EPPC*) as its neighbors. Semantic and episodic memories are stored not in the hippocampus or the EPPC, however, but in various modality and functionally specific cortical areas. Bilateral damage to the hippocampus leads to a temporally circumscribed retrograde amnesia, that is, to a loss of parts of the remote memory, as well as to *anterograde amnesia*, the inability to integrate new information into declarative memory. Within declarative memory, a distinction is made between *episodic memory*, which concerns specific events in relation to one's own person, and *semantic memory*, which pertains to facts independent of persons, locations, and time (Aggleton & Brown, 1999; Markowitsch, 1999, 2000; Tulving & Markowitsch, 1998). The storage of episodic memory is thought to depend on the hippocampus proper, whereas semantic memory is dependent on the EPPC.

A "division of labor" can be seen among the hippocampus, the EPPC, and the amygdala within the area of declarative and emotional memory. In a classical conditioning experiment, in which a fear reaction was induced in normal respondents by a loud noise, patients with bilateral damage of the amygdala were able to describe which of several sensory stimuli had been paired with the fear-inducing aversive stimulus. These patients did not show the vegetative concomitants of fear, such as an increase of the galvanic skin response (Bechara et al., 1995). Thus, they did not develop fear or startle responses and simply faced the sequence

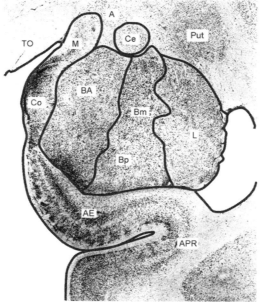

Figure 11–3.   Section through the amygdala and the adjacent medio-temporal regions. Left is medial (i.e., toward the middle of the brain); right is lateral. A = Area amygdaloidea anterior; AE = Area entorhinalis; APR = Area perirhinalis; BA = Nucleus basalis anterior; Bm = Nucleus basalis magnocellularis; Bp = Nucleus basalis parvocellularis; Ce = Nucleus centralis; Co = Nucleus corticalis; L = Nucleus lateralis; M = Nucleus medialis; Put = Putamen; TO = Tractus opticus. Modified after Drenckhahn & Zenker, 1994, from Roth & Dicke, 2005, p. 12. With permission of the authors.

of stimuli without emotions. Patients with a bilateral damage to the hippocampus, on the other hand, did not have conscious knowledge of the pairing between the conditioned and unconditioned aversive stimulus, yet they showed a pronounced autonomous reaction.

This has led to the view that the storage of the *context*, in which a negative event takes place, depends on the integrity of the hippocampus. Whenever the event is repeated, the factual as well as the emotional aspects of the event are retrieved. Negative emotions are produced by the amygdala either directly or indirectly—via the mediodorsal nucleus of the thalamus—by the cerebral cortex, especially the prefrontal cortex, and thus become accessible to consciousness.

The amygdala's counterpart is the mesolimbic system, which comprises the ventral tegmental area, the substantia nigra pars compacta, the lateral hypothalamus, the nucleus accumbens, and the adjacent parts of the ventral striatum and pallidum (Nieuwenhuys et al., 1989; Cardinal et al., 2003). The mesolimbic system is primarily responsible for the registration of positive and rewarding events and has thus been viewed as the cerebral reward system. Like the amygdala, this system entertains strong connections to the prefrontal, orbitofrontal, and cingulate cortex and is characterized by the neuromodulator dopamine. New findings suggest, however, that dopamine instead functions as a signal for the association of reward to specific events as opposed to being the "reward agent" itself. This function appears to be

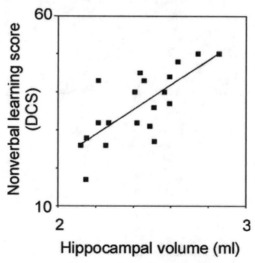

Figure 11–4.   Relationship of nonverbal learning to the volume of the hippocampus in a sample of normal elderly subjects (see Schiltz et al., 2006). DCS-Diagnosticum für cerebralschädigung (diagnostics for cerebral damage).

fulfilled by endogenous opiates, which similarly act in the mesolimbic system (Cardinal et al., 2003; Horvitz, 2000; Panksepp, 1998; Spanagel & Weiss, 1999).

The anterior cingulate gyrus (ACC; BA 25 and 32), the insular cortex, and the medial frontal and orbitofrontal cortex constitute the cortical division of the limbic system. Among the functions of the ACC is pain perception, which is carried out in conjunction with the insular cortex, the medial thalamus, and the central tegmental grey. Together with the prefrontal cortex, the ACC exerts a monitoring function specifically with regard to one's own actions (Carter et al., 1998; Gehring & Knight, 2000; Rodriguez-Fornells, Kurzbach, & Münte, 2002; Rodriguez-Fornells, Rotte, Heinze, Noesselt, & Münte, 2002). The insular cortex of the human brain (BA 13–16) is covered by parts of the frontal, parietal, and temporal lobes and is similarly part of the limbic system. Some of the many functions of the insular cortex are the representation and elaboration of gustatory experiences as well as visceral and visceral–emotional states. Furthermore, it participates in the conscious experience of pain. Pain-relevant input to the insular cortex comes from the amygdala and the lateral hypothalamus.

NEURONAL BASIS OF FEAR CONDITIONING

In recent years, extensive investigations have revealed the neural underpinnings of fear conditioning, mostly using the fear-potentiated startle response in rats (e.g., Aggleton, 1992, 2000; Fendt & Fanselow, 1999; LeDoux, 2000). The basis of this paradigm is the inborn fear reaction of rats to a loud aversive noise burst. If a neutral visual stimulus is paired with an electric shock, then the light stimulus acquires a conditioned negative meaning. In the final step of the experiment, the combination of the light stimulus and the aversive noise burst leads to an increased potentiated startle reaction (Koch, 1999).

A lesion of the entire amygdala as well as selective lesions to the central nucleus or to the ventral amygdalo–fugal pathway that targets the caudal reticular pontine nucleus abolishes all signs of conditioned fear. This is due to the fact that the central amygdala activates, via relay structures, those centers that coordinate the visceral–autonomic and motor aspects of fear and startle response. More complex forms of fear conditioning can be abolished by a circumscribed lesion to the basolateral nucleus of the amygdala, whereas simple forms of fear conditioning can be performed in the absence of an intact basolateral nucleus (Cardinal et al., 2003). The basolateral amygdala thus appears to be the locus of the association of the light (the conditioned stimulus) and the electric shock (the unconditioned stimulus). In the acoustic startle reaction the sensory input comes partially from the auditory cortex and partially via a direct input from the thalamus. Both inputs end in the basolateral amygdala. At the same time, the basolateral amygdala receives inputs from the hippocampus, which appear to transmit details about the context of the fear conditioning.

PSYCHOLOGICAL STRESS, PSYCHOLOGICAL TRAUMA, AND THEIR NEURAL UNDERPINNINGS

Psychological stress results in two different physiological responses in our nervous system and our brain. After the recognition of the stressful situation by the brain, the first reaction comprises the activation of stress-relevant subcortical and cortical brain areas. In general, the activation of subcortical areas, such as the amygdala and the hypothalamus, *precedes* that of cortical areas (LeDoux, 1996). Via the hypothalamus and other relay stations, the amygdala activates autonomous centers, mainly the locus coeruleus. This leads to the release of norepinephrine, which acts on the cortex, amygdala, hippocampus, and hypothalamus and results in an increased alertness and a preparation to act. Parallel to the action of the locus coeruleus, the sympathetic nervous system is activated by the hypothalamus via autonomous relay stations in the brain stem and the spinal cord. This leads to a release of epinephrine and norepinephrine from the adrenal glands into the bloodstream. Via the blood, epinephrine and norepinephrine reach the brain, amplify the stress symptoms just mentioned, and further increase the animal's (human's) preparation to act.

The second stress reaction, which starts a few minutes later, involves the amygdala and the hypothalamus as well as the pituitary gland and the cortex of the adrenal glands. This reaction is mediated by the *corticotropin-releasing factor* (CRF). CRF-positive neurons and fibers are found in the central nucleus of the amygdala, the arcuate nucleus, and the paraventricular parvocellular nucleus of the hypothalamus. These cells are activated by the norepinephrine from the locus coeruleus as well as the systemic release of epinephrine and norepinephrine from the adrenal glands. As a response, these cells release CRF in the median eminence of the stalk of the pituitary gland. The CRF reaches the anterior lobe of the pituitary via the portal vein system, where it promotes the release of the adreno-corticotropic hormone (ACTH) into the bloodstream. The target structure of ACTH is the cortex of the adrenal glands, where it leads to the production and release of steroid hormones, in particular of cortisol. Among the many actions of cortisol is the increase of glucose and fatty acid levels in the blood, which increases bodily performance. At the same time, cortisol inhibits the release of CRF from the hypothalamus (and thereby ACTH from the anterior lobe of the pituitary). This negative feedback loop between cortisol on the one hand and CRF and ACTH on the other hand is designed to prevent excessive release of CRF and ACTH and, finally, cortisol, in the course of a stress reaction.

In the brain, a mild elevation of cortisol leads to an increased production of neurotrophic factors, which exert a beneficiary effect on neuronal functions. Moreover, an increase in the number of glia cells (astrocytes) and signs of increased neural plasticity are found. An increase of the stress level leads not only to an increased release of CRF and norepinephrine but also to an elevated production of ß-endorphine, which is associated with a marked attenuation of pain sensations (Julien, 1997). According to current views, continuous psychological stress causes a failure of the negative feedback loop between cortisol and CRF/ACTH, leading to an excess of cortisol. This excess of cortisol appears to lead to central nervous system damage, including the shrinkage in hippocampal volume and eventual death of hippocampal neurons. This is of particular importance since it has been demonstrated that hippocampal volume positively correlates with nonverbal learning capabilities (see Schiltz et al., 2006, and Figure 11–4).

A particular reaction to stress is PTSD, which by definition is caused by one or more highly traumatic and stressful life events, such as being a victim of torture, rape, accident, or bodily assault or being involved in a catastrophe of nature (Comer, 1995; Ehlert, Wagner, Heinrich, & Heim, 1999). It is interesting that only about one quarter of people who are exposed to such extreme life events develop full-blown PTSD. PTSD leads to significant comorbidity, such as depression, substance abuse, and increased risk of suicide. PTSD is characterized by so-called *intrusions*, recurrent and highly stressful memories and dreams. During *flashbacks* the patients relive the traumatic experiences in extreme vividness and with all autonomous and emotional signs of a severe stress reaction. These memories can be triggered by certain cues. Further characteristics of the disorder are hypervigilance with increased startle reactions, scanning behavior, depersonalization symptoms, difficulties in concentrating, and insomnia.

In several groups of PTSD patients with different causes of the trauma (war experience, sexual abuse during childhood) an elevated level of CRF was found in the cerebrospinal fluid compared with non-PTSD controls and psychiatric patients with other diagnoses. At the same time, a reduced release of cortisol after stimulation with CRF was found. It is unclear whether this finding is due to the trauma or whether PTSD patients might have had an impaired function of the stress-hormone system before the trauma (cf. Ehlert et al., 1999). Additionally, an increased level of norepinephrine has been described, which could be responsible for the increased startle response in PTSD. On the other hand, however, these patients have also been found to have a reduction of the a_2-adrenergic receptors. This could be a reaction to the strong initial production of norepinephrine, but, again, a predisposition cannot be ruled out at this time.

FUNCTIONAL NEUROIMAGING OF FEAR AND PSYCHOLOGICAL TRAUMA

In a first step, we discuss how functional neuroimaging methods, such as PET and fMRI, have been used to describe the brain structures involved in the processing of fear in normal, healthy humans. Then we briefly survey the possible structural and functional imaging correlates of PTSD.

Whereas micro-electrode recordings in animals or recordings of the surface EEG or MEG in humans depict the electrical/magnetic brain activity of the human brain directly, PET and fMRI rely on the fact that neural activity leads to a local increase of cerebral blood flow and metabolism, that is, an increased use of glucose and oxygen (Münte & Heinze, 2001; Posner, 1994). For a PET scan, a positron-emitting isotope (e.g., ^{15}O in $H_2^{15}O$, or ^{18}F in fluor-desoxyglucose) is injected into the blood of the person. These tracers will reach high concentrations in those parts of the brain that either show a relatively high cerebral blood flow ($H_2^{15}O$) or metabolism (fluor-desoxyglucose). The decay of the isotope leads to a free positron that fuses with an electron, thereby emitting gamma rays. Two photons are emitted in exactly opposite directions; they are detected by an array of detectors that are positioned in a ring around the head. With the aid of a computer, the locus and the strength of decay can be determined and visualized as a three-dimensional activity map. The spatial resolution of a PET image is about 5 to 10 mm. The scanning time can vary between 45 to 90 sec for rapidly decaying tracers ($H_2^{15}O$) used for blood flow measurement to many minutes for more slowly decaying tracers (fluor-desoxyglucose). This implies that PET scans integrate the neural correlates of cognitive or emotional processes over time and do not permit a fine temporal resolution.

A main advantage of the PET technique is its versatility, as radiochemists have produced a wide variety of tracers used to investigate different transmitter systems.

Magnetic resonance tomography (MRI) relies on the fact that the nuclei of atoms align themselves parallel to the magnetic field trajectories in a strong magnetic field. If they are forced out of this position by the application of a short, high-frequency pulse, a signal is emitted when the atoms jump back to their earlier position. This signal is revealing with regard to the position and chemical nature of its origin.

Structural MRI is very sensitive to a differential content of hydrogen atoms within a tissue and therefore yields unprecedented anatomically precise pictures of the brain with a high contrast between the grey and white matter. For *functional* MRI, one takes advantage of the fact that oxygen-rich and oxygen-depleted hemoglobin have different magnetic properties. This has also been termed the *blood-oxygen-level-dependent (BOLD) effect*. If differences in the oxygen content of the blood occur as a function of differential engagement of different brain areas in a certain cognitive, emotional, or motor task, these differences can be measured, and a functional MRI image can be computed. Although the BOLD effect may appear to be only remotely related to the neural activity of interest to cognitive neuroscientists, there is ample evidence that it indeed reflects reliably differences in task-related neural activity. In recent investigations by Logothetis, Pauls, Augath, Trinath, and Oeltermann (2001; see also Arthurs & Boniface, 2002), the electrical activity of small ensembles of cell groups in the visual cortex was measured in parallel with the BOLD effect in macaques. It appears from these data that the BOLD effect corresponds best to the local field potentials, which predominantly reflect the activity of the synaptic input to the dendrites of the neurons. The correspondence of the BOLD effect with the action potentials, which reflect the output of the nerve cells, was much weaker.

Both the spatial and temporal resolution of fMRI are much better than that of PET. The temporal resolution is approximately 1 sec and is determined more by the dynamics of neurovascular coupling, that is, by the time constant of the BOLD response, than by technical limitations of the fMRI technique. The temporal resolution is thus still much worse than that of EEG- and MEG-based techniques. In spite of these limitations, there have been first attempts at mental chronometry using fMRI (Formisano & Goebel, 2003). Moreover, there is an increasing number of studies that combine methods with high temporal resolution (i.e., EEG and MEG) with fMRI, thus constructing a temporo–spatial picture of the neural events involved in certain tasks (e.g., Rodriguez-Fornells, Rotte, et al., 2002).

Büchel, Dolan, Armony, and Friston (1999) used a task that has been widely used in animal research, trace conditioning, to study the role of the amygdala and the hippocampus as well as other brain structures for the acquisition of the fear responses in healthy humans. In trace conditioning experiments the aversive stimulus (US) is presented with a certain interval, that is, without overlap, to the neutral stimulus (CS). From animal research it is known that the integrity of the amygdala and the hippocampus are necessary for the acquisition of the fear reaction under these circumstances. Büchel et al. (1999) showed in their fMRI study that the amygdala was activated for CS+ stimuli (neutral stimuli paired with the US) but not for other neutral stimuli not associated with an aversive stimulus (CS–). Moreover, their study revealed that the amygdala and hippocampus were differentially activated over the time course of the conditioning experiment. This is clear evidence for their involvement in the acquisition of the CS–US association. It is interesting that the cingulate gyrus was also activated during the acquisition.

Although this study is extremely important, because it can serve as a bridge to the animal literature, one has to keep in mind that in humans fear is not only a reflex. Instead, we can experience fear also in response to an abstract threat. An fMRI study conducted by Phelps et al. (2001) showed that the amygdala is involved in this very different kind of fear as well. These authors contrasted activations to a stimulus that signaled a threat with a stimulus that signaled safety. In the threat condition, the participants were told that they might receive an aversive stimulus, which, however, did not occur during the entire experiment. In all of their participants, Phelps et al. could demonstrate activations of the *right* amygdala.

The role of the amygdala in the perception of face stimuli has been studied extensively. It appears that the amygdala is especially responsive to threatening faces, whereas reactions to positive faces have been found less consistently (Zald, 2003). A further function that has been assigned to the amygdala is the estimation of trustworthiness (Adolphs, Tranel, & Damasio, 1998; Winston, Stranger, O'Doherty, & Dolan, 2002). Less trustworthy faces activate the amygdala on both sides and the right-sided insular cortex, which has intimate connections with the amygdala. Whether the right and the left amygdala show a functional specialization, is a matter of debate (Zald, 2003). Whereas Canli, Sivers, Whitfield, Gotlib, and Gabrieli (2002) reported that their participants showed bilateral activation of the amygdala in response to threatening faces, other authors (e.g., Hariri et al., 2003) have found a stronger activation on the right. Dolan (2000), on the other hand, found a stronger activation for the left amygdala. It is interesting that Canli et al. reported an increased activation for the left amygdala to happy faces, but only for participants with an elevated, positive mood.

Rauch et al. (2000) were able to show that the amygdala can be activated by emotionally negative items in the absence of conscious perception of these items. Their participants were exposed to negative or positive faces in some of the trials. These faces were replaced after a few milliseconds by neutral faces, such that the participants were consciously aware only of the neutral faces. Nevertheless, the amygdala showed differential activation as a function of the emotional valence of the subliminal faces. This dissociation is likely due to the fact that the amygdala receives fast (unconscious) subcortical input in addition to the slower and conscious cortical input.

A key characteristic of PTSD is the peculiar dissociation between cognitive and emotional experience. It is interesting to speculate in the face of Rauch et al.'s (2000) results that part of this dissociation might be due to a preserved subcortical, but blocked cortical, input to the amygdala in PTSD. With regard to structural changes to the medial temporal structures in PTSD, a seminal study was published by Bremner et al. (1995). These authors used structural MRI in 26 Vietnam veterans with PTSD and compared their results to those of 22 veterans without PTSD. The quantitative volumetric analysis for the right hippocampus revealed a volume that was decreased by about 8% in the PTSD group. This study also reported a correlation between the degree of atrophy and verbal memory deficits.

The finding of a smaller hippocampus in PTSD has been replicated several times in different participant groups (Bremner et al., 1997; Canive et al., 1997). Villarreal and colleagues (Villareal & King, 2001; Villareal et al., 2002) have pointed out that in PTSD not only can one find a reduction of hippocampal volume, but also the ratio of CSF volume to intracranial volume is increased, and the ratio of white matter to intracranial volume is decreased. These latter findings suggest a generalized atrophy of the white matter of the brain. The volume of the hippocampi in this cohort was still reduced after correction for the decreased total brain volume.

One should not overlook, however, the fact that not all volumetric studies have found a relation between PTSD and a reduction of hippocampal volume (see, e.g., Bonne et al., 2001). This might be due to the fact that in studies with "positive" findings, the patients with extreme traumatization (e.g., Vietnam veterans) had experienced the trauma 20 or more years ago. Moreover, it should be kept in mind that in these groups additional problems, such as alcohol and drug abuse or significant psychiatric comorbidity, are common; this might have influenced the results as well.

Therefore, important studies use different, and probably more sensitive, methods to investigate the integrity of the brain substance. Such techniques might be able to reveal a morphological substrate of PTSD without necessarily requiring a change of volume. One such technique is *magnetic resonance spectroscopy*. Like MRI, this method is based on the spin properties of protons. Specific molecules can be assigned to the peaks of the spectral response, thereby allowing an estimation of their content in different brain regions. An important molecule is N-acetyl-aspartate, which is thought to be a marker of neuronal integrity. Schuff et al. (2001) found that N-acetyl-aspartate in 18 PTSD participants was on average decreased by about 23% relative to a control group in the absence of any atrophy. This suggests that microstructural changes are present in the hippocampus of PTSD respondents in the sense of a neuronal loss that has not (yet) led to a loss volume. In a group of children who had sustained prolonged abuse, De Bellis, Keshavan, and Harenski (2001) were able to show similar changes in the cingulate gyrus. It is to be expected that these measurements will be complemented by further magnetic resonance-based methods, such as diffusion-weighted imaging, in the near future. In diffusion-weighted imaging, the signal depends on the ability of water molecules for diffusion: The larger the extracellular space, the higher the diffusion signal.

In animal studies, it has been demonstrated that an excessive release of stress hormones—in particular, cortisol—induces a neurotoxic cascade, which eventually leads to cell loss in the hippocampus and other brain areas. It is tempting to speculate that a similar mechanism might also be responsible for the (micro)-structural changes of the hippocampus in PTSD patients. In this respect, it is interesting that the CRF level in the cerebrospinal fluid of PTSD patients is moderately elevated (Baker et al., 1999). Further corroborating evidence for a role of cortisol in PTSD comes from studies that have demonstrated a shrinkage of the hippocampus in patients with hypercortisolism due to Cushing's disease. Finally, patients with major depression, for whom a chronically elevated stress level can be assumed as well, have also been found to have decreased hippocampal volumes.

Although these thoughts on the role of cortisol in hippocampal damage constitute an important hypothesis, it has to be stressed that, up to now, concise proof is missing. Moreover, all studies cited earlier dealing with hippocampal structural changes in PTSD investigated the participants at a single time point and therefore allow different interpretations. The atrophy of the hippocampus might well be the result of the psychological trauma and an elevated cortisol level. It cannot be ruled out, however, that only participants with a habitually small hippocampus might be especially vulnerable to respond to a trauma with PTSD. As we mentioned earlier, only about one quarter to one third of people develop PTSD upon the encounter of a severe trauma.

Luckily, some recent studies have tried to tackle this difficult but important research question. Bonne et al. (2001) investigated 37 persons who had suffered an acute psychological trauma. These participants were scanned twice, the first time within 1 week of the traumatization and the second time after about 6 months. Ten of the 37 participants fulfilled the criteria for PTSD at the time of the second examination. The volumetric measurements showed two main findings. First, the 10 PTSD patients did not show a smaller volume of the hippocampus and amygdala in the first scan. This argues against the hypothesis that a habitually small hippocampus might present a risk factor for the development of a PTSD. Second, the PTSD patients did not show any volume change of the hippocampus between the first and the second measurements. This finding is compatible with the assumption that a time frame of 6 months between trauma and volumetry is too short for the development of hippocampal damage. On the other hand, it might also be possible that only participants with extremely severe or prolonged traumatization will develop hippocampal atrophy.

A second study (De Bellis, Hall, Boring, Frustaci, & Moritz, 2001) followed a group of 9 children who had experienced severe abuse over at least 2 years. There was no differential development of the hippocampus compared with an age-matched control group. A different approach was followed by Gilbertson et al. (2002), who investigated 12 monozygotic pairs of twins. In each pair, one of the twins had been traumatized during the Vietnam war and showed persisting symptoms of PTSD at the time of the study, whereas the other twin had not been exposed to trauma. As an additional control, a further group of twin pairs was used. Of these control pairs, one twin had participated in the Vietnam war but had not developed a PTSD. In this study, a smaller hippocampal volume was found in the PTSD twins as well as their healthy siblings compared with the control pairs. Other twin studies have revealed that the size of the hippocampus is largely determined by genetic predisposition. Gilbertson et al. therefore tentatively concluded that a habitually small hippocampus might be a predisposing factor for a PTSD but probably only in cases with extreme traumatization and prolonged nonremitting variants of the disorder.

A recent study by Bremner et al. (2003), on the other hand, appears to support the hypothesis that prolonged stress during PTSD may lead to hippocampal damage. In this study, three groups of women were investigated (Group A had experienced sexual abuse during childhood and persisting PTSD, $n = 10$; Group B had experienced sexual abuse during childhood but no PTSD, $n = 12$; and Group C had experienced no abuse and no PTSD, $n = 11$). The hippocampal volume was determined using structural MRI. Furthermore, the functional integrity of the hippocampus was assessed with a declarative memory task that the participants had to perform within a PET scanner. The hippocampal volume of Group A was found to be smaller than that of Groups B and C by 16% and 19%, respectively. The right hippocampus was more severely affected in the volumetric measurements (22% loss in Group A vs. Group C). In the PET study, Group A participants showed a significantly lower activation of the left hippocampus, which is viewed as being important for the encoding of verbal information.

In a PET study conducted by Gilboa et al. (2004), PTSD patients were compared to healthy participants who had experienced trauma. While patients were in the PET scanner, symptoms were provoked by presenting trauma-related material. A network comprising the right prefrontal cortex, hippocampus, and visual cortex was commonly activated in both patient groups and was interpreted as a "memory network." The activation of the amygdala, anterior cingulate cortex, and premotor cortex, on the other hand, was different in the two groups. Traumatic re-experience during the scanning session appears to lead to an overactivation of the amygdala and its associated autonomous affective reactions.

Similar findings have been reported in patients with BPD, who have been shown to exhibit a bilateral excessive activation of the amygdala upon presentation of pictures with emotionally negative valence. Furthermore, a strong bilateral activation of the fusiform gyrus has been found in BPD, which is known to support the processing of emotional expression of faces (Herpertz et al., 2001). An important study with regard to the effects of psychotherapy of traumatized patients was presented by Ochsner, Bunge, Gross, and Gabriel (2002). In their fMRI investigation, a cognitive–emotional reappraisal of strongly negative pictures led to an increase of activity in lateral and medial prefrontal cortex and to a decrease of activity in the orbitofrontal cortex and the amygdala.

CONCLUSIONS

A core assumption of modern neuroscience is that all affective–emotional processes are coupled to specific neural processes in specific brain regions. These brain regions comprise the dorsolateral prefrontal, orbitofrontal, anterior cingulate, and insular cortex; the hippocampal formation; the mesolimbic system; and the amygdala. These limbic centers are strongly interconnected and constitute a network that is primarily concerned with the affective–emotional evaluation of objects and events and the evaluation of their behavioral relevance (e.g., with regard to reward or punishment entailed by these events). A certain antagonism can be seen between the dorsolateral prefrontal, orbitofrontal, and anterior cingulate cortex on the one hand and the amygdala and mesolimbic system on the other hand in that the former regions appear to exert an inhibiting and/or controlling influence on the subcortical regions. In psychiatric disorders such as PTSD, generalized anxiety disorders, or BPD, this inhibiting influence is compromised, and an overactivation of the amygdala results.

Attempts to delineate the neurobiological foundations of affective–emotional states and of psychiatric disorders with the aid of structural and functional imaging methods are still at their very initial steps. This is mainly due to methodological and experimental reasons (cf. Zald, 2003). For example, the amygdala of the human brain is quite small (about 1.3–1.9 cm in diameter), and the modulations of activity are not very pronounced and therefore difficult to detect. Moreover, the limbic centers of the brain support a wide variety of functions: The amygdala, for example, is involved in the evaluation of surprising events in general and in the processing of stimuli with positive valence, in addition to its main task of evaluating items with negative valence. This poses the difficulty of constructing stimulation scenarios that are not too simple but are demanding enough to yield a differential activation of the amygdala.

In the face of these difficulties, it is very encouraging that the available PET and structural and functional MRI investigations allow us to paint an initial picture of the involvement of the different parts of the limbic system in the appraisal of stimuli with negative valence and in psychiatric disorders such as PTSD, generalized anxiety disorder, and BPD. A source of further encouragement is the good correspondence between the neuroimaging studies and animal studies of emotional conditioning, in particular fear conditioning. Thus, there can be no doubt that—within the restricted framework chosen here—states of the psyche can be visualized by modern neuroimaging methods.

REFERENCES

Adolphs, R., Tranel, D., & Damasio, A. R. (1998). The human amygdala in social judgment. *Nature, 393,* 470–474.

Aggleton, J. P. (1992). *The amygdala: Neurobiological aspects of emotion, memory, and mental dysfunction.* New York: Wiley-Liss.

Aggleton, J. P. (2000). *The amygdala: A functional analysis* (2nd ed.). Oxford, England: Oxford University Press.

Aggleton, J. P., & Brown, M. W. (1999). Episodic memory, amnesia, and the hippocampal–anterior thalamic axis. *Behavioral Brain Sciences, 22,* 425–489.

Akert, K. (1994). Limbisches System [Limbic system]. In D. Drenckhahn & W. Zenker (Eds.), *Benninghoff, Anatomie* (Vol. 2, pp. 603–627). Baltimore: Urban & Schwarzenberg.

Anderson, S. W., Bechara, A., Damasio, H., Tranel, D., & Damasio, A. R. (1999). Impairment of social and moral behavior related to early damage in human prefrontal cortex. *Nature Neuroscience, 2,* 1032–1037.

Arthurs, O. J., & Boniface, S. (2002). How well do we understand the neural origin of the fMRI BOLD signal? *Trends in Neurosciences, 25,* 27–31.

Baker, D. G., West, S. A., Nicholson, W. E., Ekhator, N. N., Kasckow, J. W., Hill, K. K., et al. (1999). Serial CSF corticotropin-releasing hormone levels and adrenocortical activity in combat veterans with posttraumatic stress disorder. *American Journal of Psychiatry, 156,* 585–588.

Bechara, A., Tranel, D., Damasio, H., Adolphs, H. R., Rockland, C., & Damasio, A. R. (1995, August 25). Double dissociation of conditioning and declarative knowledge relative to the amygdala and hippocampus in humans. *Science, 269*, 1115–1118.

Bonne, O., Brandes, D., Gilboa, A., Gomori, J. M., Shenton, M. E., Pitman, R. K., & Shalev, A. Y. (2001). Longitudinal MRI study of hippocampal volume in trauma survivors with PTSD. *American Journal of Psychiatry, 158*, 1248–1251.

Bremner, J. D., Randall, P., Scott, T. M., Bronen, R. A., Seibyl, J. P., Southwick, S. M., et al. (1995). MRI-based measurement of hippocampal volume in patients with combat-related posttraumatic stress disorder. *American Journal of Psychiatry, 152*, 973–981.

Bremner, J. D., Randall, P., Vermetten, E., Staib, L., Bronen, R. A., Mazure, C., et al. (1997). Magnetic resonance imaging-based measurement of hippocampal volume in posttraumatic stress disorder related to childhood physical and sexual abuse—A preliminary report. *Biological Psychiatry, 41*, 23–32.

Bremner, J. D., Vythilingam, M., Vermetten, E., Southwick, S. M., McGlashan, T., Nazeer, A., et al. (2003). MRI and PET study of deficits in hippocampal structure and function in women with childhood sexual abuse and posttraumatic stress disorder. *American Journal of Psychiatry, 160*, 924–932.

Büchel, C., Dolan, R. J., Armony, J. L., & Friston, K. J. (1999). Amygdala-hippocampal involvement in human aversive trace conditioning revealed through event-related functional magnetic resonance imaging. *Journal of Neuroscience, 19*, 10869–10876.

Cahill, L., & McGaugh, J. (1998). Mechanisms of emotional arousal and lasting declarative memory. *Trends in Neurosciences, 21*, 294–299.

Canive, J. M., Lewine, J. D., Orrison, W. W., Jr., Edgar, C. J., Provencal, S. L., Davis, J. T., et al. (1997). MRI reveals gross structural abnormalities in PTSD. *Annals of the New York Academy of Sciences, 821*, 512–515.

Canli, T., Sivers, H., Whitfield, S. L., Gotlib, I. H., & Gabrieli, J. D. E. (2002, June 21). Amygdala responses to happy faces as a function of extraversion. *Science, 296*, 2191–2195.

Cardinal, R. N., Parkinson, J. A., Hall, J., & Everitt, B. J. (2003). Emotion and motivation: The role of the amygdala, ventral striatum, and prefrontal cortex. *Neuroscience and Biobehavioral Reviews, 26*, 321–325.

Carter, C. S., Braver, T. S., Barch, D. M., Bitvinick, M. M, Noll, D., & Cohen, J. D. (1998, May 1). Anterior cingulate cortex, error detection, and the online monitoring of performance. *Science, 280*, 747–749.

Comer, R. J. (1995). *Klinische Psychologie.* [Abnormal psychology]. Heidelberg, Germany: Spektrum Akademischer Verlag.

Davidson, R. J., & Irwin, W. (1999). The functional neuroanatomy of emotion and affective style. *Trends in Cognitive Sciences, 3*, 11–21.

De Bellis, M. D., Hall, J., Boring, A. M., Frustaci, K., & Moritz, G. (2001). A pilot longitudinal study of hippocampal volumes in pediatric maltreatment-related posttraumatic stress disorder. *Biological Psychiatry, 50*, 305–309.

De Bellis, M. D., Keshavan, M. S., & Harenski, K. A. (2001). Anterior cingulate N-acetyl-aspartate/creatine ratios during clonidine treatment in a maltreated child with posttraumatic stress disorder. *Journal of Child and Adolescent Psychopharmacology, 11*, 311–316.

Dolan, R. J. (2000). Functional neuroimaging on the human amygdala during emotional processing and learning. In J. P. Aggleton (Ed.), *The amygdala: A functional analysis* (2nd ed., pp. 631–653). Oxford, England: Oxford University Press.

Drenckhahn, D., & Zenker, W. (1994). *Benninghoff Anatomie Bd. 2*. Munich, Germany: Urban & Schwarzenberg.

Ehlert, U., Wagner, D., Heinrichs, M., & Heim, C. (1999). Psychobiologische Aspekte der posttraumatischen Belastungsstörungen [Psychobiological aspects of posttraumatic stress disorders]. *Nervenarzt, 70*, 773–779.

Ekman, P. (1999). Basic emotions. In T. Dagleish & M. J. Power (Eds.), *Handbook of cognition and emotion* (pp. 45–60). New York: Wiley-Liss.

Fendt, M., & Fanselow, M. S. (1999). The neuroanatomical and neurochemical basis of conditioned fear. *Neuroscience and Biobehavioral Reviews, 23*, 743–760.

Formisano, E., & Goebel, R. (2003). Tracking cognitive processes with functional MRI mental chronometry. *Current Opinion in Neurobiology, 13*, 174–181.

Gehring, W. J., & Knight, R. T. (2000). Prefrontal–cingulate interactions in action monitoring. *Nature Neuroscience, 3*, 516–520.

Gilbertson, M. W., Shenton, M. E., Ciszewski, A., Kasai, K., Lasko, N. B., Orr, S. P., & Pitman, R. K. (2002). Smaller hippocampal volume predicts pathologic vulnerability to psychological trauma. *Nature Neuroscience, 5*, 1242–1247.

Gilboa, A., Shalev, A. Y., Laor, L., Lester, H., Louzoun, Y., Chisin, R., & Bonne, O. (2004). Functional connectivity of the prefrontal cortex and the amygdala in posttraumatic stress disorder. *Biological Psychiatry, 55*, 263–272.

Hariri, A. R., Mattay, V. S., Tessitore, A., Kolachana, B., Fera, F., & Weinberger, D. R. (2003). Neocortical modulation of the amygdala response to fearful stimuli. *Biological Psychiatry, 53*, 494–501.

Herpertz, S. C., Dietrich, T. M., Wenning, B., Krings, T., Erberich, S. G., Willmes, K., et al. (2001). Evidence of abnormal amygdala functioning in borderline personality disorder: A functional MRI study. *Biological Psychiatry, 50*, 292–298.

Horvitz, J. C. (2000). Mesolimbicocortical and nigrostriatal dopamine responses to salient non-reward events. *Neuroscience, 96*, 651–656.

Julien, R. M. (1997). *Drogen und Psychopharmaka*. [A primer of drug action]. Heidelberg, Germany: Spektrum Akademischer Verlag.

Koch, M. (1999). The neurobiology of startle. *Progress in Neurobiology, 59*, 107–128.

LeDoux, J. (1996). *The Emotional Brain*. New York, NY: Simon & Schuster.

LeDoux, J. (2000). Emotion circuits in the brain. *Annual Review Neuroscience, 23*, 155–184.

Logothetis, N. K., Pauls, J., Augath, M., Trinath, T., & Oeltermann, A. (2001). Neurophysiological investigation of the basis of the fMRI signal. *Nature, 412*, 150–157.

McDonald, A. J. (2003). Is there an amygdala and how far does it extend? An anatomical perspective. *Annals of the New York Academy of Sciences, 985*, 1–21.

Markowitsch, H. J. (1999). *Gedächtnisstörungen*. [Memory disorders]. Stuttgart, Germany: Kohlhammer.

Markowitsch, H. J. (2000). The anatomical bases of memory. In M. S. Gazzaniga (Ed.), *The new cognitive neurosciences* (2nd ed., pp. 781–795). Cambridge, MA: MIT Press.

Münte, T. F., & Heinze, H.-J. (2001). Beitrag moderner neurowissenschaftlicher Verfahren zur Bewußtseinsforschung [Contribution of modern neuroscientific methods to the consciousness research]. In M. Pauen & G. Roth (Eds.), *Neurowissenschaften und Philosophie* (pp. 298–328). München, Germany: UTB-W. Fink.

Nieuwenhuys, R., Voogd, J., & van Huijzen, C. (1991). *The human central nervous system.* New York: Springer.

Ochsner, K. N., Bunge, S. A., Gross, J. J., & Gabrieli, J. D. E. (2002). Rethinking feelings: An fMRI study of the cognitive regulation of emotion. *Journal of Cognitive Neuroscience, 14,* 1215–1229.

Panksepp, J. (1998). *Affective neuroscience: The foundations of human and animal emotions.* Oxford, England: Oxford University Press.

Petrides, M. (2000). The role of the mid-dorsolateral prefrontal cortex in working memory. *Experimental Brain Research, 133,* 44–54.

Petrides, M., & Pandya, D. N. (1999). Dorsolateral prefrontal cortex: Comparative cytoarchitectonic analysis in the human and the macaque brain and corticocortical connection patterns. *European Journal of Neuroscience, 11,* 1011–1036.

Phelps, E. A., O'Connor, K. J., Gatenby, J. C., Gore, J. C., Grillon, C., & Davis, M. (2001). Activation of the left amygdala to a cognitive representation of fear. *Nature Neuroscience, 4,* 437–441.

Posner, M. I. (1993, October 23). Seeing the mind. *Science, 262,* 673–674.

Rauch, S. L., Whalen, P. J., Shin, L. M., McInerney, S. C., Macklin, M. L., Lasko, N. B., et al. (2000). Exaggerated amygdala response to masked facial stimuli in posttraumatic stress disorder: A functional MRI study. *Biological Psychiatry, 47,* 769–776.

Robbins, T. M., & Everitt, B. J. (1995). Arousal systems and attention. In M. S. Gazzaniga (Ed.), *The cognitive neurosciences* (pp. 243–262). Cambridge, MA: MIT Press.

Rodriguez-Fornells, A., Kurzbuch, A. R., & Münte, T. F. (2002). Time course of error detection and correction in humans: Neurophysiological evidence. *Journal of Neuroscience, 22,* 9990–9996.

Rodriguez-Fornells, A., Rotte, M., Heinze, H. J., Noesselt, T., & Münte, T. F. (2002). Brain potential and functional MRI evidence for how to handle two languages with one brain. *Nature, 415,* 1026–1029.

Rolls, E. T. (1999). *The brain and emotion.* Oxford, England: Oxford University Press.

Roth, G. (2003). *Fühlen, Denken, Handeln.* [Feeling, thinking, acting]. Frankfurt a. M. Main, Germany: Suhrkamp.

Roth, G. & Dicke, U. (2005). Funktionelle neuroanatomie des limischen systems [Functional anatomy of the limbic system]. In H. Foerstl, M. Hautzinger, & G. Roth (Eds.), *Neurobiologie psychischer störungen* [Neurobiology of psychic disorders]. Heidelberg, Germany: Springer, 1–74.

Schiltz, K., Szentkuti, A., Guderian, S., Kaumann, J., Munte, T. F., Heinze, H.-J., et al. (2006). Relationship between hippocampal structure and memory function in elderly humans. *Journal of Cognitive Neuroscience, 18,* 990–1003.

Schuff, N., Neylan, T. C., Lenoci, M. A., Du, A. T., Weiss, D. S., Marmar, C. R., & Weiner, M. W. (2001). Decreased hippocampal N-acetyl aspartate in the absence of atrophy in posttraumatic stress disorder. *Biological Psychiatry, 50*, 952–959.

Spanagel, R., & Weiss, F. (1999). The dopamine hypothesis of reward: Past and current status. *Trends in Neurosciences, 22*, 521–527.

Tulving, E., & Markowitsch, H. J. (1998). Episodic and declarative memory: Role of the hippocampus. *Hippocampus, 8*, 198–204.

Villarreal, G., Hamilton, D. A., Petropoulos, H., Driscoll, I., Rowland, L. M., Griego, J. A., et al. (2002). Reduced hippocampal volume and total white matter volume in posttraumatic stress disorder. *Biological Psychiatry, 52*, 119–125.

Villarreal, G., & King, C. Y. (2001). Brain imaging in posttraumatic stress disorder. *Seminar in Clinical Neuropsychiatry, 6*, 131–145.

Winston, J. S., Stranger, B. A., O'Doherty, J., & Dolan, R. J. (2002). Automatic and intentional brain responses during evaluation of trustworthiness of faces. *Nature Neuroscience, 5*, 277–292.

Zald, D. H. (2003). The human amygdala and the emotional evaluation of sensory stimuli. *Brain Research Reviews, 41*, 88–123.

12

Brain Imaging Methods and the Study of Cognitive Processes: Potentials and Limits

Rainer M. Bösel
Free University of Berlin, Germany

W hat kind of realization of psychological facts is possible using imaging methods compared with using other psychological methods? Current popular literature informs us about such things as brain localization of intelligence or moral conscience. Naturally, questions arise concerning the relationship between the topography of brain processes and the topology of cognitive structures. Behind the scenes, we argue about the usefulness of excessive technology in psychological research and about some deviant pathways on which biomedical techniques embark. Given these considerations, the main question to discuss here is how to measure cognition.

Cognition in a narrow sense means to realize things. From the viewpoint of neuropsychology, in cognition objective and subjective conditions are linked. To elucidate the nature of this link, most research looks at localization within the brain and at the time course of cognitive processes. In accordance with the history of neuropsychology, I begin with a discussion of the psychological view on localization of cognition.

Long ago, a connection between brain and thought was proposed by Alkmaion (500BC). Assumptions about a relationship between brain anatomy and individual characteristics and skills, such as the ability of causal thinking, social support, imitation, or cautious planning, were expressed much later, in the 18th century, by Franz Joseph Gall in Vienna (Hagner, 1997). Gall's theoretical approach was later called *phrenology*. When in 1796 the Académie française requested a detailed look at Gall's theory, he was cautious enough to present only his anatomical studies and not his functional assumptions.

At this time, empirical data were usually recorded only for single cases. One fruitful observation was made by the British physician John Harlow on his patient Phineas Gage (Damasio, 1994, chaps. 1–2). Gage, who worked as a blaster, was severely injured by an explosion in 1848. An iron pole with a thickness of about 3 cm went through his brain and lesioned his frontal cortex. The injury altered Gage's character: He mainly showed a loss of responsibility and pleasantness and his sense of fairness. In general, the birth of neuropsychology is associated with the Parisian psychiatrist Pierre Paul Broca. In 1861, he claimed a relationship between aphasias of speech and lesions of the left frontal cortex. In the following years, he bolstered this thesis with the description of 12 cases of aphasic patients (Harrington, 1987).

More recently, Sandra Witelson and her colleagues surveyed Albert Einstein's brain (Witelson, Kigar, & Harvey, 1999) and found that it had partly greater brain volume around the gyrus supramarginal than is commonly found in other brains. Similar results were obtained for Karl Friedrich Gauß's brain; however, these findings were met with derision, because the gyrus supramarginalis is known for imagery of motions. Today, we know that reasoning engages, in part, the same brain resources as imagery of motions. Despite the long history of knowledge about localization of function in the human brain, there are still many unanswered questions. The time has come, once again, to think about the location of mental processes within the brain.

First of all, we have to recognize that scientific measuring of mental processes is a common procedure in psychology. According to the ophthalmologist Donders (1868), it seems to be indisputable for reaction time research to assume that there is a mental course beginning with detection and followed by selection and decision. Simple decisions require less time than multiple-choice reactions. Certainly, we also reach a limit, assuming that reaction is determined by the strongest signal without knowledge about the power behind it. Nevertheless, technologies for measuring mental processes seem to be fruitful for psychological theories, and theories about brain functioning may be fruitful for neuropsychological practice.

We cannot ignore the importance of measuring mental processes by measuring brain activity. But how well can we determine the location of any ongoing mental process within the brain?

LOCATING MENTAL FUNCTIONS WITH NEUROPSYCHOLOGICAL METHODS

The basis for measurements on the working brain is the assumption that information processing by nerve cells is related to electrical and metabolic changes within the brain. Measurements of the electrical or magnetic field on the scalp show fluctuations in the frequency range of 0 to 60 Hz. These fluctuations are related to wakefulness and to observable changes of stimuli or motor actions. The source of potential changes within the brain can be computed; however, an exact localization is not easily practicable because this source is only the sum of an unknown number of unknown positions of real dipole generators within the cortex. Nevertheless, we can analyze the time course of brain activation up to a range of milliseconds by the use of electrophysiological methods.

Measurements of the metabolic responses induced by active brain regions are realizable with different methods. A commonly used method is *functional magnetic resonance imaging* (fMRI), based on the determination of actual oxygen disposal and metabolism in certain brain regions. In fMRI, properties of hydrogen atoms in hemoglobin molecules are measured. These properties can be measured only from a small percentage of molecules and change very slowly within 5 to 6.5 sec. Nevertheless, we can analyze the location of activation very precisely, up to millimeters. It should be mentioned that recently developed methods such as event-related optical signal processing (Gratton & Fabiani, 2003) promise a resolution up to 25 mm in space and 100 msec in time.

There is, however, a marked trade-off between the measures of locations and times. Besides these uncertainties, different methods seem to produce commensurable results, and psychological facts can often be related to the localization of brain activity. Therefore, psychologists are called upon to be open to these methods. Medical scientists and psychologists use these methods, contributing to 50% of publications each, or publishing in teams. Psychologists are requested to design paradigms for testing selected brain regions. Psychological research should be helpful in the realization of imaging-based diagnostics.

At this point in the usefulness discussion, we have to consider three basic restrictions in interpreting local brain activations: (a) anatomical variability, (b) variable distribution of the cognitive structure according to the individual learning history, and (c) differing functional signifi-cance of activated areas for understanding psychological processes.

Anatomical brain differences between subjects require allometric in-terpolations in the determination of brain areas with uncertain validity. Moreover, conceptual representations seem to be located in wide-spread, distributed ensembles. For instance, the gyrus fusiformis is well known as an area involved in face recognition (the "fusiform face recog-nition area"). Lesions here have long been supposed to cause an inabil-ity to recognize faces (so-called *prosopagnosia*). Also within this area, some nerve modules are activated when buildings are recognized (Haxby et al., 2001). In general, as revealed by neuronal network mod-els, the exact pattern of distribution is determined by the individual's learning history. Newer findings give rise to the assumption that prosop-agnosia is more often caused by certain lesions in a network involved at an earlier stage in visual processing (cf. Barton, Cherkasova, Press, Intrilligator, & O'Connor, 2003). Similar problems occur in dyslexia. Reading skills have to be localized in a widespread network. It is very dif-ficult to predict particular symptoms from distinct lesions. In this case, network models are more helpful for a thorough understanding than pure anatomy (Plaut & Shallice, 1993).

An additional problem occurs with the interpretation of parts of acti-vation patterns as representing factors or stages of cognitive processes. Blood and Zatorre (2001) investigated activation patterns in the brain during pleasurable experiences (i.e., listening to classical music). They found parts of the brain to be active that are usually involved in effort and social behavior, and other parts to be inactive, such as control of avoidance behavior or other executive functions (see Fig. 12–1). It re-mains unclear, however, whether the sum of these activations or a part of them represents a true image of aesthetic perception (Bösel, 2003). Indeed, "The fact that area F becomes active during happiness does not imply that happiness is localized to area Φ" (Sarter, Berntson, & Cacioppo, 1996, p. 20).

Supposing that patterns of coincident activations are representative for a certain mental stage, a lot of methods are used for imaging coher-ences of electrical brain activity. Highly coherent patterns are indeed strongly related to certain gestalt perceptions (Tallon-Baudry, Bertand, Delpuech, & Pernier, 1996). Synchronous oscillations in the so-called "gamma band" of the electroencephalographic (EEG) signal seem to be good candidates for indexing binding of detected features into holistic percepts. Binding processes can be assumed to be correlated to con-scious phenomena. Unfortunately, a lot of literature gives rise to the as-sumption that synchronous oscillations are in fact a necessary but not a sufficient condition for gestalt experience.

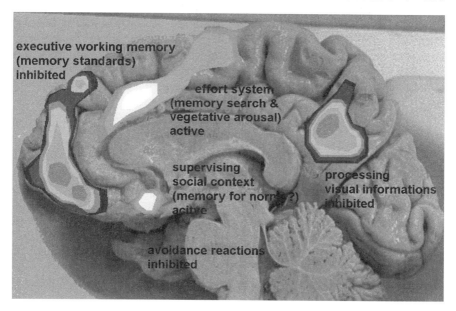

Figure 12–1. Example of an imaging pattern representing a complex brain state in aesthetic perception. Is the sum of activated and inhibited parts of the processing structure shown equivalent to a state of aesthetic experience? Data are in accordance with Blood and Zatorre (2001). From "Ästhetisches Empfinden: Neuropsychologische Zugänge" (p. 279), by R. M. Bösel, In J. Küpper and C. Menke (Hrsg.), *Dimensionen ästhetischer Erfahrung* [Dimensions of aesthetic experience], 2003, Frankfurt a. M. Main, Germany: Suhrkamp. Copyright 2003 by Rainer Bösel. Adapted with permission.

Localizing brain activation is not always instrumental in exploring factors that influence cognitive functioning or mental steps. The reader may remember Leonardo da Vinci's paintings by the use of the *camera obscura*. This technique—as perfect as it was—opened a door to distortion, faking, and fiction. Perhaps we have at present a similar problem of changing technology in cognitive sciences. On the other hand, many psychologists are worried about the possible loss of traditional psychological research fields to neurophysiology or brain research more generally. As demonstrated early in the philosophy of science, it is not possible to prevent ourselves from drawing false conclusions on the basis of precise findings (Wind, 1930/2001). Some scientists warn against *pseudo-empirical findings*—that is, the false interpretation of empirical results determined by a priori assumptions about the object being measured. How useful is it in psychology to know where cognitive processes are localized? The question of the usefulness of topographic methods arises in psychology quite apart from the medical applications of such methods in neurosurgery, pain research, or the diagnosis of cerebral dysfunction. Undoubtedly, there is a relationship of some kind between the dynamic of activations over time and the changing patterns of mental states due to the progress of ongoing information processing; however, what precisely that relationship might be remains unclear.

RELATIONSHIP BETWEEN BRAIN DYNAMICS AND INFORMATION PROCESSING

To understand brain dynamics, we usually differentiate between data-driven processes that work bottom-up in encoding and top-down processes of controlled attention and working memory actions (see Fig. 12–2; cf. Desimone et al., 1995). Interactions between early processes in perception and higher level dynamics are in most cases not observable and have to be interpreted post hoc according to a common psychological validity.

The fundamental problem of reconstructing brain dynamics from imaging data can be discussed in two steps. First, brain areas that are representative for interactions between bottom-up and top-down processing

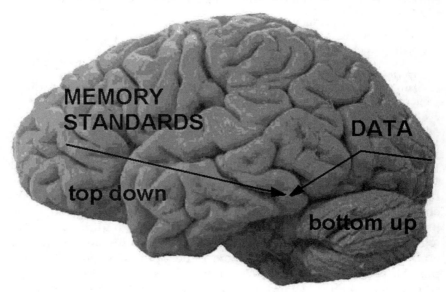

Figure 12–2.   Brain dynamics is composed of an interaction of bottom-up and top-down processes. The time course of dynamics and involvement of brain structures depends on the actual setting demands as well as on the individual cognitive set determined by learning history and habitual or instructed strategies.

are usually less active than areas activated by mismatch detection or automatic attention. For example, this has been shown in a recognition paradigm. Consider research participants who familiarize themselves with certain abstract geometric figures in a training phase. The following day, many more figures are presented, and participants have to decide whether they have seen these figures before. Executive processes are supposed to control reward behavior according to the match between presented figures and memory standards. This match is seen by fMRI halfway between primary sensory area and motor cortex, located in a pathway known for object recognition (Bösel, 2001, Fig. 25.4). Unfortunately, this location shows only a small amount of activity because broad memory activations as seen for mismatches (new stimuli) are suppressed in the case of matches (old stimuli). Moreover, the location for recognition changes slightly among participants according to their subjective memory structure.

Another problem is the partly unknown causes of activity patterns. Consider a person who is monitoring a video showing a fast ride through a winding tunnel simulating sliding in a pipe like those found in a water park. In most cases, people experience the feeling of bodily locomotion instead of the perception of moving features on a screen. To analyze brain mechanisms of this illusion phenomenon, we imaged cerebral activity using fMRI during a film presentation. Two brain areas were active for the comparison between movement perception and perception of a still picture: (a) the supramarginal gyrus and (b) the premotor cortex (see Fig. 12–3). Doubtlessly, the path of information can be interpreted as proceeding from supramarginal to premotor areas, explaining unwilled compensatory movements. However, perceptions of bodily locomotion also occur in cases without automatic compensatory movements. Two questions remain. First, what gives rise to these premotor activations? Second, is there a retrograde influence on the supramarginal imagery area producing the illusory phenomena? Unfortunately, these questions cannot be answered by brain imaging methods.

It should be mentioned that other neuropsychological methods are more closely related to the assumed underlying mental processes, illustrating the time course of brain activation patterns. In a recent experiment, we showed two or more digits of the same numeric value on screen. Participants had to make decisions about the numerical amount of either the digit frequency or the digit value. This condition was compared to a more difficult one, in which they had to decide whether the numerical amount was larger for the digit frequency or the digit value. In the harder condition, participants had to perform at least one additional cognitive operation before response execution compared with the simple condition, namely, the comparison be-

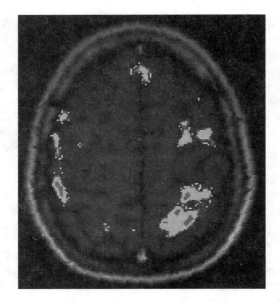

Figure 12–3.   Activated brain structures in monitoring a video showing a ride through a winding tunnel as revealed by functional magnetic resonance imaging. Subjective experience is dominated by the illusory perception of locomotor movement. A region below in the right hemisphere is activated within the gyrus supramarginalis, an important part in mental imagery of movements. The activation in the middle of the right hemisphere shows participation of the premotor cortex, commonly active in movement performance. What kind of interaction between these brain parts may produce the occurring illusory phenomenon? Data presented with permission of Mareike Heß.

tween the former two judgments. We hope to see exactly this in the time course of a certain EEG frequency power obtained from attention controlling parts of the executive cortex (see Fig. 12–4). However, evidence for a correspondence between EEG power changes and mental activity has not yet appeared.

At this point of the discussion we have to ask what level of cognitive dynamics can be mapped by imaging techniques. For this, we must turn to the problem of the time course and the chronometry of mental processes.

LOCATIONS AND THE TIME COURSE OF MENTAL PROCESSING

Let us consider that mental phenomena are matters of subjective experience that have to be commensurate with objective facts. Cognition is determined by the architecture of the brain. But how do we find out the best parameters for mapping cognitive dynamics?

Cognitive dynamics can be illustrated by considering a fact, that could be described verbally by three to five sentences, each containing about 10 words. Verbal description takes about 10 sec, given a speech speed with three to five words per second. However, mental dynamics are considerably faster. To feature the mental dynamics representing the same fact, we may consider a complex choice reaction upon this fact, lasting about 500 to 1,000 msec. Subtracting the encoding time, we can assume a time course lasting about at least 300 to 350 msec to build up a mental image of the fact. This process in cognition is called *microgenesis*, resulting in a mental state.

Brain dynamics are essentially faster. Each cortical neuron is connected to another one by at least three to four synapses. Given the synaptic delay of some milliseconds plus the nerve conductance speed of 25 to 50 msec, we can assume a resulting delay of more than 300 msec between the starting point of the brain process and the beginning of conscious mental events.

The negative time lag between mental states and the rise of the related physiological process of at least 300 msec can be observed by certain methods. In event-related potential research, a positive deflection

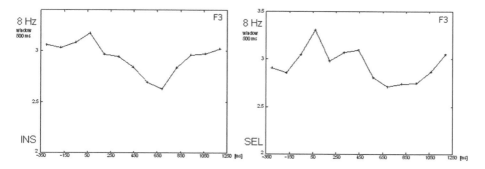

Figure 12–4. Brain dynamics in decision making: time course of electroencephalogram power of 8-Hz frequency value at frontal sites (F3), indicating mental concentration. Stimuli consisted of two or more digits of the same value (e.g., 4 4). Two response conditions are compared: (a) INS, to find out the numerical amount the digit value/frequency, and (b) SEL, to find out the greater/smaller amount of digit value/frequency. A one-step decision, as in INS—for example, deciding amount of value or frequency—corresponds to one phase of brain activation. Decisions requiring two mental steps, as in SEL—for example, deciding amount of value and frequency and comparing them—at least correspond to two phases of brain activation. Here, activation of selected brain areas is less informative than the time course. Data presented with permission of Sascha Tamm.

of the derived signal occurring more than 300 msec after stimulus onset (P300) gives reference to a conscious perception of the stimulus. Libet (1985, 1999) has found voluntary acts to be delayed by about 350 msec compared with the related unconscious cerebral activities.

We cannot know exactly to what extent this negative time delay determines the degree of freedom for intentional thoughts (in the sense of will). Intentional thoughts depend on ongoing working memory processes, and it is very hard to predict subjective associative connections and their related activity within the individual memory. This remains an open question, especially in the planning phase of convergent thinking (after having "crossed the rubicon," according to Heckhausen's [1989] model). Nevertheless, there is a strong determination by brain processes for voluntary acts (Bieri, 2001). Potentials for acts are matters of objective fact, whereas potentials for thoughts are matters of social judgments, revealed by reasoning and predictions against the background of common norms.

CRITIQUE AND OUTLOOK

Most of our concepts of human behavior and subjective experience are highly abstract and are derived from myriad features. Social constructs such as creativity, qualia, or reality filters do not exist within the brain, whereas things such as concept formation or episodic reconstruction do.

An anecdote may illustrate the problem of social judgments about cognition and cognitive abilities in neuropsychology. The British neurologist John Lorber (1915/1996) reported on a young student at his university. This student had an IQ of 126, had gained a first-class honors degree in mathematics, and was socially completely normal. And yet the boy had virtually no brain. When Lorber did a brain scan on him, he saw that instead of the normal 4.5 mm-thick brain tissue between the ventricles and the cerebral surface, there was just a thin layer of mantle measuring 1 mm or so. The cranium of the student was mainly filled with cerebrospinal fluid (Lewin, 1980).

To bridge the gaps between subjective experience, cognitive psychology, and neurology, we urgently need more data derived from self-report in neuropsychological research. In psychology, we need concepts with a good perspective for a possible implementation in the real neural networks of the brain. In using biomedical methods, we have to develop better techniques for mental chronometry, particularly for induced (non-phase-locked) brain processes. In general, we need more than peaceful coexistence of different methods within psychological research. We also need fruitful cooperation between traditional and biomedical research, with each controlling the other's research goals and theoretical implications. In the end, it should be possible to describe human behavior and consciousness based on the functioning of approximately 20 billion cortical neurons.

REFERENCES

Barton, J. J. S., Cherkasova, M., Press, D. Z., Intriligator, J., & O'Connor, M. (2003). Developmental prosopagnosia: a study of three patients. *Brain and Cognition, 51*, 12–30.

Bieri, P. (2001). *Das Handwerk der Freiheit. Über die Entdeckung des eigenen Willens.* [Trades of freedom: On the discovery of one's own will]. München, Germany: Hanser.

Blood, A. J., & Zatorre, R. J. (2001). Intensely pleasurable responses to music correlate with activity in brain regions implicated in reward and emotion. *Proceedings of the National Academy of Sciences of the U.S.A., 98*, 11818–11823.

Bösel, R. M. (2001). *Denken.* [Thinking]. Göttingen, Germany: Hogrefe.

Bösel, R. M. (2003). Ästhetisches Empfinden: Neuropsychologische Zugänge [Aesthetic feeling: Neuropsychological perspectives]. In J. Küpper & C. Menke (Hrsg.), *Dimensionen ästhetischer Erfahrung* (pp. 264–283). Frankfurt a. M. Main. Germany: Suhrkamp.

Damasio, A. (1994). *Descartes' error: Emotion, reason, and the human brain.* New York: Avon Books.

Desimone, R., Miller, E. K., Chelazzi, L., & Lueschow, A. (1995). Multiple memory systems in the visual cortex. In M. S. Gazzaniga (Ed.), *The cognitive neurosciences* (pp. 475–486). Cambridge, MA: MIT Press.

Donders, F. C. (1868). Die Schnelligkeit psychischer processe [The speed of mental processes]. *Archiv für Anatomie, Physiologie und wissenschaftliche medicin (Leipzig)*, 657–681.

Gratton, G., & Fabiani, M. (2003). The event-related optical signal (EROS) in visual cortex: Replicability, consistency, localization, and resolution. *Psychophysiology, 40*, 561–571.

Hagner, M. (1997). *Homo cerebralis: Der Wandel vom Seelenorgan zum Gehirn.* [Homo cerebralis: The conversions of soul's organ to brain]. Berlin, Germany: Berlin Verlag.

Harrington, A. (1987). *Medicine, mind and the double brain.* Princeton, NJ: Princeton University Press.

Haxby, J. V., Gobbini, M. I., Furey, M. L., Ishai, A., Schouten, J. L., & Pietrini, P. (2001, September 28). Distributed and overlapping representations of faces and objects in ventral temporal cortex. *Science, 293*, 2425–2430.

Heckhausen, H. (1989). *Motivation und Handeln* (2nd ed.). [Motivation and action]. Berlin, Germany: Springer.

Lewin, R. (1980, December 12). Is your brain really necessary? *Science, 210*, 1232–1234.

Libet, B. (1985). Unconscious cerebral initiative and the role of conscious will in voluntary action. *Behavioral and Brain Sciences, 8*, 529–566.

Libet, B. (1999). How does conscious experience arise? The neural time factor. *Brain Research Bulletin, 50*, 339–340.

Plaut, D. C., & Shallice, T. (1993). Deep dyslexia: A case study of connectionist neuropsychology. *Cognitive Neuropsychology, 10*, 377–500.

Sarter, M., Berntson, G. G., & Cacioppo, J. T. (1996). Brain imaging and cognitive neuroscience: Toward strong inference in attributing function to structure. *American Psychologist, 51*, 13–21.

Tallon-Baudry, C., Bertrand, O., Delpuech, C., & Pernier, J. (1996). Stimulus specificity of phase-locked and non-phase-locked 40 Hz visual response in human. *Journal of Neuroscience, 16*, 4240–4249.

Wind, E. (2001). *Das Experiment und die Metaphysik.* [Experiment and metaphysics]. Frankfurt a. M. Main, Germany: Suhrkamp. (Original work published 1930)

Witelson, S. F., Kigar, D. L., & Harvey, T. (1999). The exceptional brain of Albert Einstein. *The Lancet, 353*, 2149–2153.

13

Mind Reading, Brain Mirror, Neuroimaging: Insight Into the Brain or the Mind?

Michael Hagner
Eidgenössische Technische Hochschule Zürich, Switzerland

MIND READING AND THE UNCANNY

Mind reading is an ambivalent cultural phenomenon. At times, one can say admiringly to someone else, "You are a mind reader," when that person has guessed what one is thinking at the moment without the use of words, gestures, or other expressive signals. However, as soon as one goes beyond such coincidences, one no longer knows exactly what is going on. Extrasensory perception, charlatanry, or pathology are possible conventional explanations. Others might think of hidden mechanisms that cannot be explained rationally. This uncertainty about a phenomenon that appears to be such a riddle often leads to a feeling of the uncanny.

That uncertainty and a sense of the uncanny have something to do with one another is not new. S. Freud wrote in his essay, "The Uncanny"

(1955/1919), that "a particularly favourable condition for awakening uncanny feelings is created when there is an intellectual uncertainty whether an object is alive or not, and when an inanimate object becomes too much like an animate one" (p. 233). A feeling of the uncanny arises when two things come together that do not belong together according to previous experience, where something happens that is thought not to be possible, or where a certain order of things appears to be put in question. As examples Freud cited so-called "doubles" (*Doppelgängers*) and telepathy. When someone appears to have immediate contact with the thoughts or experiences of another person, when a doubling of the self appears to be happening, there is fertile ground for feelings of the uncanny. Mind reading is one variant of such contact, but thoughts are invisible. No one can say in what characters they are written. Reading is dependent on visibility. Whoever wants to read my thoughts may not necessarily want to attack me physically, but he or she definitely wants to cross a boundary. Whoever goes unbidden behind the door with the "No Admittance" sign on it acquires a sort of access that transforms my secure inner space into a zone of uncanniness.

Brain mirrors are anything but irrational or pathological, and yet they have something to do with mind reading. Brain mirrors, encephaloscopes, and cerebroscopes are apparatuses with which the world in our heads can be represented visually, without necessarily having to open the skull. Such apparatuses have been possible only for a little more than 100 years. There were twp presuppositions for them: (a) the idea that neurophysiological processes in the brain take place in direct relation to mental life, which today is largely undisputed and (b) that brain mirrors can represent these processes reliably and can therefore make direct statements about mental life, a claim that remains a topic of controversy until today. However that may be, the working mind is now under observation. The professionals interested in a rational, demystified form of mind reading—the military and secret service agencies, the courts and the police, anatomists and psychophysiologists—all of them have been trying for a long time to identify the writing of the nerve cells as legible thoughts. For this no magicians or psychics are needed but instead complex technologies of visualization and a code that makes the secret writing in the head legible. Even now it is foreseeable that lies will no longer be exposed with conventional lie detectors but instead—and with far greater effort—with the help of new, computer-aided brain imaging techniques.

One would think that this technological form of mind reading no longer allows any space for the uncanny, because, for better or for worse, it appears to be entirely open and above board. Nonetheless, traces of the uncanny are visible in various ways even in this scenario; the feeling of insecurity inserts itself into the technological insights and expectations, precisely at the point diagnosed by Freud, because different things come together that do not seem to belong together, things that, when they show up in a common context, do not seem to be opportune. This constellation can be made clear with a brief history of the brain mirror, which can be divided into three periods. First, in the early 19th century, there are *fictions*, presented at an informed distance from *science*. Then, from the late 19th century, the story becomes a tale of *science fiction*, told by both scientists and literary writers. In the past few years, the brain mirror has become a topic of science itself, but one with strongly fictional elements.

Whether it will ever be possible to make the content of thoughts visible—and I would like to doubt that—does not really matter in this context, because both the stimulus and the uncanniness of the brain mirror lie in the possibility that it could perhaps make thoughts legible. The mirror thus remains located on the boundary between reality and fantasy, in spite of all the technical developments of the past 100 years. Even those scientists who think they can, or once thought that they could, develop a brain mirror are therefore acting within the field of science fiction, in which *science* is the nurturing soil of fantasy and *fiction* can be understood as commentary on, exaggeration of, and future perspectives for the science. Only so long as the brain mirror remains in the realm of possibility can it stimulate feelings of the uncanny. Should such an apparatus become reality one day, which appears to me, as stated above, to be improbable, the feeling of the uncanny would disappear immediately. The scientifically protected and explainable participation in mind reading could then still spread fear and loathing, but such feelings would no longer be located in the grey area that is the necessary location for feelings of the uncanny.

FICTIONS WITH SCIENCE: *DANTON'S DEATH*

For technologically protected mind reading there is a primal scene in Georg Büchner's drama *Danton's Death*, which is not really a primal scene, because a feeling of the uncanny cannot occur because of the brutality of the idea being proposed. Büchner, who was both a brain anatomist and a poet, makes a drastic suggestion for how to observe thoughts where they take place: "Know one another? We'd have to crack open our skulls and drag each other's thoughts out by the tails"[1] (Büchner, 1963, p. 3). Danton, in whose mouth Büchner places this

---

[1]The original reads as follows: "Wir müßten uns die Schädeldecken aufbrechen und die Gedanken einander aus den Hirnfasern zerren" (Büchner, 1992, p. 13).

sentence, makes this demand in reaction to the impossibility of truly knowing another person. On this account, the authentic and undisguised truth can be not found in words and looks, gestures and deeds, but only in the brain itself, as though one could search for thoughts there and could actually understand them if they actually were in that place, as though the brain fibers, which are beyond good and evil, lies or truth, could give us information about the content of thoughts.

Leaving aside the fact that the truth about brain fibers has not really been understood either in Büchner's time or today, his vivisectionist anatomy links an axiomatic certainty with desire, a topographical approach with a utopia. For Büchner and the science of his day, the certainty was that they connected thinking, experience, and sensation with the brain as a matter of course. The desire was the utopian wish to untie the puzzling knot of thought and brain. Büchner went beyond the diagnostic claims of the so-called "physiognomics" of his time, the aim of which was to read a person's character from his or her facial expressions; he also went beyond the skull diagnostics of phrenology, the aim of which was to discover people's interests, qualities, and talents by reading their skulls. Looking into the living brain is supposed here to discover the cerebral correlate of each individual thought: one fiber, one thought. Already in the late 18th century the doctrine of sensualism assumed that for each individual sense impression a single brain fiber existed. According to this view, the brain was a conglomerate of innumerable fibers, which were gradually filled with sense impressions (Bonnet, 1769, pp. 18–27). That was a beautifully simple theory, which was attractive for poets after 1800, but which presented considerable problems for increasingly empirically oriented brain research.

Although the poet Büchner could easily cite the brain fibers he had learned about in his medical studies, he and his contemporaries had little to say as anatomists. Instead, they worked incessantly on the question of whether the individual convolutions in the brain actually corresponded to specific mental functions, as phrenologists claimed. Many anatomists busied themselves for decades with the effort to bring some sort of consistent order into the confusing convolutions of the brain. And even when they had some success in individual cases, the variability among individuals was so great that the legibility of the cerebral cortex remained a notoriously difficult enterprise. This was true in incomparably greater measure for the innumerable smaller fibers, the paths of which could not be followed with the microscopes of that time.

Büchner's rough-hewn version of mind reading is a special case. He was not without historical predecessors—for example, the French scientist Maupertuis's demand that vivisection experiments be carried out on the brains of criminals who had been condemned to death

(Maupertuis, 1768, p. 410), or the galvanic experiments conducted on freshly guillotined heads during and after the French Revolution (Borgards, 2004; Hagner, 1997, p. 185–193; Jordanova, 1989). However, this imaginary vivisectionist's reach into the brain, which turns mind reading into a nearly cannibalistic act, is so unmistakably clear in its metaphorical force and in its absurdity that it cannot be located on the boundary between science and fiction but must rather be placed clearly in the realm of fiction. In such an unambiguous space, however, the phenomenon of the uncanny cannot prosper. Instead, it reappears at the moment when the hard, bloody form of grasping for thoughts is replaced by soft, media-based insight. Not cutting into the wet ware, but rather the regime of optics, would decide the future of mind reading.

SCIENCE FICTION: READING BRAINS AND MINDS FROM THE 19TH TO THE 20TH CENTURIES

The 19th century was the century of optical instruments, of visualization beyond previously known limits and supposedly insuperable obstacles. This meant primarily the visualization of the interior and internal workings of the human body. The spectacular beginning was Hermann Helmholtz's invention of the ophthalmoscope in 1853, which made visible the interior of the eye, including its blood vessels. At the end of the century, in 1895, came Conrad Wilhelm Röntgen, with his discovery of X rays, which made the skeleton and some internal organs, such as the heart and the lungs, visible, although not the muscles, the stomach, the liver, or the brain. However, even before Röntgen's entrance the ophthalmoscope, the laryngoscope, and the otoscope had so increased trust in the scopic power of instruments that even the brain mirror seemed possible after all. The fascination of medical scientists and the wider public for the new visual media can also be seen in the lectures of the Vienna experimental pathologist Salomon Stricker, held with the aid of an instrument called an *epidiascope*, in which students sitting in a darkened room attentively observed the projected image of a brain (see Fig. 13–1).

Vienna was a good place for visual and other projections. The fictional birth of the brain mirror lies chronologically between Helmholtz and Röntgen; it took place in Vienna, and a surgeon functioned as the midwife, who developed his vision without either scalpel or a slice in the flesh. In 1884, Vienna surgeon Eduard Albert presented the brain mirror in a public lecture in the following words:

> Let us allow our imaginations to run free. Let us imagine how these things will look after a thousand or ten thousand years. In that time a pro-

Figure 13–1. The pathologist Salomon Stricker projects the image of a brain onto a screen with the aid of an epidiascope, ca. 1885. Source: Institute for the History of Medicine, University of Vienna. Published in E. Freud, Freud, and Grubrich-Simitis (1976, p. 83).

cedure will be discovered to make transparent the living skull, including the brain. A light will be produced that will be so strong, that it can penetrate the entire skull. With a single instrument called the encephaloscope the interior of the brain will be projected into the air in enlarged format, so that during a popular lecture everyone present will see everything. (Albert, 1885, p. 96)

Albert may have erred somewhat in the chronology of his prognosis for the realization of such an apparatus, but it is clear that he understood the illumination of the skull to be the royal road to the reading of the mind. In this he found himself fully within the scientific and cultural horizon of the late 19th century. This was true for his ideas about what was to be seen in such an image in real time and for the question regarding with whom one was allowed to perform such investigations. Albert's setting fit in quite comfortably with the mores of his educated upper middle class Vienna public. This began with his choice of experimental subjects. As he said, adults "do not like to have their interiors shown" (Albert, 1885, p. 96). This sentence is best understood in light of the fact that hypnosis was flourishing at the time, a procedure that made public the will-less and uncontrolled interior of the hypnotized. One year later, in 1886, the young Sigmund Freud became involved in a passionate controversy over the reliability and permissibility of hypnosis with his former teacher, the psychiatrist and brain anatomist Theodor Meynert (Mayer, 2002, pp. 138–140, 146–153). Albert seems to have wanted to avoid any controversy, so in his little science fiction he lets a child instead of an adult come onto the stage, and he asks the child to perform the most typical of all activities for members of the educated middle classes: The child recites a poem, while it's brain is illuminated by the brain mirror.

Albert asks his public to concentrate its attention on the third left frontal convolution, that is, the region that the Parisian physical anthropologist and physician Paul Broca had localized the motoric language center of the brain in 1861. And the public sees, according to Albert, the following:

> As the child begins to speak, an indescribable movement begins in that place; the molecules vibrate at a great rate, some move about in circles, others in ellipses, etc. Suddenly he child hesitates, because it has forgotten a word or line; it turns red from embarrassment and becomes excited, the molecules shoot irregularly toward one another, and suddenly they follow regular pathways again, the blood circulates more regularly in the blood vessels; the child continues speaking. (Albert, 1885, p. 96)

One could describe a functional magnetic resonance tomography in this way today, if it were to produce not only images but a film in real time. The play of the represented elements would be similar, if meditating monks, punishing altruists, or love-smitten youths would be studied in the tomograph while gazing at a picture of a loved one or of a child reciting a poem according to the script just described. The molecules would be the oxygen atoms, the enrichment of which in certain activated zones is being measured; whether their staggering motions correspond to insecurity in speech flow, to the inner mood of the monks in prayer, to the self-punishment of the altruists, or to being in love, is another question. Albert at least plainly assumes a correspondence between the order of the molecules and that of thoughts. He even believes that the equivalent of thought contents can be seen in the play of the molecules and thinks it possible that "one would recognize and be able to conclude what the observed person thinks, the way one can conclude from spoken words often, but not always what the speaker thinks" (Albert, 1885, p. 96).

With this consideration the surgeon brushes against the boundary to the uncanny, but then he immediately steps back from the edge when he adds that "one will never be able to observe the actual inner state, the processes of consciousness with the senses." (Albert, 1885, p. 97). Why the thought processes just described do not belong to the processes of consciousness proper remains the speaker's secret. At least the idea of seeing the soul appears to cause him to shudder, while a thought process can be deduced from the encephaloscope just the way it can from an ordinary speech. But Albert does not touch on this point again; by choosing a child as an experimental subject he avoided the possible embarrassment that an adult might notice a contradiction between the spoken word and the brain image. A possible feeling of uncanniness that could have come from the idea that public participation in the brain processes of a child has nothing secret or intimate about it is suppressed from the start. The apparently visible onrush of emotions indicated by the turbulence of the molecules betrays nothing more than reddening and stuttering due to forgetting a line of poetry. The uncanny would come into play only when something could be seen in the brain image that was supposed to be hidden from view. That cannot happen, according to Albert, but nonetheless he makes no attempt actually to explore the full potential of his brain mirror.

Albert's optical fantasies were not accidental. The idea of illuminating the brain and its supposed thought contents was repeated in different versions after Röntgen's discovery. The precarious status of revealing the mind's intimate affairs, so carefully suppressed by Albert, soon came to be central to the question of illuminating the brain. This can be seen also in the field of so-called "thought photography" which was in fashion briefly after the discovery of X rays. After 1895, many scientists actually believed in the possibility of representing thoughts in photographic images (for further discussion, see Chéroux, 1997; Fischer, 2004). William Crookes, an important English chemist and physicist, predicted in 1897 that photography of the interior of the skull would soon take place and that in this manner the mechanisms of thinking would become understandable. He made this prediction in a lecture before the London Society of Psychical Science, the center of mesmerism, telepathy, and parapsychology in Britain. For a brief moment, it appeared that the fantasies of the spiritists had been fulfilled by the optical technologies of the turn of the 20th century. After the French psychiatrist Hippolyte Baraduc, who worked after all at the famous Salpetrière clinic, heard of Röntgen's new discovery, he began to work in a field that he called *thought photography*. His method was in principle the same as that of Röntgen. He fixed a sensitive photographic plate onto the forehead of a subject and waited for a time. Baraduc was convinced that rays streamed from the body carrying substances too fine to be visible with the naked eye but that might be captured on the photographic plate. He attributed the images that he produced with this method to cerebral discharges. In 1896, he wrote: "When a thought is fixed in an image, this photograph, the glowing covering of our thought, will produce a photochemical effect that is strong enough to make an impression on gelatine film—albeit in a way that is not visible to the human eye. The images thus obtained I have called psychicons, glowing and living images of thought" (cited in Chéroux, 1997, p. 15).

Unfortunately, the images were somewhat disappointing compared with this hopeful statement. They showed contingent patterns of light and shadow, and not even Baraduc was able to interpret his results in detail. Another experimenter, Louis Darget, appeared to be luckier, because he could show pictures with apparently more realistic forms. Röntgen had merely illuminated his wife's hand and published the image, but Darget presented a thought photo of his wife, while she was in a hypnotic sleep. *Dream* and *eagle* were the words that Darget noted on his picture (see Fig. 13–2), which he produced only 4 years before the publication of Freud's *Interpretation of Dreams*. However, Darget did not go into further detail about the meaning that the idea of an eagle could have for his hypnotized wife.

Of course, the parallels between Röntgen and the French experimenters should not be emphasized too heavily, because the latter believed in rays that flowed from the body instead of rays that could be projected into the body. This claim led to considerable controversy in Paris. Critics showed that perspiration, heat, electricity, and the handling of the photographic plate sufficed completely to explain these pictures. Despite this result, which was so embarrassing for the spiritists, the idea of being able to produce visual images of thoughts was not given up. Instead, it traveled from experimental photography into literature.

At the turn of the 20th century, the philosopher and storyteller Kurt Laßwitz wrote a fairy tale with the title "The Brain Mirror" (Laßwitz, 1928). In this text, too, an intense light—but not X rays—penetrates the skull, when the subject first ingests a chemical substance called *Craniophane*, which makes bone transparent. The first-person narrator of the short story meets a friend, who reports to him the following event. He is invited to see his Uncle Pausius, an ingenious tinkerer, in order to examine a spectacular invention—indeed, a brain mirror—about which, however, the nephew knows nothing when he enters the darkened room into which Pausius invites him. The surprise is complete: "Finally I recognize a weakly illuminated screen and on it—I am not a little shocked—my own form" (Laßwitz, 1928, p. 99). The inventor, who at this point is invisible, asks his nephew, where his wife, who was supposed to accompany him, might be. Immediately the image of the wife appears alongside that of the man on the screen. The nephew demands an explanation. Pausius has demonstrated in an experiment on himself

Figure 13–2.   Louis Darget, photography of thinking, 1896. Source: Institut für Grenzgebiete der Psychologie und Psychohygiene, Freiburg im Breisgau, Germany. Published in Fischer (2004, p. 149).

that he can localize and make visible his own optical images in the brain. Even before the nephew has actually entered the darkened room, he is already there in the mind of his uncle. Because this inner brain image can be projected onto the screen, the nephew sees himself when he enters the room: "What you are thinking now, so to speak—yes, I can even photograph that" (Laßwitz, 1928, p. 101).

In this case the visual image is one of something that someone expects to see, but in principle any possible inner images can be transferred to the screen, and from this Laßwitz gains storytelling capital, with which he also brings the feeling of the uncanny into the game. Finally the nephew's wife appears, as expected, but she is worried because she has lost her key. In this situation the brain mirror is just the right thing. Pausius recommends that the woman place herself in front of the apparatus and take *Craniophane*, in order to make the key visible as a memory image and in this way to identify its location. What happens now shows Laßwitz's feeling for the dialectic between the practical or even therapeutic usefulness of the apparatus and the undesired effects it can also have. On the screen appears not the key, but the head of a man—the first person narrator, at which point the husband loses his composure, because he suspects that his wife is cheating on him with his best friend. Just then it occurs to his wife that she has misplaced the key at home by hanging it on the wall behind the photograph of the friend. The husband rushes home and actually finds the key. His suspicion has evaporated, but there remains an uncomfortable feeling: "Suddenly an uncanny feeling of anxiety overcame me [...] the thought that I should suddenly see what my wife can imagine in her inmost thoughts [...] no one can know, what secrets she has in her head" (Laßwitz, 1928, p. 104).

Laßwitz took the story of the brain mirror seriously at the point at which Albert had turned away from it. The visualization of the intimate and the scandalous, of the feared adultery, has brought the husband a kind of participation in his wife's thoughts that he does not want to have at all, but which for a moment had put the entire order of his life in doubt. By means of this insight into the inner thought world of the wife, which neither of them wants to acquire, the uncanny is raised to an ordering principle. Here too the uncanny enters at the moment when it is uncertain whether the image shown by the brain mirror is real or unreal. Laßwitz's sophisticated construction is to use a media technique to introduce the mistake. The difference between a real person and his or her photograph is eliminated in the cerebral representation. Although it is true that the subject can say before the brain mirror whether he or she is thinking of a person in a real situation or of that person's photographic portrait, in the brain image this distinction disappears. What the brain mirror makes visible on the screen is the image of the person of whom the subject is thinking at the time, no more.

We could put it this way: For the neurons in the brain it matters not at all whether a real, a filmed, or a photographed person is being represented. For them it is all the same. The important implications of this fact for the idea of brain imaging was first recognized, so far as I can see, neither by a brain researcher nor by a philosopher, but by a popular medical writer, Fritz Kahn (1929). In 1929, in his widely distributed book, *Human Life*, he imagined the brain mirror as an X ray microscope that follows the nervous excitations in the brain. Accordingly, it would be possible to determine with this apparatus "whether a person is speaking or playing the piano, whether he is writing or playing cards" (Kahn, 1929, p. 184). Everything seems to point to a direct correspondence among experience, action, and brain process, but according to Kahn this is mistaken. The active nerve cells in the brain never come into contact with the external world; they only receive information from other nerve cells. How can they know whether, for example, the experience "elephant," decoded by the brain mirror, represents the image of a real elephant or is only being imagined? Not at all, says Kahn, because a nerve cell makes no distinction between reality, imagination and dreams:

> Life is a dream and a dream is life, a true experience, excitation of the cortex, excitation of nerve cells [...] The X-ray microscopist, who follows the brain excitation, can perhaps some day in a far off utopia recognize the following: in the optical memory cells the picture of an elephant appears, the motor cells of the nerves in the hand "grasp," the nerve cells of the leg "climb," but he will never be able to succeed in deciding whether the brain dreams or has real experiences. (Kahn 1929, p. 184)

The brain organizes itself. That is how current neuroscientists would also put it. Nerve cells communicate with one another, not with the outside world. Nonetheless, a brain would soon give up the ghost, so to speak, if it were isolated from the environment. Brains are arranged for a high level of plasticity, which means that they want to be fed not with significance, deeper meaning, jokes or irony but with impulses that neurons can do something with, that keep a sort of permanent dynamics in play. Presumably it is the case that continuous change is needed in order to keep cerebral status intact. However, none of the meaningful connections or contexts of our life world can be completely represented in these neuronal processes, as the examples from Laßwitz and Kahn have already suggested.

The uncanny is to be sought neither in our daily experience—to which we have immediate access—nor in the activity of the brain itself—which we can measure—but rather in the space between them, the logic of which is hidden from us and from the measuring devices. We surely tend to base our ordering of the world on the distinction between dream and real experience, meaning experience of reality in the waking state. When we cannot make this distinction for the organism, which like no other is the basis for our ability to think and have sensations or feelings, then an obvious gap exists, which could be bridged easily with a strictly dualistic position on the relation of body and mind. If we do not accept such a dualism, because it has not made a single coherent argument for the idea of a soul independent of the brain, then a feeling remains that can be located with Freud in the zone of the uncanny, but in a sense opposite to the one Freud had in mind. Here things are not being brought together that do not actually belong together. Instead, some things obvious belong together, that seem to fit together less and less well, the more details we learn over their exceedingly complex connection with one another.

In 1929, when Kahn published his volume about the nervous system, the Jena psychiatrist Hans Berger also published his first article on electroencephalography (EEG; Borck, 2005b). Even though Kahn presumably did not know of this text when he wrote his chapter, his considerations on the observation and observability of neuronal activity went in a direction similar to that which led to the EEG. Naturally, there are differences: The EEG records the activity not of individual nerve cells but of the mass action of many neurons. Nonetheless, some important brain researchers were convinced that the recorded brain waves offered insight into mental life. Among them was the mathematician and cyberneticist Norbert Wiener (for the following, see Borck, 2005a, pp. 296–300). He not only assumed that the brain worked like a computer but also asserted that EEG curves revealed, in a certain sense, the language of the brain. He was particularly interested in the so-called "alpha wave," which he associated at first with form perception, because "it partakes of the nature of a sweep rhythm, like the rhythm shown in the scanning process of a television apparatus" (Wiener, 1961, p. 141). However, the analogy between television and brain became doubtful when Wiener's coworkers found that there are significant individual differences in the alpha rhythms of experimental subjects. Wiener was not easily intimidated, however, and proposed the hypothesis that an individual's alpha rhythm was an expression of that person's intelligence. He then planned a new research project, in which the EEG curves of three geniuses were recorded: Wiener himself, John von Neumann, and Albert Einstein. Naturally, Einstein's EEG got the largest amount of public attention. During the recording session, he was asked to think either about relativity theory or about nothing at all. The curves differed from one another, and those of Einstein, Wiener, and von Neumanns actually differed somewhat from those of so-called "normal" subjects. But not even the *New York Times* wanted to conclude from this data that the curves represented relativity theory or the genius of its creator.

NEUROIMAGING: SCIENCE, THE MEDIA, AND A REALM OF (UNCANNY) POSSIBILITIES

After this rather peculiar episode, the idea that the EEG could depict thoughts was finally given up. Put more generally, the cognitive neurosciences kept rather quiet about the visualization of thoughts for several decades. This situation has changed fundamentally in the past 15 years. Now, at the beginning of the 21st century, talk about mind reading is more popular than ever. The explanation lies, of course, in the new computer-aided methods of neuroimaging, such as functional magnetic resonance tomography. In this new kind of brain mirror the distribution of oxygen atoms is measured by activating a strong magnetic field. The data are then transformed into images by means of complicated mathematical operations. The procedure is called imaging (*Bildgebung* [picture giving] in German); this term is supposed to make clear that a direct image of the object is not involved, but rather something produced or achieved indirectly from signals. The correspondence between measured data and mental process is supposed to be secured by mathematical operations, and no longer by optical procedures as before. However, despite all of the scientific and technical sophistication being brought to bear there is here, too, a place where science is transformed into fiction, and again the ambivalent concept of mind reading plays an essential role.

"Supercomputer makes thoughts visible"—so, for example, runs the headline of a recent article in a German weekly newsmagazine about a new model magnetic resonance tomography that can produce magnetic fields with an intensity of 9.4 Tesla, three to six times stronger than the equipment currently in use (Spiegel online, 2004). The same metabolic processes are measured as before, clearly with higher resolution, but metabolic processes are not thoughts. It appears that no technical innovation in this field, no matter how positive, can be presented to the public today without indulging in such fundamental category mistakes or producing science fiction. This is legitimation by illusion, and such procedures are among the most notorious in today's knowledge society.

The results of neuroimaging studies are presented to the public in much the same way. Here is a drastic example from the "brave neuro world": A Canadian neurologist pushes test participants into a scanner, shows them pornographic films, and measures the increase of activity in the so-called emotional areas of their brains, when the participants become sexually excited by a scene. The reporter, obvious stimulated himself by such studies, then turns to his or her readers and asks: "And what about you? Do you excite men, women—or maybe even both sexes? Does cuddling sex turn you on, or do you prefer S and M?" (Kraft, 2004, p. 29). These appear to be important questions that can be answered by magnetic resonance tomography. The reporter forgets to add that simply reaching beneath someone's underwear under the same experimental conditions would produce the same result. The genitals do not lie and can hide nothing, and a study using direct genital stimulation would no doubt be much cheaper than one using such an apparatus.

The problematic character of studies such as the one just cited cannot be located in sensationalist journalistic reporting on them alone but begins with the studies themselves, because they have been designed by the scientists involved in such a way that they will get media attention. This collaborative game played by science and the public (and assisted by the media) would have to be analyzed in more detail than can be provided here, in order to understand better the current fascination of cognitive neuroscience. Nonetheless, it is already clear without such an analysis that the price of this public fascination is a noticeable reduction in the precision, skepticism, and clarity of scientific research itself in this field. Yet again we find that the boundary between science and fiction lies at the point at which a space of possibility has been created. No one, and certainly no machine, can read thoughts, and yet the possibility of doing so is being presented to us yet again. Does this also mean that the brave new world of the brain's interior that is now being made visible with the new model brain mirror lead us back to a zone of the uncanny? Let us return to Freud's discussion.

S. Freud (1919/1955) emphasized

> that an uncanny effect is often and easily produced when the distinction between imagination and reality is effaced, as when something that we have hitherto regarded as imaginary appears before us in reality, or when a symbol takes over the full functions of the thing it symbolizes, and so on. It is this factor which contributes not a little to the uncanny effect attaching to magical practices. (p. 244)

Neuroimaging is not a magical practice, but the effect with respect to thought reading is much the same. The brain image is a symbol that is supposed to represent the achievement and significant of the object allegedly being symbolized, meaning a thought or thought process. In the reality of our experience only the thought appears to us, while the underlying brain activity remains invisible, as long as we are not connected with a measuring device. And even then, to get from one situation to the next, we refer to thoughts, not to patterns of cerebral activity. However, if we believe some brain researchers, then this relationship must be reversed with the visualization of brain processes that occur during thought. For them, the neuronal chatter is real, and the thoughts are in the realm of fantasy. According to this logic, we are all illusionists living in a realm of metaphysical uncanniness. But this visually evoked reversal also lies on the boundary of science and fiction. To maintain such a position, a machine like the brain mirror is required, along with the wish to be able to read minds. In other words, we must link two things with one another that do not belong together in ordinary experience, and we find ourselves yet again in the realm of the uncanny.

ACKNOWLEDGMENT

Translated by Mitchell G. Ash.

REFERENCES

Albert, E. (1885). *Gehirn und Seele.* [The brain and the soul]. (*Schriften des Vereins zur Verbreitung naturwissenschaftlicher Kenntisse in Wien*, Vol. 25). Vienna: Braumüller.

Bonnet, C. (1769). *La palingénésie philosophique, ou idées sur l'état passé et sur l'état futur des êtres vivans.* [The philosophical palingenesis, or Ideas on the condition of living beings in the past and in the future]. (Vol. 1). Geneva, Switzerland: Philibert & Chirol.

Borck, C. (2005a). *Hirnströme: Eine Kulturgeschichte der Elektroenzephalographie.* [Brain currents. A cultural history of electroencephalography]. Göttingen, Germany: Wallstein.

Borck, C. (2005b). Writing brains: Tracing the psyche with the graphical method. *History of Psychology, 8*, 79–94.

Borgards, R. (2004). Kopf ab. Die Zeichen und die Zeit des Schmerzes in einer medizinischen Debatte um 1800 und Brentanos Kasperl und Annerl [Beheading. Signs and time of pain in a medical debate around 1800 and Brentano's Kasperl and Annerl]. In G. Brandstetter & G. Neumann (Eds.), *Romantische Wissenspoetik. Die Künste und die Wissenschaften um 1800* (pp. 123–150). Würzburg, Germany: Königshausen & Neumann.

Büchner, G. (1963). Danton's death. In *Complete plays and prose* (R. Mueller, Trans.) (pp. 11–90). New York: Hill & Wang.

Büchner, G. (1992). Dantons Tod. In *Sämtliche Werke* (Vol. 1). Frankfurt a. M. Main, Germany: Deutscher Klassiker Verlag.

Chéroux, C. (1997). Ein Alphabet unsichtbarer Strahlen. Fluidalfotografie am Ausgang des 19. Jahrhunderts [An alphabet of invisible rays. Fluid photography at the end of the nineteenth century]. In A. Fischer & V. Loers (Eds.), *Im Reich der Phantome. Fotografie des Unsichtbaren* (pp. 11–22). Ostfildern, Germany: Ruit.

Fischer, A. (2004). "La Lune au front." Remarques sur l'histoire de la photographie de la pensée ["The moon at the front." Remarks on the history of photography of thought]. In C. Cheroux & A. Fischer (Eds.), *Le troisième oeil. La photographie et l'occulte* (pp. 139–153). Paris: Gallimard.

Freud, E., Freud, L., & Grubrich-Simitis, I. (Eds.). (1976). *Sigmund Freud. Sein Leben in Bildern und Texten.* [Sigmund Freud. His life in pictures and texts]. Frankfurt a. M. Main, Germany: Suhrkamp.

Freud, S. (1955). The uncanny. In *The standard edition of the complete psychological works of Sigmund Freud* (Vol. XVII, pp. 219–252; J. Strachey, Ed.). London: Hogarth. (Original work published 1919)

Hagner, M. (1997). *Homo cerebralis. Der Wandel vom Seelenorgan zum Gehirn.* [Homo cerebralis. The transformation from the organ of the soul to the brain]. Berlin, Germany: Berlin Verlag.

Jordanova, L. (1989). Medical mediations: Mind, body and the guillotine. *History Workshop Journal, 28,* 39–52.

Kahn, F. (1929). *Das Leben des Menschen.* [The life of man]. (Vol. 4). Stuttgart, Germany: Kosmos.

Kraft, U. (2004). Schöne neue Neuro-Welt [Brave new neuro world]. *Gehirn & Geist, 6,* 20–29.

Laßwitz, K. (1928). Der Gehirnspiegel [The brain mirror]. In *Traumkristalle. Neue Märchen* (9th–10th ed., pp. 97–108). Berlin, Germany: Felber.

Maupertuis, P. L. M. de. (1768). Lettre sur le progrès des sciences [Letter on the progress of the sciences]. In *Oeuvres* (Vol. 2, pp. 373–431). Lyon, France: Bruyset.

Mayer, A. (2002). *Mikroskopie der Psyche. Die Anfänge der Psychoanalyse im Hypnose-Labor.* [Microscopy of the psyche. The beginnings of psychoanalysis in the laboratories of hypnosis]. Göttingen, Germany: Wallstein.

Spiegel online. (2004). *Supermagnet macht Gedanken sichtbar.* [Super magnet makes thoughts visible]. Retrieved June 14, 2006, from http://www.spiegel.de/wissenschaft/mensch/0,1518,319057,00.html

Wiener, N. (1961). *Cybernetics: Or control and communication in the animal and the machine* (2nd ed.). Cambridge, MA: MIT Press.

14

Tools = Theories = Data?
On Some Circular Dynamics
in Cognitive Science

Gerd Gigerenzer
Max Planck Institute for Human Development, Germany

Thomas Sturm
Max Planck Institute for the History of Science, Germany

Where new auxiliary means become fruitful for research in a certain domain, it is a frequently occurring phenomenon that the auxiliary means are sometimes also confused with the subject matter.

Daß man, wo neue Hilfsmittel für die Forschung innerhalb eines bestimmten Gebietes fruchtbar werden, gelegentlich auch einmal das Hilfsmittel mit der Sache verwechselt, ist ja eine oft genug vorkommende Erscheinung.
> —(Wundt, 1921, Vol. I, p. 148; translated by T. Sturm)

Scientific inquiry is often divided into two great domains: (a) the context of discovery and (b) the context of justification. Philosophers, logicians, and mathematicians claimed justification as a part of their territory and dismissed the context of discovery as none of their business, or even as "irrelevant to the logical analysis of scientific knowledge" (Popper, 1935/1959, p. 31). Concerning discovery, there still remains a mystical darkness where imagination and intuition reigns, or so it is claimed. Popper, Braithwaite, and others ceded the task of an investigation of discovery to psychology and, perhaps, sociology, but few psychologists have fished in these waters. Most did not care or dare.

Inductivist accounts of science, from Bacon to Reichenbach and the Vienna School, often focus on the role of data but do not consider how the data are generated or processed. Neither do the anecdotes about discoveries, such as Newton watching an apple fall in his mother's orchard while pondering the mystery of gravitation; Galton taking shelter from a rainstorm during a country outing when discovering correlation and regression toward mediocrity; and the stories about Fechner, Kekulé, Poincaré, and others, which link discovery to beds, bicycles, and bathrooms. These anecdotes report the setting in which a discovery occurs, rather than analyzing the process of discovery.

The question "Is there a logic of discovery?" and Popper's (1935/1959) conjecture that there is none have misled many into assuming that the issue is whether there exists a logic of discovery or only idiosyncratic personal and accidental reasons that explain the "flash of insight" of a particular scientist. However, formal logic and individual personality are not the only alternatives (Nickles, 1980). The process of discovery can be shown to possess more structure than thunderbolt guesses but less definite structure than a monolithic logic of discovery of the sort for which Hanson (1958) searched. The present approach lies between these two extremes.

In this chapter, we argue that, in part, the generation of new theories can be understood by a *tools-to-theories* heuristic. This proposed heuristic (not logic) of theory development makes use of various tools of justification that have been used by scientific communities. By *tools* we mean both analytical and physical instruments that are used to evaluate given theories. Analytical tools can be either empirical or nonempirical. Examples of analytical methods of the empirical kind are tools for data processing, such as statistics; examples of the nonempirical kind are normative criteria for the evaluation of hypotheses, such as logical consistency. Examples of physical tools are measurement instruments, such as clocks.

The main goal of this chapter is to show that some tools can provide metaphors that become concepts for psychological theories. We will discuss the heuristic role, as well as the possibilities and problems, of two tools developed during, as it has been called retrospectively, the *cognitive revolution* in the American psychology of the 1960s: inferential statistics and the digital computer. The cognitive revolution was more than an overthrow of behaviorism by mental concepts. Mental concepts have been continuously part of scientific psychology, even coexisting with American behaviorism during its heyday (Lovie, 1983). The cognitive revolution did more than revive the mental; it changed its meaning. The two new classes of theories that emerged, and partially overlapped, pictured the mind as an "intuitive statistician" or a "computer program."

This chapter is structured as follows. First, we outline how tools inspire new theories, both on an individual level and on the level of a scientific community (Section I). Second, we sketch the possible value for the present explanatory approach for a critical evaluation of theories (Section II). After this, we analyze in greater detail the two examples of inferential statistics (Section III) and the digital computer (Section IV). We close with a reconsideration of the issue of the generation of psychological theories (Section V). In doing so, we aim to show how ongoing psychological research sometimes can, and should, integrate considerations concerning its history and philosophy, rather than outsourcing them to other disciplines.

I. TOOLS, METAPHORS, AND THEORY DEVELOPMENT

Conceiving the mind in terms of scientific tools may seem strange. However, understanding aspects of mental life in such ways might be rooted in our common-sense thinking or in our intellectual history.

For instance, before psychology was institutionalized as a discipline in the latter half of the 19th century, many investigations of our sensory capacities could be found in astronomical and optical writings. Investigations of human capacities were often driven by methodological needs of other sciences, and so the senses of human beings were viewed as instruments functioning more or less properly (Gundlach, 1997, 2007). The astronomer Tobias Mayer developed a series of what we would characterize as psychophysical experimental analyses of visual acuity, although his main goal was to develop a "science of errors" (Mayer, 1755; Scheerer, 1987). He aimed at an investigation of the weaknesses of our eyes, comparing their role with that of the instruments used in the observation of heavenly bodies. When Johann Heinrich Lambert tried to measure the intensity of light, he complained that there did not yet exist a photometer comparable to the thermometer in the theory of heat. Hence, the eye had to be used as the measuring device, despite its familiar limitations (Lambert, 1760/1892). Much talk of a "sensory apparatus" derives from such contexts; nowadays, this is ordinary, largely innocent talk, hardly recognizable in its metaphorical origins. Rhetoricians speak of "dead metaphors" here—a misleading metaphor itself, because the metaphors are better characterized as alive, although they are no longer noticed as such. These metaphors inform and shape the content of the terms we take to be as literally referring. The same can be, and often is, true in scientific theories. As W. V. O. Quine (1978) said, metaphors are "vital ... at the growing edges of science" (p. 159). It would be thus a mistake to ignore or prohibit the use of scientific tools for trying to conceive the mind in new ways.

To at least some extent, such a successful transfer of meaning is possible only if one does not understand the functioning of metaphors in traditional ways. It has often been claimed that metaphors work in one direction only, as when the metaphor "Achill is a lion" is teased out to give "Achill is like a lion in the following regards ..." This functioning of metaphor is didactical rather than heuristical; its goals are more understanding and teaching than research and discovery. However, metaphors frequently involve an interaction between the terms that are explained metaphorically and the metaphorical terms themselves, by which various meanings are picked out, emphasized, later on rejected, and remembered again. Both our understanding of what was originally referred to metaphorically and the metaphorical expressions are reshaped (Black, 1962; Draaisma, 2000, chap. 1). Such interaction is especially possible in the long-term developments of science and language. However one thinks of the functioning of metaphors in general, the interaction theory is adequate for the heuristically useful metaphors in science.

Not all scientific tools can play this heuristic role for science in general or for psychology in particular. The simple pieces of round white paper that were used in the Paris Academy in the 17th century to produce the impression of the blind spot in the visual field did never support the generation of new concepts of vision (Mariotte, 1668); neither did the early apparatuses used to experimentally present and measure the temporal persistence of visual sensations (D'Arcy, 1765; Sturm, in press), and so on, for many later psychological tools such as the simple weights used by E. H. Weber and G. T. Fechner in their psychophysiological experiments, the Hipp chronoscope in reaction time measurement, or, more recently, instruments for visual imaging such as positron emission tomography or functional magnetic resonance imaging.

But the tools-to-theories heuristic applies for various innovative theories within psychology (Gigerenzer, 1991). For instance, Smith (1986) argued that Tolman's use of the maze as an experimental apparatus transformed Tolman's conception of purpose and cognition into spatial characteristics, such as cognitive maps. Similarly, he argued that Clark L. Hull's fascination with conditioning machines shaped Hull's thinking of behavior as if it were machine design. The tools-to-theories heuristic also applies, as we will argue, in the cases of inferential statistics and digital computer programs.

The tools-to-theories heuristic is twofold:

1. *Generation of new theories*: The tools a scientist uses can suggest new metaphors, leading to new theoretical concepts and principles.
2. *Acceptance of new theories within scientific communities*: The new theoretical concepts and assumptions are more likely to be accepted by the scientific community if the members of the community are also users of the new tools.

This heuristic explains not the discovery but the generation or development of theories (theoretical concepts and claims). Talk of discovery tends to imply success (Arabatzis, 2002; Curd, 1980; Papineau, 2003; Sturm & Gigerenzer, 2006), but it should be treated as an open question whether theoretical notions and assumptions inspired by scientific tools might have led to good research programs or not. For a similar reason, we speak here not of *justification* but of *acceptance*. A scientific community might be justified from its own current point of view in accepting a theory, but such acceptance might later be found to be in need of further revision.

A highly difficult question is that of how, as it is claimed in Step 1, tools can begin to be used as new metaphors. How is a new theoretical concept, as inspired by a tool, originally generated in a scientist? We think that it is important to note here that it is not tools *simpliciter* that suggest new concepts, but the way a tool is used. When tools of justification are used metaphorically to conceptualize the mind, a new, deviant use of the tools comes into play. Such a deviant use becomes possible if the scientist has a practical familiarity with a tool. A sophisticated understanding of the tool is not necessary. A scientist who knows how to successfully apply a given method to analyze his data may start to compare other systems with the functioning of his tool and then to interpret these systems in terms of the tool. Some such psychological processes should play a role, and they are themselves in need of a better explanation: Are there highly general principles or mechanisms that guide all such processes of theory generation? Or is the nature of these processes more strongly constrained by the specific tools that are used as metaphors, and the psychological phenomena that are conceptualized thereby? Surely such an explanatory task is too complex to be fully addressed here. We wish to emphasize that, first, it is the practical familiarity with the tool that can inspire a new metaphor. Second, it is important that even the ordinary use of a tool—its use for the justification of empirical claims or for the evaluation of a general hypothesis—is not always one and the same. Methods of statistical inference, for instance, have been used for various purposes and in various ways: For example, one might use methods of statistical inference to test hypotheses, or to check the data. It is important to clarify which of these options have also entered the cognitive theories of human thought and behavior that were developed on the background of the metaphor of the mind as an intuitive statistician. This general point applies to the case of the metaphor of mind as computer as well. We return to this later.

II. THE CRITICAL VALUE OF AN EXPLANATION OF THEORY GENERATION

Within the class of tools that can play a metaphorical role, some are better suited for this than others, much as some metaphors in general can be better than others. Once this is recognized, it becomes clear that the tools-to-theories heuristic may be of interest not only for an a posteriori understanding of theory development, or for a psychology of scientific creativity (e.g., Gardner, 1988; Gruber, 1981; Tweney, Dotherty, & Mynatt, 1981). It may also be useful for a critical understanding of present-day theories and for the development of new alternatives. We shall illustrate this by three closely related topics: the justification of these theories; the realistic interpretation of these theories; and the complex relation between theory, data, and tools.

First, let us go back to the distinction between *discovery* and *justification*. It is important here not to view it as a distinction between different processes, let alone processes of a specific temporal order: First comes discovery, then justification. We should rather emphasize that there are different types of questions we can ask with regard to scientific propositions. For any given claim p, we can always ask "Is p justified?" This question differs in principle from the question "How did someone come to accept that p?" (Hoyningen-Huene, 1987; Reichenbach, 1938; Sturm & Gigerenzer, 2006).

Hans Reichenbach and other adherents of the discovery–justification distinction often assume that the critical task of evaluating a scientific claim can be pursued quite independently of knowledge about the origins of that claim. This is why defenders of the distinction hardly found it necessary to pursue research about what brings about new discoveries. Here we disagree. It seems plausible that sometimes a good criticism of a theoretical assumption will profit from such knowledge, if not be impossible without it. The reason for this claim is the following: The heuristic function of tools in theory generation involves a metaphorical transfer of meaning. Metaphorical transfer of meaning from one context to another is often advantageous, but it can also include losses. S. Freud famously compared the relation between the two systems of perception–consciousness and memory to the *Wunderblock* or "mystic writing pad." On such a pad, consisting of a wax layer, a wax sheet, and a transparent celluloid paper, one can erase text by simply pulling the paper free of the wax layer. When one pulls the paper, however, at a deeper level a trace of what had been written is stored. Freud also pointed out that, unlike our capacity of memory, the pad cannot reproduce the erased text from inside (Draaisma, 2000). Metaphors emphasize some aspects and leave others out. Especially in cases of the more successful metaphors in science, such partiality can easily be forgotten. The more aware we become that there has been, and continues to be, a use of tools in the development of theoretical concepts or assumptions, the better we can take care of the pitfalls contained in influential theoretical concepts and assumptions.

Second, the tools-to-theories explanation of theory generation has caused some worries among realistically inclined philosophers. Thus, it has been maintained that tools have been merely necessary conditions of the generation and the factual acceptance of the theories that we will discuss:

> How can cognitive scientists possibly be tracking the truth, if they can be persuaded to believe given theories by institutional developments which have no apparent connection with the subject matter of those theories? … It would indeed be damning if the institutional developments in question were *sufficient* to determine theory acceptance. But their being necessary leaves it open that other factors might also have been necessary, and in particular proper empirical support might have been necessary too. (Papineau, 2003, pp. 146–147)

Such worries are inspired by debates about realism and antirealism in the philosophy of science (see Hacking, 1983; Kitcher, 1993, chap. 5; Papineau, 1996). Here it is important to see, first, that we keep up the traditional distinction between discovery and justification in a certain sense. From the fact that the generation of the new theories is to be (in part) explained on the basis of the tools-to-theories heuristic, it does not follow that the theories are correct. A main goal of this chapter is to make psychologists aware of where crucial new ideas of the cognitive revolution came from and that these origins are by no means innocent. Second, the view that theoretical models were inspired by certain methodological tools by no means implies that the models must be incorrect either. The explanation of the development of new theories leaves open the question of whether they "map" an independent reality or whether the claims of the theory are true or correct.

This reply leads to the crucial worry. The debates between scientific realism and antirealism mainly concern the meaning of *theoretical* terms and statements. Can terms such as "electron" or "DNA" be interpreted realistically? That is, do they refer to mind-independent objects and properties? And can the statements in which such terms occur be true or false in the same way in which more mundane observational statements, such as "The cat is on the mat," can be, or are they simply efficient instruments of prediction and explanation of the phenomena?

There are no simple answers to such questions. We should hardly be surprised if it is an open question whether current theories of cognitive science can be understood realistically. We should also resist the assumption that one either has to be a scientific realist *tout court* or one has to accept antirealism. One may defend a realistic interpretation of, say, *electron* without thereby being a realist with regard to all theoretical parts of the various sciences. The difficult task is to identify criteria for a realistic interpretation and to show that these criteria apply.

As cited earlier, Papineau (2003) suggested that the relevant cognitive theories might have been accepted not only because scientists were fond of their tools but also because there was proper empirical support. However, that is much too simplistic. We argue later in this chapter that some types of empirical evidence were possible only because the theories were already assumed to be correct, and so the reference to empirical evidence needs additional qualifications at least. Also, some alternative theories of cognitive processing (e.g., different statistical models) can make some data virtually disappear. Stated generally, talk of proper empirical support cannot do the real job. It might also lead to a merely instrumentalist, antirealistic interpretation of the theoretical concepts and claims.

In fact, the defense of a realistic interpretation of any particular theory depends on more complex arguments and is itself a matter of piecemeal, long-term research. Typical kinds of arguments that support realism about a given theory involve *extrapolation*, as when microscopic phenomena are legitimately understood in terms of macroscopic phenomena; or *circumstantial evidence*, which may be illustrated by the case of the quite heterogeneous discoveries in support of an atomistic theory of matter. In physical and chemical theories of matter of the 18th and 19th centuries it was found out independently that substances react in fixed numerical proportions; that solid bodies must be viewed as structures of elements that do not allow for arbitrary combinations, a fact that excluded theories of matter as a continuous entity; that the number of particles in a chemical substance could be determined by Avogadro's number, and so on. Such heterogeneous discoveries supported a realistic understanding of the term "atom," but this was a hard-fought-for achievement (Krüger, 1981). Knowing the origins of some theoretical concepts better might help us to think critically about such issues and reflect whether such criteria apply: Is it, or is it not, a legitimate extrapolation to view some aspects of thought and behavior in terms of information processing or statistics? Is there any circumstantial evidence for this theoretical vocabulary?

One might try to avoid such difficult problems by biting the antirealistic bullet. Is it not better to view the theoretical concepts and claims of cognitive psychology as "mere" constructs or as "as-if" models? One may do so, but there is a price to be paid here. For instance, we mentioned earlier that behaviorists did use a mentalistic vocabulary. However, for them mentalistic terms did not really refer to intervening variables that are crucial for a cognitivist approach to the explanation of psychological phenomena. Only the latter approach takes seriously the view that mental states play real causal roles. Empiricists within current psychology who wish to treat talk of information processing or of the mind as a computer as merely a model or as merely metaphorical face a similar problem. Their explanations remain on a purely empirical level of generalization, at the risk of being mere redescriptions instead of real explanations. One takes a step back if one does not try to substantiate the pretensions of the cognitive revolution. Again, however, even a moderate realism about cognitive theories cannot be hoped for if one has not critically reflected where theoretical concepts came from, how they have spread over the scientific community, and what their possible problems and limitations are.

Third, the generation of theories through tools leads to possibly problematic relations between theory, data, and tools which should be highlighted in advance. The familiar theory-laden ness of data and instruments already questions simple views about the relation between theory and data (Figures 14–1 and 14–2). Now, the fact that certain theories are inspired by the tools scientists favor makes things even more difficult, because scientists are rarely aware of the metaphorical origins, and possible pitfalls, of their theories. Neither are they always clear that their favorite tools, theories, and data might be supporting one another, in ways that leave other, and perhaps more fruitful, research directions out of sight (see Fig. 14–3).

We do not claim that the circularity indicated in Figure 14–3 must always occur, or that its problems cannot be avoided. On the other hand,

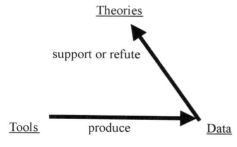

Figure 14–1.   The standard view of the relation among tools, data, and theories. According to this view, scientific instruments can be used to produce data, which are then used to support or refute theories, in a neutral or unbiased way.

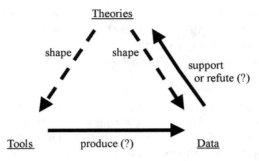

Figure 14–2. The well-known theory-laden-ness of data and instruments questions the standard view. Are data produced in theory-neutral ways? If not, can they be used to support or refute theories? How can theories then be understood realistically?

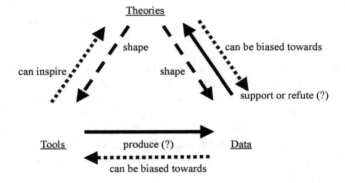

Figure 14–3. The possibly circularity among tools, theories, and data. Theoretical concepts and claims are often inspired by the scientists' favorite research tool, theories are not supported or tested by theory-neutral data, and tools tend to favor certain data and to leave others out. If that is so, do then tools, theories, and data justify one another in a circular or self-vindicating way?

we do not see any general procedure for solving the problems. The best thing seems to be to learn from historical case studies and to make scientists aware of the potentially circular relation among tools, theories, and data. This said, we turn to the two tools that have turned into psychological theories: (a) inferential statistics and (b) the digital computer.

III. COGNITION AS INTUITIVE STATISTICS

In American psychology, the study of cognitive processes was suppressed in the early 20th century by the allied forces of operationalism and behaviorism. The operationalism and the inductivism of the Vienna School, *inter alia*, paved the way for the institutionalization of inferential statistics in American experimental psychology between 1940 and 1955 (Gigerenzer, 1987a; Toulmin & Leary, 1985). In experimental psychology, inferential statistics became almost synonymous with the scientific method. Inferential statistics, in turn, provided a large part of the new concepts for mental processes that have fueled the cognitive revolution since the 1960s. Theories of cognition were cleansed of terms such as *restructuring* and *insight*, and the new mind has come to be portrayed as drawing random samples from nervous fibers, computing probabilities, calculating analyses of variance, setting decision criteria, and performing utility analyses.

After the institutionalization of inferential statistics, a broad range of cognitive processes were reinterpreted as involving *intuitive statistics*. For instance, W. P. Tanner and his coworkers assumed in their theory of signal detectibility that the mind "decides" whether there is a stimulus or only noise, just as a statistician of the Neyman–Pearson school decides between two hypotheses (Tanner & Swets, 1954). In his causal attribution theory, Harold H. Kelley (1967) postulated that the mind attributes a cause to an effect in the same way as behavioral scientists have come to do, namely, by performing an analysis of variance (ANOVA) and testing null hypotheses. These influential theories show the breadth of the new conception of the "mind as an intuitive statistician" (Gigerenzer & Murray, 1987).

Three points need to be argued for in closer detail here. First, the development of theories based on the conception of the mind as an intuitive statistician caused discontinuity in theory rather than being merely a new, fashionable language. Second, there was an inability of researchers to accept the conception of the mind as an intuitive statistician before they became familiar with inferential statistics as part of their daily routine. Third, we will show how the tools-to-theories heuristic can help us to see the limits and possibilities of current cognitive theories that investigate the mind as an intuitive statistician.

Discontinuity in Cognitive Theory Development

The spectrum of theories that model cognition after statistical inference ranges from auditory and visual perception to recognition in memory, and from speech perception to thinking and reasoning. The discontinuity within cognitive theories can be shown in two areas: (a) stimulus detection and discrimination and (b) causal attribution.

What intensity must a 440-Hz tone have to be perceived? How much heavier than a standard stimulus of 100 gm must a comparison stimulus be in order for a perceiver to notice a difference? How does one understand the elementary cognitive processes involved in those tasks, known today as *stimulus detection* and *stimulus discrimination*? Since Herbart (1816), such processes have been explained by using a threshold metaphor: Detection occurs only if the effect an object has on our nervous system exceeds an absolute threshold, and discrimination between two objects occurs if the excitation from one exceeds that from another by an amount greater than a differential threshold. Weber's and Fechner's laws refer to the concept of fixed thresholds, Titchener (1896) saw in differential thresholds the long-sought-after elements of mind (he counted approximately 44,000), and classic textbooks such as Brown and Thomson's (1921) and Guilford's (1954) document methods and research.

Around 1955, the psychophysics of absolute and differential thresholds was revolutionized by the new analogy between the mind and the statistician. W. P. Tanner and others proposed a *theory of signal detectability* (TSD), which assumes that the Neyman–Pearson technique of hypothesis testing describes the processes involved in detection and discrimination. Recall that in Neyman–Pearson statistics two sampling distributions (hypotheses H_0 and H_1) and a decision criterion (which is a likelihood ratio) are defined, and then the data observed are transformed into a likelihood ratio and compared with the decision criterion. Depending on which side of the criterion the data fall, the decision "reject H_0 and accept H_1" or "accept H_0 and reject H_1" is made. In straight analogy, the TSD assumes that the mind calculates two sampling distributions, for "noise" and "signal plus noise" (in the detection situation), and sets a decision criterion after weighing the cost of the two possible decision errors (Type I and Type II errors in Neyman–Pearson theory, now called *false alarms* and *misses*). The sensory input is transduced into a form that allows the brain to calculate its likelihood ratio and, depending on whether this ratio is smaller or larger than the criterion, the participant says "No, there is no signal" or "Yes, there is a signal." Tanner (1965) explicitly referred to his new model of the mind as a *Neyman–Pearson detector* and, in unpublished work, his flow charts included a drawing of a homunculus statistician performing the unconscious statistics in the brain (Gigerenzer & Murray, 1987, pp. 43–53).

The new analogy between mind and statistician replaced the old concept of a fixed threshold by the twin notions of observer's attitudes and observer's sensitivity. Just as the Neyman–Pearson technique distinguishes between a subjective part (e.g., selection of a criterion dependent on cost–benefit considerations) and a mathematical part, detection and discrimination became understood as involving both subjective processes, such as attitudes and cost–benefit considerations, and sensory processes. Swets, Tanner, and Birdsall (1964, p. 52) considered this link between attitudes and sensory processes to be the main thrust of their theory. The analogy between technique and mind made new research questions thinkable, such as "How can the mind's decision criterion be manipulated?" A new kind of data even emerged: Two types of errors—false alarms and misses—were generated in the experiments, just as the statistical theory distinguishes two types of error. The development of TSD was not motivated by new data; instead, the new theory motivated a new kind of data. In fact, in their seminal article, Tanner and Swets (1954) admitted that their theory "appears to be inconsistent with the large quantity of existing data on this subject," and they proceeded to criticize the "form of these data" (p. 401).

The Neyman–Pearsonian technique of hypothesis testing was subsequently transformed into a theory of a broad range of cognitive processes, ranging from recognition in memory (e.g., Murdock, 1982; Wickelgreen & Norman, 1966) to eyewitness testimony (e.g., Birnbaum, 1983) and discrimination between random and nonrandom patterns (e.g., Lopes, 1982).

The second example concerns theories of causal reasoning. Albert Michotte (1946/1963), Jean Piaget (1930), the Gestalt psychologists, and others had investigated how temporal–spatial relationships between two or more visual objects, such as moving dots, produced phenomenal causality. For instance, research participants were made to "perceive" that one dot launches, pushes, or chases another. After the institutionalization of inferential statistics, Harold H. Kelley (1967) proposed in his *attribution theory* that the long-sought laws of causal reasoning are in fact the tools of the behavioral scientist: R. A. Fisher's ANOVA. Just as the experimenter has come to infer a causal relationship between two variables from calculating an ANOVA and performing an F test, the man in the street infers the cause of an effect by unconsciously doing the same calculations. By the time Kelley developed the new metaphor for causal inference, about 70% of all experimental articles already used ANOVA (Edgington, 1974).

The theory was quickly accepted in social psychology; Kelley and Michaela (1980) reported more than 900 references in 10 years. The vision of the Fisherian mind radically changed the understanding of causal reasoning, the problems posed to the participants, and the explanations looked for. Here are a few discontinuities that reveal the fingerprints of the tool.

1. ANOVA needs repetitions or numbers as data to estimate variances and covariances. Consequently, the information presented to the participants in studies of causal attribution consists of information about the frequency of events (e.g., McArthur, 1972), which played no role in either Michotte's or Piaget's work.

2. Whereas Michotte's work still reflects the broad Aristotelian conception of four causes (see Gavin, 1972), and Piaget (1930) distinguished 17 kinds of causality in children's minds, the Fisherian mind concentrates on the one kind of causes for which ANOVA is used as a tool (similar to Aristotle's "efficient cause").

3. In Michotte's view, causal perception is direct and spontaneous and needs no inference, as a consequence of largely innate laws that determine the organization of the perceptual field. ANOVA, in contrast, is used in psychology as a technique for inductive inferences from data to hypotheses, and the focus in Kelley's attribution theory is consequently on the data-driven, inductive side of causal perception.

The last point illustrates that the specific *use* of a tool, that is, its practical context, rather than merely its mathematical structure, can also shape theoretical conceptions of mind. What if Harold Kelley had lived 150 years earlier than he did? In the early 19th century, significance tests (similar to those in ANOVA) were already being used by astronomers (Swijtink, 1987). However, they used their tests to reject data, so-called "outliers," and not to reject hypotheses. At least provisionally, the astronomers assumed that the theory was correct and mistrusted the data, whereas the ANOVA mind, following the current statistical textbooks, assumes the data to be correct and mistrusts the theories. So, to our 19th-century Kelley, the mind's causal attribution would have seemed expectation driven rather than data driven: The statistician homunculus in the mind would have tested the data and not the hypothesis.

Before the Institutionalization of Inferential Statistics

There is an important test case for the present hypothesis: (a) that familiarity with the statistical tool is crucial to the generation of corresponding theories of mind and (b) that the institutionalization of the tool within a scientific community can strongly further the broad acceptance of those theories. That test case is the era before the institutionalization of inferential statistics. Theories that conceive of the mind as an intuitive statistician should have a very small likelihood of being discovered and even less likelihood of being accepted. The two strongest tests are cases where (a) someone proposed a similar conceptual analogy and (b) someone proposed a similar probabilistic (formal) model. We know of only one case each, which we will analyze after defining first what is meant by the term *institutionalization of inferential statistics*.

Statistical inference has been known for a long time. In 1710, John Arbuthnot proved the existence of God using a kind of significance test; as mentioned earlier, astronomers used significance tests in the 19th century; G. T. Fechner's statistical text *Kollektivmasslehre* (1897) included tests of hypotheses; W. S. Gosset (using the pseudonym "Student") published the *t* test in 1908; and Fisher's significance testing techniques, such as ANOVA, as well as Neyman–Pearsonian hypothesis testing methods, have been available since the 1920s (see Gigerenzer et al., 1989). Bayes's theorem was known since 1763. Nonetheless, there was little interest in these techniques in experimental psychology before 1940 (Rucci & Tweney, 1980).

By 1942, Maurice Kendall (1942) could comment on the statisticians' expansion: "They have already overrun every branch of science with a rapidity of conquest rivaled only by Attila, Mohammed, and the Colorado beetle" (p. 69). By the early 1950s, half of the psychology departments in leading American universities offered courses on Fisherian methods and had made inferential statistics a graduate program requirement. By 1955, more than 80% of the experimental articles in leading journals used inferential statistics to justify conclusions from the data (Sterling, 1959), and editors of major journals made significance testing a requirement for the acceptance of articles submitted (e.g., Melton, 1962).

The year 1955 can be used as a rough date for the institutionalization of the tool in curricula, textbooks, and editorials. What became institutionalized as the logic of statistical inference was a mixture of ideas from two opposing camps, those of R. A. Fisher, on the one hand, and Jerzy Neyman and Egon S. Pearson (the son of Karl Pearson) on the other.

Genesis and Early Rejection of the Analogy

The analogy between the mind and the statistician was first proposed before the institutionalization of inferential statistics, in the early 1940s, by Egon Brunswik at Berkeley (e.g., Brunswik, 1943). As Leary (1987) showed, Brunswik's probabilistic functionalism was based on a very unusual blending of scientific traditions, including the probabilistic worldview of Hans Reichenbach and members of the Vienna School, and Karl Pearson's correlational statistics.

The important point here is that in the late 1930s Brunswik changed his techniques for measuring perceptual constancies, from calculating (nonstatistical) *Brunswik ratios* to calculating Pearson correlations, such as *functional* and *ecological validities*. In the 1940s, he also began to think of the organism as "an intuitive statistician," but it took him several years to spell out the analogy in a clear and consistent way (Gigerenzer, 1987b).

The analogy is this: The perceptual system makes inferences from its environment from uncertain cues by (unconsciously) calculating correlation and regression statistics, just as the Brunswikian researcher does when (consciously) calculating the degree of adaptation of a perceptual system to a given environment. Brunswik's "intuitive statistician" was a statistician of the Karl Pearson school, like the Brunswikian researcher. Brunswik's intuitive statistician was not well adapted to the psychological science of the time, however, and the analogy was poorly understood and generally rejected (Leary, 1987).

Brunswik's analogy came too early to be accepted by his colleagues of the experimental discipline; it came before the institutionalization of statistics as the method of scientific inference, and it came with the "wrong" statistical model: correlational statistics. Correlation was an indispensable method not in experimental psychology but in its rival discipline, known as the *Galton–Pearson program* or, as Cronbach (1957) put it, the "Holy Roman Empire" of correlational psychology. The schism between the two disciplines had been repeatedly taken up in presidential addresses before the American Psychological Association (Dashiell, 1939; Cronbach, 1957) and had deeply affected the values and the mutual esteem of psychologists (Thorndike, 1954). Brunswik could not succeed in persuading his colleagues from the experimental discipline to consider the statistical tool of the competing discipline as a model of how the mind works. Ernest Hilgard (1955), in his rejection of Brunswik's perspective, did not mince words: "Correlation is an instrument of the devil" (p. 228).

Brunswik, who coined the metaphor of "man as intuitive statistician," did not survive to see the success of his analogy. It was accepted only after statistical inference became institutionalized in experimental psychology and with the new institutionalized tools rather than (Karl) Pearsonian statistics serving as models of mind. Only in the mid-1960s, however, did interest in Brunswikian models of mind emerge (e.g., Brehmer & Joyce, 1988; Hammond, Stewart, Brehmer, & Steinmann, 1975).

Probabilistic Models Without the "Intuitive Statistician"

Although some probabilistic models of cognitive processes were advanced before the institutionalization of inferential statistics, they were not interpreted using the metaphor of the mind as intuitive statistician. This is illustrated by models that use probability distributions for perceptual judgment, assuming that variability is caused by lack of experimental control, measurement error, or other factors that can be summarized as experimenter ignorance. Ideally, if the experimenter had complete control and knowledge (e.g., Laplace's superintelligence), all probabilistic terms could be eliminated from the theory (Laplace 1814-1951, p. 1325). This does not hold for a probabilistic model that is based on the metaphor. Here, the probabilistic terms model the ignorance of the mind rather than that of the experimenter; that is, they model how the "homunculus statistician" in the brain comes to terms with a fundamental uncertain world. Even if the experimenter had complete knowledge, the theories would remain probabilistic, because it is the mind that is ignorant and needs statistics.

The key example is L. L. Thurstone, who in 1927 formulated a model for perceptual judgment that was formally equivalent to the present-day TSD. However, neither Thurstone nor his followers recognized the possibility of interpreting the formal structure of their model in terms of the intuitive statistician. Like TSD, Thurstone's model had two overlapping normal distributions, which represented the internal values of two stimuli and which specified the corresponding likelihood ratios, but it never occurred to Thurstone to include the conscious activities of a statistician, such as the weighing of the costs of the two errors and the setting of a decision criterion, in his model. Thus, neither Thurstone nor his followers took—with hindsight—the small step to develop the "law of comparative judgment" into TSD. When Duncan Luce (1977) reviewed Thurstone's model 50 years later, he found it hard to believe that nothing in Thurstone's writings showed the least awareness of this small but crucial step. Thurstone's perceptual model remained a mechanical, albeit probabilistic, stimulus–response theory without a homunculus statistician in the brain. The small conceptual step was never taken, and TSD entered psychology by an independent route.

To summarize: There are several kinds of evidence for a close link between the institutionalization of inferential statistics in the 1950s and the subsequent broad acceptance of the metaphor of the mind as an intuitive statistician: (a) the general failure to accept, and even to understand, Brunswik's intuitive statistician before the institutionalization of the tool, and (b) the case of Thurstone, who proposed a probabilistic model that was formally equivalent to one important present-day theory of intuitive statistics but was never interpreted in this way.

Limitations and Possibilities of Current Research Programs

How can the preceding analysis be of interest for the evaluation of current cognitive theories? One has to recognize that tools like statistics are not theoretically inert. They come with a set of assumptions and interpretations that may be smuggled, in Trojan horse fashion, into the new theories and research programs. Tools may have the advantage of opening new conceptual perspectives or making us see new data, but they may also make us blind in various ways.

There are several assumptions that became associated with the statistical tool in the course of its institutionalization in psychology, none of them being part of the mathematics or statistical theory proper. The first assumption can be called "There is only one statistics." Textbooks on statistics for psychologists (usually written by nonmathematicians) generally teach statistical inference as if there existed only one logic of inference. Since the 1950s and 1960s, almost all texts teach a mishmash of R. A. Fisher's ideas tangled with those of Jerzy Neyman and Egon S. Pearson, but without acknowledgment. The fact that Fisherians and Neyman–Pearsonians could never agree on a logic of statistical inference is not mentioned in the textbooks; neither are the controversial issues that divide them. Even alternative statistical logics for scientific inference are rarely discussed (Gigerenzer, 1993). For instance, Fisher (1955) argued that concepts such as Type II error, power, the setting of a level of significance before the experiment, and its interpretation as a long-run frequency of errors in repeated experiments, are concepts inappropriate for scientific inference—at best, they could be applied to technology (his pejorative example was Stalin's). Neyman, for his part, declared that some of Fisher's significance tests are "worse than useless" (because their power is less than their size; see Hacking, 1965, p. 99). Textbooks written by psychologists for psychologists usually present an intellectually incoherent mix of Fisherian and Neyman–Pearsonian ideas, but a mix presented as a seamless, uncontroversial whole (Gigerenzer et al., 1989, chaps. 3 and 6).

This assumption that "statistics is statistics is statistics" reemerges at the theoretical level in current psychology (Gigerenzer, 2000). For instance, research on so-called "cognitive illusions" assumes that there is one and only one correct answer to statistical reasoning problems. As a consequence, other answers are considered to reflect reasoning fallacies. Some of the most prominent reasoning problems, however, such as the cab problem (Tversky & Kahneman, 1980, p. 62), do not have just one answer; the answer depends on the theory of statistical inference and the assumptions applied. Birnbaum (1983), for example, showed that the "only correct answer" to the cab problem claimed by Tversky and Kahneman, based on Bayes's rule, is in fact only one of several reasonable answers—different ones are obtained, for instance, if one applies the Neyman–Pearson theory (Gigerenzer & Murray 1987, chap. 5).

A second assumption that became associated with the tool during its institutionalization is that "there is only one meaning of probability." For instance, Fisher and Neyman–Pearson had different interpretations of what a level of significance means. Fisher's was an epistemic interpretation; that is, that the level of significance tells us about the confidence we can have in the particular hypothesis under test, whereas Neyman's was a strictly frequentist and behavioristic interpretation that claimed that a level of significance tells us nothing about a particular hypothesis but about the long-run relative frequency of wrongly rejecting the null hypothesis if it is true. In textbooks, these alternative views of what a probability (e.g., level of significance) could mean are generally neglected—not to speak of the other meanings, subjective and objective, that have been proposed for the formal concept of probability (Hacking, 1965).

Many of the so-called cognitive illusions were demonstrated using a subjective interpretation of probability, specifically, asking people about the probability they assign to a single event. When instead researchers began to ask people for judgments of frequencies, these apparently stable reasoning errors—the conjunction fallacy and the overconfidence bias, for example—largely or completely disappeared (Gigerenzer, 2000, chap. 12; 2001). Untutored intuition seems to be capable of making conceptual distinctions of the sort statisticians and philosophers make, such as between judgments of subjective probability and those of frequency (e.g., Cohen, 1986; Lopes, 1981; Teigen, 1983). These results suggest that the important research questions to be investigated are "How are different meanings of 'probability' cued in every-day language?" and "How does this affect judgment?" rather than "How can we explain the alleged bias of 'overconfidence' by some general deficits in memory, cognition, or personality?"

To summarize: Assumptions entrenched in the practical use of statistical tools—which are not part of the mathematics—can re-emerge in research programs on cognition, resulting in severe limitations in these programs. This could be avoided by pointing out these assumptions, and this may even lead to new research questions.

IV. MIND AS COMPUTER

Prehistory

The relation between conceptions of the mind and the computer has had a long history, involving an interaction among social, economical, mental, and technological contexts (see Gigerenzer, 2003). Here, we concentrate on the period of time since the cognitive revolution of the 1960s when the computer, after becoming a standard laboratory tool in this century, was proposed and, with some delay, accepted, as a model of mind. In particular, we focus on the development and (delayed) acceptance of Herbert Simon and Allen Newell's brand of information processing psychology (Newell & Simon, 1972).

The invention of the first modern computers, such as the ENIAC and the EDVAC at the University of Pennsylvania during and after the second world war, did not lead immediately to a view of the mind as a computer. There were two groups drawing a parallel between the human and the computer, but neither used the computer as a theory of mind. One group, which tentatively compared the nervous system and the computer, is represented by the mathematician John von Neumann (1903–1957). The other group, which investigated the idea that machines might be capable of thought, is represented by the mathematician and logician Alan Turing (1912–1954). Von Neumann, known as the father of the modern computer, wrote about the possibility of an analogy between the computer and the human nervous system. He thus drew the comparison on the level of the hardware. Turing (1950), in contrast, thought the observation that both the digital computer and the human nervous system are electrical, is based on a "very superficial similarity" (p. 439). He pointed out that the first digital computer, Charles Babbage's Analytical Engine, was purely mechanical (as opposed to electrical) and that the important similarities to the mind are in function, or in software.

Turing discussed the question of whether machines can think rather than the question of whether the mind is like a computer. Thus, he was looking in the opposite direction than psychologists were going the cognitive revolution and, consequently, he did not propose any theories of mind. He argued that it would be impossible for a human to imitate a computer, as evidenced by humans' inability to perform complex numerical calculations quickly. He also discussed the question of whether a computer could be said to have a free will, a property of humans (many years later, cognitive psychologists, under the assumptions that the mind is a computer and that computers lack free will, pondered the question of whether humans could be said to have one). And, most famously, the famous Turing test is about whether a machine can imitate a human mind, but not vice versa.

Turing (1969) anticipated much of the new conceptual language and even the very problems Newell and Simon were to attempt, as we will see. With amazing prophecy, Turing suggested that many intellectual issues can be translated into the form "find a number n such that ..."; that is, that "search" is the key concept for problem solving, and that Whitehead and Russell's (1935) *Principia Mathematica* might be a good start for demonstrating the power of the machine (McCorduck, 1979, p. 57). Still, Turing's work had practically no influence on artificial intelligence in Britain until the mid-1960s (McCorduck, 1979, p. 68).

Newell's and Simon's New Conception: Meaning and Genesis

Babbage's mechanical computer was preceded by human computers performing highly limited tasks of calculation. Similarly, Newell and

Simon's first computer program, the Logic Theorist (LT), was preceded by a human computer. Before the LT was up and running, Newell and Simon reconstructed their computer program out of human components (namely, Simon's wife, children, and several graduate students), to see if it would work. Newell wrote up the subroutines of the LT program on index cards:

> To each member of the group, we gave one of the cards, so that each person became, in effect, a component of the LT computer program—a subroutine—that performed some special function, or a component of its memory. It was the task of each participant to execute his or her subroutine, or to provide the contents of his or her memory, whenever called by the routine at the next level above that was then in control.

> So we were able to simulate the behavior of the LT with a computer consisting of human components ... The actors were no more responsible than the slave boy in Plato's Meno, but they were successful in proving the theorems given them. (Simon, 1991, p. 207)

As in Babbage's engine, the essence of the functioning of the LT is a division of labor—each human actor requiring little skill and repeating the same routine again and again. Complex processes are achieved by an army of workers who never see but a little piece of the larger picture.

However, there is an important difference between Babbage's mechanical computer and Simon's LT (and their human precursors). Babbage's engine performed numerical calculations; Simon's computer matched symbols, applied rules to symbols, and searched through lists of symbols—what is now generally known as *symbol manipulation*.

An important precondition for the view of mind as a computer is the realization that computers are symbol manipulation devices, in addition to being numerical calculators: As long as computers are viewed as being restricted to the latter, and as long as mental activities are seen as more complex than numerical calculation, it is hardly surprising that computers are not proposed as a metaphor for the mind. Newell and Simon were among the first to realize this. In interviews with Pamela McCorduck (1979, p. 129), Allen Newell recalled, "I've never used a computer to do any numerical processing in my life." Newell's first use of the computer at RAND corporation—a prehistoric card-programmed calculator hooked up to a line printer—was calculating and printing out symbols representing airplanes for each sweep of a radar antenna.

The symbol-manipulating nature of the computer was important to Simon because it corresponded to some of his earlier views on the nature of intelligence:

The metaphor I'd been using, of a mind as something that took some premises and ground them up and processed them into conclusions, began to transform itself into a notion that a mind was something which took some program inputs and data and had some processes which operated on the data and produced output. (cited in McCorduck, 1979, p. 127)

It is interesting to note that 20 years after seeing the computer as a symbol manipulating device, Newell and Simon came forth with the explicit hypothesis that a physical symbol system is necessary and sufficient for intelligence.

The LT generated proofs for theorems in symbolic logic, specifically, the first 25 or so theorems in Whitehead and Russell's (1935) *Principia Mathematica*. It even managed to find a proof more elegant than the corresponding one in the *Principia*.

In the summer of 1958, psychology was given a double dose of the new school of information-processing psychology. One was the publication of the *Psychological Review* article "Elements of a Theory of Human Problem Solving" (Newell, Shaw, & Simon, 1958). The other was the Research Training Institute on the Simulation of Cognitive Processes at the RAND institute, which we discuss later.

The *Psychological Review* article is an interesting document of the transition between the view that the LT is a tool for proving theorems in logic (the artificial intelligence view) and an emerging view that the LT is a model of human reasoning (the information-processing view). The authors go back and forth between both views, explaining that "the program of LT was not fashioned directly as a theory of human behavior; it was constructed in order to get a program that would prove theorems in logic" (Newell, Shaw, & Simon, 1958, p. 154) but later that LT "provides an explanation for the processes used by humans to solve problems in symbolic logic" (Newell et al., 1958, p. 163). The evidence provided for projecting the machine into the mind is mainly rhetorical. For instance, the authors spend several pages arguing for the resemblance between the methods of LT and concepts such as set, insight, and hierarchy, described in the earlier psychological literature on human problem solving.

In all fairness, despite the authors' claim, the resemblance to these earlier concepts as they were used in the work of Karl Duncker, Wolfgang Köhler, and others, is slight. It is often a useful strategy to hide the amount of novelty and claim historical continuity. When Tanner and Swets, 4 years earlier, also in *Psychological Review*, proposed that another scientific tool, Neyman–Pearsonian techniques of hypothesis testing, would model the cognitive processes of stimulus detection and discrimination, their signal detection model also clashed with earlier notions, such as the notion of a sensory threshold. Tanner and Swets (1954, p. 401), however, chose not to conceal this schism, explicitly stating that their new theory "appears to be inconsistent with the large quantity of existing data on this subject." There is a different historical continuity in which Simon and Newell's ideas stand: the earlier Enlightenment view of intelligence as a combinatorial calculus. What was later called the "new mental chemistry" pictured the mind as a computer program:

> The atoms of this mental chemistry are symbols, which are combinable into larger and more complex associational structures called *lists* and *list structures*. The fundamental "reactions" of the mental chemistry use elementary information processes that operate upon symbols and symbol structures: copying symbols, storing symbols, retrieving symbols, inputting and outputting symbols, and comparing symbols. (Simon, 1979, p. 63)

This atomic view is certainly a major conceptual change in the views about problem solving compared with the theories of Köhler, Wertheimer, and Duncker. But it bears much resemblance to the combinatorial view of intelligence of the Enlightenment philosophers.[1]

The different physical levels of a computer led to Newell's cognitive hierarchy, which separates the knowledge-level, symbol-level, and register-transfer levels of cognition. As Arbib (1993) pointed out, the seriality of 1971-style computers is actually embedded in Newell's cognitive theory.

One of the major concepts in computer programming that made its way into the new models of the mind is the decomposition of complexity into simpler units, such as the decomposition of a program into a hierarchy of simpler subroutines, or into a set of production rules. On this analogy, the most complex processes in psychology, and even scientific discovery, can be explained through simple subprocesses (Langley, Simon, Bradshaw, & Zytkow, 1987).

The first general statement of Newell and Simon's new vision of mind appeared in their 1972 book, *Human Problem Solving*. In this book, the authors argue for the idea that higher level cognition proceeds much like the behavior of a production system, a formalism from computer

---

[1]The new view was directly inspired by the 19th-century mathematician George Boole who, in the spirit of the Enlightenment mathematicians such as Bernoullis and Laplace, set out to derive the laws of logic, algebra, and probability from what he believed to be the laws of human thought (Boole, 1854/1958). Boole's algebra culminated in Whitehead and Russell's (1935) *Principia Mathematica*, describing the relationship between mathematics and logic, and in Claude E. Shannon's seminal work (1938), which used Boolean algebra to describe the behavior of relay and switching circuits (McCorduck, 1979, p. 41).

science (and before that, from symbolic logic) that had never been used in psychological modeling before:

> Throughout the book we have made use of a wide range of organizational techniques known to the programming world: explicit flow control, subroutines, recursion, iteration statements, local naming, production systems, interpreters, and so on .... We confess to a strong premonition that the actual organization of human programs closely resembles the production system organization. (Newell & Simon, 1972, p. 803)

We will not attempt to probe the depths of how Newell and Simon's ideas of information processing changed theories of mind; the commonplace usage of computer terminology in the cognitive psychological literature since 1972 is a reflection of this. It seems natural for present-day psychologists to speak of cognition in terms of encoding, storage, retrieval, executive processes, algorithms, and computational cost.

New Experiments, New Data

New tools can transform the kinds of experiments performed and the data collected. This happened when statistical tools turned into theories of mind, and a similar story is to be told with the conceptual change brought about by Newell and Simon—it mandated a new type of experiment, which in turn involved new kinds of subjects, data, and justification. In academic psychology of the day, the standard experimental design, modeled after the statistical methods of Ronald A. Fisher, involved many subjects and randomized treatment groups. The 1958 *Psychological Review* article uses the same terminology of *design of the experiment* and *subject* but radically changes their meanings. There are no longer groups of human or animal subjects. There is only one subject: an inanimate being named LT. There is no longer an experiment in which data are generated by either observation or measurement. Experiment takes on the meaning of simulation.

In this new kind of experiment, the data are of an unforeseen type: computer printouts of the program's intermediate results. These new data, in turn, require new methods of hypothesis testing. How did Newell and Simon determine whether their program was doing what minds do? There were two methods. For Newell and Simon, simulation was a form of justification itself: a theory that is coded up as a working computer program shows that the processes it describes are, at the very least, sufficient to perform the task, or, in the more succinct words of Simon (1992), "A running program is the moment of truth" (p. 155). Furthermore, a stronger test of the model is made by comparing the computer's output to the think-aloud protocols of human participants. Newell and Simon put their subject, the LT, as a coauthor of a paper submitted to the *Journal of Symbolic Logic*. Regrettably, the paper was rejected (as it contained no new results from modern logic's point of view), and the LT never tried to publish again.

The second dose of information processing (after the *Psychological Review* article) administered to psychology was the Research Training Institute on the Simulation of Cognitive Processes at the RAND institute, organized by Newell and Simon. The institute held lectures and seminars, taught IPL-IV (Information Processing Language-IV) programming, and demonstrated LT, the General Problem Solver, and the EPAM (Elementary Perceiver and Memorizer) model of memory on the RAND computer. In attendance were some figures who would eventually develop computer simulation methods of their own, including George Miller, Robert Abelson, Bert Green, and Roger Shepard.

An early, but deceptive, harbinger of acceptance for the new information-processing theory was the publication, right after the summer institute, of *Plans and the Structure of Behavior* (Miller, Galanter, & Pribram, 1960), written mostly by George Miller. This book was so near to Newell and Simon's ideas that it was at first considered a form of theft, although the version of the book that did see the presses is filled with citations recognizing Newell, Shaw, and Simon. Despite the 1959 dispute with Newell and Simon over the ownership and validity of the ideas within, this book drew a good deal of attention from all of psychology.

It would seem the table was set for the new information-processing psychology; however, it did not take hold. Simon complained of the psychological community who took only a cautious interest in their ideas. Computers were not yet entrenched in the daily routine of psychologists.[2]

---

[2]Another evidence for this view is that a similar development within the philosophy of mind of the 1960s did not support the acceptance of the computer metaphor within the psychological community either. Hilary Putnam's articles on the status of psychological predicates, and on the relevance of Turing's work for a better understanding of the relation between the mind and the brain, became quickly influential among philosophers. In particular, Putnam's work explained a crucial weakness of mind–brain identity theories that had been quite widespread during the 1950s. Putnam argued for a distinction between mind and brain in terms of the difference between software and hardware, thus showing that mental states can be realized in quite different physical systems (Putnam, 1960, 1967a, 1967b, all reprinted in Putnam, 1975). Such an abstract argument could influence the philosophical debate, because it was restricted to a principled, ontological understanding of the mind–body relation. The new (computer) functionalism was also quickly seen as a good basis for the autonomy of psychology in relation to other sciences such as biology or neurophysiology. However, even this did not help the computer metaphor to become more popular within psychology. Although the metaphor was available, and although it had started to do some fruitful work within a different community, the psychological community remained reluctant or ignorant.

No Familiar Tools, No Acceptance

We take two institutions as case studies to demonstrate the part of the tools-to-theories heuristic which concerns acceptance: (a) the Center for Cognitive Studies at Harvard, and (b) Carnegie Mellon University. The former never came to fully embrace the new information-processing psychology. The latter did, but after a considerable delay.

George Miller, the cofounder of the Center at Harvard, was certainly a proponent of the new information-processing psychology. Given Miller's enthusiasm, one might expect the center, partially under Miller's leadership, to blossom into information-processing research. It never did. Looking at the *Annual Reports* of the center from 1963–1969, we found only a few symposia or papers dealing with computer simulation.

Although the center had a PDP—4C computer, and the reports anticipated the possibility of using it for cognitive simulation, as far as 1969 it never happened. The reports mention that the computer served to run experiments, to demonstrate the feasibility of computer research, and to draw visitors to the laboratory. However, difficulties involved with using the tool were considerable. The PDP saw 83 hours of use, on an average week in 1965–1966, but 56 of these were spent on debugging and maintenance. In the annual reports are several remarks of the type "It is difficult to program computers ... Getting a program to work may take months." They even turned out a 1966 technical report called "Programmanship, Or How to Be One-Up On a Computer Without Actually Ripping Out Its Wires."

What might have kept the Harvard computer from becoming a metaphor of the mind was that the researchers could not integrate this tool into their everyday laboratory routine. The tool turned out to be a steady source of frustration. Simon (1979) took notice of this:

> Perhaps the most important factors that impeded the diffusion of the new ideas, however, were the unfamiliarity of psychologists with computers and the unavailability on most campuses of machines and associated software (list processing programming languages) that were well adapted to cognitive simulation. The 1958 RAND Summer Workshop, mentioned earlier, and similar workshops held in 1962 and 1963, did a good deal to solve the first problem for the 50 or 60 psychologists who participated in them; but workshop members often returned to their home campuses to find their local computing facilities ill-adapted to their needs. (p. 365)

At Carnegie Mellon, Newell, Simon, a new information processing-enthusiastic department head, and a very large National Institute of

Mental Health grant were pushing "the new [information-processing] religion" (H. A. Simon, personal communication, June 22, 1994). Even this concerted effort failed to proselytize the majority of researchers within their own department. This again indicates that entrenchment of the new tool into the everyday practice was an important precondition for the spread of the metaphor of the mind as a computer.

Acceptance of Theory Follows Familiarity With Tool

In the late 1950s, at Carnegie Mellon, the first doctoral theses involving computer simulation of cognitive processes were being written (H. A. Simon, personal communication, June 22, 1994). However, this was not representative of the national state of affairs. In the mid-1960s, a small number of psychological laboratories were built around computers, including Carnegie Mellon, Harvard, Michigan, Indiana, MIT, and Stanford (Aaronson, Grupsmith, & Aaronson, 1976, p. 130). As indicated by the funding history of National Institute of Mental Health grants for cognitive research, the amount of computer-using research tripled over the next decade: In 1967, only 15% of the grants being funded had budget items related to computers (e.g., programmer salaries, hardware, supplies); by 1975, this figure had increased to 46%. The late 1960s saw a turn toward mainframe computers, which lasted until the late 1970s, when the microcomputer started its invasion of the laboratory. In the 1978 Behavioral Research Methods & Instrumentation conference, microcomputers were the issue of the day (Castellan, 1981, p. 93). By 1984, the journal *Behavioral Research Methods & Instrumentation* appended the word *Computers* to its title to reflect the broad interest in the new tool. By 1980, the cost of computers had dropped an order of magnitude from what it was in 1970 (Castellan, 1981, 1991). During the last 20 years, computers have become the indispensable research tool of the psychologist.

Once the tool became entrenched into everyday laboratory routine, a broad acceptance of the view of the mind as a computer followed. In the early 1970s, information-processing psychology finally caught on at Carnegie Mellon University. Every Carnegie Mellon authored article in the 1973 edition of the Carnegie Symposium on Cognition mentions some sort of computer simulation. For the rest of the psychological community, who were not as familiar with the tool, the date of broad acceptance was years later. In 1979, Simon estimated that, from about 1973 to 1979, the number of active research scientists working in the information processing vein had "probably doubled or tripled."

This does not mean that the associated methodology became accepted as well. It clashed too strongly with the methodological ritual that was institutionalized during the 1940s and 1950s in experimental psychology. We use the term *ritual* here for the mechanical practice of a curious mishmash between Fisher's and Neyman–Pearson's statistical techniques that was taught to psychologists as the sine qua non of scientific method. Most psychologists assumed, as the textbooks have told them, that there is only one way to do good science. However, their own heroes—Fechner, Wundt, Pavlov, Köhler, Bartlett, Piaget, Skinner, and Luce, to name a few—never had used this ritual, but some had used experimental practices that resembled the newly proposed methods used to study the mind as computer.

Pragmatics

Some have objected to this analysis of how tools turned into theories of mind. They argue that the tool-to-theories examples are merely illustrations of psychologists being quick to realize that the mathematical structure of a tool (e.g., ANOVA, or the digital computer) is precisely that of the mind.

This repeats a simplistic version of realism we have already criticized (see section II). Now, we can add that the assumption that new theories just happen to mirror the mathematical structure of the tool overlooks the important pragmatics of a tool's use (which is independent of the mathematical structure). The same process of projecting pragmatic aspects of a tool's use into a theory can be shown for the view of the mind as a computer. One example is Levelt's (1989) model of speaking. The basic unit in Levelt's model, which he calls the *processing component*, corresponds to the computer programmer's concept of a subroutine. The model borrowed not only the subroutine as a tool but also the pragmatics of how subroutines are constructed.

A subroutine (or *subprocess*) is a group of computer instructions, usually serving a specific function, which is separated from the main routine of a computer program. It is common for subroutines to perform often-needed functions, such as extracting a cube root or rounding a number. There is a major pragmatic issue involved in writing subroutines that centers around what is called the *principle of isolation* (Simon & Newell, 1986). The issue is whether subroutines should be black boxes. According to the principle of isolation, the internal workings of the subroutine should remain a mystery to the main program, and the outside program should remain a mystery to the subroutine. Subroutines built without respect to the principle of isolation are *clear boxes* that can be penetrated from the outside and escaped from the inside. To the computer, of course, it makes no difference whether the subroutines are isolated or not. Subroutines that are not isolated work just as well as those that are. The only difference is a psychological one. Subroutines that violate the principle of isolation are, from a person's point of view, harder to read, write, and debug. For this reason, intro- ductory texts on computer programming stress the principle of isolation as the essence of good programming style.

The principle of isolation—a pragmatic rule of using subroutines— has a central place in Levelt's model, where the processing components are "black boxes" and constitute what Levelt considers to be a definition of Fodor's notion of *informational encapsulation* (Levelt, 1989, p. 15). In this way, Levelt's psychological model embodies a maxim of good computer programming methodology: the principle of isolation. That this pragmatic feature of the tool shaped a theory of speaking is not an evaluation of the quality of the theory. In fact, this pragmatic feature of the subroutine has not always served the model well: Kita (1993) and Levinson (1992) have attacked Levelt's model at its Achilles heel—its insistence on isolation.

Limitations and Possibilities of Current Research Programs

The computer metaphor has been so successful that many find it hard to see how the mind could be anything else: to quote Philip John- son-Laird (1983), "The computer is the last metaphor; it need never be supplanted" (p. 10). Such a stunningly realistic attitude interpretation overlooks that the computer metaphor, as every metaphor, has some important limitations. They can be inferred from two main discrepan- cies: First, human minds are much better at certain tasks than even the most developed computer programs and robots; second, digital com- puters are much better at certain tasks than human minds. Although human minds are still much better in, say, pattern recognition, the un- derstanding of emotion and expressions, or in the learning of fast in- tentional bodily movement (as in sports), computer programs succeed in complex arithmetical calculations (e.g., Churchland, 1995, chap. 9). The important task is to understand why the differences ob- tain.

Alan Turing predicted in 1945 that computers will one day play very good chess; and others have hoped that chess programming would con- tribute to the understanding of how humans think. Turin's prediction turned out to be correct, as shown by the famous defeat of world chess champion Garry Kasparov against the IBM computer program Deep Blue in 1997. The other hopes did not turn out to be correct, and this signals one of the limitations of the computer metaphor.

Consider the different heuristics chess computers and human beings use. Both have to use heuristics, because there is no way to fully compute all possible moves in order to figure out the best strategy to win a given game. Both need to pursue intermediate goals that offer some probability of leading to success if repeatedly achieved. The heuristics computers and human beings use are different because they work on different capacities. Deep Blue has the enormous power to go through 200 million operations every second and uses a relatively simple heuristic to compute how good each of these moves is. Human chess experts do not generate all these possible moves but use the capacity of spatial pattern recognition, which is unmatched by any existing computer program. Kasparov once said that he thinks only 4 or 5 moves ahead, whereas Deep Blue can look ahead about 14 turns. Also, Herbert Simon has tried to take the opposite direction of Turing's suggestion, that is, Simon and his colleagues interviewed human chess experts in order to extract their heuristics and then implement them on chess computers. These programs did not play very well, however. The heuristics used in computer programs and in human minds are not identical.

The current alternative to the digital computer is *connectionism*, or models of parallel distributed processing. These have various advantages over traditional computer models, and they have important applications within artificial intelligence research. However, as models of the mind they are not without limitations either. For instance, connectionist researchers have been unable to replicate so far the nervous system of the simplest living things, such as the worm *Caenorhabdis elegans*, which has 302 neurons, even though the patterns of interconnections are perfectly well known (Thomas & Lockery, 2000; White, Southgate, Thomson, & Brenner, 1986). We should not adopt, certainly not by now, a realistic interpretation of the computer and connectionist models of the mind.

Other objections have been advanced against the program of artificial intelligence, but we are skeptical about these. For instance, John Searle has advanced the argument that computer programs do not, and cannot, realize true mentality. His argument is that they merely perform syntactical operations upon symbols, whereas real minds additionally possess a semantic understanding of symbols and symbolic operations (Searle, 1984). Most critical in this argument is the unquestioned assumption of a certain theory of meaning or intentionality. And there are other skeptical arguments. They concern the question of whether, say, computer algorithms can ever reveal the full mathematical capacities of human beings, or whether computers or artificial neural networks possess the phenomenal or qualitative features that accompany many mental states, such as perceptions or feelings. What connects these objections is that they are based on unquestioned intuitions about human minds and computers or artificial neural networks

(Churchland, 1995, chap. 9). To find out real differences between about minds and computers (or artificial neural networks), we should not rely on mere intuitions but instead try to empirically identify the various heuristics used by them. Moreover, we must show how human (and other living) minds differ not only in their functional architecture but also in their physical architecture from computers and connectionistic networks. We must work out how the software depends on the hardware.

V. THE GENERATION OF THEORIES RECONSIDERED

The tools-to-theories heuristic is about scientists' practice, that is, the analytical and physical tools used in the conduct of empirical research. This practice has a long tradition of neglect. The very philosophers who called themselves logical empiricists had, ironically, no interest in the empirical practice of scientists. Against their reduction of observation to pointer reading, Kuhn (1970) has emphasized the theory-ladenness of observation. Referring to perceptual experiments and Gestalt switches, he wrote, "scientists see new and different things when looking with familiar instruments in places they have looked before" (p. 111). Both the logical empiricists and Kuhn were highly influential on psychology (see Toulmin & Leary, 1985), but neither view has emphasized the role of tools and experimental conduct. Only recently have they been scrutinized more closely, both in the history of psychology and generally in the history and philosophy of science as well (Danziger, 1985, 1987, 1990; Galison, 1987; Hacking, 1983; Lenoir, 1986, 1988). Without being able to discuss such analyses here, it can be pointed out that they have made it highly plausible that theory is often inseparable from instrumental practices.

Should we go on telling our students that new theories originate from new data? If only because "little is known about how theories come to be created," as Anderson introduces reader to his *Cognitive Psychology* (1980, p. 17)? On one widespread view, theories are simply "guesses guided by the unscientific" (Popper, 1935/1959, p. 278). Against this, we wish to emphasize that in order to understand the generation of theories appropriately, the familiar theory–data relation should be supplemented by a third factor: the use(s) of tools. Moreover, it cannot be overemphasized that some guesses are better than others from the very beginning. Even when rational evaluation of theories has not been achieved, the question of which theories are plausible and serious candidates must have its own rationale. The tools-to-theories heuristic is one possible answer, even if the metaphorical use of tools requires continuous critical reflection.

ACKNOWLEDGMENTS

This article is in part based on G. Gigerenzer (2003) and on Sturm & Gigerenzer (2006).

REFERENCES

Aaronson, D., Grupsmith, E., & Aaronson, M. (1976). The impact of computers on cognitive psychology. *Behavioral Research Methods & Instrumentation, 8,* 129–138.

Anderson, J. R. (1980). *Cognitive psychology and its implications*. San Francisco: Freeman.

Arabatzis, T. (2002). On the inextricability of the context of discovery and the context of justification. In J. Schickore & F. Steinle (Eds.), *Revisiting discovery and justification* (pp. 111–123). Berlin, Germany: Max Planck Institute for the History of Science.

Arbib, M. A. (1993). Allen Newell, unified theories of cognition. *Artificial Intelligence, 59,* 265–283.

Birnbaum, M. H. (1983). Base rates in Bayesian inference: Signal detection analysis of the cab problem. *American Journal of Psychology, 96,* 85–94.

Black, M. (1962). *Models and metaphors*. Ithaca, NY: Cornell University Press.

Boole, G. (1854/1958). *An investigation of the laws of thought on which are founded the mathematical theories of logic and probabilities*. New York: Dover. (Reprinted from London: Walton).

Brehmer, B., & Joyce, C. R. B. (Eds.). (1988). *Human judgment: The SJT view*. Amsterdam: North-Holland.

Brown, W., & Thomson, G. H. (1921). *The essentials of mental measurement*. Cambridge, England: Cambridge University Press.

Brunswik, E. (1943). Organismic achievement and environmental probability. *Psychological Review, 50,* 255–272.

Castellan, N. J. (1981). On-line computers in psychology: The last 10 years, the next 10 years—The challenge and the promise. *Behavioral Research Methods & Instrumentation, 13,* 91–96.

Castellan, N. J. (1991). Computers and computing in psychology: Twenty years of progress and still a bright future. *Behavior Research Methods, Instruments, & Computers, 23,* 106–108.

Churchland, P. M. (1995). *The engine of reason, the seat of the soul*. Cambridge, MA: MIT Press.

Cohen, L. J. (1986). *The dialogue of reason*. Oxford, England: Clarendon.

Cronbach, L. J. (1957). The two disciplines of scientific psychology. *American Psychologist, 12,* 671–684.

Curd, M. (1980). The logic of discovery: An analysis of three approaches. In T. Nickles (Ed.), *Scientific discovery, logic, and rationality* (pp. 201–219). Dordrecht, The Netherlands: Reidel.

Danziger, K. (1985). The methodological imperative in psychology. *Philosophy of the Social Sciences, 16,* 1–13.

Danziger, K. (1987). Statistical method and the historical development of research practice in American psychology. In L. Krüger, G. Gigerenzer, & M. S. Morgan (Eds.), *The probabilistic revolution: Vol. II. Ideas in the sciences* (pp. 35–47). Cambridge, MA: MIT Press.

Danziger, K. (1990). *Constructing the subject*. Cambridge, England: Cambridge University Press.

D'Arcy, P. (1765). Memoire sur la durée de la sensation de la vue [A disquistition concerning the duration of the sensation of sight]. *Histoire de l'académie royale des sciences avec les mémoires de mathématique & de physique, 82*, 439–451.

Dashiell, J. F. (1939). Some rapprochements in contemporary psychology. *Psychological Bulletin, 36*, 1–24.

Draaisma, D. (2000). *Metaphors of memory*. Cambridge, England: Cambridge University Press.

Edgington, E. E. (1974). A new tabulation of statistical procedures used in APA journals. *American Psychologist, 29*, 25–26.

Fechner, G. T. (1897). *Kollektivmasslehre* [The measurement of collectivities]. Leipzig, Germany: W. Engelmann.

Fisher, R. A. (1955). Statistical methods and scientific induction. *Journal of the Royal Statistical Society (B), 17*, 69–78.

Galison, P. (1987). *How experiments end*. Chicago: University of Chicago Press.

Gardner, H. (1988). Creative lives and creative works: A synthetic scientific approach. In R. J. Sternberg (Ed.), *The nature of creativity* (pp. 298–321). Cambridge, England: Cambridge University Press.

Gavin, E. A. (1972). The causal issue in empirical psychology from Hume to the present with emphasis upon the work of Michotte. *Journal of the History of the Behavioral Sciences, 8*, 302–320.

Gigerenzer, G. (1987a). Probabilistic thinking and the fight against subjectivity. In L. Krüger, G. Gigerenzer, & M. S. Morgan (Eds.), *The probabilistic revolution: Vol. II. Ideas in the sciences* (pp. 11–33). Cambridge, MA: MIT Press.

Gigerenzer, G. (1987b). Survival of the fittest probabilist: Brunswik, Thurstone, and the two disciplines of psychology. In L. Krüger, G. Gigerenzer, & M. S. Morgan (Eds.), *The probabilistic revolution: Vol. II. Ideas in the sciences* (pp. 49–72). Cambridge, MA: MIT Press.

Gigerenzer, G. (1991). From tools to theories: A heuristic of discovery in cognitive psychology. *Psychological Review, 98*, 254–267.

Gigerenzer, G. (1993). The superego, the ego, and the id in statistical reasoning. In G. Keren & G. Lewis (Eds.), *A handbook for data analysis in the behavioral sciences: Methodological issues* (pp. 311–339). Hillsdale, NJ: Lawrence Erlbaum Associates.

Gigerenzer, G. (2000). *Adaptive thinking*. New York: Oxford University Press.

Gigerenzer, G. (2001). Content-blind norms, no norms or good norms? A reply to Vranas. *Cognition, 81*, 93–103.

Gigerenzer, G. (2003). Where do new ideas come from? A heuristic of discovery in cognitive science. In M. C. Galavotti (Ed.), *Observation and experiment in the natural and social sciences* (pp. 1–39). Dordrecht, The Netherlands: Kluwer.

Gigerenzer, G., & Murray, D. J. (1987). *Cognition as intuitive statistics.* Hillsdale, NJ: Lawrence Erlbaum Associates.

Gigerenzer, G., Swijtink, Z., Porter, T., Daston, L., Beatty, J., & Krüger, L. (1989). *The empire of chance.* Cambridge, England: Cambridge University Press.

Gruber, H. (1981). *Darwin on man, a psychological study of scientific creativity* (2nd ed.). Chicago: University of Chicago Press.

Guilford, J. P. (1954). *Psychometric methods* (2nd ed.). New York: McGraw-Hill.

Gundlach, H. (1997). Sinne, Apparate und Erkenntnis: Gibt es besondere Gründe dafür, weshalb die neue Psychologie apparativ wurde? [The senses, apparatuses, and knowledge: Are there specific reasons why the new psychology became apparatus-driven?] In D. Albert & H. Gundlach (Eds.), *Apparative Psychologie: Geschichtliche Entwicklung und gegenwärtige Bedeutung* (pp. 35–50). Lengerich, Germany: Pabst Science.

Gundlach, H. (2007). What is a psychological instrument? In M. G. Ash & T. Sturm (Eds.), *Psychology's territories: Historical and contemporary perspectives from different disciplines.* Mahwah, NJ: Lawrence Erlbaum Associates.

Hacking, I. (1965). *Logic of statistical inference.* Cambridge, England: Cambridge University Press.

Hacking, I. (1983). *Representing and intervening.* Cambridge, England: Cambridge University Press.

Hammond, K. R., Stewart, T. R., Brehmer, B., & Steinmann, D. O. (1975). Social judgment theory. In M. F. Kaplan & S. Schwartz (Eds.), *Human judgment and decision processes* (pp. 271–312). New York: Academic.

Hanson, N. R. (1958). *Patterns of discovery.* Cambridge, England: Cambridge University Press.

Harvard University Center for Cognitive Studies. (1963). *Third annual report.*

Harvard University Center for Cognitive Studies. (1964). *Fourth annual report.*

Harvard University Center for Cognitive Studies. (1966). *Sixth annual report.*

Harvard University Center for Cognitive Studies. (1968). *Eighth annual report.*

Harvard University Center for Cognitive Studies. (1969). *Ninth annual report.*

Herbart, J. F. (1816). *Lehrbuch zur Psychologie.* Königsberg, Germany: August Wilhelm Unzer.

Hilgard, E. R. (1955). Discussion of probabilistic functionalism. *Psychological Review, 62,* 226–228.

Hoyningen-Huene, P. (1987). Context of discovery and context of justification. *Studies in the History and Philosophy of Science, 18,* 501–515.

Johnson-Laird, P. N. (1983). *Mental models.* Cambridge, England: Cambridge University Press.

Kahneman, D., Slovic, P., & Tversky, A. (Eds.). (1982). *Judgment under uncertainty: Heuristics and biases.* Cambridge, England: Cambridge University Press.

Kelley, H. H. (1967). Attribution theory in social psychology. In D. Levine (Ed.), *Nebraska Symposium on Motivation* (Vol. 15, pp. 192–238). Lincoln: University of Nebraska Press.

Kelley, H. H., & Michaela, I. L. (1980). Attribution theory and research. *Annual Review of Psychology, 31,* 457–501.

Kendall, M. G. (1942). On the future of statistics. *Journal of the Royal Statistical Society, 105,* 69–80.

Kita, S. (1993). *Language and thought interface: A study of spontaneous gestures and Japanese mimetics*. Unpublished doctoral dissertation, University of Chicago.

Kitcher, P. (1993). *The advancement of science*. Oxford, England: Oxford University Press.

Krüger, L. (1981). Vergängliche Erkenntnis der beharrenden Natur [Transitory knowledge of permanent nature]. In H. Poser (Ed.), *Wandel des Vernunftbegriffs* (pp. 223–249). Freiburg, Germany: Alber.

Kuhn, T. (1970). *The structure of scientific revolutions* (2nd ed.). Chicago: University of Chicago Press.

Lambert, J. H. (1892). *Photometrie* (E. Anding, Ed. and Trans.). Leipzig, Germany: W. Engelmann. (Original work published 1760)

Langley, P., Simon, H. A., Bradshaw, G. L., & Zytkow, J. M. (1987). *Scientific discovery*. Cambridge, MA: MIT Press.

Laplace, P.-S. (1995). *A philosophical essay on probabilities* (F. W. Truscott and F. L. Emory, Trans.). New York: Springer (Original work published 1814)

Leary, D. E. (1987). From act psychology to probabilistic functionalism: The place of Egon Brunswik in the history of psychology. In M. G. Ash & W. R. Woodward (Eds.), *Psychology in twentieth-century thought and society* (pp. 115–142). Cambridge, England: Cambridge University Press.

Leary, D. E. (Ed.). (1990). *Metaphors in the history of psychology*. Cambridge, England: Cambridge University Press.

Lenoir, T. (1986). Models and instruments in the development of electrophysiology, 1845–1912. *Historical Studies in the Physical Sciences, 17*, 1–54.

Lenoir, T. (1988). Practice, reason, context: The dialogue between theory and experiment. *Science in Context, 2*, 3–22.

Levelt, W. J. M. (1989). *Speaking: From intention to articulation*. Cambridge, MA: MIT Press.

Levinson, S. (1992). *How to think in order to speak Tzeltal*. Unpublished manuscript, Cognitive Anthropology Group, Max Planck Institute for Psycholinguistics, Nijmegen, The Netherlands.

Lopes, L. L. (1981). Decision making in the short run. *Journal of Experimental Psychology: Human Learning and Memory, 7*, 377–385.

Lopes, L. L. (1982). Doing the impossible: A note on induction and the experience of randomness. *Journal of Experimental Psychology: Learning, Memory, and Cognition, 8*, 626–636.

Lovie, A. D. (1983). Attention and behaviorism—Fact and fiction. *British Journal of Psychology, 74*, 301–310.

Luce, R. D. (1977). Thurstone's discriminal processes fifty years later. *Psychometrika, 42*, 461–489.

Mariotte, E. (1668). *Nouvelle découverte touchant la veüe*. Paris.

Mayer, T. (1755). Experimenta circa visus aciem [Experiments on visual acuity]. *Commentarii Societatis Regiae Scientiarum Gottingensis, Pars physica et mathematica, 4*, 97–112.

McArthur, L. A. (1972). The how and what of why: Some determinants and consequents of causal attribution. *Journal of Personality and Social Psychology, 22*, 171–193.

McCorduck, P. (1979). *Machines who think*. San Francisco: Freeman.

McCulloch, W. S. (1965). *Embodiments of mind*. Cambridge, MA: MIT Press.

Melton, A. W. (1962). Editorial. *Journal of Experimental Psychology, 64*, 553–557.

Michotte, A. (1963). *The perception of causality*. London: Methuen. (Original work published 1946)

Miller, G. A., Galanter, E., & Pribram, K. H. (1960). *Plans and the structure of behavior*. New York: Holt, Rinehart & Winston.

Mises, R. von. (1957). *Probability, statistics, and truth*. London: Allen and Unwin.

Murdock, B. B., Jr. (1982). A theory for the storage and retrieval of item and associative information. *Psychological Review, 89*, 609–626.

Neumann, J. von. (1958). *The computer and the brain*. New Haven, CT: Yale University Press.

Newell, A., Shaw, J. C., & Simon, H. A. (1958). Elements of a theory of human problem solving. *Psychological Review, 65*, 151–166.

Newell, A., & Simon. H. A. (1972). *Human problem solving*. Englewood Cliffs, NJ: Prentice Hall.

Neyman, J. (1937). Outline of a theory of statistical estimation based on the classical theory of probability. *Philosophical Transactions of the Royal Society (Series A), 236*, 333–380.

Neyman, J., & Pearson, E. S. (1928). On the use and interpretation of certain test criteria for purposes of statistical inference: Part I. *Biometrika, 20A*, 175–240.

Nickles, T. (1980). Introductory essay: Scientific discovery and the future of philosophy of science. In T. Nickles (Ed.), *Scientific discovery, logic, and rationality* (pp. 1–59). Dordrecht, The Netherlands: Reidel.

Papineau, D. (Ed.). (1996). *The philosophy of science*. Oxford, England: Oxford University Press.

Papineau, D. (2003). Comments on Gerd Gigerenzer. In M. C. Galavotti (Ed.), *Observation and experiment in the natural and social sciences* (pp. 141–151). Dordrecht, The Netherlands: Kluwer.

Piaget, J. (1930). *The child's conception of causality*. London: Kegan Paul.

Popper, K. (1959). *The logic of scientific discovery*. New York: Basic Books. (Original work published 1935)

Putnam, H. (1960). Minds and machines. In S. Hook (Ed.), *Dimensions of mind* (pp. 138–164). Albany: State University of New York Press.

Putnam, H. (1967a). The mental life of some machines. In H.-N. Castaneda (Ed.), *Intentionality, mind and perception* (pp. 177–200). Detroit, MI: Wayne State University Press.

Putnam, H. (1967b). Psychological predicates. In W. H. Capitan & D. D. Merrill (Eds.), *Art, mind and religion* (pp. 37–48). Pittsburgh, PA: University of Pittsburgh Press.

Putnam, H. (1975). *Mind, language and reality: Philosophical papers* (Vol. II). Cambridge, England: Cambridge University Press.

Quine, W. V. O. (1978). A postscript on metaphor. In S. Sacks (Ed.), *On metaphor* (pp. 159–160). Chicago: University of Chicago Press.

Reichenbach, H. (1938). *Experience and prediction*. Chicago: University of Chicago Press.

Rucci, A. J., & Tweney, R. D. (1980). Analysis of variance and the "second discipline" of scientific psychology: A historical account. *Psychological Bulletin, 87*, 166–184.

Scheerer, E. (1987). Tobias Meyer—Experiments on visual acuity. *Spatial Perception, 2*, 81–97.

Searle, J. (1984). *Minds, brains and science.* Cambridge, MA: Harvard University Press.

Shannon, C. E. (1938). A symbolic analysis of relay and switching circuits. *Transactions of the American Institute of Electrical Engineers, 57*, 713–723.

Simon, H. A. (1969). *The sciences of the artificial.* Cambridge, MA: MIT Press.

Simon, H. A. (1979). Information processing models of cognition. *Annual Review of Psychology, 30*, 363–96.

Simon, H. A. (1991). *Models of my life.* New York: Basic Books.

Simon, H. A. (1992). What is an "explanation" of behavior? *Psychological Science, 3*, 150–161.

Simon, H. A., & Newell, A. (1986). Information Processing Language V on the IBM 650. *Annals of the History of Computing, 8*, 47–49.

Smith, L. D. (1986). *Behaviorism and logical positivism.* Stanford, CA: Stanford University Press.

Sterling, T. D. (1959). Publication decisions and their possible effects on inferences drawn from tests of significance or vice versa. *Journal of the American Statistical Association, 54*, 30–34.

"Student" (W. S. Gosset). (1908). The probable error of a mean. *Biometrika, 6*(1), 1–25.

Sturm, T. (in press). Is there a problem with mathematical psychology in the eighteenth century? A fresh look at Kant's old argument. *Journal of the History of the Behavioral Sciences.*

Sturm, T., & Gigerenzer, G. (2006). How can we use the distinction between discovery and justification? On the weaknesses of the Strong Programme in the sociology of scientific knowledge. In J. Schickore & F. Steinle (Eds.), *Revisiting discovery and justification* (pp. 133–158). New York: Springer.

Swets, J. A., Tanner, W. D., & Birdsall, T. G. (1964). Decision processes in perception. In J. A. Swets (Ed.), *Signal detection and recognition in human observers* (pp. 3–57). New York: Wiley.

Swijtink, Z. G. (1987). The objectification of observation: Measurement and statistical methods in the nineteenth century. In L. Krüger, L. J. Daston, & M. Heidelberger (Eds.), *The probabilistic revolution. Vol. 1: Ideas in history* (pp. 261–285). Cambridge, MA: MIT Press.

Tanner, W. P., Jr. (1965). *Statistical decision processes in detection and recognition* (Technical Report). Ann Arbor: University of Michigan, Sensory Intelligence Laboratory, Department of Psychology.

Tanner, W. P., Jr., & Swets, J. A. (1954). A decision-making theory of visual detection. *Psychological Review, 61*, 401–409.

Teigen, K. H. (1983). Studies in subjective probability IV: Probabilities, confidence, and luck. *Scandinavian Journal of Psychology, 24*, 175–191.

Thomas, J. H., & Lockery, S. R. (2000). Neurobiology. In I. A. Hope (Ed.), *C. elegans: A practical approach* (pp. 143–180). Oxford, England: Oxford University Press.

Thorndike, R. L. (1954). The psychological value systems of psychologists. *American Psychologist, 9,* 787–789.

Thurstone, L. L. (1927). A law of comparative judgement. *Psychological Review, 34,* 273–286.

Titchener, E. B. (1896). *An outline of psychology.* New York: Macmillan.

Toulmin, S., & Leary, D. E. (1985). The cult of empiricism in psychology, and beyond. In S. Koch (Ed.), *A century of psychology as science* (pp. 594–617). New York: McGraw-Hill.

Turing, A. M. (1950). Computing machinery and intelligence. *Mind, 59,* 433–460.

Turing, A. M. (1969). Intelligent machinery. In B. Meltzer & D. Michie (Eds.), *Machine intelligence* (Vol. 5, pp. 3–23). Edinburgh, Scotland: Edinburgh University Press.

Tversky, A., & Kahneman, D. (1974). Judgment under uncertainty: Heuristics and biases. *Science, 185,* 1124–1131.

Tversky, A., & Kahneman, D. (1980). Causal schemata in judgments under uncertainty. In M. Fishbein (Ed.), *Progress in social psychology* (Vol. 1, pp. 49–72). Hillsdale, NJ: Lawrence Erlbaum Associates.

Tversky, A., & Kahneman, D. (1982). Judgments of and by representativeness. In D. Kahneman, P. Slovic, & A. Tversky (Eds.), *Judgment under uncertainty: Heuristics and biases* (pp. 84–98). Cambridge, England: Cambridge University Press.

Tversky, A., & Kahneman, D. (1983). Extensional versus intuitive reasoning: The conjunction fallacy in probability judgment. *Psychological Review, 90,* 293–315.

Tweney, R. D., Dotherty, M. E., & Mynatt, C. R. (Eds.). (1981). *On scientific thinking.* New York: Columbia University Press.

White, J. G., Southgate, E., Thomson, J. N., & Brenner, S. (1986). The structure of the nervous system of the nematode *Caenorhabditis elegans. Philosophical Transactions of the Royal Society London B, 314,* 1–340.

Whitehead, A. N., & Russell, B. (1935). *Principia mathematica* (2nd ed., Vol. 1). Cambridge, England: Cambridge University Press.

Wickelgreen, W. A., & Norman, D. A. (1966). Strength models and serial position in short-term recognition memory. *Journal of Mathematical Psychology, 3,* 316–347.

Wundt, W. (1921). *Logik* [Logic] (4th ed.). Stuttgart, Germany: Enke.

15

Reflexivity Revisited: Changing Psychology's Frame of Reference

James H. Capshew
Indiana University

REFLEXIVITY REVISITED

After the shock and awe of the greatest conflict in history—the killing and maiming of millions of human beings in the second world war—psychologists found it impossible to return to the academic life they had left a few years earlier. That world was gone forever. In the United States, at least, casualties were relatively low. With the nightmare of the Great Depression fading and the perception of the righteousness of Allied military might, psychologists shared in the buoyant mood. However, the specter of atomic warfare hung over all. Now psychologists, along with scientists and citizens everywhere, were caught up in the challenges of a new era of global insecurity.

In the fertile ground of postwar America, psychological applications sprouted like mushrooms. Built on a substrate of experimental and psychometric findings, psychologists were eager to focus on the task of personal rehabilitation and social reconstruction. Psychologists as diverse as

Gordon Allport, George Kelly, Kurt Lewin, Carl Rogers, and B. F. Skinner believed that they were cultivating investigations that would foster psychological health and satisfaction if applied generally. Collectively, with the rebirth of the American Psychological Association (APA) and strong federal support for psychological applications, American psychologists were entering a period of sustained growth in personnel and public influence. The opportunities seemed endless (Capshew, 1999).

The expansion in clinical applications was especially robust. With thousands of neuropsychiatric patients in the hospitals of the Veterans Administration, the federal government was footing the bill to train and employ clinical psychologists as an essential component of the mental health team. The Veterans Administration, along with allied programs of the U.S. Public Health Service, virtually created the specialty of clinical psychology. Psychologists were involved hand-in-glove with these developments, devising curricula, programs, and internships to mold this interest. Epistemologically, clinical psychology, especially psychotherapy, raised questions about the adequacy of laboratory methods and the utility of experimental data and focused attention on how subjectivity and interpersonal relations could be woven into the scientific fabric of psychology.

Even psychoanalysis, long suspect in psychology's academic circles, was enjoying a revival of public interest and increasing use among clinical and applied psychologists in the wake of its perceived wartime success. As early as 1940, Harvard University experimentalist Edwin G. Boring shared his analytic experience in the pages of the *Journal of Abnormal and Social Psychology* (Boring, 1940) as part of a symposium of "Psychoanalysis as Seen by Analyzed Psychologists." The forum provided an opportunity for academic psychologists to come to grips with Freudian theory by discussing their individual experiences. Although the participants focused on questions of scientific validity, the essentially subjective nature of their evidence was a substantial departure from conventional standards of experimental proof. It also suggested a reflexive turn in psychologists' thinking about themselves and their work that was demonstrated in Boring's transmutation of his idiosyncratic encounter with psychoanalysis into a matter of broad professional import.

Reflexivity—the idea that the psychologist is the object of his or her own study—can serve as a heuristic to interpret the proliferation of psychological applications and technologies to manage the self, in both individual and collective registers. Not a type or category of applied psychology per se, reflexivity can be conceptualized as a form of metadiscourse, whether acknowledged or not, by psychologists as they work with human participants. This had the effect of placing the psychologist into the equation of their theoretical constructions and practical interventions. Such efforts can be viewed as attempts to develop an applied psychology of the psychologist.

Historical analysis reveals several varieties of psychological reflexivity in postwar America. They range from a general atmosphere of professional self-awareness to an explicit attempt to generate a reflexive psychological theory and therapeutic technique. Reflexive thinking is also reflected in the vast quantities of psychological self-help books, including ones authored by nonpsychologists. Indeed, some critical theorists and postmodern philosophers argue that we live in an era of "extreme reflexivity" in which "thought and action are constantly refracted back upon one another" (Giddens, 1990, p. 38). Such self-referencing perspectives create problems of infinite regress and provide few conceptual anchors to veridical reality. However, as stimulating as these postmodern musings are (see Lawson, 1985), this chapter will neglect philosophy in favor of history and point out some interesting features of psychology's postwar ecology.

After the behaviorist revolution banished experimental introspection following World War I, scientific self-awareness was expressed through ruminations on method and autobiography of professional careers. Morawski (1992, 2007) evokes the differentiation of the psychologist's scientific self from their investigational subjects and their subsequent identification with scientific method. When the behaviorist "age of learning" was in full swing, a dozen article-length personal reflections by prominent psychologists from the United States and Europe were published in *A History of Psychology in Autobiography* (Murchison, 1930). The title suggests the conceptual rationale that the story of scientific psychology can be best told by those who have contributed most to its development and that the microcosm of an individual can illuminate the macrocosm of the discipline. These "human interest" accounts would not only tell something about the people behind the research but also keep the reflexive gaze within the manageable boundaries of experimental design. The series struck a vein of interest and, by 1936, two other volumes were published. The series continues today.

In 1933, Saul Rosenzweig proposed a reflexive study of the psychological laboratory. He raised the possibility that biased attitudes, conscious or not, on the part of the experimenter or the participant might influence the outcome of the experiment. He pointed out the special challenge of psychological research: "When one works with human materials one must reckon with the fact that everyone is a psychologist" (1933, p. 342). He went on to outline ways to explore such influences systematically as a hedge against experimental error. Rosenzweig did not question the conventional distinction between experimenter and subject, or the epistemological validity of the psychological experiment, but sought to turn reflexive features of the laboratory situation to constructive use as a way to improve research.

Such uses of reflexivity became part of the management of the psychologist's scientific identity. The irreducibly human elements behind the research were circumscribed within conventional personal narratives emphasizing the psychologist's fidelity to method and growth in scientific virtuosity. For the most part, one looks in vain for accounts of family dynamics or emotional life in the volumes of *A History of Psychology in Autobiography*. The genre soon assumed a ritual significance, teaching by example each generation of psychologists about how to behave as scientists. Rosenzweig's prewar work on the social psychology of the psychological experiment lay fallow for several decades until it was rediscovered as a precursor to the study of experimenter effects and the "artifact threat" (see Suls & Rosnow, 1988). In general, such work was aimed toward eliminating or minimizing experimental "artifacts" through refinements in method rather than toward consideration of their epistemological implications. Thus reflexive character of the psychological experiment was brought under control by inscribing it as a scientific problem, to be managed by technical methods.

APPROACHES TO REFLEXIVITY IN POSTWAR AMERICAN PSYCHOLOGY

It can be argued that Gordon Allport, in his 1939 APA presidential address, "The Psychologist's Frame of Reference," brought reflexive issues to the forefront in his championing of the *idiographic* approach (i.e., a focus on individual cases) to augment the prevailing *nomothetic* orientation (i.e., the search for general principles). On the basis of a review of the psychological literature of the past 50 years (Bruner & Allport, 1940), he noted that "the development of a notable schism between the psychology constructed in a laboratory and the psychology constructed on the field of life" (Allport, 1940/1978, p. 383). Allport claimed that psychologists had hardly improved upon plain common sense in being able to usefully predict behavior. What was needed was more attention to the specifics of single cases and the contexts in which they were embedded. Moreover, psychologists had hindered their comprehension by not considering sufficiently the participant's point of view or frame of reference and by interpreting their research findings within narrow methodological constraints. Allport thought one way to bridge that gulf was further development of idiographic psychology in an effort to generate practical control of human affairs. His election to the APA presidency was indicator of the rise of social psychology and the study of personality in the 1940s (for further discussion, see Pandora, 1997).

Social psychologist Kurt Lewin was heartened by wartime developments that had brought theory and practice closer together. Toward the end of the war, he urged even closer collaboration: "This can be accomplished in psychology, as it has been accomplished in physics, if the theorist does not look toward applied problems with highbrow aversion or with a fear of social problems, and if the applied psychologist realizes that there is nothing so practical as a good theory" (Lewin, 1944/1951, p. 169). To further that vision, Lewin founded the Research Center for Group Dynamics at MIT in 1945 and set an ambitious program of "action research" in motion. The following year, he supervised a leadership workshop for the Connecticut State Inter-Racial Commission. The 41 participants, about half of whom were African American or Jewish, were drawn mainly from the ranks of educators and social service workers, with a few others from business and labor. Members of the workshop

> hoped to develop greater skill in dealing with other people, more reliable methods of changing people's attitudes, insight into reasons for resisting change, a more scientific understanding of the causes of prejudice, and a more reliable insight into their own attitudes and values. (Marrow, 1969, p. 211)

Lewin and his colleagues considered the workshop a large-scale "change" experiment in which the process of training could be monitored and evaluated on an ongoing basis to provide research data on group dynamics. At the end of each daily session, staff members would review and discuss their observations of the trainees' behavior. In the course of one of these postsession conferences, a few of the trainees happened to be present. As they shared with the assembled psychologists their perceptions of what had transpired, it was clear that they interpreted things differently than the experts. Far from rejecting this unexpected information, Lewin and company continued the discourse with their putative participants and came to the conclusion that the very process of analyzing leadership-training sessions with members of the group could have a therapeutic function. This was an example of how social psychological research could, through a process of mutual feedback, lead to desirable changes both in the personalities of individual participants and in their interpersonal relations within the group. The reflexive implication was clear: The investigation as well as the enhancement of group dynamics went hand in hand.

The initial experiment was so successful that the approach was institutionalized in the National Training Laboratories, established in 1947 in Bethel, Maine, with initial funding from the Office of Naval Research. Here "T" (for *training*) group research and practice continued, contributing to the spread and proliferation of "sensitivity training" in various forms (Back, 1972). By the late 1960s, clinical psychologist Carl Rogers was calling the technique "the most significant social invention of this century" (Rogers, 1968, p. 265).

Rogers himself was guided by a similar reflexive ethos of practice in constructing a psychology of the person. By the late 1930s, he was beginning to articulate his nondirective, or client-centered approach to psychotherapy. In his 1942 book, *Counseling and Psychotherapy*, he took an explicitly scientific stance presenting his work as a "series of hypotheses" (Rogers, 1942, p. 17). Perhaps his most fundamental assumption was that the client was the best guide to the identification and solution of his or her own problems. In establishing a therapeutic relationship with the client, the role of the counselor was to provide unlimited positive regard. *Client-Centered Therapy* (1951) further developed the idea that the therapist was supposed to become an agent of psychological change by embodying certain values and orientations, not simply by applying methods or techniques of psychotherapy. In Rogers's words, the effective counselor "holds a coherent and developing set of attitudes deeply imbedded in his personal organization" (Rogers, 1951, p. 19). In other words, the psychotherapist—as a person—served instrumental purposes in promoting positive psychological change in the client.

Prompted by the competing demands of scientific research and professional practice, Rogers reported experiencing ambivalence between "sensitive subjective understanding" and "detached objective curiosity" about people. In 1955, he expressed his concerns in the pages of the *American Psychologist* as a philosophical choice between "Persons or Science?" (Rogers, 1955). Like the Lewinians, Rogers found ways to incorporate experiential, idiographic data as he developed his theories and techniques of psychotherapy.

In the evolving work of Lewin and Rogers one can see the operation of a constitutive reflexivity, an awareness of the reflexive nature of individual self-consciousness and human relations. Both of these psychologists, I argue, were led to a reflexive position by their practical scientific investigations and interventions. This reflexive ethos of practice depended on both the scientist and the participant contributing to the reframing of psychological activity. However, the psychologist retained the role of expert by virtue of professional preparation, credentialing, and knowledge.

Yet another variety of reflexivity can be found in the work of George A. Kelly, who attempted to construct an explicitly reflexive theory of personality. Sensitized before the second world war to the incompatibilities of viewing "the person as a laboratory subject, as a statistical case, and as a clinical client" (Kelly, 1939, p. 186), and distressed at the way psychology textbooks described scientific behavior vis-à-vis the behavior of ordinary individuals, he took reflexivity as a scientific imperative. His 1955 book, *The Psychology of Personal Constructs* (Kelly, 1955), was founded on a reflexive thesis. It developed a theory of human nature that viewed people as if they behaved like scientists, making hypotheses about the world and then testing them against experience. For Kelly, humans seek cognitive control of their world by construing events and fitting them into a framework of *personal constructs* that give them meaning. The system carried explicit therapeutic implications: Desired personality changes could be effected by adopting new personal constructs, with or without the aid of a psychotherapist.

Kelly, in his nomothetic drive to unify idiographic phenomena, turned to his own experience of being a scientist, reflecting on his own behavior and giving it wider significance. As one of his disciples put it:

> In inventing personal construct theory, [Kelly] set out to depict all persons as scientists or, for that matter, all scientists as persons. He strove to build a reflexive theory; a theory that would account for its own creation and its creator and use one language only to describe all human endeavor and confusion. By arguing that our desire to understand and anticipate is at the center of our human nature, Kelly judged science to be only a Sunday-best version of an everyday activity. (Bannister, 1985, p. xi)

Kelly's conceptual move stripped scientific investigation of its special separate status in the repertoire of human action and recast it as the general foundation of all behavior.

Another notable feature of the personal construct system was its quality of open-endedness "that makes possible a *study* of value attitudes rather than a mere dictation of values from a point outside the theory" (Oliver & Landfield, 1962, p. 120). Such a perspective could be applied equally to the psychologist and to the layperson alike.

The autobiography of neobehaviorist B. F. Skinner (1976, 1979, 1983) returns to earlier reflexive themes of the management of the psychologist's identity as a scientist. However, because of its length and unconventional form, it deserves special consideration. Beginning in the 1930s, Skinner developed the experimental analysis of behavior in the laboratory, featuring operant conditioning as a key concept. During the war, he extended his efforts to real life settings in such diverse projects as Project Pigeon, the Air Crib, and the utopian novel *Walden Two* (Capshew, 1993). After the war, Skinner continued his laboratory work and became a spokesman for the behaviorist point of view, promoting his ideas in the pages of psychological journals as well as books for the public.

When asked for a contribution to APA's self-survey of psychological science in the mid—1950s, Skinner responded by penning an ironic account of his own behavior as a working scientist in "A Case History in Scientific Method" (Skinner, 1956/1972). In a wicked parody of the stuffy formalisms about scientific method common among philosophers of science as well as the general public, Skinner portrayed himself as an opportunistic individualist in the laboratory. He also attacked the increasing domination of statistics in research design and data analysis, suggesting it had attained the status of a shibboleth to scientific orthodoxy. He then described his own behavior as an experimenter, deriving some unformalized principles of scientific methodology. Skinner concluded his self-analysis with a strong reflexive twist: "The organism whose behavior is most extensively modified and most completely controlled in research of the sort I have described is the experimenter himself" (Skinner, 1956/1972, p. 122).

What began as a scientific self-description in literary form in the 1950s would later blossom into a full-scale autobiographical study in the 1970s, when Skinner sought to describe his life history using behaviorist concepts and language. For more than a decade, he was occupied with his autobiography, which grew into perhaps his largest and most sustained literary production. (Skinner had long-standing literary ambitions.) Eschewing analysis of his motives or inner life, he attempted to describe his life objectively, from the perspective of an outside observer. He used the terminology of behavioral analysis—*contingencies, reinforcement, shaping*—to convey the sense that his life was the result of environmental forces acting upon his biological endowment. His message was that a person's "life" was merely a convenient shorthand label for the nexus of behavioral events impinging upon an individual.

In Skinner's hands, the particular idiosyncrasies of his life, writ large, became exemplars of the universal principles revealed by behavioral psychology. Thus the tale of the scientist's behavior was transformed into a vehicle for telling the story of behavioral science. What makes Skinner's autobiographical project different from most others in this genre is not simply its length but the claim that his life was an instantiation of his behavioral theory, thus providing evidence for the support of his scientific system. In an earlier personal narrative (Skinner, 1967), he reflected: "Whether from narcissism or scientific curiosity, I have been as much interested in myself as in rat and pigeons. I have applied the same formulations, I have looked for the same kind of causal relations, and I have manipulated behavior in the same way and sometimes with comparable success" (p. 407). This reflexive bootstrapping, in which psychologists use their own self-awareness and self-referencing action as an integral part of their theory, illustrates yet another variety of reflexive dynamics in psychology.

This brief survey of the varieties of reflexive practices in postwar American psychology suggests that reflexivity is not only an interesting historical topic but also a theme that cross-cuts traditional psychological categories. The preceding examples suggest some of the manifold ways in which psychologists managed reflexive dynamics, ranging from the circumscription of professional self-consciousness and autobiography, to an ethos of practice in psychotherapy and group dynamics, and to reflexivity as an epistemological value and explicit theoretical goal.

WIDER CONTEXTS OF REFLEXIVITY

Reflexive dynamics have been little noted in psychology (Oliver & Landfield, 1962), either as a basic epistemological issue (Barker, 1989; Flanagan, 1981) or as an aspect of professional practice (Steier, 1991). By contrast, in anthropology (Marcus, 2001; Ruby, 1982) and sociology, reflexive themes have a rich tradition of analysis and debate, perhaps aided by traditional methods of participant observation and a commitment to relativism. Sociologists of science have been particularly concerned about reflexivity, but much of that discussion is sterile (Ashmore, 2001), veering off into experimental literary forms that might dazzle but are lacking in historical utility (Ashmore, 1989; Woolgar, 1988). In this context, Lynch (2000), in "Against Reflexivity as an Academic Virtue and Source of Privileged Knowledge," provided a useful categorization of different kinds of reflexivity as he argues for the deflation of the "'epistemological' hubris that often seems to accompany self-consciously reflexive claims" (p. 47). Instead, he adopted an ethnomethodological framework in which reflexivity is an ordinary feature of discourse and action, the analysis of which may (or may not) reveal attributes of interest.

Morawski's (1992) observation that strong versions of reflexivity "challenge the very foundations of psychological knowledge" (p. 285) provides a clue to explain this lack of attention. By bringing reflexive dynamics to awareness, the psychologist may well have to embrace a transactional model of mind rather than continue with the individualistic one that has been dominant. This "cultural" approach to psychology has been strongly argued by Bruner (1986, 1990), and might be usefully applied internally to the normative expectations (or the "folk psychology") of the psychological community. These types of collective behavior patterns are not visible until some member of the community transgresses the norm or behaves in unexpected ways. On this view, reflexivity is part of the epistemological background that every psychologist acquires in the course of his or her education and training, literally unremarkable until some individual disturbs the status quo.

When psychologists moved from their animal laboratories to working with human beings as a result of World War II, reflexive dynamics came to the fore and were expressed and managed in different ways. Confronted with the challenges of personnel, group relations, and clinical work, there were strong incentives to incorporate personal and interpersonal subjectivity into psychology. Before the war, as Morawski (1992) noted, reflexive aspects of psychology were "denied, erased, displaced, or forgot[ten]" (p. 286) as the psychologist's identity as objective scientist was formed and regulated. These distancing mechanisms were still in operation after the war, but some psychological work depended on embracing aspects of reflexive understanding, albeit intuitive or unacknowledged by the researcher.

This perspective sheds light on a persistent puzzle of postwar American academic psychology and the rise of the "psychological society" (see Ash, 2003; Capshew, 1999). Much of the development in the psychological profession in this period was fueled by the scientization of personal thoughts, feelings, and beliefs into a sprawling system of clinical techniques and social interventions, both in the United States and abroad. As Roger Smith (1997) noted, in such a society "everyone became her or his own psychologist, able and willing to describe life in psychological terms" (p. 577). Several authors (e.g., Herman, 1996, 2003; Rose, 1996) have traced out the connections among knowledge, power, and identity that have gone into the construction of the modern self. Seen in this context, psychologists have been at the center of the expanding personal growth industry, attempting to shape its contours and forms while at the same time existing in its pervasive culture, much to the dismay of critics (see Milton, 2002; Moskowitz, 2001). Psychotherapy, beginning with Freudian psychoanalysis, depended on the generation of a narrative, a coherent "story" that allowed the client to make sense out of his or her difficulties. Woolfolk (1998) argued "that settling on a 'salutary' story is an essential aspect of therapy even when the therapy does not emphasize the construction or reconstruction of personal histories" (p. 100).

From this historical perspective, reflexivity provided a bridge, an epistemological "trading zone" (Galison, 1997) between two major ways of knowledge making in psychology: the paradigmatic and the narrative. Scientific knowledge is usually seen as paradigmatic, with the interrelated qualities of logic, conceptual analysis, and universalism. Much of the history and philosophy of science is focused the development and status of this kind of esoteric knowledge. Indeed, Thomas

Kuhn's famous 1962 book, *The Structure of Scientific Revolutions*, has engendered 40 years of debates and interpretations on the role of paradigms in science. That discussion has had special relevance for psychology, for Kuhn (1962/1970) implied that the social sciences were pre-paradigmatic: "It remains an open question what parts of social science have yet acquired such paradigms at all" (p. 15). That struck a nerve, rallying psychologists to proclaim yet once again that their relatively new discipline was a part of the venerable family of science.

Although philosophers were quick to point out that Kuhn applied the term *paradigm* in multiple, sometimes conflicting ways (see Masterman, 1970), most psychologists did not follow that philosophical debate but used his conceptual scheme superficially (Coleman & Salamon, 1988; see Peterson, 1981) or took the view that psychology had several paradigms (Burgess, 1972). However, alternate ways of knowing in psychology have increased in scope and power since the 1940s, and narrative approaches have grown alongside the prevailing scientific ideology of paradigmatic knowledge. Indeed, the rapprochement between "hard" science (e.g., experimental psychology) and "soft" approaches (e.g., psychotherapy) that occurred in the 20th century provides an indicator of such intradisciplinary dynamics.

Within the framework of the narrative approach of Bruner and others (e.g., Gergen & Gergen, 1988) to an investigation of the cultural history of psychology, one might suggest that reflexivity can be understood best not only as a conceptual and logical issue but also as a resource for the generation of authoritative accounts of psychology and its practitioners and their audiences. Perhaps such narratives gain power precisely to the extent that they are part of the background, woven into the very fabric of theory, psychotherapy, and practice. On this view, narratives of psychology's history can reinforce its prevalent scientific ideology, for example, in the proliferation of standard "history and systems" textbooks (see Ash, 1983) or, alternately, provide new frames of meaning for the intellectual and social role of psychologists.

As scholars seek to explain psychology, then "taking psychologists seriously in our historical investigations requires taking reflexivity seriously" (Morawski, 1992, p. 304). Whether considered as an aspect of theory construction, as a research technique, as a badge of professional identity, or as a goal to be achieved with clients, the management of reflexivity can serve as a useful historical indicator, marking a viaduct between the knowledge and the knower. Understanding the role of reflexive practices in psychological investigations, in the evolution of professional identities in psychology, and in the social surroundings of the field could provide a crucial element in explaining psychology's ascendancy and ubiquity in the 20th century.

REFERENCES

Allport, G. W. (1978). In E. R. Hilgard (Ed.), *American psychology in historical perspective: Addresses of the Presidents of the American Psychological Association, 1892–1977* (pp. 371–395). Washington, DC: American Psychological Association. (Original work published 1940)

Ash, M. G. (1983). The self-presentation of a discipline: History of psychology in the United States between pedagogy and scholarship. In L. Graham, W. Lepenies, & P. Weingart (Eds.), *Functions and uses of disciplinary histories* (pp. 143–189). Dordrecht, The Netherlands: Reidel.

Ash, M. G. (2003). Psychology. In T. M. Porter & D. Ross (Eds.), *The modern social sciences* (Vol. 7, pp. 251–274). Cambridge, England: Cambridge University Press.

Ashmore, M. (1989). *The reflexive thesis: Wrighting the sociology of scientific knowledge.* Chicago: University of Chicago Press.

Ashmore, M. (2001). Reflexivity, in science and technology studies. In N. J. Smelser & P. B. Baltes (Eds.), *International encyclopedia of the social and behavioral sciences* (Vol. 19, pp. 12881–12884). Amsterdam: Elsevier.

Back, K. (1972). *Beyond words: The story of sensitivity training and the encounter movement.* New York: Russell Sage Foundation.

Bannister, D. (1985). Foreword. In R. A. Neimeyer (Ed.), *The development of personal construct psychology* (pp. xi–xii). Lincoln: University of Nebraska Press.

Barker, P. (1989). The reflexivity problem in the psychology of science. In B. Gholson, W. R. Shadish, Jr., R. A. Neimeyer, & A. C. Houts (Eds.), *Psychology of science: Contributions to metascience* (pp. 92–114). Cambridge, England: Cambridge University Press.

Boring, E. G. (1940). Was this analysis a success? *Journal of Abnormal and Social Psychology, 35,* 4–10.

Bruner, J. S. (1986). *Actual minds, possible worlds.* Cambridge, MA: Harvard University Press.

Bruner, J. S. (1990). *Acts of meaning.* Cambridge, MA: Harvard University Press.

Bruner, J. S., & Allport, G. W. (1940). Fifty years of change in American psychology. *Psychological Bulletin, 37,* 757–776.

Burgess, I. S. (1972). Psychology and Kuhn's concept of paradigm. *Journal of Behavioural Science, 1,* 193–200.

Capshew, J. H. (1993). Engineering behavior: World War II, Project Pigeon, and the conditioning of B. F. Skinner. *Technology and Culture, 34,* 835–857.

Capshew, J. H. (1999). *Psychologists on the march: Science, practice, and professional identity in America, 1929–1969.* New York: Cambridge University Press.

Coleman, S. R., & Salamon, R. (1988). Kuhn's *Structure of scientific revolutions* in the psychological journal literature, 1969–1983: A descriptive study. *Journal of Mind and Behavior, 9,* 415–445.

Flanagan, O. J., Jr. (1981). Psychology, progress, and the problem of reflexivity: A study in the epistemological foundations of psychology. *Journal of the History of the Behavioral Sciences, 17,* 375–386.

Galison, P. (1997). *Image and logic: A material culture of microphysics.* Chicago: University of Chicago Press.

Gergen, K. J., & Gergen, M. (1988) Narrative and the self as relationship. In. L. Berkowitz (Ed.), *Advances in experimental and social psychology* (Vol. 21, pp. 17–56). New York: Academic.

Giddens, A. (1990). *The consequences of modernity*. Stanford, CA: Stanford University Press.

Herman, E. (1996). *The romance of American psychology*. Berkeley: University of California Press.

Herman, E. (2003). Psychologism and the child. In T. M. Porter & D. Ross (Eds.), *The modern social sciences* (Vol. 7, pp. 649–662). Cambridge, England: Cambridge University Press.

Kelly, G. A. (1939). The person as a laboratory subject, as a statistical case, and as a clinical client [Abstract]. *Proceedings of the Indiana Academy of Science, 48*, 186.

Kelly, G. A. (1955). *The psychology of personal constructs* (2 vols.). New York: Norton.

Kuhn, T. S. (1970). *The structure of scientific revolutions* (2nd ed.). Chicago: University of Chicago Press. (Original work published 1962)

Lawson, H. (1985). *Reflexivity: The post-modern predicament*. London: Hutchinson.

Lewin, K. (1951). Problems of research in social psychology. In D. Cartwright (Ed.), *Field theory in social science: Selected theoretical papers by Kurt Lewin* (pp. 155–169). New York: Harper & Row. (Original work published 1944)

Lynch, M. (2000). Against reflexivity as an academic virtue and source of privileged knowledge. *Theory, Culture & Society, 17*, 26–54.

Marcus, G. E. (2001). Reflexivity and anthropology. In N. J. Smelser & P. B. Baltes (Eds.), *International encyclopedia of the social and behavioral sciences* (Vol. 19, pp. 12877–12881). Amsterdam: Elsevier.

Marrow, A. (1969). *The practical theorist: The life and work of Kurt Lewin*. New York: Basic Books.

Masterman, M. (1970). The nature of a paradigm. In I. Lakatos & M. Musgrave (Eds.), *Criticism and the growth of knowledge* (pp. 59–90). Cambridge, England: Cambridge University Press.

Milton, J. (2002). *The road to malpsychia: Humanistic psychology and our discontents*. San Francisco: Encounter Books.

Morawski, J. G. (1992). Self-regard and other-regard: Reflexive practices in American psychology, 1890–1940. *Science in Context, 5*, 281–308.

Morawski, J. G. (2007). Scientific selves: Discerning subjects and experimenters in experimental psychology in the United States, 1900–1935. In M. G. Ash & T. Sturm (Eds.), *Psychology's territories: Historical and contemporary perspectives from different disciplines* (pp. 342–355). Mahwah, NJ: Lawrence Erlbaum Associates.

Moskowitz, E. S. (2001). *In therapy we trust: America's obsession with self-fulfillment*. Baltimore: Johns Hopkins University Press.

Murchison, C. (Ed.). (1930). *A history of psychology in autobiography*. Worcester, MA: Clark University Press.

Oliver, W. D., & Landfield, A. W. (1962). Reflexivity: An unfaced issue in psychology. *Journal of Individual Psychology, 18*, 114–124.

Pandora, K. A. (1997). *Rebels within the ranks: Psychologists' critique of scientific authority and democratic realities in New Deal America*. Cambridge, England: Cambridge University Press.

Peterson, G. L. (1981). Historical self-understanding in the social sciences: The use of Thomas Kuhn in psychology. *Journal for the Theory of Social Behaviour, 11*, 1–30.

Rogers, C. R. (1942). *Counseling and psychotherapy*. Boston: Houghton Mifflin.

Rogers, C. R. (1951). *Client-centered therapy: Its current practice, implications, and theory*. Boston: Houghton Mifflin.

Rogers, C. R. (1955). Persons or science? A philosophical question. *American Psychologist, 10*, 267–278.

Rogers, C. R. (1968). Interpersonal relationships U.S.A. 2000. *Journal of Applied Behavioral Science, 4*, 265–280.

Rose, N. (1996). *Inventing ourselves: Psychology, power, and personhood*. New York: Cambridge University Press.

Rosenzweig, S. (1933). The experimental situation as a psychological problem. *Psychological Review, 40*, 337–354.

Ruby, J. (Ed.). (1982). *A crack in the mirror: Reflexive perspectives in anthropology*. Philadelphia: University of Pennsylvania Press.

Skinner, B. F. (1972). A case history in scientific method. In *Cumulative record: A selection of papers* (3rd ed., pp. 101–124). New York: Appleton-Century-Crofts. (Original work published 1956)

Skinner, B. F. (1967). B. F. Skinner. In E. G. Boring & G. Lindzey (Eds.), *A history of psychology in autobiography* (Vol. 5, pp. 385–413). New York: Appleton-Century-Crofts.

Skinner, B. F. (1976). *Particulars of my life*. New York: Knopf.

Skinner, B. F. (1979). *The shaping of a behaviorist*. New York: Knopf.

Skinner, B. F. (1983). *A matter of consequences*. New York: Knopf.

Smith, R. (1997). *The Norton history of the human sciences*. New York: Norton.

Steier, F. (Ed.). (1991). *Research and reflexivity*. London: Sage.

Suls, J. M., & Rosnow, R. L. (1988). Concerns about artifacts in psychological experiments. In J. G. Morawski (Ed.), *The rise of experimentation in American psychology* (pp. 163–187). New Haven, CT: Yale University Press.

Woolfolk, R. L. (1998). *The cure of souls: Science, values, and psychotherapy*. San Francisco: Jossey-Bass.

Woolgar, S. (Ed.). (1988). *Knowledge and reflexivity: New frontiers in the sociology of knowledge*. London: Sage.

Author Index

Subject Index

A

Action 7, 9, 10–14, 16, 20, 23, 37, 40–43, 45–60, 69–77, 79, 81, 82, 84–86, 89–96, 98–103, 105–108, 115–116, 118–120, 122, 131, 134–135, 137–139, 148, 165, 170, 178, 183–186, 232, 254, 298, 345, 347, 349, 351
  decisions for, 75–82
  different from behavior, 70, 92–94, 98–101
  evaluation of, 70–71
  explanation of, 9, 12, 52–53, 57–59, 69–70, 99, 105–108, 173, 254
  first Person and, 182–183
  scientific experiments as a kind of, 91, 93–98
  see also freedom of will, Intentional/Intentionality, Logical connection argument, Self
Aesthesiometer, 205–206
American Psychological Association, 147, 165, 320, 344, 354
Amygdala, 254–260, 263–265, 267–273
Analytical engine, 324–325
Analysis of variance (ANOVA), 291, 303, 315, 317–319, 332, 341
Apparatus, 14–15, 17–18, 41, 43, 140, 196–197, 199, 206–207, 218–220, 288–289, 292, 297–299, 301, 307–308, 338
  apparatus-driven research, 15, 218
  see also Instruments
Apperception, 34, 37–40, 49
Artifacts, 7, 83, 148, 170, 346, 356
Artificial intelligence, 99–100, 324, 326, 334
  see also Intelligence, Computer
Asking questions, 16, 224–227, 229, 231, 233, 235, 237, 239, 241, 243, 245
  see also Questionnaire
Attention, 11, 31–48, 53, 55, 58, 60, 61, 71, 131, 142, 160, 162–163, 186, 212, 240, 245, 256, 280–282, 293
  attention deficit disorder (ADD), 160, 162–163
  differentiated analyses of, 36–40
  first experimental research on, 33
  neuropsychological research, 256, 280–282, 293
  its possible effect on social control, 41–43
  its problematic effects on psychological tests and interviews, 240, 245
  problems of experiments on, 36–37, 43–45, 212
  its role for the control of mental states, 53, 55, 58, 186